California Mennonites

YOUNG CENTER BOOKS IN ANABAPTIST & PIETIST STUDIES

Donald B. Kraybill, *Series Editor*

California Mennonites

Brian Froese

JOHNS HOPKINS UNIVERSITY PRESS
Baltimore

© 2015 Johns Hopkins University Press
All rights reserved. Published 2015
Printed in the United States of America on acid-free paper

2 4 6 8 9 7 5 3 1

Johns Hopkins University Press
2715 North Charles Street
Baltimore, Maryland 21218-4363
www.press.jhu.edu

Library of Congress Cataloging-in-Publication Data

Froese, Brian, 1969– author.
California Mennonites / Brian Froese.
pages cm. — (Young Center books in Anabaptist & Pietist studies)
Includes bibliographical references and index.
ISBN 978-1-4214-1512-3 (hardcover) — ISBN 1-4214-1512-7 (hardcover) —
ISBN 978-1-4214-1513-0 (electronic) — ISBN 1-4214-1513-5 (electronic)
1. Mennonites—California—History. 2. California—Church history. I. Title.
BX8117.C2F76 2014
289.7'794—dc23
2014002821

A catalog record for this book is available from the British Library.

All photographs courtesy of the Mennonite Library & Archives, Fresno Pacific University.

*Special discounts are available for bulk purchases of this book. For more information,
please contact Special Sales at 410-516-6936 or specialsales@press.jhu.edu.*

Johns Hopkins University Press uses environmentally friendly book materials,
including recycled text paper that is composed of at least 30 percent
post-consumer waste, whenever possible.

To Lorelee and Benson

Whoever will, let him read history.
—Menno Simons, "Reply to Gellius Faber," 1554

The analyst of California is like a navigator who is trying to chart
a course in a storm: the instruments will not work; the landmarks are lost;
and the maps make little sense.
—Carey McWilliams, *California: The Great Exception*, 1949

Contents

Preface

In 1949 Carey McWilliams, the influential social commentator on California society, asked, "Is there really a state called California or is all this boastful talk?"[1] California was, in the mid-twentieth century, still defined by dreams of gold, movie magic, and endless sunshine. That the world moved in was testament to the drawing power of California as both a place and an exportable idea. McWilliams brought his perceptive eye to bear on the religious environment of Southern California by countering the romantic mythologies surrounding the Spanish Catholic missions and Aimee Semple McPherson, founder of the Foursquare Church. Though separated in time, that juxtaposition of images—the mission of the old established church and the new religious movement—has largely defined California religious historiography. In the first half of the twentieth century, thousands of Mennonites moved to California, joining the millions of people from all over America and the world making the same trip.[2] Of course, there really was, and is, an American state called California. What millions of people found, however, were countless interpretations, understandings, and manifestations of what that state could be.

Historian and former state librarian Kevin Starr once observed, "Unlike New Englanders or the citizens of Oregon and Utah, Californians could not justify themselves on the basis of founding ideals . . . those who reflected upon experience from the vantage point of an ennobling ideology did not set the tone of society, or, indeed, have much to say about its direction."[3] California is characterized by a lack of religious hegemony, which for some has provided freedom, for others, concern. Mennonites expressed both.

In this book, I examine the Mennonite experience in California through 1975 and in a brief epilogue add an update into the twenty-first century. Although we know of a few Mennonites who dug for gold in the 1850s, the real story of Mennonite religious experience in California began in the 1890s with westward migrations for fertile soil and healthy sunshine. By the mid-twentieth century, the Mennonite story in California develops into an interesting tale of religious conservatives, traditionally agrarian, finding their way in an increasingly urban and always religiously pluralistic California. In the geographically and spiritually wide open spaces of California, Mennonites, like many other ethnic, national, and religious groups from the world over, by necessity managed the pressures of modernity.

By choosing to migrate to and remain in California, I argue, Mennonites employed several strategies to bring together religious identity, accommodation, and practice so that their Mennonitism could take root in the Golden State. The plurality of their responses and strategies demonstrates the freedoms and concerns the far west frontier provided for a small group of ethno-religious agrarians well into the twentieth century. Indeed, by the 1960s, California Mennonites were well on their way to becoming as racially and ethnically diverse as the state around them. Summarily described as Anabaptist, evangelical, or secular, California Mennonites often situated themselves among these three categories to denote their religious identity: historically rooted in the sixteenth-century Reformation ideals of the early Anabaptists (pacifism, congregationalism, discipleship); in twentieth-century American evangelicalism (evangelism, missions, Billy Graham); and in a commitment to social justice that involved practical ties to government programs and a quiet connection to religion.

Mennonites are a religious group born of primarily Dutch and Swiss descent—forged in the flurry of sixteenth-century European Protestant reformations and in the fury of its persecutions—that espoused anticlericalism, adult baptism, bibliocentrism, and eventually pacifism. Mennonites moved throughout Europe seeking safe havens from religiously motivated persecutions, which largely dissipated during the seventeenth century. About the time Spain colonized present-day California, Dutch Mennonites who sought employment and escape from tribulation moved eastward from the Netherlands to North Germany. These Mennonites, along with other German and Swiss Mennonites, were eventually recruited to William Penn's colony, and some migrated to Pennsylvania in the early eighteenth century.

Additionally, numerous Dutch Mennonites migrated to the Vistula Delta, and in the late eighteenth century, at the invitation of Catherine the Great, settled the steppes of the Russian Ukraine. These Russian Mennonites began migrating to North America in the 1870s. During the nineteenth century, as California went through several political permutations and a gold rush before becoming an American state in 1850, many Swiss—South German Mennonites migrated to and settled mostly in the eastern and midwestern United States. In the late nineteenth and early twentieth centuries, Russian Mennonites from the Ukraine migrated largely to the American Midwest and western states.[4]

To oversimplify these histories, Dutch and Swiss—South German Mennonites migrated from Germany to Pennsylvania during America's colonial period, Swiss—South German Mennonites migrated from Switzerland to Pennsylvania and to the American Midwest—then to the western frontier—during America's period of westward expansion, and Russian Mennonites migrated from the Ukraine to America's Midwest and western states during America's Gilded Age and Progressive Era.

Although a few Mennonites were present at the gold rush, their real story begins in the last decade of the nineteenth century and accelerates with many twentieth-century transformations. In California, the Mennonites take us to cities like Los Angeles, but mostly to cities and towns in the Great Central Valley, where the vast majority of California Mennonites chose to live. California history has largely been the history of gold mines in the Sierra, the Los Angeles basin, the San Francisco Bay area, and the capitol building in Sacramento. In the Mennonite story, those three great city centers pulse in the background as the main events unfold largely on a stage from Bakersfield to Fresno in the fertile San Joaquin Valley, revealing in the process of assimilation a demonstration of the powerful influences of religious freedom, tolerance, and secularism.

To tell the story, I focus on Mennonites who migrated to California and integrated into its social, political, and cultural environment. During the middle decades of the twentieth century, Mennonites in California went through a modernizing transformation that included significant changes in the religious symbols and images they used to identify themselves and their new home. These changes came through experiences in which various historical themes and pressures—gender, migration, and war—came together.

Mennonites do not number large enough to merit attention from most historians of California, and they share a similar fate as that of other

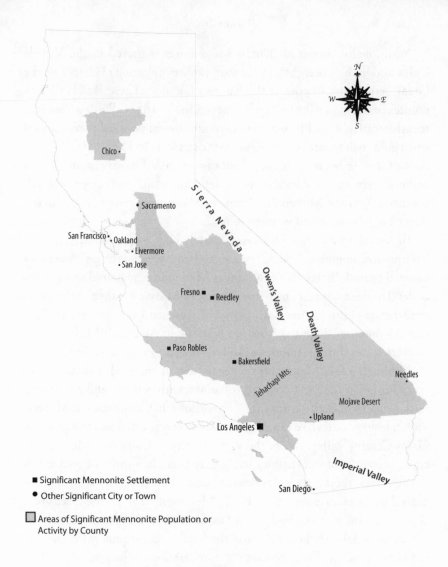

■ Significant Mennonite Settlement

● Other Significant City or Town

□ Areas of Significant Mennonite Population or Activity by County

Mennonites in California, 1890–1970. *Source:* Prepared using public domain data made available by the California Spatial Information Library (CaSIL), http://gis.ca.gov.

religious groups whose national denominational histories have only recently discovered the Pacific Coast.[5] To be fair, California is not the only state with a concentration of Mennonites largely overlooked by historians; Texas and Florida also warrant close study but have not received it. As historian Rod Janzen observes, "The California experience has been given

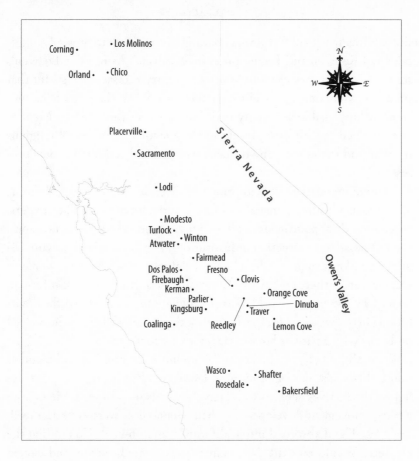

• Significant Mennonite Cities and Towns

Mennonites in the Central Valley, 1890–1970. *Source:* Prepared using
public domain data made available by the California Spatial
Information Library (CaSIL), http://gis.ca.gov.

short shrift in most works of Mennonite history."[6] This book addresses
that shortcoming.

As a group, Mennonites generally play the role of ethno-religious pacifist agrarians for American religious historians, but in California that role
quickly collapses.[7] Here Mennonites embraced modernity, marked by
urbanization and professionalization, often sooner than elsewhere. However, in that embrace they made significant symbolic actions of resistance.
Providing continuity through this transition were religious symbols that

shifted from images of California's natural environment to those of American Civil Religion and Protestant evangelicalism.[8] As Royden Loewen's study of Mennonites in mid-twentieth-century Kansas suggests for that state, the Mennonites in California may have taken the role of "barometer," making visible seemingly invisible pressures there.[9] How Mennonites evolved in California speaks to the assimilative power of religious freedom and the moderating influences of material and institutional success.

Mennonites arrived in California with wonder in their eyes, desirous of freedom, a healing climate, and fertile agricultural land. They experienced some disappointment but reified their desires through a continuous, even ritualistic, construction of institutions. Institutions such as sanitariums, mental health hospitals, schools, social relief organizations, women's societies, and others embraced the promise and problems of Californian society. By the end of World War II, Mennonites rationalized the devils lurking in the wilderness of early twentieth-century California into social problems with a patient hope of transforming society.[10]

From 1850 to 1975, American Mennonites migrated to and blended into California's social and cultural landscape. By the 1960s, when religious distinctives seemed to be mostly words on a page, a Mennonite heritage movement developed. By then Mennonites were Americanized, assimilated, and absorbed into California's environment. Countering the pressures of cultural drift, Mennonites took symbolic action and named college buildings and quads after sixteenth-century heroes; they also took concrete action and built an archive to house their records and memories.

The Protestant mainstream actively embraced, if not pursued, modernity for most of the twentieth century. Many of the values of "modernized Protestantism" can be found in the California Mennonites, especially the "ecumenism, actionism, and pluralism" so important to mainline American Protestantism in defining their religion and even their national identity.[11] For Mennonites in California the choice to become modern fit with their evangelical Anabaptist Mennonite religious faith, especially as they embraced change—lauded by both evangelical religion and modernity.[12]

In California, Mennonites were active. Upon arriving they almost immediately developed a variety of social and religious institutions. First came churches and church networks, followed quickly by parachurch institutions: hospitals, schools, and social relief organizations. Sometimes Mennonites intended these institutions solely to serve co-religionists, but they expanded their concern to the larger world in the case of hospitals and social relief endeavors. This socio-religious activism challenges any perception that agrarian sectarians resisted social change.

This study comprises the three major Mennonite denominations, which represent different approaches to American culture. In order from largest to smallest nationwide, they are the Mennonite Church, the General Conference Mennonites, and the Mennonite Brethren.[13] In California, however, the size order is reversed, with the Mennonite Brethren becoming the largest in the course of the twentieth century, as shown in table 1. (Small Mennonite groups in California outside the scope of this project include an attempted Amish settlement,[14] the Krimmer Mennonite Brethren, the Brethren In Christ, and the Holdeman, or Church of God In Christ Mennonites.)

The Mennonite Church, at the turn of the twentieth century, was largely an ethnically homogenized group descended from the Swiss and South German Mennonite migrations of the seventeenth to early nineteenth centuries.[15] These Mennonites were more sectarian, kept stricter boundaries with the larger culture, and had a stronger regional conference governance structure than other Mennonite groups.

The General Conference Mennonites formed in 1860 in an effort to unite several smaller Mennonite groups while remaining flexible on questions of polity, ethnic identity, and theology. They represented an "open door," or "open tent," commitment to that flexibility. Despite providing a denominational canopy to cover congregations across the theological spectrum, or maybe because of such accommodation, many Mennonites have considered the General Conference to be the most "liberal" Mennonite denomination and, initially, the least defined by ethnic origins. Beginning in the 1870s, a significant percentage of Mennonites who came from Russia later joined the General Conference.[16]

The Mennonite Brethren were the most evangelical, pietistic, and individualistic of all Mennonite groups. They originated in Russia in an 1860 split from the larger Mennonite community along lines of piety, land ownership, and social standing. They migrated to the United States and Canada in several waves in the late nineteenth and early twentieth centuries to avoid economic dislocation and a changing attitude on behalf of the Russian government toward Mennonite nonparticipation in the military. Of all Mennonite groups, the Mennonite Brethren have the largest percentage of members in California. By the end of the 1950s, two significant

Mennonite churches and members in California, 1905–2012

Denomination	1905		1960		2000		2012	
	Churches	Members[a]	Churches	Members	Churches	Members	Churches	Members
Mennonite Church	0[b]	<100	5[c]	291[c]	40[d]	1,954[d]	33[e]	2,367[e]
General Conference	2[b]	ca. 150	9[f]	1,518[g]	—	—	—	—
Mennonite Brethren	1[h]	ca. 100	24[h]	5,144[i]	62[j]	8,612[j]	72[k]	10,200[k]
Total	3	<350	38	6,953	102	10,566	105	12,567

Notes: Numbers from 1905 are imprecise because record keeping was not as consistent as later in the century. In the early 2000s the Mennonite Church and the General Conference Mennonites merged to form Mennonite Church USA (MCUSA).

[a] Gary B. Nachtigall, "Mennonite Migration and Settlements of California," M.A. thesis (California State University, Fresno, 1972), 71.

[b] L. R. Just and Clayton Auernheimer, "California (State)," *Global Anabaptist Mennonite Encyclopedia Online*, 1987, www.gameo.org/encyclopedia/p331.html.

[c] Minutes of the Annual Meeting of the South Pacific Conference, Nov. 24–26, 1960, "Conference Statistics for 1960," II15-3.6 SWMC Secretary, Theron Weldy, 1960–63, box 2, 1961 Conference Downey, MCA-G.

[d] James E. Horsch, ed., *Mennonite Directory 2001*, vol. 3 (Scottdale, PA: Faith and Life Resources, 2001).

[e] MCUSA online directory, www.mennoniteusa.org/online-directory (accessed Oct. 15, 2013).

[f] *Handbook of Information of the General Conference of the Mennonite Church of North America, 1959–1960*, 69–70. This number is from 1958.

[g] Samuel Floyd Pannabecker, *Open Doors: The History of the General Conference Mennonite Church* (Newton, KS: Faith and Life Press, 1975), 144–45.

[h] "Pacific District Conference Congregations," Center for Mennonite Brethren Studies, Archival Collections: Pacific District Conference of Mennonite Brethren Churches, www.fresno.edu/library/cmbs/archives/pacific_district_conference.asp (accessed Feb. 20, 2007).

[i] Numbers derived from Kevin Enns-Rempel, "Making a Home in the City: Mennonite Brethren Urbanization in California," in *Bridging Troubled Waters: The Mennonite Brethren at Mid-Twentieth Century*, ed. Paul Toews (Winnipeg, MB: Kindred Productions, 1995), 214.

[j] *2000/2001 Planner Directory* (Winnipeg, MB: Board of Resource Ministries General Conference of Mennonite Brethren Churches, Kindred Productions, 2001), 118–26.

[k] *2012/2013 Planner Directory* (Winnipeg, MB: Board of Resource Ministries General Conference of Mennonite Brethren Churches, Kindred Productions, 2012), 100.

streams of Mennonitism ran through Mennonite Brethren leadership in California: a tendency to "secularism" and a desire to reclaim "evangelical Anabaptism" from an encroaching fundamentalism. Both were attempts to articulate religious ideals while entering Californian society.[17] Moreover, as the demographics in table 2 indicate, the California Mennonite story in the last half of the twentieth century is largely about the Mennonite Brethren.

In his analysis of twentieth-century American religious history, Martin Marty uses the images of cocoon, canopy, and carapace to interpret denominational relationships to the wider society.[18] The *cocoon* describes the process whereby a religious group attempts to protect itself from outside influences. It keeps outsiders out and insiders in as the group mediates change, though it is a permeable boundary permitting some passage both ways. The *canopy* describes groups in the process of providing a religious shade of protection from outsiders, although the winds of modernity nonetheless blow through its sides. Denominations protect their beliefs in this model while increasingly tolerating outside influences in support of their grander ideals. This may occur, for example, when religious groups drop traditional markers of identity—including ethnic identifications—to demonstrate the universal applicability of their theological convictions, especially as a group modernizes.[19] The *carapace* is a hardened denominational response to the permeable boundaries set by the cocoon and the virtual absence of distinctives created by the canopy. Marty calls this "reactive Protestantism" and likens it to a tortoise shell, where "outside influences are unable to penetrate and people within have made their aggressive choice to keep only each other's spiritual company."[20] Marty includes such "hardened" positions as biblical inerrancy, Pentecostalism, and premillennialism as examples of this stance. California Mennonites spanned the entire spectrum of Marty's typology.

Mennonites in California responded to modernity in complex ways as they both embraced and resisted their modern world. Mostly, however, they came to terms with living in a modern society through a religious network that included churches, schools, and hospitals as integral to their lives. These Mennonites found strength in evangelical religion, were less concerned about integrating into society on professional and business levels, but were more anxious about assimilating some social practices— weddings, for example—and embracing religious pluralism.

Early Mennonites moving to California at the turn of the last century did so often for reasons of climate and economic advantage. Significantly, many also came as tourists. Tourism signaled mobility, acceptance of certain aspects of modern culture and consumer practice, and the enjoyment of an economic position that made such trips possible. More than simple pleasure, early twentieth-century Mennonite tourists often published

Mennonite denominational membership in California and the United States, 1970–2012

Denomination	1970[a]		2000		2012	
	California	U.S.	California	U.S.	California	U.S.
Mennonite Church	418	85,343	1,954[b]	120,381[c]	2,367[d]	103,245[e]
General Conference	1,543	36,337	—	—	—	—
Mennonite Brethren	5,747	15,120	8,612[f]	22,072[f]	10,200[g]	35,488[h]
Total	7,708	136,800	10,566	142,453	12,567	138,733

Note: In the early 2000s the Mennonite Church and the General Conference Mennonites merged to form Mennonite Church USA (MCUSA).

[a] Gary B. Nachtigall, "Mennonite Migration and Settlements of California," M.A. thesis (California State University, Fresno, 1972), 69.

[b] James E. Horsch, ed., *Mennonite Directory 2001*, vol. 3 (Scottdale, PA: Faith and Life Resources, 2001), 104–8.

[c] Horsch, *Mennonite Directory 2001*, vol. 3, 391.

[d] MCUSA online directory, www.mennoniteusa.org/online-directory/ (accessed Oct. 15, 2013).

[e] Mennonite World Conference, *World Directory 2012*, 31.

[f] *2000/2001 Planner Directory* (Winnipeg, MB: Board of Resource Ministries General Conference of Mennonite Brethren Churches, Kindred Productions, 2001), 118–26.

[g] *2012/2013 Planner Directory* (Winnipeg, MB: Board of Resource Ministries General Conference of Mennonite Brethren Churches, Kindred Productions, 2001), 100.

[h] Mennonite World Conference, *World Directory 2012*, 32.

reports of their adventures in denominational newspapers, illustrating the multivariate nature of these excursions as an amalgam of prosperity, consumerism, piety, and communalism.

This book explores the transformation of Mennonite culture in the middle decades of the twentieth century. Historians almost uniformly consider these decades to be a watershed in North American history.[21] Mennonites in California lived through the tensions and transformations wrought by a constellation of economic prosperity and social optimism following World War II. They employed a variety of strategies to navigate these changes, all the while trying to balance the goals of trying to be both good Mennonites and good Americans.

Some Mennonites found a way through the transitions via conservative evangelicalism; others found it by reclaiming the examples of sixteenth-century Anabaptists. Still other Mennonites found meaningful religious experience by entering deeper into society through social service and action to the extent that they even appeared "secularized." Yet lived experience is not always this simple, and many found their way through a mixture of these categories. Evangelical, Anabaptist, and secular—the responses cover a broad spectrum, yet represent a selective retaining and discarding of Mennonite religious practices and expressions. All these creative responses to modern society, changing economies, and shifting mores came with forms of accommodation and resistance.

Regional histories tell us about people living in particular places, but it is misleading to consider experiences, however geographically defined, as peculiar only to a singular place. Thus, some of the topics examined in this book speak to the California experience, which at times is particular and at times partners with national trends. On this point I follow Eldon Ernst's caution against writing something approaching "Californiology."[22] For example, Civilian Public Service (CPS) had units in regions of the United States other than just California. In the religious history of California Mennonites, however, CPS connects with themes that reach deep into the Mennonite psyche, especially that of pacifism. Thus, while CPS was administered nationally, it had California units filled with men from across the country. The California context flavored their experience in a particular way, as it also did with other Mennonite institutional developments such as women's societies and mental health hospitals.

Without claiming that what happens in California only happens in California, this book explores the complex world of mid-twentieth-century California Mennonites through several selected themes. These topics, while appearing arbitrary or episodic in nature, emerge from two major considerations: the nature of the source material and the questions asked of cultural history.

The use of denominational print media and archival records placed constraints on this project in several important ways. It privileged materials collected and archived in an institutional world often governed by male leaders and administrators. However, the source materials also document the lives of people with significant involvement in their local church communities. The people whose voices are heard in this book worked on committees, wrote to denominational newspapers, and engaged their religious culture through traditional churchly practices. This has its strengths for a book about religious transformations, but its weaknesses are here acknowledged, for religious culture is also about religion lived beyond the church's institutional shadow. Although there are hints at such lived practices, they are not a primary focus here. Such histories remain to be written of California Mennonite agriculture, business, family, and politics, and I hope they will be someday. Second, while archival sources move the historian in particular directions, the questions the historian asks are significant and are posed here in the context of cultural history. Therefore, this book explores themes of gender, race, conflict, religious practice, and religious imagination, though shaped by the archival record.

This book—in twelve chapters and an epilogue—provides a contextualized study of Mennonite religious and cultural transformations in mid-twentieth century California. The context is set in the opening chapters, where Mennonite life in California is explored through the establishment of a physical institutional presence in which churches, conferences, schools, health care facilities, and relief agencies provide the contours of a life lived in society through religious motivation. In addition to institutions, Mennonites also articulated a sense of place and identity as they encountered and responded to California's urban and natural environments as migrants and tourists from the Canadian prairies, American Midwest, and Russia. Yet changing concepts of place and identity went further than West Coast urbanism and agriculture; it also included religious pluralism and even changing concepts of insider and outsider status among themselves. Through such religious and cultural conflicts concerning Pentecostalism, liberalism, and evangelicalism—at times refracted through lenses crafted by different generations and shaped by formal education—Mennonites in California worked toward an integrated identity with the world in which they lived. The story opens with a chapter that sketches the setting of Mennonite life in California, providing a religious and cultural context where Mennonites established a physical institutional presence primarily through the construction of churches and regional conferences. Chapters 2 and 3 examine Mennonite understandings of California's urban and natural environments as migrants and tourists from the Canadian prairies, American Midwest, and Russia. The changing concepts of insider and outsider status for the Mennonites are explored in chapter 4 through such issues as Pentecostalism and heresy.

As religious pluralism raised important questions for Mennonites, so too did race. Chapter 5 explores the question of racial and religious identity as it developed for Mennonites in Los Angeles and the San Joaquin Valley. In relating to racial and religious "others," Mennonites found themselves making decisions common to other Anglo-European—based denominations, decisions that often included moving to new neighborhoods and engaging others primarily through mission work.

The next three chapters investigate the California experience in conjunction with the larger American Mennonite experience. Alongside the question of racial identity and relationship, in chapter 6, gendered experiences are explored in the context of women's missionary societies, where, in the quest for religious experience and lived faith commitments, questions of expanding roles for women in church were confronted. Pacifism is considered in chapter 7 through Mennonite experiences with CPS, an alternative to military service, and a highly publicized case of naturalization. In both these situations, Mennonites debated what it meant to be good Mennonites and good Americans at a time when such soul searching · came with real-world consequences. Chapter 8 examines the creation and early years of the mental health institute Kings View Homes (KVH), born out of the CPS experience and the presence of "secular" Mennonitism.

In chapter 9, I describe the development of the West Coast Regional Office of the social relief agency Mennonite Central Committee (MCC) and its clothing center—where we find the evolution of a bureaucracy as a strategy for realizing objectives of religious faith and modernization. The Mennonite Brethren attempted to establish a distinct presence with a subtle embrace of California's religious culture through the creation of two postsecondary schools: Pacific Bible Institute (PBI) and Mennonite Brethren Biblical Seminary (MBBS); this experience is covered in chapter 10 and updated in the epilogue. The question of higher education is important because church-related schools are part of a deliberate engagement with society. In the schools, we find Mennonites clarifying definitions of what type of education is desirable for Mennonite young people and how to achieve it. These are "finishing schools," not to cultivate manners, but to prepare Mennonite young people for living in a professional world defined much less, if at all, by religious norms, let alone Mennonite ones.

Chapter 11 presents a case study of how different generations of Mennonites in eastern states imaginatively constructed California. It follows the experience of eastern visitors to California in the early 1970s as they discover a different form of Mennonitism than they expected in migrant labor disputes. In the final chapter, the threads of this project are pulled together to reveal something of the fabric of California Mennonite life, a culture and people continually transformed. The epilogue briefly updates the story into the twenty-first century.

Throughout this story, we will find a dynamic people who did not simply become modern but who actively shaped their experience to do so on their own terms.

Acknowledgments

In the process of writing this book, my debts of gratitude increased, and I owe thanks to several individuals and organizations that lent their support and encouragement. I am grateful to Donald B. Kraybill, senior fellow and series editor, and Cynthia Nolt, research and editorial associate, at the Young Center for Anabaptist and Pietist Studies at Elizabethtown College, for their patient editorial advice, as well as Greg Nicholl, formerly assistant editor at Johns Hopkins University Press, for guiding the project through the approval stages. This book had its beginnings as a doctoral dissertation, and I am grateful to my professors at the Graduate Theological Union in Berkeley, who helped shape my interest in history and religion in California and the American West, especially my advisor, Randi Walker, and Eldon Ernst. Kerwin Lee Klein at the University of California in Berkeley and Paul Toews at Fresno Pacific University also deserve special thanks for their comments and insights.

In addition, I benefited greatly from Kevin Enns-Rempel, archivist at the Center for Mennonite Brethren Studies at Fresno Pacific University. He provided me with much insight in our many conversations on California and California Mennonite history. Kevin also brought to my attention source material I either had missed or would not have thought to explore; as well, I appreciate his help with the photos, their captions, and his close reading of an earlier version of the manuscript. The reference and public services librarian of the Hiebert Library at Fresno Pacific University, Anne Guenther, also provided helpful assistance in using the library's collections. In Fresno, Jane Friesen provided me with warm accommodation on many of my research visits.

I have been the fortunate recipient of financial support in the form of research grants from the California Mennonite Historical Society and the Mennonite Historical Society, as well as benefiting from a Newhall Research Fellowship from the Graduate Theological Union and a Canadian Mennonite University Faculty Research Grant. I visited several archives and found their respective staffs helpful and resourceful. I thank the kind and engaging staff at the Mennonite Church USA Archives in Goshen, Indiana—John E. Sharp, director; Dennis Stoesz, archivist; and Ruth Schrock and Cathy Hochstetler, archives assistants—for their aid. In Goshen, I enjoyed the hospitality of Ken and Rebecca Horst. The staff at Mennonite Church USA Archives in North Newton, Kansas—John Thiesen, archivist, and James Lynch, assistant archivist—were helpful in tracking down leads on the California experience. Peggy Goertzen, director of the Center for Mennonite Brethren Studies at Tabor College in Hillsboro, Kansas, assisted me with the Henry J. Martens Collection. I am also grateful to the staff at the Fresno County Public Library in Reedley, California, and to Corinna Siebert Ruth, archivist at First Mennonite Church in Reedley. In Winnipeg I received welcome assistance toward the end of the project from Korey Dyck and Conrad Stoesz at the Mennonite Heritage Centre Archives and from Jon Isaak at the Centre for Mennonite Brethren Studies.

At several conferences, where I presented research undertaken for this project, I received helpful feedback. In particular, I thank Amanda Porterfield, Florida State University, Tallahassee; the late Ferenc Morton Szasz, University of New Mexico; and Susan Yohn, Hofstra University, for helpful comments at three such gatherings. The editorial staff at the *California Mennonite Historical Society Bulletin* kindly granted permission to use parts of two articles in this book. I wish to thank those who read the manuscript in various stages in whole, or in part, providing helpful comments: Kevin Enns-Rempel, Rod Janzen, Eveyln Labun, Valerie Rempel, Janis Thiessen, and Pat Sanders. Furthermore, I extend my appreciation to Allyssa Rempel, at Trinity Designs in Winnipeg, who produced the maps.

Along the way, I have enjoyed the encouragement of family, friends, and colleagues. Above all, I want to express my deepest appreciation and greatest debt of gratitude to my wife, Lorelee, and son, Benson, for their patience and unwavering support while living with this manuscript for such a long time; to them I dedicate this book.

California Mennonites

CHAPTER 1

Going to California

The Mennonite Migration

Souls are starving for . . . the bread of life.
—Mennonite immigrant, 1909

A New Start

California for much of its history was a powerfully attractive force for people around the world, where Russian, Spanish, and Native American societies at one time existed in relative proximity. After Mexican independence from Spain in 1821, California was a Mexican province for a quarter century, before becoming an independent republic for about a month in summer 1846, when the United States annexed it. The discovery of gold in 1848 at Sutter's Mill in Coloma sparked a global rush of people to extract the precious metal. As a result, California bypassed territory status to become, in 1850, the thirty-first state of the United States. Since statehood, California has profoundly influenced American society through its predominance in a wide range of sectors, including mass entertainment, technology, industry, politics both liberal and conservative, youth culture, and viniculture.

The Central Valley, to which many Mennonites migrated, is large. About 450 miles long and ranging anywhere between 40 and 120 miles in width, it contains some 15 million acres of tremendously fertile land if heavily irrigated, making it one of the most significant agricultural regions in the country.[1] Mennonites, like countless others, moved to California for reasons of economics, health, and climate. They mostly came from the Great Plains. In the years 1887 to 1939, for instance, Oklahoma, Kansas, and Nebraska represented 43.5 percent of the total Mennonite migration to California.[2] That Mennonites, a traditionally rural people, were attracted to California is not surprising. Nor were the early settlements exceptional in what is now the Los Angeles basin, an agricultural region in the early twentieth century.[3] The migratory experience for the Mennonites was not new either. Moving to California was part of a long history of uprooting and seeking new homes from Europe to North America and now beyond the American Midwest. Those rural experiences, however, quickly became urban ones. In the twentieth century, massive immigration and rapid urbanization shaped California. Although California represented less than 2 percent of the national population in 1900, by the early twenty-first century that proportion increased sixfold, as seen in table 3. Mennonites responded to these developments through strategies that embraced modernity. Their strategies ultimately reshaped traditional identities and made Mennonites active participants in larger society.[4]

Mennonite Forty-Niners

Before Mennonites settled permanently in California, some came searching for gold.[5] Johannes Dietrich Dyck was most likely the first Mennonite in California. Our only source of his experience is the narration given by his great-grandson, Cornelius J. Dyck, based on his elder's diary. Johannes Dyck, born in West Prussia in 1826, arrived in New York on November 2, 1848. Soon, news of golden riches in California drifted his way, and he dreamed of returning to his fiancée in Prussia with a fortune in hand. By February 1850 he had earned enough money to travel to California. Dyck actually struck gold and three years later planned the long return trip to Prussia. Shortly thereafter, he lost all his gold in a Native American attack. Returning to the mines, he worked on and off for several years but never struck it rich. Finally he generated enough income to return to Prussia in 1858, when he married his fiancée of ten years.[6]

Joseph Summers was another Mennonite forty-niner. According to his obituary, he was born on October 11, 1823, in Lancaster County, Pennsylvania. After he married on December 8, 1846, he and his wife moved to Holmes County, Ohio, where they settled on a farm for seventeen years.

Population of California and the United States, 1900–2010

Year	U.S. population (in millions)	California population (in millions)	California as % of U.S. population
1900	76.2	1.5	1.97
1910	92.2	2.4	2.60
1920	106.0	3.4	3.21
1930	123.2	5.7	4.63
1940	132.2	6.9	5.22
1950	151.3	10.6	7.01
1960	179.3	15.7	8.76
1970	203.2	20.0	9.84
1980	226.5	23.7	10.46
1990	248.7	29.8	11.98
2000	281.4	33.9	12.05
2010	308.7	37.3	12.08

Source: California Population of Counties by Decennial Census: 1900 to 1990, compiled and edited by Richard L. Forstall, Population Division, US Bureau of the Census, March 27, 1995, www.census.gov/population/cencounts/ca190090.txt; 2000 and 2010, www.census.gov/prod/cen2010/briefs/c2010br-01.pdf, p. 2.

During this time, Summers made two trips to California, one to start a mining company and the other simply to "live there." In fall 1850, he and twelve other men from Zanesville, Ohio, arrived in Dry Town, California, to start the Zanesville Mining Company. The obituary gives no details as to his success or failure but simply recounts, "His anecdotes of this journey and the valuable lessons he drew from his observations afforded many an hour's profitable entertainment."[7] His second trip was a six-year move, and there his story falls silent.

These two documents, the diary and the obituary, offer virtually no detail of California life but are effective symbols for the place of California in Mennonite historiography.[8] In sketching out the setting of early Mennonite settlement in California, this chapter explores their beginnings in Southern California and the San Joaquin Valley. Though I follow these experiences along lines of specific denominational development—General Conference (GC), Mennonite Brethren (MB), and Mennonite Church (MC)—a strict chronology becomes fluid for clarity.

Beginnings in Southern California

By the late 1880s and 1890s, a trickle of Mennonites were moving to Southern California in search of what many other Americans and migrants from around the world also sought: improved health, improved economic status—primarily through agriculture for the Mennonites—and to start life over.[9] Perhaps in response to falling commodity prices in the Midwest and the economic contractions of the 1890s, migration to California became more attractive. Mennonites moving to Los Angeles in the final dozen years of the nineteenth century found themselves in the midst of a phenomenal population explosion. From 1880 to 1890 Los Angeles's population grew by 351 percent, and in the next decade another 103 percent; by 1910 the number of residents increased by another 212 percent. Outside of New York and Pennsylvania, four of the top six states exporting people to Southern California were in the Midwest, and all had significant Mennonite populations. The call to California was not only loud but also well received. By the time Mennonites began to move and settle in, the religious and racial diversity of the Los Angeles area was staggering for its time, as was the speed of its development. Furthermore, various denominations perceived that new, some would call looser, methods of religious ministry and practice were necessary to account for the relative isolation, climate, and frontier qualities of Southern California.[10]

Large-scale Protestant migration to Southern California did not begin until the 1860s, and it took until the late 1880s for it to displace Roman Catholicism in terms of political influence. When the Southern Pacific Railroad and Santa Fe line reached Los Angeles in 1876 and 1885, the movement of peoples from other states intensified. Many of these stateside migrants were religious, likely Protestant, and in 1890, 36 percent of Los Angeles's 50,395 inhabitants were churchgoers. Los Angeles was in a state of dissonance at the start of the twentieth century. By the measure of church attendance, it was among the most religious cities of the American West, with an ever-growing religious diversity, and yet it was a frontier town replete with much gambling, prostitution, alcohol, and political graft. Through it all, Protestants struggled to have an influence on the City of Angels.[11]

Jacob Hege was an early GC leader of a congregation near Paso Robles, the first recognized Mennonite congregation in California. He was a pastor

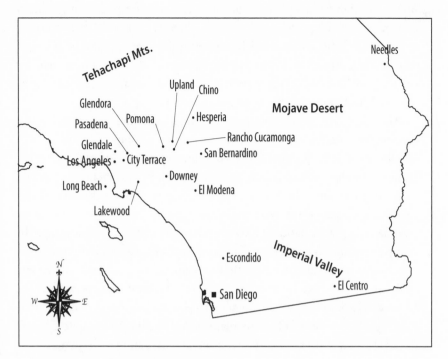

● Significant Mennonite Settlement
■ Other Significant City or Town

Mennonites in Southern California, 1890–1970. *Source:* Prepared using
public domain data made available by the California Spatial
Information Library (CaSIL), http://gis.ca.gov.

from Wisner, Nebraska, who became interested in California through his
brother-in-law, Dr. Jacob Horsch. Hege visited Horsch, already living in
California, who introduced him to a man selling land in San Luis Obispo
County. Afterwards, Hege decided to move and invited other Mennonites
to join him, describing the land he saw as ideal for farming and the mild
coastal climate as perfect for the sick and elderly.[12] The sale deadline was
July 1, 1896. He hoped to hear of people willing to move by at least May 15.
Not until June, however, did he receive a letter from Jacob Claassen
of Beatrice, Nebraska, who wanted to join him. That October, they, with
their families, apparently purchased land and boarded a train headed
west. They arrived in San Miguel on November 1, 1896. Other Men-

nonite families followed, and within a year, they formed a congregation east of Paso Robles. Hege, who arrived in 1897, became their minister and helped fulfill an assumed Mennonite practice: "Wherever Mennonites settled, they always held Sunday services."[13] This pattern of combining the pursuit of new opportunities with traditional religious practices repeated itself well into the twentieth century.

Also that year, 1897, another group of Mennonites—comprising six families from Beatrice, Nebraska, led by Aron J. Wiebe—settled ten miles northwest of Paso Robles. The two groups agreed to start a church together.[14] Though two different settlements, they saw themselves as the same congregation—the San Marcos Mennonite Church. Because of the geographic distance between them, they maintained separate meetings and meeting places, holding a co-operative monthly "union meeting." In 1903, they called a joint council meeting to discuss their relationship. Despite some discussion to merge, they formalized their separate identities, as the geographic distance between proved too significant. Thus, the San Marcos Mennonite Church dissolved. The more eastern group, which then moved into Paso Robles, reorganized as the First Mennonite Church of Paso Robles, with twenty-five charter members and Jacob Hege as their minister, until 1906, when he left for Idaho.[15] The northwestern group reorganized and in 1904 reclaimed the name San Marcos Mennonite Church, then moved to Willow Creek. They became, in 1943, the Second Mennonite Church of Paso Robles and in 1954 renamed themselves Willow Creek Mennonite Church.[16]

At about the same time as the early developments in the Paso Robles area, in the late 1880s and 1890s, approximately 240 miles south, Mennonites seeking improved health were coming to Southern California. In 1887, Henry Rees, from Ashland, Ohio, moved to Pomona, California, and over the next six years found company with other Mennonite families, who came mostly from Illinois. These families, independent of each other, moved throughout Southern California to places like Pomona, Cucamonga, and Pasadena. Finally, in 1897, a large enough group settled in Upland that a church was created a few years later. In an early 1898 report to the Board of Home Missions of the General Conference, J. B. Baer, home mission and field secretary for the General Conference, noted there was a congregation in "St. Louis, Obispo County" (sic) with fifty members who were confident more families would come and settle there. They became the Upland First Mennonite Church in 1903.[17] The General Conference was optimistic about their future in California, and they established a number of churches by the mid-1930s. These churches were located in cities and towns such as Los Angeles (1918), Winton (1921), and Shafter (1935). By 1955, however, their numbers totaled only sixteen hundred.[18]

A series of similar events occurred in Los Angeles, leading eventually to the creation of a new church. Though some Mennonites in Los Angeles were meeting informally in 1902, General Conference work began there in the years 1909 to 1914, "seeing the need for aggressive work among the Mennonites coming to Los Angeles."[19] In early 1909, the Home Missions Board sent Rev. and Mrs. E. F. Grubb to Los Angeles at the request of the denomination to assist local Mennonites by providing a Mennonite place of worship and spiritual leadership. A year later, a location was found for their mission in a former pool hall, and they called it the River Station Mission. Due to "industrial expansion in the vicinity," in 1914 the mission moved and renamed itself Whosoever Will Mission.[20]

The mission held its first public service on May 8, 1910, which it adopted as its official date of origin, despite meeting informally as early as 1902. In 1924, the mission expanded and the group built a new church building at Seventy-Ninth and Stanford, naming it Immanuel Mennonite Church, thus closing the Whosoever Will Mission chapter of its history. This group, which received financial support for nearly twenty years from the General Conference, became self-supporting in 1931.[21] In the early decades of the twentieth century, Mennonite mission work in California was not an enterprise among non-Christians, or the "unchurched"; rather, it serviced a critical mass of Mennonites living in a region without a Mennonite church.[22]

Immanuel Mennonite Church made an intentional connection between historical identity and twentieth-century evangelical openness in their fiftieth-anniversary publication, which included "The Purpose, Plan and History of this Church." It was a reprint of a 1924 announcement by Reverend Claassen, who explained to the local community, "The members of this church lived scattered throughout this and adjoining cities. A large number of them live here in the southern part of Los Angeles and for this reason we decided on this location, . . . [to] humbly serve the Lord Jesus." Moreover, they welcomed everyone to worship at the church. The publication explained the name "Mennonite" as given by the persecutors of "our ancestors," while noting, "Our denominational existence antedates the Reformation period. We find our forefathers in the faith in those old evangelical bodies which blazed the way to the Reformation."[23] Immanuel was a rare case in California, where a Mennonite church situated and marked itself both historically Mennonite and open with an active evangelical sense of mission.

As Mennonites settled permanently and established churches, by the late 1890s, the General Conference national body responded to these developments in the Paso Robles area and Southern California by creating the Pacific District Conference. This was an organizing body, defined regionally, to help coordinate Mennonite religious activity. Unlike the large administrative bureaucratic structure that it is today, at the turn of the last century it existed somewhat informally, providing largely financial and spiritual assistance to new congregations. It went about its work with a threefold rationale: "promote fellowship" among Mennonites in the Pacific region, coordinate missionary efforts in the far west, and integrate the Pacific Coast Mennonites into the structure of the national denominational body.[24] It was the smallest of the six General Conference Mennonite regional conferences by population, but largest in area. The increasing stream of General Conference Mennonites to Southern California from the 1880s to the early 1900s led to quick denominational response to address their religious needs and extend denominational oversight.[25]

Beginnings in the San Joaquin Valley

In 1903, Daniel Eymann and his family moved to Upland from Kansas. Having bought a twenty-acre orange grove, they headed west for warmer winters. A few months later, they decided to move again, this time north to Reedley, just over a hundred miles away over the Tehachapi Mountains. The rest of the family boarded a train while two sons made the ten-day trip from Upland by four-horse wagon to their new home. Arriving in Reedley was exciting, as one son, Ernest, recalled later in life. Ernest was particularly impressed by the saloons; he recalled that his first memory of the town was a large brawl near one involving several men and their dogs in the middle of Main Street.[26]

The Eymanns had become "dissatisfied with orange growing" because of high costs in Southern California.[27] The Santa Fe Immigration Department, which promoted settlement along the San Joaquin Valley line, prompted their move to Reedley. As Mennonites moved to Reedley largely for its agricultural promise, they brought with them religious practices, and they gathered for worship. Early participants in this congregation came from Kansas, Minnesota, and Ohio.[28] By 1906, these settlers formally organized their congregation with the denomination and in 1908 built their first church building. Within fifty years, First Mennonite Church of Reedley had a membership of 593, made up primarily of South German and Russian immigrant Mennonites and their descendants, most of whom were fruit farmers who lived in nearby rural areas.[29]

The Eymanns may have been at the start of Mennonite migration to the area, but they were not alone. Shortly after their move to California, their old pastor, Reverend Schellenberg of Moundridge, came to visit them and other midwestern migrants from his flock. Mennonites were on the move west.[30] When Mennonites began moving to the Reedley area, there was already a substantial Finnish settlement formed by Finns escaping a Russian program of russification in the late nineteenth century. They were settling the area along with a Lebanese-Syrian colony, Armenians, Mexicans, Japanese, Danish, Filipinos, and soon Koreans. A direct result of the railroad, Reedley's growth was diverse and rapid.[31]

The Eymanns' role in Reedley was, as noted by archivist Kevin Enns-Rempel, much more involved than agriculture. In those early years, people moved to Reedley primarily from Ohio, Missouri, Kansas, Montana, the Dakotas, and Minnesota, with backgrounds in many lines of work that were of use in the growing town: farming, business, and law. Though the Eymanns moved to farm in the area, and the Mennonites in and around Reedley organized into a religious fellowship, the Eymanns' children, in what was atypical for American Mennonites at this time, entered professions in politics and law. The Eymann family was noteworthy for their extensive public service: producing Reedley's first and fifth mayor, a district attorney, and a superior court judge.[32]

It was not just a single family branching out from the usual Mennonite work. Later, as Earl Eymann entered real estate in 1930, other Mennonites began automobile dealerships in the early 1930s: Martens Chevrolet and Oldsmobile in 1930, and Enns Pontiac, Buick and GMC in 1931. Mennonites were moving to California in the early 1900s and thriving in agriculture, business, banking, and politics.[33] These were thrilling times for Reedley. It was growing, businesses were expanding, and consumer goods increasing. As rail transportation improved through new bridge construction and increased train stops, Reedley saw its star rising.[34]

Mennonite Brethren Beginnings

Near the same time as GC families such as the Eymanns arrived, Mennonite Brethren began moving to Reedley, in the early 1900s, leaving, like so many others, midwestern winter cold to farm and ranch in California. In the Reedley area they came as farmers, and they built up ranches, working fourteen-hour days picking almonds and fruit, irrigating vineyards and orchards, cutting alfalfa, and milking cows. Although some were beef and dairy farmers, most were grain farmers to the north and east of town, or orchard and vineyard growers to the south and west. Early church meetings were held in the home of D. T. Enns, a member of one of the early families to arrive from Kansas, who, before leaving, was "charged by Elder Abraham Schellenberg, founder of Ebenezer MB Church near Buhler [Kansas], of the spiritual welfare of the pioneer families moving here." He took the charge seriously.[35] These early settlers organized the Reedley Mennonite Brethren Church in 1905 and met in the Windsor Grammar School until they constructed a building in 1908.[36]

In the early twentieth century, the Reedley Mennonite Brethren thought it necessary for their children to receive an education to help with Mennonite cultural retention. By 1910, classes in religion and German began. From 1912 to 1928, the German school benefited from the serendipitous arrival of three educated Russian migrants, all accomplished educators. By the early 1920s, plans were made to create a system of education in California that included a college similar to the liberal arts school Tabor College in Kansas, though that would not take shape until the 1940s, with the creation of Pacific Bible Institute. In the mid-1920s, when the Reedley Mennonite Brethren Church split over internal divisions regarding polity and Pentecostal influences, control of the school shifted between the two factions. In 1938, the Reedley Mennonite Brethren Church opened a rival Bible academy, though in 1941, the two schools merged as Immanuel Bible School.[37] Eventually, Immanuel became a local high school as educational needs changed.[38]

Reedley Mennonite Brethren Church was the first MB congregation in California and soon the largest Mennonite congregation in North America, with a membership reflecting its rural roots in Kansas, Oklahoma, Nebraska, Minnesota, and Russia. With fewer than 20 charter members at its start, the church grew to 1,436 members by 1957.[39] By 1955, the Reedley MB Church understood itself as a "lighthouse" to the world, drawing people in from all over with the "light of the gospel."[40] Self-identifying as a beacon on the West Coast calling the world to Christ was certainly in keeping with exceptionalist imagery for Mennonite religious missions, California cultural identity, and American evangelicalism.

Further north, Lodi represents an early instance of denominational diversity in a Mennonite Brethren church. The congregation there formed in 1907 when three Mennonites—Ludwig Reimche, Jacob Knoll, and George Bechtold—and their families arrived from Harvey, North Dakota. Initially they attended the evangelical church in nearby Victor. Striking out on their own, in 1911 they rented a house for religious services, and in 1912 organized as a Mennonite Brethren church. The membership in Lodi was composed mainly of Mennonites, Lutherans, and Baptists with Germanic background as part of the immigration from Russia to the United States in the early decades of the twentieth century. Filled to capacity at 350 in the 1920s, inner strife caused the membership to decline to about 110 in 1954. By the late 1950s, attendance hovered at about 200, giving some cause for optimism. The Lodi congregation has its roots in the Woodrow Gospel Chapel in North Dakota. Many Mennonites and other German-speaking immigrants from South Russia came between 1874 and 1888, and many of those in Woodrow in the early twentieth century from that migration to North Dakota moved to either Lodi or Saskatchewan. In the 1920s, North Dakota churches experienced a drain due largely to "California fever," though many also moved to Saskatchewan. Eventually these two streams out of North Dakota—to Saskatchewan and to California—met in Lodi. In the Lodi MB Church records, these two migratory streams converged with hints of tensions between them.[41]

Some Mennonite Brethren congregations, such as those in Rosedale and Bakersfield, trace their beginnings to relocated victims of the debacle at Martensdale. What has become known as the "Henry J. Martens Land Scheme" was a case of land speculation gone awry. In 1909, Henry Martens sold land in California to Mennonite families in the Midwest, going to the effort of bringing some Mennonites by rail to California to inspect the land. Although he appeared to have arranged to purchase just over 5,000 acres in California, the Mennonites involved settled on someone else's property and were forced to move, having lost their land in the Midwest and owning none in California.[42]

Otto and Lydia Boese, original Martensdale members, reflected on

Reedley Mennonite Brethren Church children on their way to a Sunday school picnic, ca. 1922.
Source: Records of Reedley Mennonite Brethren Church.

their experiences in Bakersfield at the church's fiftieth anniversary. The
Boeses recalled that they moved from Pueblo, Colorado, to California,
because California had "a magic ring to it." After the collapse of Martensdale, the Boese family moved with other families to Bakersfield, where
the Kern County Land Company donated land for them to build a church.
By 1915, five years after forming a congregation and six years after forming a house group, the Bakersfield Mennonite Brethren Church formally
organized, began holding street meetings, and started a jail and hospital
visitation program.[43]

Ten miles west of Bakersfield, Rosedale Mennonite Brethren Church,
also born directly from the Martensdale scheme, held the preliminary sessions in 1911 for the first Mennonite Pacific District Conference (PDC)
session held a year later.[44] In Shafter, the Mennonite Brethren built their
"tabernacle" in 1919, also on land donated by the Kern County Land
Company; by 1957, it boasted a membership of 522.[45]

Members of the Reedley Mennonite Brethren Church posing for a panoramic
photo (undated). Note photographer in foreground on truck. *Source:* Records of
Reedley Mennonite Brethren Church.

At the first gathering of the Mennonite Brethren Pacific District Conference (PDC) in Reedley in 1912, organizers were concerned that delegates would not attend from as far away as Lodi and Escondido. If the
fifteen miles between the San Marcos and Paso Robles General Conference congregations was too far for regular meetings, the 160 miles from
Lodi and the 320 miles from Escondido to Reedley at this time were considerable. Nevertheless, attendance was overflowing. Despite concerns of
the scattered and geographically isolated Mennonite Brethren congregations, PDC became the largest Mennonite Brethren district conference
in the United States. Though that was not obvious at the start, due to
the small number of Mennonite Brethren in California during the years
1909 to 1911, congregations could choose which district to join—Middle
or South. Although that option to choose was short-lived, within half a

century, prodigious population growth, primarily through immigration, catapulted California into the position of largest Mennonite Brethren district in the nation.[46]

Traveling Evangelists

In the early 1900s, Mennonite Church congregations in California did not have locally established ministers; they were served by traveling ministers called "evangelists." The isolation Mennonites experienced along with their lack of influence among the local population heightened their sense of religious mission. To help stabilize new congregations, traveling evangelists were sent at times by denominational conferences to hold church services and offer pastoral support to congregations. In the Pacific Coast region, these evangelists traveled along a well-worn circuit through Oregon, California, Idaho, Washington, and back to Oregon. However, sometimes these evangelists traveled on their own initiative.

Revival meetings held by the traveling evangelists were used to attract people to join the local congregations. As Timothy Smith argues, revivalism was "not 'individualistic' in the usual sense that term suggests; though they made faith a profoundly personal experience, their aim and outcome was to bind individuals to new communities of belief and action."[47] The individualistic component of revivalism aided the modernization of the community to which one was "bonded" through the focus on individual conversion as prescribed by the group's precepts.[48]

Appreciation was expressed for any traveling evangelist who came to California. In Corning, for example, Emanuel Stahly reported that they warmly welcomed the visit of two preachers from Millersville, Pennsylvania. On two consecutive evenings, sermons were preached on Hebrews 2:1 and Revelations 3:8, with the theme of the "Open Door, and [he] earnestly admonished all to come to Christ before He would shut the door." Stahly also made it clear that his congregation believed "it would be well if more of our eastern ministers would visit the churches west of the Rocky Mountains. We had some very warm weather, but for some time now the weather is cool and pleasant."[49] Before Christ shuts the door, the call went out, please visit us.

One popular Mennonite Church evangelist was John P. Bontrager from Albany, Oregon. Local congregations naturally used his visits to entice the churched and unchurched in their communities to attend their church. In

1908, Mennonites in Dinuba hoped Bontrager would visit their congregation, and the next year he came.[50] Bontrager's 1909 sermons in Dinuba were well attended: "We as a little band were very much encouraged and strengthened in the faith. Sinners were under deep conviction but would not yield." The Mennonite Church in Dinuba had organized with seventeen members, held Bible meetings every Wednesday, and ran a Sunday school in addition to a Sunday service.[51]

Despite this religious activity, the Dinuba congregation reported, "We are much in need of help . . . being without a minister, and extend a hearty invitation to all west-bound ministers to make this one of their stopping points. We will gladly correspond with any one who is interested in this work, country, etc." The plea from Dinuba spoke of a need for mission to a lost humanity in their midst: "Doors are wide open to our church in California. The doctrines of our church are known to very few in the state. Souls are starving for want of the bread of life. We as a church claim to teach a pure and entire Gospel. If we are right, then many, many are living deceived." The writer asked, "In view of this fact, can it be right in the sight of God for three and four ministers to occupy the same pulpit Sunday after Sunday, year in and year out? Is that going into all the world and preaching the Gospel to every creature?"[52]

On the same 1909 visit to Dinuba, Bontrager also visited Porterville, where "twelve souls confessed Christ" and many more wrestled with an awakened awareness of sin. Moreover, Porterville "extend[ed] a hearty welcome to all coming to California to give us a visit."[53] Another evangelist, J. C. Springer from Upland, preached in Corning on September 25, 1909, and again on his way back home from Oregon and Washington on October 23. As a result of his visit, local citizens reminded eastern Mennonites that "it would be well if more of our ministering brethren would visit the small bands scattered over the Pacific Coast from time to time."[54]

Correspondence to the *Gospel Herald* that described visits such as those made by Allen Erb of La Junta, Colorado, and Bontrager, often concluded with requests that readers pray for the California church and its success in God's work. While Bontrager was in Pasadena for revival meetings in 1913, he brought a message of encouragement from other churches for them, as they were "far from our church homes."[55] In 1929 Bontrager and Erb visited Los Angeles. Erb gave a series of "soul-stirring and convicting" sermons on topics such as the life of Christ, baptism of the Holy Spirit, and the Second Coming of Christ, followed by Bontrager's sermon. The

Mennonite Church, with its small and scattered population, depended on the social network provided by the traveling evangelists, who carried messages and news from other places and maintained an apocalyptic urgency to the church's aloneness in California. The General Conference and Mennonite Brethren also used traveling ministers, but their larger numbers facilitated an easier creation of more extensive church networks.[56]

By the 1930s, the focus of church work in California shifted from the traveling evangelist to organizing churches. The Mennonite Church in Winton, organized in 1931, was made up of forty-two original members who transferred their church memberships to Winton from Sacramento, Modesto, Terra Bella, Dinuba, Lemon Cove, and Los Angeles. The Winton congregation continued the process of organizing their identity around typical American Protestant development when they held their first Mission Day meeting in 1931. Mission Day was an all-day affair with sermons and a program, which became a quarterly event. The congregation also held mid-week prayer meetings and biweekly Bible study class.[57]

As Winton developed institutionally, the Mennonite population became increasingly racially diverse, however slightly. In 1932, the congregation's aggressive mission outreach to the local community resulted in several Filipino attendees. That year they baptized a Filipino man and were excited by his desire to return to the Philippines to evangelize.[58] J. J. Reber, a congregant of Winton, focused on the baptism of the Filipino: "We praise God for the spiritual blessings received during the revival meetings [in Winton]. Also for a Filipino brother who was received into our beloved church by water baptism on Jan. 6. We have quite a number of Filipinos who attend regularly at our services." Significantly, despite Filipinos attending the church, it was not until one was baptized that the wider church learned of their presence, though the baptismal candidate was never named.[59]

With local churches building social networks through traveling evangelists and eventually organizing formally, the development of regional governing bodies began. The Pacific Coast Conference of the Mennonite Church was organized on November 1, 1906, with California, Arizona, and New Mexico joining later. In 1948, New Mexico, Arizona, and Southern California formed their own conference: the South Pacific Mennonite Conference. The South Pacific Mennonite Conference changed its name to Southwest Mennonite Conference (SWMC) a few years later, because of the great distances needed to travel for the Pacific Coast Mennonite Conference meetings.[60]

Members of the SWMC came from all parts of the country and in-cluded "Navajo Indians, Blacks, and Spanish Americans . . . There are many families from outside Mennonite backgrounds among us." This multiculturalism was a point of pride: "We are cosmopolitan. This is to us a fulfillment of the commandment of Christ."[61] Religious pluralism was at times threatening for the Mennonite Church, but racial diversity under-stood as cosmopolitan and deeply Christian was a badge of honor. Despite an evolving urban sophistication, the Mennonite Church's presence in California was always small, and several congregations attempted in Di-nuba, Corning, and Terra Bella failed for reasons ranging from expensive land to malaria to competition from other churches.[62]

Congregations that Disappeared

Mennonite successes in settling California were only part of the story, for the simple reality was that some congregations failed to survive. In 1907, a Mennonite Brethren group that had formed near San Diego in Escondido began its slow journey to oblivion. Traveling missionaries served them as they hoped for a permanent leader to move to their vicinity. That year, Elder Abraham Schellenberg, a prominent Mennonite Brethren leader, arrived, giving the small group a prominence it otherwise would not have enjoyed. The Escondido group dispersed in the early 1920s, however, af-ter consecutive years of citrus-destroying frost.[63]

The General Conference, in 1912, also attempted a congregation in Escondido under the guidance of Michael M. Horsch of Upland. After several families moved away, this church closed in 1934.[64] Escondido pro-vides an example of how the pressures of numerous religious options in an area can influence a small congregation. General Conference Mennonites were moving to the Escondido region by 1911. Shortly after building a church, GC membership dissipated throughout Southern California and parts of the San Joaquin Valley. In 1923, the local German Methodist church attempted to absorb the Mennonites who remained in the Es-condido region. That action encouraged Mennonites from as far away as Upland to support their co-religionists. With such support, the General Conference church in Escondido survived until the early 1930s, when it became too expensive to maintain a congregation of only eleven mem-bers. From local historians we learn that after the sale of the Escondido building, Los Angeles Mennonite ministers visited the Mennonites who remained. The Mennonites who stayed were discouraged, even homesick, and eventually dispersed among other churches.[65]

Northward, in the San Joaquin Valley, the establishment of a Mennonite institutional presence was tied directly to the availability of water for agricultural use. In the early decades of the twentieth century, the Central Valley Water Project was planned and constructed to bring enough water to the Central Valley to support an agricultural economy. By 1930 there had been so much groundwater pumping in the Central Valley that its agricultural economy was set to collapse. As a six-year drought began in 1929, agricultural interests and water access began to dominate state politics. Finally, in 1933, Sacramento passed the massive Central Valley Project Act. Because of the Depression, the bonds needed to finance the Central Valley Project (CVP) did not sell well, and President Franklin Roosevelt, through the U.S. Bureau of Reclamation, took control of the project. All this occurred as a historic drought crushed the Great Plains, and Oakies (migrant farm workers from Oklahoma) hit the road for California. After much political struggle over funding and land reclamation, and fierce opposition by privately held utilities, CVP construction began in 1937, and it finally brought water to the San Joaquin Valley in 1951.[66]

Economic struggles and a lack of water conspired to make life difficult. One church established in Dos Palos, Merced County, in 1930, lasted only until 1933. Despite initial optimism, "it was discontinued because of failure of promised water for irrigation."[67] As one Mennonite correspondent wrote, "California is not worth 5c[ents] an acre if it has no water. Water is the gold of California."[68] Without the promised water, the community crumbled.[69]

The Dos Palos story is part of California's troubled history with water. Donald Worster argues that in a society formed around centralized water control, the power to succeed or fail was often in the impersonal hands of the few who managed that "coercive, monolithic, and hierarchical system."[70] When it was clear that the water promised Dos Palos was a mirage, Mennonite farmers out of necessity moved away.

The Mennonite Brethren also attempted to settle Dos Palos and failed. Water and isolation did to them as to the others. Entreaties to send religious and spiritual assistance made by the Mennonite Brethren in Reedley to the Pacific District Conference resulted in quarterly song festivals, prayer, and preachers; none of it helped. In 1933, with no irrigation, a depressed economy, and neighbors moving away as land was repossessed, the

Dos Palos Mennonite Brethren group disbanded. Two denominations attempted simultaneous settlements at Dos Palos and both failed. As Kevin Enns-Rempel observes, Dos Palos was "a victim of economic hardship and spiritual isolation," exacerbated by a land company that failed to provide water.[71]

Religious Options

A significant part of the California context was the variety of religious options. Some saw the challenge of these options as especially powerful. By the late 1930s, Pastor D. D. Eitzen observed that Mennonite identity in Los Angeles was fluid and loyalty to the denomination weak. He estimated that about half of the Mennonites in the Los Angeles area attended the Church of the Open Door, which was affiliated with the fundamentalist Bible Institute of Los Angeles (BIOLA). Other churches that attracted Mennonites included the Presbyterian Church of Glendale, Christian Science churches, and Aimee Semple McPherson's Foursquare Gospel churches, along with "innumerable cults that thrive in this favorable California climate." Mennonite churches in the eastern states paid "little or no attention" to the condition of Mennonites in California, who were vulnerable to myriad religious alternatives.[72]

Though Eitzen gave no specific reasons for the dissatisfaction of Mennonites with their churches, they were nonetheless attracted to evangelical and conservative congregations that were very much part of the larger history of Southern California's development. Weakened ties with eastern denominational structures lent itself to a fervent entrepreneurial spirit that was part of the California religious context. The absence of the General Conference Mennonite establishment, which was centered in the Midwest, combined with a rich diversity of available religious alternatives permitted Mennonites in Southern California to avail themselves of the religious options in a pluralistic society—similar to a canopy through which the winds of society blew freely.[73]

North in the San Joaquin Valley, economic realities and religious options took a toll on a GC church in Shafter. Henry Krehbiel, an early twentieth-century General Conference leader, came to California in 1908 for the climate and stayed as a pastor in Reedley. As pastor, he bought and tended "several California fruit orchards" and lived in the area of Reedley locally known as "Mennonite Row." He was the pastor of Reedley

Jacob J. and Lena Reimer family in their home at Escondido.
Source: General Photograph Collection.

General Conference Mennonite Church until 1927, when he suffered
a severe heart attack. He died October 5, 1940.[74] Krehbiel also led the
development of the Shafter First Mennonite Church (GC), which served
Mennonites who migrated to the area in 1918–1919. The Shafter church
fell victim to the Depression when low fruit prices and increased irrigation costs devastated the local economy. Some Mennonites moved away,
and the rest joined other denominations as the church was dissolved. The
church's story did not end there, however; in 1935 Krehbiel returned to
Shafter, restarted the church, and two years later, attracted enough Mennonites to join that they built their own building.[75]

Mennonites Engage Modernity?

Churches, schools, and regional governing bodies mediated the migrants'
experience with California society through social networks and recog-

nizable religious structures. Change was not the nemesis of Mennonite cultural and religious identity, though it was often suspect and anxiety producing. A mixing of traditional Mennonite "ethnic" concerns with religious markers of identity propelled Mennonites in California to look more to the future and less to the past.[76] As they became acculturated Americans, their concerns were often the worldly present and the future, while attempting to remain faithful to their spiritual inheritance. The traveling evangelists, the Reedley school, and the general Mennonite emphasis on organizing communities around churches helped set boundaries with the wider world and provided institutional context to their religious and cultural identity.

The Mennonite Brethren, the largest Mennonite group in California, were largely evangelical and congregated mostly in the San Joaquin Valley, where they constructed institutions that helped to negotiate their boundaries with the larger world. Ironically, after World War II, this strategy encouraged their assimilation into California's social and evangelical culture. In the early period of their California experience, their school, which was constructed to teach German and the Bible, in fact became a community high school.

Timothy Smith argues that such a theologically informed process contradicts a secularization interpretation.[77] In some realms of the Mennonite experience, accommodation was made between religious impulses and secular society to such an extent that little distinction could be made between them. Secularization marks a realignment of identity, seeking justification more from society and less from religion. A Kansas Mennonite in the early 1950s observed that the distinctive Californian social environment was known well enough in other parts of the country: "It might be well for the rest of the Mennonites to look to the California churches who have had to face the trend to urbanization for some time both on the farm and in the city."[78] Mennonites looking westward in the postwar period understood that something was happening in California that would soon happen in the east.

Thus, during the early decades of the twentieth century, California Mennonites not only explored their new environment through a religious and spiritual language, which is explored in chapters 2 and 3, but also set about constructing an institutional culture. By the 1930s, Mennonites had organized several churches and created regional governing bodies, which always grouped California with neighboring states. Thus, Mennonites made visible their sense of religious and cultural identity. This institutional development also expanded to include other visible manifestations of Mennonitism, including health care and higher education.

Deep in these congregational and denominational stories, however, was the siren call of California's arcadian climate, which at times resulted in dramatic church growth, and at other times, tremendous loss, even failure. As I discuss in the next chapter, California was simultaneously Promised Land, Paradise Lost, healer, feverish swamp, fertile, and parched. California was also a place where religious boundaries within conservative Protestantism were porous and geographic distances great—exacerbating existing cultural-religious anxieties. Yet, it provided a natural canvas on which Mennonites illustrated their cosmology. As they set about the day-to-day tasks of settling in a new home, a rich sense of religious identity was unintentionally drawn out.

CHAPTER 2

Alone in the Garden

Boosters, Migrants, and Refugees

Finally we entered this land of "Milk and Honey"
with all its oranges and grapes.
—Mennonite immigrant, Thanksgiving Day, 1922

Garden of Eden and Forbidden Fruit

In the late 1970s, Daniel Hertzler, editor of the Mennonite weekly *Gospel Herald*, toured Mennonite congregations throughout the United States and Canada. When he visited one in Clovis, California, a congregant took him to nearby Reedley. Hertzler described the scene outside the car window: "It was fruit blossom time and with a little imagination we could have been led to believe that the Garden of Eden was in the San Joaquin Valley and the forbidden fruit a plum."[1] Although Hertzler's trip to California came approximately 130 years after the first Mennonite arrived, his two images of California—paradise and sin—were not new. Boosters and Mennonite settlers in the early twentieth century promoted a mythology of California as both Edenic paradise and forbidden fruit.

Throughout California's history, people often portrayed it in images crackling with cosmic significance. Turn-of-the century boosters promoted California as a natural arcadia. Many who made the journey to its utopian promise found their dreams, but others found disappointment or worse.[2] This chapter, sorting through the representations of California in the promotional literature of boosters commonly known to Mennonites and their own immigrant memoirs, shows the development of Mennonite visions of California and the Mennonites' place within it. The promises and failures of booster promotion and the refraction of memory through memoirs of those who moved to California—from the North American plains and Russian steppes—illustrates the power California held over Mennonite imaginations.

Hertzler's binary impression demonstrates how geography helps construct identity. In fact, the Janus-faced reality of California beguiled evangelicals, who saw promise and threat co-mingling there.[3] Philosopher José Ortega y Gasset argues that land has powerful symbolic meanings because its significance is predicated on the freedom people have (or some have) to choose where they live. He observes, "It is not simply that the land makes man, but that man *elects* his land, that is, his landscape, that portion of the planet where he finds his ideal or life-project symbolically prefigured."[4] This symbolic relationship extends to religion, where, as historian Laurie F. Maffly-Kipp observes, "Geographic placement is an important factor in understanding religious behaviors and beliefs."[5] As Hertzler so clearly illustrated, environment and religion are intimately connected. The Mennonites who came decades before him experienced this existentially as loneliness and spiritually as divine mission.

In a popular survey of Mennonite history, C. Henry Smith notes that the Mennonite Brethren had been largely attracted to California, especially to Fresno, since 1942.[6] Although the 1940s was a time of tremendous institutional development, California had been a favored destination for Mennonite Brethren long before then. The attraction for Mennonites, as for most everyone else, was prosperity, health, and climate. When these early Mennonite Brethren wrote to denominational newspapers, however, the dominant themes were social isolation, natural abundance, and moral depravity. As Willard Smith argues, the entire western migration of Mennonites in America is about isolation. Scattered Mennonite communities "illustrate[d] the spiritual problems of Mennonites who migrated west to areas where there were no Mennonite churches and little or no prospect of organizing them."[7] In the early decades of the twentieth century, Mennonites felt alone in a fecund garden.

Mennonite historians have typically understood Mennonite migrations as a religious response to persecutions or to thwart temptations to compromise core principles, especially pacifism. Once in North America, their westward movement and colonizing efforts were often interpreted as cultural-religious attempts to maintain traditional communities.[8] The leading American Mennonite historian of the mid-1900s, Harold S. Bender, summarized Mennonite identity: "Perhaps on the whole, however, the members of no religious or social group have seemed so much [as Mennonites] to be pilgrims and strangers on the earth rather than partakers of the life and culture of the men and nations among whom they have lived."[9] Bender's observation was upended in California.

In the early decades of the twentieth century, Mennonites moved to California primarily to improve their economic status and physical health; it was not a religious reaction to government policy, threatened principles, or persecution—save one important exception from Russia. Those who came to California often wrote about their experiences and thoughts concerning their new homes in a rhetorical mix of wonder and pain. Before they came, they listened to boosters who promoted California throughout North America as an arcadian garden. Many enjoyed those soothing pitches, and later some suffered the consequences of the hype. However, when Mennonites came, they brought their religion with them and easily mixed their hope for a Christian society with desires for health, sunshine, and prosperity.

Boosterism: Selling Sunny California

Water: The New California Gold

Companies attempting to lure Mennonites to California typically stressed three points: fabulous weather, agricultural productivity, and ethno-religious community. The Kern County Land Company claimed in an 1895 promotional pamphlet published specifically for Mennonites: "Along the coast the sea breeze softens the climate, therefore, in summer and winter it feels warmer than places with similar latitudes further inland." With idyllic climate also came health: "The dryness in the summer does not let malaria and related diseases arise, whereas consumption (tuberculosis), rheumatism, and lung illnesses are soon healed under such climatic conditions."[10] Though California was the second largest state in the Union and the first in produce, and Mennonites were agriculturalists, the final point was social stability and community. The need for fellowship, in a place so far away from the familiar, was not lost on land companies eager to promote California as an open paradise. Thus they claimed that several Mennonite families were already living there in absent-minded bliss (zerstreut).[11]

In 1896, other Mennonites made an investigative trip to Southern California and responded in prose sacralizing water and irrigation. They interpreted Southern California's aridity and need for irrigation through the prophetic writings of Isaiah 41:18 and 43:19. These two biblical passages describe God's promise to turn the wilderness into a "pool of water and the dry land springs of water," and, "I [God] will even make a way in the wilderness and rivers in the desert."[12] The ambition of human engineering, called on here to transform arid Southern California, was sacralized by these words of an ancient Hebrew prophet. The visiting Mennonites even observed that providentially the land was flat, "as if intended especially for irrigation."[13]

Irrigation was not an end but a means, and here it would turn a desert into a garden, where "large colonies of our people can be located."[14] This idea of transformation through irrigation was not peculiar to Mennonites. Universalist minister Thomas Starr King embraced the powerful myth of "deliverance through irrigation," earlier in the 1860s, when he described the transformation of desert into a garden as doing God's work. Nor were these rhetorical flourishes of an earlier time. An article in *Mennonite Community*, a Mennonite church publication of the 1950s, describes a congregation in Los Angeles accompanied by thirteen photos. One photo features a stream and lush vegetation with the caption, "California is beautiful[;] with artificial watering, the desert becomes lush woodland."[15] Mennonites enacted their own desert redemption through the tilling of gardens and construction of communities anchored by churches, schools, and socially oriented ministries. The Central Valley was truly a garden, albeit manufactured, and by the 1950s, there was little desert left to see.[16]

Spiritual Teacher for Tourists

Travel diaries, letters to newspapers, and serialized accounts of Mennonites who vacationed in California demonstrate further the grip California's natural environment held on Mennonite imaginations. Agnes Albrecht Gunden, on a trip from Peoria, Illinois, to Los Angeles, listed the many attractions her and her group visited. Upon reaching Corning, she described the scenery, "Palm trees, orchards of figs, peaches, pears, olives, almonds, and oranges were seen in abundance. Peaches and pears were ripe," and juxtaposed this garden image with the observation that no organized Mennonite church existed there.[17]

John Peters standing by his pumping plant at Fairmead, 1913.
Source: Papers of Julius Siemens.

In Southern California, Gunden went up Mount Lowe, took a trolley ride through Los Angeles, visited Long Beach, and went over to Catalina Island. On the way to Catalina Island, she reflected, "It was the nicest scenery we have seen since on our trip or before." Before her return home, she expressed her gratitude: "We have had a nice stay at Los Angeles and we thank the giver of all good for the privilege of seeing what we have seen and for getting into a good hotel." For Gunden, California was the apex of sacred natural scenery.[18]

Though nature captivated the senses, Mennonite visitors still considered California a lonely place without much by way of churchly infrastructure. C. Z. Yoder was part of a traveling party from the Midwest to the Pacific Coast in 1908. Yoder serialized his account of the trip in the *Gospel Herald* that same year. In Corning, he wrote, "Here grow without any winter protection the orange, lemon, fig, palm and eucalyptus trees, the last-named shed its bark annually, but not its leaves. The raisin grapes grow here in abundance and are dried in the sun, as well as other fruit." As they headed to Dinuba, Yoder observed the isolation experienced by Mennonites living there: "These brethren are here without a resident minister. These congregations appreciate visitors from the same faith in a way that large congregations do not understand." Along the way, they passed through San Francisco, saw some damage from the 1906 earthquake and fire, and visited "Bro[ther]" D. E. Conrad of the Bay Area, who was "deprived of the privilege of attending services with his brethren in the faith."[19]

A common Mennonite practice at the time was to visit churches while vacationing. In addition to the stop in Dinuba, Yoder and his party visited Mennonites in Los Angeles and Upland. He observed: "In visiting these brethren and the small congregations on the Pacific coast, having no resident minister, we are again reminded of the great need of workers." While thinking of the denominational response, he writes, "May the Lord hasten the day when our Churches, conferences and mission Board, will put forth greater efforts to send out laborers in the great harvest field to watch over the shepherd less ones and to see the lost and dying." Yet landscape was the image of California that Yoder held on to as he departed: "On Sept. 24, [1908], we left our friends at Upland, Calif. In a few hours we miss the beautiful orange groves, the flowers and the evergreen trees, and instead are passing through a barren land for hundreds of miles where water is shipped on the railroad and sold to the consumers. How thankful we should be for the abundant supply of good, refreshing water."[20]

There was also a tendency by migrants and tourists alike to see in California's natural environment a moral and spiritual teacher. When, for example, Helen Stoesz and her family moved from Minnesota to California in approximately 1920, she reflected on their arrival: "The roses were in full bloom and the tall stately palm trees all helped to make the trip enjoyable. Besides that, we had left Minnesota in a snow storm . . . I still remember how we walked on the sandy beach and watched the ever present sea gulls dashing down when the ocean tide had washed various small sea life onto the sandy beach; then the sea gulls would have their feed." Yet she concludes on a pious note: "What a wonderful Lord we have! He takes care of the birds of the air, who do not toil nor need to work for . . . daily food."[21]

Anna Nissley, from Lancaster County, Pennsylvania, took a trip to the coast and wrote three articles of her experience exploring the landscape and reflecting on its meaning. In the Sierra Madre, at Cucamonga Canyon, a bridge of logs Nissley and her friends tried to build across a stream washed away. She concluded, "The thought presented to me, that Satan will take us just as quickly down the current of endless woe if we allow him to lift our feet from the rock." Likewise, after she took a drink of water, she was reminded "that God was the Giver of all, and the Creator of the surroundings which were very picturesque."[22]

Nissley made two other trips that year. On one she took the electric car to the summit of Echo Mountain and "realizing the great depth below us almost caused us to shudder, yet perfectly safe, knowing no condemnation resting on our souls. We could sing praises to God for the privilege to behold the beauty of His works."[23] The Pacific Ocean offered a grand view, an afternoon of hunting seashells, and a visit to Catalina Island; it also reminded Nissley of "the benighted heathen on the other side. And our minds wandered from place to place where our missionaries are stationed." California was not only a natural paradise, it was a constant reminder of God's creative power and salvation, and that near the continent's edge were the heathen. The question of California's abundance nagged her as she traveled north through the San Joaquin Valley towards Oregon: "We all gazed with great admiration and wondered why the Creator put so much beauty at one place."[24] It was a marvelous landscape evoking for Mennonite travelers the temptations of Satan, the power of God the creator, and their responsibility for mission.

In some ways, she answered her own question with her pious outpourings of spiritual lessons gleaned from California's natural world. Nissley was not the only Mennonite to explore California and make such spiritual connections. Frank and Mary Smucker on vacation drew similar conclusions: "A person stands by the seashore and views the mighty ocean and the great mountain peaks [and] it causes us to think more and more of the One who created both the heavens and the earth."[25] As another tourist observed, next to the Pacific Ocean, "We feel the littleness of our insignificant self," while God was its creator and controller.[26]

California was both a marvel to behold and an existential puzzle. After crossing the Colorado River into Bagdad, California, Oswald Goering described his first impressions of California in guarded tones: "Mountains, no plants—little vegetation—at places nothing but rocks and sand. Even bare mountains are beautiful as far as forms go but how the few people live is a question." Goering, arrested by paradise, wrote, "We stopped to look at ocean within 15 feet of water (and then I put my hand in the water, I had my hand in the Pacific Ocean.) . . . trees [were] loaded with oranges."[27] The Pacific Ocean was not only an important destination, but also a mystical experience. Through a fusion of evangelical Mennonite biblicism and pietistic emphasis on experiential theologizing, these moments were much more than emotional tourism.

Even when visitors encountered discouraged MC Mennonites, in places like Dinuba, the fecundity of the environment often took precedence in their reporting. S. B. Zook from Hubbard, Oregon, took a trip to Los Angeles and returned through Porterville, Dinuba, and San Francisco. Although the MC Mennonites in Dinuba were "discouraged," Zook was particularly impressed with the valley's flatness, and how "with the aid of irrigation system it is made quite productive." In addition to alfalfa, there were the oranges, peaches, and figs to admire, grown in rich sandy soil in a warm climate. According to Zook, the land surrounding Dinuba was the "greatest . . . in central California for all kinds of fruit growing."[28] Los Angeles, Zook effused, was Edenic: "The climate is invigorating, the atmosphere pure and balmy, the fruit trees laden with tropical fruit, and the evergreen shade trees and the flowers of every color are all around us, it truly makes us feel that it is good to be here."[29] For tourists, as with migrants, California's environment was a spiritually transformative force.

Travels to church conferences were also occasions for Mennonites to wax eloquently on California's wonders. J. C. Mehl, a Mennonite reporter at the 1910 General Conference Pacific District Conference in Upland, observed the "rich delights as we rushed along past lemon and orange groves, through alfalfa fields and walnut orchards—many of these being bordered by rows of palms or acacia trees, or by beds of roses, geraniums, dahlias or other blooming plants." Mehl's description of Los Angeles itself focused on water, specifically the once controversial Owens River aqueduct, transporting water hundreds of miles to "Angel City," diminishing "that deceptive mirage of the desert which has lured many a sun-scorched traveler to a tragic death." The route through the Tehachapi was "tortuous" and then "as though being weary of its awful contortions the train shoots out like an arrow into the beautiful San Joaquin valley."[30] Similarly, on a trip in 1930 from Colorado to California, Dora Shantz Gehman invoked not only natural abundance, but also the Native American presence. She reported on "eating more grapes . . . [seeing] many Indians, goats and cattle—adobe houses," and in so doing, captured 1930 California in terms of fruit production and Native architecture.[31] These travel narratives covered similar themes as found in early Mennonite reports: natural abundance, exotic newness, wonderful irrigation, and lessons from heaven.

New Ethno-Religious Colonies

In the early twentieth century, companies such as the Rawlings Land Company and Kern County Land Company as well as individuals such as Karl Pohl, of Kerman, California, continued to use such booster tropes of nature, prosperity, and ethno-religious community. The Rawlings Land Company advertised in the *Steinbach Post*, a weekly German-language newspaper serving a primarily Mennonite community in southern Manitoba, Canada. Teasingly the ad asked: "Have you heard of the new German Mennonite settlement in Littlefield, Texas?" Rawlings claimed that "over 50 families from Kansas, Oklahoma, California, North Dakota and Manitoba" had already bought land here both "fertile and flat."[32]

Karl Pohl—more aggressive in his advertising—used an outline similar to the Kern County Land Company, which underscored nature, production, and community. Attempting to reach the frostbitten Mennonites in southern Manitoba, Pohl spoke of California as having "no winter" and possessing a "sunny climate [which] offers you God's beautiful nature." Of course, warm weather was only part of the story. In Kerman a farmer could make with 20 acres in raisins what 640 acres of grain anywhere else could produce. To believe this, one must come and see the "pure land" located "in the heart of the most fertile valley in America, the San Joaquin Valley." Finally, to make the pitch irresistible, Pohl declared Kerman to be "The new German colony," where twenty acres of raisins, alfalfa, or fruit could establish a secure home.[33]

Building great and prosperous colonies in California was also a task for Mennonite land promoters. In 1908 Julius Siemens, an enterprising Mennonite land promoter, was corresponding with the California Irrigated Land Company of San Francisco regarding land in Tehama County.

From 1910 to 1911, he promoted land in Los Molinos, Tehama County, in an attempt to create the "greatest Mennonite settlement in California." He even attempted a second colony in Fairmead, Madera County.[34] Siemens and his partners were so sure of this venture that when two men took a financial loss and pulled out of the deal, all he said was, "The weather here is simply beautiful and I do not see how a man could return to Ritzville [Washington] where no work can be done for several months."[35] More appropriately, for Siemens, was the response of a delegation from Hillsboro, Kansas. After a tour of the San Joaquin Valley and San Francisco, the delegation wrote a thank-you letter saying California was so impressive that when they stopped in New Mexico they were not enchanted.[36]

In a 1913 promotional pamphlet for his settlement at Fairmead, Siemens answered people's questions. He described the land as flat and even, like that of the Red River Valley in Canada and North Dakota, or the Molotschna in Russia—all areas of successful Mennonite settlements. The Fairmead colony, he assured them, was in the most beautiful and fruitful part of the San Joaquin Valley, with up to three alfalfa harvests a year. For the farms to succeed, however, each family needed to set up their own irrigation at their own expense, at an estimated cost of ten to fifteen dollars per acre. Siemens advised Mennonites that they would save money if they did it themselves during the winter, when twenty acres could be set up for irrigation.[37]

Siemens assured his audience that twenty Mennonite Brethren and five General Conference families were already settled there, holding religious services. Fairmead was not only beautiful; it was also only three miles from the nearest Mennonite settlement. To underscore the desirability of the soil there, Siemens claimed that many traveled thousands of miles to purchase this land, where water already came from a canal off the Kings River. It was perfect, where the crops were plentiful, the water accessible, and the people living there German speaking.[38]

To press his point, Siemens described the climate as the best in North America, with no winter, in contrast to Siberia, Canada, or the midwestern states. He even made the improbable claim that the summer sea breeze coming out of San Francisco's Golden Gate moderated Fairmead's climate. Having addressed the concerns of climate, economics, and ethno-religious community, Siemens ended his promotion with the grand declaration that his settlement in Fairmead would be "die groeszte deutsche Ansiedlung in Kalifornien," or "the greatest German Settlement in California."[39]

A pump and canal on the Wittenberg farm at Fairmead, 1913.
Source: Papers of Julius Siemens.

Despite boosterism, sacred readings of the environment, and the ambitions of Mennonite land promoters, Mennonite desire for westward expansion was met with some disapproval. In 1909 J. M. Brunk, likely from Colorado, criticized westward-migrating Mennonites for alienating other Mennonites with what he saw as materialist expansionism. He described the early twentieth century as a time of "restlessness and dissatisfaction with present locations." Brunk continued, "While we heartily endorse the idea of evangelization by colonization . . . we feel that the time is here when we should raise our voices against the modern church-destroying

Cornelius Siemens and Abraham Siebert working the land at Fairmead, 1913.
Source: Papers of Julius Siemens.

spirit of restlessness and land craze about which we have been hearing so much the past few years." The destructive spirit Brunk described was found "especially among the smaller congregations of the West . . . [who were] ready to respond to any call which may come from some brother who has found a beautiful oasis where he hopes to plant a colony of Mennonites."[40]

Brunk even called Mennonites hypocrites who were involved in the westward expansion and colonization of the American West, a process contributing to the scattering of Mennonites. It was hypocrisy, he argued, to constantly change location, invoking the "direct leadings of God," only to move elsewhere after a series of crop failures. The westering phenomena was dismissed by Brunk as foolish: "Experience has proven that it is very unwise for individuals or even families to isolate themselves from all others of like faith, and endeavor to cope with the battles of life on the frontier." Although Brunk did not explain what the frontier battles were, he insisted that financial reasons should be secondary to religious reasons for moving. He was particularly frustrated by the glowing letters read back east: "In the midst of our work, letters would come to some of the brethren, painting such glowing financial pictures of distant localities that we found it difficult to keep the pulse of some of the brethren normal even in the midst of our meetings."[41] Despite the quickened heartbeats of eastern Mennonites, and Brunk's heavy pronouncements, many Mennonites moved, and some were fleeced because of their California fever.

Scandalized California Fever

Several Mennonite families suffered in what is known as the Henry J. Martens Land Scheme. Henry J. Martens boasted of and sold land in the western states, primarily in California, to Mennonites in the Great Plains. One such farmer described the mood in 1909: "Because of the ongoing unmerciful storm and continuing drought, we have gotten the blues and already have strong symptoms of the California fever ... We are reading that Mr. Martens will make another excursion there in September. Then not all our hope will vanish if he gives us an opportunity to go along and the California fever has not left us by then; for now the fever here is very high."[42] Intoxicated with "California fever," many were receptive to his sales pitch.

Martens swept through the Midwest, peddling the fifty thousand acres of California land he claimed to own. He regaled Mennonites in Oklahoma, Kansas, Nebraska, and South Dakota with stories of fabulous wealth awaiting those who ventured west. Despite his claims, Martens, it seems, had arranged to purchase 5,120 acres in California, and he exchanged them for farmers' acres in the Midwest. He brought these families in by train and ensured that they were well treated.[43] It was the beginning of Martensdale.

Martens's scheme developed to such proportions that some of the Mennonites who moved to Martensdale began meetings—with Martens—to start a Bible college. A college board was formed; Martens donated land and pledged to meet any fiscal shortfall—up to three thousand dollars. The board set March 1, 1910, as their "no later" date by which to begin construction.[44] However, before any construction began, Martensdale collapsed as the scheme became apparent.

After they arrived, Martens gave the Mennonites maps to their land. By Christmas 1909, the newly arrived Mennonites learned they were living on someone else's property. In many cases, Mennonites had built houses that now needed to be transferred onto wagons as they looked for

Henry J. Martens excursion group in front of the San Gabriel Mission, 1909—
the group was on its way to see Martens' land in Kern County.
Source: Papers of Regina Becker.

a new place to live. A victim of the scandal reported: "Our joy had turned
to sorrow—we could not stay here. Every day the little homes were set
on wagons and taken to Rosedale or Bakersfield by the owners . . . The
land deal was unsatisfactory, so in June we moved the house with all its
contents, including the family, to a lot not far from the present Beardsley
School, in northern Bakersfield." In a final blow, the writer noted that because of "much swampland along the Kern River[,] John, Marie, Regina
and I contracted Malaria fever. We were compelled to move again."[45] Indeed, California fever became malarial fever.

Some people later in life reflected on their experiences at Martensdale
and used biblical texts to make sense of the disaster. J. P. Nord, for example, cited Psalm 46:1, "God is our refuge and strength, a very present
help in trouble," and P. P. Elrich cited Numbers 13:17 for what he thought
to be an appropriate description of the Mennonite "exodus" to California:

"When Moses sent them to spy out the land of Canaan, he said to them, 'Go up there unto the Negev; then go up into the hill country.' "[46] As these Mennonite migrants reflected on California, the biblical images are interesting: a place of trouble, the Promised Land, Canaan, relocating from one place to another. The Promised Land of California was Paradise Lost.

In these reports and letters—from early settlers, tourists, church correspondents, concerned readers, and victims—one set of Edenic images was counteracted with a dim view of American expansion. If the boosters and promoters lured many Mennonites from winter windchill to winter sea breeze, concerned readers such as J. M. Brunk saw something altogether different at work. In what appears to be a recalling of the biblical prophecy that in the last days people will move about freely, quickly, and often (Daniel 12:4), Brunk reminds his readers that destruction lies nearby. By taking an active role in the westward march across the North American continent—to the disregard of spiritual maturity that comes with stable settlement—their excited march was a harbinger of church destruction, absorbing lost battles endemic to frontier life, and hypocrisy. Those who actually migrated to California, however, were unambiguous in their desires, and when a few wrote their memoirs later in life, many kept the florid flourishes—even if tempered by time.

The Promised Land: End of a Westward Journey

Mennonite journeys to California were numerous and varied. Although some migrated from Russia to California via New York and Mexico, with one coming to Reedley from Mexico by taxi,[47] most are stories of immigration cast in exodus or eschatological imagery. John J. Gerbrandt, in his concise narrative of packing the car and driving west, bathes it in natural imagery and biblical symbolism. When the Gerbrandts arrived in South Dakota from Manitoba, after a delay due to car trouble, he recalled, "We had so much hoped that we would be farther along to the land of eternal summer by this time."[48] California as the land of "eternal summer," or the land without winter, was a powerful image not only for the Mennonites in Manitoba, as illustrated earlier in the advertisements land companies and boosters used, but for many other years later.

Throughout Gerbrandt's memoir, the excitement of moving westward was captured by the repeated use of phrases like "turned west," "faces were turned west," "point of no return," and "determined to continue

The Excursion to California

Aug. 1909.

Henry J. Martens excursion group in White's Park in Riverside, California,
August 1909; possibly the same group as at the San Gabriel Mission.
Source: General Photograph Collection.

west." Their excitement grew the nearer they came to California, "as we
headed west to lower elevations with expectations of reaching our 'Promised Land', our spirits rose . . . closer and closer we came to the Promised
Land." Finally the great day came, when they crossed the border into
Needles, California, and "oh how we all rejoiced when finally we entered
this 'Land of Milk and Honey' with all the oranges and grapes we had heard
about!" They rejoiced in the belief that God had brought them to Reedley,
on Thanksgiving Day, in 1922. It was an adventure filled with optimism
and hope in what the Promised Land of California could be.[49] Though Gerbrandt combined an excited reading of the exodus motif with an important
national feast day, not all Mennonite accounts were so extravagant.[50]

Most memoirs from Kansas and Oklahoma primarily described agricultural activity, climate, and the business scene in Reedley. As one re-counted, "After they [male family members who took a trip to California] returned from their trip, all we heard for days, especially from my father, Daniel T. Eymann, was about the wonders of California and its marvelous climate."[51] Climate as a motivator was common, as clear in the explanation given by Marie Eymann-Marlar, an early Mennonite settler in Reedley, for their decision to move: "Having spent many years in the rigors of Kansas climate, my parents spent several weeks during the winter in various cities in California," and that was all they needed to be convinced.[52]

Regina Becker, whose family came from Oklahoma in 1909, wrote a family history in 1974. Taking the long view, she opens with a fifteen-page account of church, Anabaptist, and American Mennonite history. The chapter "California Fever 1912–1918" describes why several of her relatives sold their homesteads and moved to California: "[On] April 11, 1912 Uncle Frank wrote a letter from El Modena, Calif. praising the comfortable weather—not too hot, not too cold. No wind storms, little weather damage 'that beats Oklahoma.'"[53]

Carl Pankratz was seventeen in 1937 when he and his family left their farm in Oklahoma for better luck in California. After years of drought and grasshoppers, the dust bowl finally became too much, and the Pankratz family pulled up and moved. In Reedley young Carl Pankratz worked digging ditches for irrigation pipelines, pruning fruit trees, toiling in packing sheds, and picking cotton near Firebaugh. In just a few years during that terrible decade, the Pankratzes went from growing cotton in Oklahoma to picking it in California.[54]

The 1930s did, however, shape Carl's religious outlook for life. After the Great Depression and World War II passed, Carl and his brother, Abe Pankratz, struck out on their own and purchased fifty acres to grow primarily sweet potatoes. After marrying, Carl sold his interest, and he and his wife, Mildred, settled in Reedley, where he took up carpentry and house building. Mildred raised up to 4,000 chickens after they purchased a cotton farm and chicken ranch, pushing Carl's carpentry to the side. Over the decades of the 1950s to the 1980s, they were heavily involved with the Mennonite Disaster Service (MDS), an interdenominational Mennonite agency to assist those caught in mostly natural disasters. Late in life, Carl attributed his interest in working for MDS, including in its top levels of administration in California, to his participation in the dust bowl migration of the 1930s.[55]

Despite the preponderance of affection given to California climate and geography, weather was the least of concerns for Mennonites elsewhere in the world who came to California.

The Promised Land: The End of a Journey for Soviet Refugees

During the winters of the 1920s, Mennonites crossed the frozen Amur River on the border of Manchuria and the eastern Soviet Union, fleeing Communist oppression for American freedom via Harbin, China.[56] Aided by J. J. Isaac, a physician in Harbin, they contacted Mennonite relief agencies in the United States and in Europe. Between two and three hundred Mennonites were granted admission to the United States, and they settled mostly in California. Those who did not go to California went to Washington, Paraguay, or Brazil.[57]

Peter C. Hiebert, through the inter-Mennonite relief agency, the Mennonite Central Committee (MCC), appealed to President Herbert Hoover to help bring over the Harbin Mennonites. Hoover agreed to bring the three hundred Mennonites to America in small groups month by month. They arrived at San Francisco, and while MCC was responsible for logistics upon their arrival, Hiebert suggested they write a thank-you letter to Hoover. Over the course of a year, the Mennonites who arrived in California settled mostly in Reedley, where they "adjusted to the American way of life and became prosperous." Twenty-five years later, the Harbin Mennonites held a reunion in Dinuba and honored Hiebert.[58]

Several survivors and descendants of the Harbin refugees wrote memoirs. H. P. Isaak wrote of his family's adventure in *Our Life Story and Escape* (1976). Isaak's family received permission in 1930 to travel to "the glorious Beulah land of America." When "the day and hour had come where we also would leave for the beloved land where gold and honey flowed," on April 4, 1930, they boarded a ship for San Francisco. It was "like a dream, as also the fact that we were actually on our way to the 'Promised Land,' the United States; where the people tell no lies, no one steals, and none are poor!"[59] Isaak's infectious optimism was soon dampened. He was nearly deported from Angel Island, the immigration-processing center near San Francisco, and later tricked out of his fruit-picking wages. His youthful enthusiasm now tempered later in life, he wrote: "We also believed that the American dollar was worth more than a gold dollar, that the President

Mennonite immigrants from Harbin picking fruit near Orange Cove, ca. 1930s.
Source: Records of Reedley Mennonite Brethren Church.

of the United States [Herbert Hoover] must be like unto the angels, that on some streets the surface was covered with gold, and that all one had to do was to bend down and pick it up. We had some grandiose preconceptions and I believed them all."[60] Other Harbin migrants wrote less apocalyptically about what America and by extension California meant symbolically, but the metaphors of exodus and the Promised Land remained.

Herb Neufeld's family history, for example, describes the flight from Russia to America, "the land of freedom and peace," to escape the oppressive government policies of post–1917 Revolution Russia. Once in Harbin, in winter 1929, Herb's father, Jacob, recalled that his brother had a daughter, Elisabeth Neufeld, in either Shafter or Reedley. Jacob wrote letters to both Mennonite Brethren churches hoping to find her to ask for a travel loan. Elisabeth Neufeld, from Shafter, received one of the letters in time and raised money for their passage to America.[61]

In September 1930, with travel documents and money received, they gladly set sail for America: "Even though they were unable to get much food, they knew they could endure anything, now that they were leaving for America!" Herb further exclaimed: "As the ship sailed into San Francisco Bay, Jake and Corney stood on the deck and took in all the marvelous sights: the beautiful bay with ocean liners and cargo ships, the islands —Angel Island, Treasure Island and Alcatraz—all resting in the middle of glistening blue water . . . They marveled at the scene before them and thought it was the most beautiful sight they had ever seen. This was America!"[62]

They docked at Angel Island. After some confusion regarding their country of origin, and facing possible deportation to Russia because they had left without permission, their sponsors from Shafter intervened. While in custody, the Neufelds were permitted to stay together as a family, and they were fed large meals and given beds and blankets. Helena (Herb's mother) reacted "sternly" to the immigration official when informed of their likely deportation to Russia. Only after this confrontation did their sponsoring relatives from Shafter arrive. The family wrote a letter to President Hoover and believed he personally responded, despite a lack of any evidence, for in only one week they were granted admission.[63]

There are conflicting stories of their gaining admission. In another account, the family made a request to the Department of Immigration. When the commissioner could not act on their request, senators Hiram Johnson and Samuel Shortridge were petitioned for assistance. One of the senators sent a telegram to Washington, as did Representative H. Barbour of Fresno, and the matter was cleared up after a bond for one thousand dollars was posted.[64] Nonetheless, the Neufelds arrived in Shafter on November 1, 1930, and immediately gave thanks to God: "Now they were finally safe and free from oppression, thanks to the wonderful people in Shafter and the generosity of the government of the United States and the president." Mennonites in Shafter gave them furniture, clothes, food, and jobs for the men. The family soon took English lessons at the local elementary school. Three months after their arrival, Helena gave birth to a son named Herbert, after the president.[65]

Not all Mennonites who fled Soviet oppression at this time came via Harbin. Arthur Rempel, likely no relation to the Neufeld family above, like other memoirists began his family history with the sixteenth-century radical reformation in Holland but focused on events in the twentieth century, conflating religious and historical genealogies. In 1922, in Gnaden-feld, Ukraine, Arthur's uncle Wilhelm and aunt Margaret Neufeld, from Reedley, came bringing food to help the family, who were caught in fam-ine. That fall the Rempels left for America. "As we reached the western Atlantic . . . Soon we sighted land, and not much later, land flanked us on both sides as we glided up Long Island Sound and ended our sea voyage when the skyscrapers of New York reached up toward the sky before our eyes. We had reached America!"[66] The Neufeld family cleared Ellis Is-land, took a Southern Pacific train to California, and arrived in Reedley in February 1923. Arthur's relatives lent them a cottage on their farm, where he noticed the "arid subtropical climate of the San Joaquin Valley." The palm, eucalyptus, lemon, and orange trees growing alongside the magno-lias were all new to him.[67]

Contrasting Immigrant Visions

The trope of suffering in the migration stories of coming to California permeated the psychic foundation of Mennonite presence in California.[68] Mennonites came because of economic dislocation, religious persecution, dust bowl drought, and physical illness. They came by train from the Great Plains and Midwest, car from Canada, hired taxi from Mexico City, in sleds over frozen Russian rivers, through the Russian refugee haven of Harbin, China, just ahead of the Japanese invasion of Manchuria in 1931, and across oceans with hearts full of hope for a new life in America and anxiety for not having exit visas.

Even the cover art used by the two groups of Mennonite migrants for their memoirs reveals significantly different understandings of their jour-neys. Herb Neufeld's memoir has a red outline of a man running against a black background, which gives a bold impression to the subtitle of the book, *Escape from Communist Russia*. Other titles, such as *Escape to Freedom*, with the Golden Gate Bridge superimposed onto an American Flag on the cover, or *From Despair to Deliverance*, with a cover depicting a dark green-gray dense forest giving way to a light blue-white mountain vista, or John Block's eschatological laden *Escape: Siberia to California—The 65 Year Provi-dential Journey of Our Family*, all come with symbols of spiritualized place identity. Mennonites from the Great Plains spoke more to an image of rugged individualism with titles such as *Water from the Well: The Recollec-tions of a Former Plowboy*; Auernheimer's *Memories of a Farm Boy*; Becker's,

A Bundle of Living: Recollections of a Shafter Pioneer; the autobiography *JB: The Autobiography of a Twentieth-Century Mennonite Pilgrim;* and Hofer's, *Accepting the Challenge: The Autobiography of David L. Hofer.* Where the original covers exist, they are usually photographs of the author; Auernheimer's uses four photographs of highlights of his life. It should be noted that J. B. Toews was part of the Soviet refugee story in his coming to America, and as many Mennonites did, he lived a life of frequent migratory moves, eventually coming to California from the Midwest, where he had become a Mennonite Brethren leader.[69]

Both sets incorporate biblical imagery in describing California. Soviet refugees, who moved from politically oppressive and economically depressed situations to a prosperous and safe country, employed an apocalyptic narrative of providence and destiny. Midwestern and Canadian prairie migrants, who moved to California on account of climate and depressed farming conditions—but favorable political contexts—used a narrative reflective of the Hebraic exodus story of suffering, migration, and deliverance. The difference between the two exodus-type accounts is the apocalyptic tone of the Soviet refugee Mennonites, reflective of the arduous, even desperate, conditions of their migratory experience.[70] The borrowing of the Hebraic exodus story by North American Mennonites was significant for their emphasis on prosperity and appropriating that biblical story as a rhetorical device to sacralize hard economic realities and a fertile Promised Land.

Mennonite historian Harold S. Bender's description of the Mennonites wandering the earth in search of a home and not partaking of the culture of nations never applied in California. With the exception of a few hundred Harbin refugees, Mennonites moved to California for economic and climatic reasons.[71] Boosters and migrants alike interpreted California and the process of migrating there through an array of religious images denoting an early strategy of becoming part of California society. Attempting to make sense of their experiences as migrants and new residents, these images mixed various Christian and California visions of a natural utopia, mystical journey, and spiritual teacher. They linked their visions of California to providence and freedom. As we will see in the next chapter, these same migrants soon published images of California as a dystopic society. Mennonites in the early decades of twentieth-century California found an Edenic garden. Like Hertzler in the 1970s, they also found paradise to be both soothing and harrowing.

CHAPTER 3

Urban Dystopia and Divine Nature

The Early Mennonite Colonies

We are living in an age much like Rome.
—Mennonite visitor at the 1915 San Francisco World Fair

Loneliness in Paradise

John Ratzlaff and his family moved from Henderson, Nebraska, to Glendora, California, in the late nineteenth century. He wrote of life in California since their big move as comfortable, as were their "earthly relationships" (*irdischer Beziehung*), and they enjoyed an abundance of fruit from their harvest in 1895. Life was still difficult, and the Ratzlaffs felt isolated and lonely despite fine relationships and harvests. They hoped other Mennonites would move to their area and that they would also spiritually grow to become more dependent on the Lord, or "childlike" (*kindlich*). If those two things happened, Ratzlaff thought, God would never leave them alone.[1] This mixing of abundance and forlornness with invitations for others to visit, move, or simply write letters to alleviate the loneliness of the Californian garden was common. As another family explained, they would have reported on their experiences more often except that the alfalfa harvest took so much time, but they still needed letters for encouragement.[2]

Letters written to denominational magazines as well as memoirs penned for posterity provide immediacy to early Mennonite responses to California's urban and natural environments. The religious imagination

of Mennonites regarding their new lives in California was not limited to
awe at the scenery. There were problems in California that needed understanding, and a dichotomy between "nature" and "city" emerged. In these
reflections, authors often expressed an internal conflict pitting the joy of
California's abundance and climate against a deep sense of isolation. In
some cases, the conflicting symbols and images describe a spiritual battle
at the intersection of social isolation and sacralized environment.

Loneliness, isolation, and invitations for co-religionists to visit were
common themes in religious letter writing in the early twentieth-century
American West and not limited to Mennonites or California. Colin Goodykoontz describes this as a persistent trait among "missionaries" to the
American West, where they often asked Christians, mostly from their
own denomination, to move and help "form centers of Christian influence."[3] This attempt to create centers of Christian influence was a Mennonite imperative even as they emphasized the abundant natural environment and social isolation in their invitations. Of the three Mennonite
groups, the Mennonite Church wrote most extravagantly of the loneliness
suffered and expressed most deeply their sense of apocalyptic expectation.

L. A. Weaver, from Dinuba, wrote several letters to Mennonite Church
newspapers, *Gospel Herald* and *Gospel Witness,* and consistently mentioned
loneliness. Weaver sighed in 1908, "We do not like to be so far away from
the rest, but perhaps the Lord has something in it for us that we cannot
now see. We know the Lord makes no mistakes so we want Him to lead
and direct our way."[4] A year later, he somberly reminded co-religionists of
their existence and evangelical errand, that they were "among the living
. . . There are not many outsiders attending here, but we are not ashamed."
Saddened by his social isolation and the lack of "outsider" presence in
his church—implying the importance of the church's mission—Weaver
plaintively stated, "When we read of preachers going from place to place
visiting the churches, we wish we might be favored with a visit from some
of them."[5] However, the Weavers lived "out among the foothills at present,
so far away from our congregation." Finally, at the end of their capacity
to be so far from even their own local church, they considered moving.[6]
Tied to the lingering sadness of their living arrangements was the relent-
less march of time and the hope of an afterlife: "We are still getting older
every year. Work goes harder this year than it has, yet [it] makes us feel
glad our time is coming to leave this earthy tabernacle and go home where
there is no sorrow, and no old age."[7]

Isolation was exacerbated by the lack of ministers and visitors. As the Mennonite correspondent from Corning, north of Sacramento, wrote, "We believe it would be well if more of our eastern ministers would visit the churches west of the Rocky Mountains."[8] This complaint of a lack of ministers willing to move to California was not limited to the remote Mennonite Church in Corning. The more established group in Upland, in Southern California, had the same issue. They numbered eleven but planned to organize as a congregation; therefore, they requested that a minister come and settle with them. In what appears to be an attempt to make Upland more attractive, B. P. Swartzendruber, a deacon, followed up the request for a minister: "The Lord is blessing our brethren in material things at Upland and we are glad to note that they are willing to give the Lord a return of the same." In addition to material blessings, there were also evangelistic meetings held by traveling evangelists, all indicating activity and potential for Mennonites in the region.[9] Such preoccupations with loneliness and isolation from co-religionists came naturally enough with calls for ministers and others to visit.

Coinciding with lonely isolation was a sense of evil lurking nearby. In 1909, Mary Schrock wrote from Corning, "Though we are thousands of miles apart, yet we worship the same Lord and He is holding out before us the glorious light of the Gospel, shielding us against the fiery darts of the evil one. We may be surrounded by trials and temptations, but we are cheered by the presence of the Holy Comforter."[10] Mennonites were not the only ones migrating to California, and the growing presence of others was threatening. In a 1909 article, "The Heathen Invasion of America," the spiritual situation in California is depicted as troubling, for "Buddhists have their shrine in California." America's first Buddhist temple had been dedicated in San Francisco. Moreover, "The number of Hindus in America has been increasing since 1900 and there are now seventeen Hindu students in the University of California alone."[11] There were California Mennonites, like Elmer Isgrigg, who believed "the Devil is trying to defeat us" and hoped "to have any of God's children visit."[12] Believing they were in a spiritual battle—sometimes against the Devil, sometimes against a racialized adversary—provided occasions to invite others to move or visit.[13] The very attraction of California and its early experience in multiculturalism was as much a draw as it was a concern.

For some Mennonites, many people in California seemed impervious to the gospel. Orva Kilmer, from Portersville in 1910, exclaimed, "Oh, that souls would choose the right path before it is forever and eternally too late! Oh, that we had more good workers among us. The people in this vicinity have such hard hearts," and "My prayer is that many souls will turn to God before it is too late. Any dear ones coming to our far away country stop with us."[14] Kilmer used similar tropes of isolation and religious mission when people moved away, "so that leaves us here alone, and as we feel our weakness we ask an interest in all your prayers that we may ever be found faithful," followed by a request for visitors.[15]

It was not just Kilmer, for when Porterville changed correspondents to J. R. Miller, in 1912, similar concerns, though in less dramatic form, were still expressed. In fact, Miller replaced the spiritual battles with awe for the climate, though the loneliness remained the same.[16] Mollie Hartzler, in 1917, reported similar experiences from Terra Bella, where the people, "are growing more careless about their souls' welfare while growing deeper and deeper ingrossed [sic] in the things of this world."[17] Unfortunately, for Isgrigg, Kilmer, and Hartzler, many Mennonites who came to California arrived for reasons other than battling evil. They came to improve their health or economic status, or in a few cases, to escape Communist Russia.

Perceptions of tensions between an attractive Californian environment and its attendant despairing spiritual state persisted. John and Maria Braun, Mennonite Brethren from Lodi, wrote in 1914 that although they liked the Lodi area very much, they reserved their enthusiasm for their "heavenly homeland" (himmlische Heimat). Nevertheless, they declared their intention to strive to be children of God, and they ended their letter with a commitment based on 2 Corinthians 5:1, to live in Lodi "to the end."[18] In East Bakersfield writers spoke well of the "beautiful summer weather" (wunderschönes Sommerwetter), even in January, but noted the irreligious nature of Californian life. B. H. Nikkel, in 1913, spoke of Californians as having no need for God, as living "without God in the world" (Sie leben ohne Gott in der Welt), sad people who frequented movie theaters and saloons.[19] In 1912, a Mennonite Brethren couple in Atwater observed that although the Los Molinos area was paradise, many were sick there with malaria, which made for a clear lesson: despite malaria, God was with them to the end.[20] Lonely, isolated, sick, and on a mission to unreceptive people, these Mennonites found that the wonder of California did not seem to apply to humanity; in the cities it only got worse.

Urban Dystopia: Moral Depravity

God Shakes San Francisco

Descriptions of the Mennonite experience in California, focused on abundance, isolation, and spiritual battle, were paralleled by descriptions of urban California in stark, often moralized dystopic terms. However, large urban areas, such as Los Angeles, becoming home to many Mennonites indicated an ambiguity in their responses to urban malaise.[21]

For many people, the 1906 San Francisco earthquake was a moral event.[22] It was even God's judgment, as in the opinion of M. S. Steiner, a Mennonite minister from Ohio.[23] In an article, "The Naked Truth as to San Francisco," he concluded that—considering the deplorable moral conditions of the city evidenced by ethnic and racial pluralism, Chinatown, prostitution, drug abuse, a lack of churches, an abundance of saloons, gambling, and thievery—San Francisco got off easy with its earthquake. Furthermore: "The horrors that come to our ears from the Pacific coast were simply another example of the uncertainty of pride and spiritual drowsiness in high places." The earthquake posed a profound question for Steiner: "The question that arises in my mind is, was the earthquake and the fire that uprooted and consumed a great part of San Francisco a blessing or a curse? Can more good come from the suffering of the innocent and the unfortunate than could have come by prosperity and plenty of the wicked?"[24] A mixture of pious moralism and anti-Chinese racism informed the disaster for Steiner.

Steiner believed that the primary reason for the earthquake was the Chinese: "No man, no officer of the law, it seems, could probe the depth of the wickedness of 'Chinatown.' There the vicious of every shade and color found a harboring place. There were dark passageways tunneled from one building to another and sometimes at a depth of a hundred feet. It was an 'underground city,' often two and three stories deep." Later the offenses of Chinatown were simply too great for human intervention: "No human power, it seems, dared to molest or interfere. What man could not, the earthquake exposed and the flames purified. Tunnels served as chimneys and dens as fuel, while the depraved and wretched denizens fled like rats from their hiding places when ferreted out by an enemy."[25] Steiner concluded his diatribe against the moral decay and Chinese residents of San Francisco by quoting at length from an editorial in the *Toledo Times* (Ohio) of April 30, 1906: "Physically and morally San Francisco was built on mud." In the article, divine judgment remained a clear interpretive possibility: "Leaving the theologians to quarrel over the proposition that this catastrophe was a vengeful visitation of divine wrath, it is a fact that no modern city better deserved the fate of Gomorrah than beautiful San Francisco."[26]

Continuing from the *Toledo Times*, Steiner presents the sins of San Francisco in a fully racialized narrative reflective of strong anti-Chinese sentiment at the time:

> [San Franciso] was notorious for her harboring and laxity toward the social evil—white, black, yellow and brown. She had more murders per 1,000 than any other city in the nation . . . She had one saloon for every 250 citizens, one church for every 2,500 . . . She harbored unspeakable Chinese and Japanese infamies that would not be tolerated a day in China or Japan . . . On the second day, when the ground shook with more earthquake and the dynamiting of buildings, while the flames threw a curtain of blood-red over everything, and columns of smoke charged up and down the business thoroughfares, the street railway platforms of Market Street were covered with men dead drunk—scores of them, vomiting, cursing and howling. They knew the wickedness of the city and thought God was striking it both from above and below.[27]

Steiner was only one voice trying to interpret the earthquake. From the Mennonite General Conference perspective, the 1906 earthquake was truly a tragedy that deserved sympathy and empathy. Like Steiner, George Scott, in the *Mennonite*, celebrated that saloons were closed in the wake of the earthquake and fire, and hoped they would continue to be into the future. Unlike Steiner, however, Scott and others highlighted the human spirit of "unselfish social interest" in the many who helped San Francisco. These Mennonites considered the temporary prohibition a "blessing in disguise" but never glorified the city's destruction.[28]

The demonizing of San Francisco was not just over a major earthquake. On May 23, 1908, a news story in the *Gospel Herald* reported, "San Francisco has declared a war of extermination upon the rat. This disease-spreading, pestiferous rodent has become so abominable that a systematic crusade of extermination has been organized against him." Later, "Poisons that drive rats out of their holes and prevent the festering of their bodies in their nests is to be used in large quantities together with all means known to bring about the end of the rat tribe. Let moral infection be treated in the same way."[29] Other news reports from California described floods, bribery scandals, and two "slight" earthquakes in San Francisco.[30] Mennonite editors presented urban California as morally depraved, existing on the cusp of harsh divine judgment.

If earthquakes and rats were signs of God's wrath, the 1915 World Fair signified San Francisco's recovery. For Mennonite Church correspondent Aldus Brackbill, however, it was an occasion for scornful condemnation. He warned that although a trip to California for health reasons may be appropriate, to come for the fair was a waste of money. Brackbill's indictment of the fair was historical in scope: "We are living in an age much like Rome when the only show worthwhile was a man fighting a wild beast. It is popular today for society women to have a baby lion for a pet." Brackbill concluded, "We are living in perilous times. I am told that they say that an earthquake cannot throw these fair buildings down. Surely that is defying God. This seems to be the center of the commercial, religious, and social realms of the Pacific coast . . . The automobile demonstrates more fully Nah[um]. 2:3, 4 [where chariots rush to and fro] than any place yet."[31] Interpreting early twentieth-century cities in apocalyptic terms was not simply a Californian practice. As demonstrated by Dora Dueck, correspondents to the *Zionsbote* recounted a visit to the Kremlin tower in Moscow as something akin to experiencing the New Jerusalem, whereas, at the same time, visitors to the 1915 World's Fair combined the magnificent beauty of San Francisco with God's impending judgment.[32]

Moral Malaise in Other Cities

Brackbill not only castigated San Francisco for its decadence and arrogance but also addressed Southern California. Unmoved by the Mennonite desire to form a mission there, Brackbill offered solutions characterized by a racialized rhetoric both dominant and condescending. What was really needed, he argued, was a solid church and Sunday school, where every member was a missionary to "teach these foreigners our language, and in order to do that one must show them a kindness. We have had the privilege to talk to Chinaman and Hindu from India and to address Japanese; so that one's life can be used in more ways than simply in the pulpit."[33]

Similar racializing of religion developed in Reedley, where General Conference pastor H. J. Krehbiel was praised for his insight in treating home missions as foreign missions, as "millions of foreigners, who come to this country [will] heathenize us, if we do not Christianize them."[34] The spiritual needs of Southern and central California were racialized and the solution an assertion of guarding American society predicated on religious and national exceptionalism.

There was more to his outlook on America. Krehbiel was a proud American. He defended his patriotism from accusations of divided loyalty as a Russian Mennonite during the acrimonious Reedley elections of 1913 and 1914, and when traveling abroad in Europe maintained his enthusiastic view of American exceptionalism.[35] In 1925, H. J. Krehbiel took a several-week trip to Europe. He wrote and published a travel journal of the excursion, and among his descriptive, at-times humorous reflections of his adventures were fragments of social commentary. As he compared Parisian and Reedlian women, Krehbiel observed, "But before we leave Paris I must say that our ladies in the United States did not get their hair-bobbing custom from here, for here very few ladies have their hair bobbed. The custom of immodest dress for ladies who appear on the stage did not come from Paris either, for we attended the Grand Opera here . . . not one of them [performers] was as immodestly clad as some of the singers who appear on the lyceum course in Reedley." He walked through ruins from World War I and reflected on the skeletons he saw on a battlefield. This was proof, he wrote, of war being among the greatest of sins. The Great War was caused, Krehbiel argued, by financiers and diplomats, and he concluded by calling on people to the "Christian conviction" to "let the capitalists and militarists fight it out"; if everyone else stayed out, war would cease. To this end, he lamented the American refusal to join the League of Nations. Krehbiel wished America would adopt the European model of state ownership of railroads to subsidize ticket prices for travelers, especially so that schoolchildren could take group tours.[36]

Despite his extremely thoughtful and pleasant trip through Europe, Krehbiel found that it affirmed his love for America, even though he appreciated the efficiencies of state ownership of the rails and the geopolitics of the nascent League of Nations. While in Donnersberg, Germany, he exclaimed, "I thanked God that my ancestors went to America." In Hamburg, he came across a man speaking on a soap box in a park in front of a crowd extolling the virtues of Russian Communism. After twenty minutes Krehbiel could take no more and took his turn to speak. After identifying himself as a Californian, he was mocked for it and then replied, "that in spite of Charlie Chaplin and Hollywood and the Darwin trial in Tennessee, there were a great many very sane people in the United States"—so sane, he explained, that when people like socialist Bill Haywood and anarchist Emma Goldman could only speak of the "heaven like in Russia," they were deported so as to enjoy their collectivist paradise.[37]

Upon returning to New York, his heart soared at the sight of the Statue of Liberty. He quoted a few lines of Sir Walter Scott's poem "Patriotism" and boarded a train for Reedley. Upon their arrival in Reedley station, another poem crossed Krehbiel's lips, John Howard Payne's popular "Home, Sweet Home": "A charm from the sky seems to hallow us there, / Which, seek through the world, is ne'er met with elsewhere."[38]

Though Krehbiel's view of America shifted in tone when across the ocean, Los Angeles earned its share of moral derision from him and other Mennonite writers, and the culprits were typically decadence, movies, unemployment, charismatic religion, and earthquakes. A. R. Kurtz of Los Angeles observed that when twelve people died in 106-degree heat, the only thing they had in common was having drunk whiskey that day. Kurtz reported that despite such deaths, the number of saloons in Los Angeles was not as high as in other cities, and one could make a decent living in agriculture there. He criticized the local religious elements that stressed "second blessing"—a holiness teaching where a new convert is sanctified by the Holy Spirit after conversion—while Kurtz himself prepared for Christ's Second Coming.[39]

Despite warnings about strong drink and charismatic Christianity, Los Angeles was also the place where movies, which ruined the lives of young people, were made. Catering to an "evil minded public," movies seduced the young to aspire to become actors, succumb to awakened desires, and go out on the town at late hours. Los Angeles, by the 1920s, had replaced San Francisco as the concourse of depravity. Combined, the influence of moves, saloons, nightlife, a series of earthquakes, and wars in Europe all appeared to fulfill biblical prophecy, which for Kurtz signaled the approaching end of days.[40]

As with San Francisco, when Los Angeles experienced an earthquake on March 10, 1933, killing hundreds of people, Mennonites interpreted it as an apocalyptic sign: "It is a reminder of the helplessness of man when God stretches forth His hand of mighty power . . . it is a reminder that the masses are not prepared to meet the final coming Storm. Such occurrences are of ever increasing frequency, and point to the fact that the end is nearing."[41] Moreover, Los Angeles experienced increasing unemployment, water and power shortages, and drought. Kurtz, fourteen years after the whiskey-related deaths and four years after waiting for Jesus to return, simply recommended that people stop moving to Los Angeles altogether.[42]

Brackbill's dystopic vision of 1915 California was that of a "garden of Eden" cluttered with human wreckage. The manufacture of beer destroyed homes and brought upon the area a misery that "all the glory and grandeur of the Pacific coast could not repay." Los Angeles was wonderful for its abundance of strawberries and flowers, and for bathing in the ocean. It was also home to several businesses and churches of all denominations; however, it was isolating for Mennonites. Kurtz did not recommend others to follow, and reported that many sobbed after making the mistake of moving to a place where it was difficult to be taught "of our people." Those inclined to move to Los Angeles, however, were cautioned to consider "church privileges" (unnamed) that would be lost moving to California.[43]

Less dramatic was D. H. Bender of Hesston, Kansas. He found the blessings of Southern California to be its vices. First, there was the reality of geographic disconnection, for "the Pacific Coast district is separated from the rest of Mennonite territory by the Rocky Mountains." Then there was the seeming contradiction of paradise as problem: "It is a district noted for its fertile fields, romantic scenery, thriving cities, and a fluctuating population. It is the home of the tourist from the East . . . [Los Angeles] is both a summer and a winter resort. The problem of reaching and holding this fluctuating population which is largely on pleasure and recreation bent is no small one."[44]

In this fluid and unstable place, with morality seen to be as unsteady as the earth's crust, Mennonites lamented their inability to influence the surrounding society. A. R. Kurtz, of El Centro, even apologized: "We are sorry that California has no Sunday law, as there is so much unnecessary work done on the Lord's day."[45] Considering the experiences of the Mennonite Church and General Conference Mennonites, the tensions of both rural and urban California were a mixture of attraction and anxiety. There were fertile harvests and plump fruit, but Mennonites seemed to be eating alone.

Nature's Utopia

Pious Pleasure

There were counter-narratives to the despair of the human condition worsened by cities: climate and environment. These spiritual understandings of nature were not an indication of latent pantheism or biocentric environmentalism; rather, they were a combination of Mennonite understandings of God's creation and California booster mythologies. California was a terrestrial paradise that teased the imagination with images of life in a lush garden. Mennonites in California consistently reminded others that the state was the best place to live, even if it was lonely and irreligious.[46]

Many reports highlighted the spiritual aspect of California life. David Garber, a Mennonite Church bishop, who moved from Nampa, Idaho, to Hesperia at the turn of the century, wrote an open letter in 1905.[47] He described California as undeveloped and un-modern: "We enjoy our new home so far, not because the country is well developed; or because of our fine houses with modern conveniences; or because we have a number of congregations with many brethren and sisters of our faith, with whom we can meet occasionally, and mingle our voices in songs of praise, and prayer. No," declared Garber, "these things we have not; but because we feel that God is with us, and that the angels of the Lord encamp round about those that fear Him, and because we believe we are engaged in a work which the Lord can look upon with pleasure, and bless." Nevertheless, Garber estimated that two to three thousand acres had been "filed on [purchased] by our people." California, he warned, will be a disappointment to those "from a well developed country . . . because it is just in its infancy of development." Garber's belief was that with patience and hard work, California could experience a "great change" in five years.[48]

The appeal of California in Garber's "Open Letter" was the weather—"our summers are not extremely hot, because of the sea or mountain breeze—and the availability of free homes provided by the government." Garber then introduced the reader to "another colony," the larger Mennonite population in Reedley. The existence of these two "colonies"—Reedley and Southern California—for Garber demonstrated that the entire western region of America should have more Mennonite colonies. For him, these colonies protected Mennonite doctrines carried from the Reformation era to the present. Not only would these colonies preserve Mennonite thought, but they would help promote Mennonitism in the trans-Mountain West.[49]

Such efforts, Garber assured, would be rewarded. "Eternity will reveal that our humble efforts were not in vain, even in Southern California." Despite his optimism for the future of American Mennonitism in California, Garber ended his letter with an image of California as spiritual failure: "[It is] a shameful fact, that we have not been diligent enough in 'Our Father's business,' in being Gospel witnesses, even in our own homeland."[50] California was an undeveloped, un-modern country full of spiritual promise and wonderful weather, but also a place where lonely Mennonites lamented having little influence in shaping their new homeland.

Mennonites piously enjoyed nature. The first ever mention of California in the General Conference *Mennonite Yearbook and Almanac* was in 1905, with the article, "California Mennonites on a Picnic." It recounted a brief history of the First Mennonite Church in Upland, California, and described Pastor M. M. Horsch, who "came to California on account of his wife's health a little more than two years ago." On January 4, 1903, the Upland Mennonites organized into a congregation and later that year held a picnic. On that day, "all work and care [were] laid aside and the congregation as a whole spent the day in recreation and the enjoyment of climbing the rugged hills by the side of a babbling stream." They held a worship service, sang two hymns, read Psalm 104, and listened to a sermon preached from John chapter four. "After this impressive service was ended, the well-filled lunch baskets were emptied, after which the wonders of nature were viewed and social groups gathered for the after-dinner expressions of their appreciation of such a day's outing."[51] It was a scene to rival a booster pamphlet: Mennonites at a social gathering enjoyed nature and read the Bible, and linking the activities was a sermon derived from a Psalm that spoke apocalyptically of never hungering or thirsting again.

General Conference Mennonites wrote about the beauty of California's natural environment without the isolation, sense of evil, or apocalyptic rhetoric of MC Mennonite writing. A 1904 example by an anonymous correspondent from Upland said, "Southern California has bathed her beautiful garment of emerald in a splendid rain, which we had lately, washing all the dust from the trees and plants." It continued, "The mocking bird is singing gleefully in the pepper tree under which we are preparing this correspondence, basking in the warm California sun, enjoying the bracing and invigorating air from the snow clad mountains which shine forth in all their glory since the clouds have left them bare to the brilliant rays of the sun."[52] Correspondence in the *Mennonite* throughout the early decades of the twentieth century was similar in content, though by the 1930s, it shifted to describe church activities, and the wonder expressed earlier at the environment subsided.[53]

Christian celebrations, such as Christmas and Easter, were also described with an emphasis on nature. They observed Christmas "amid sunshine and roses," and Easter was filled with flowers of all types—roses, callas, geraniums, cannas—and the scent of lemon and orange blooms filled the air. California was a lush garden sometimes without the pain of loneliness.[54] As their fellow Mennonites in the Midwest froze under blankets of snow, in Cucamonga, they were "still having warm sunny weather. Roses in bloom, children running barefooted, windows and doors open and the busy bee is humming in the blossoming rosebushes."[55] The same themes of church and climate dominated the correspondence from Reedley, the main General Conference center in the San Joaquin Valley.[56] By the 1930s letter writers here too used less effusive language to describe natural California, focusing increasingly on the daily activities of churchgoers.

There appeared to be less a sense of isolation among the Mennonite Brethren. In Reedley, for example, they initially wrote about the mild climate, health, the new irrigation canal, and their excitement over building a church through voluntary labor.[57] During the second decade of the twentieth century, Mennonites in Lodi wondered aloud who from the Midwest would move in next. Yet this query was not characterized by the same painful sense of isolation or loneliness as with other Mennonite groups. The difference for the Mennonite Brethren was likely due to their much greater numbers in California as compared with other Mennonite groups (see table 1). Climate was an important aspect of California life to share, especially with those living elsewhere, as Ludwig Seibel of Lodi observed in 1914, when he reported that it was very nice in December, while in North Dakota—where many Lodi Mennonites came from—there was a blizzard.[58]

During the Depression of the 1930s, climate continued to be a primary lens through which to observe life in California.[59] Mrs. Jacob Shetler, in 1936, wrote, "How calm and serene, as we open the door of our quiet and cozy little cottage that we call home here in Pasadena . . . California is very beautiful. We are having sunshine every day; some very warm days, but cool at night." The only concern she noted was that not everyone in Pasadena went to church, despite the city having a large number of churches.

Dietrich M. and Sarah Enns family, Reedley, 1912. *Source:* Records of
Reedley Mennonite Brethren Church.

While the environment was abundant—"How God has divided His own
universe that a small amount of ground between the mountains can be
used to feed the many thousands of people"—the people were decadent:
"Pasadena has so many thousands of people. You may see where any of
them are as you are driving along and see the many parks. To eat a lunch is
all right, but to see the card players and smokers, a Christian has no desire
to stay."[60] This was similar to the rhetorical construction of natural wonder and human depravity noted in the Sacramento Valley by Orva Kilmer
three decades earlier.

Physical Healer

During America's westward expansion, Carey McWilliams observed
how California's climate was considered exceptional: "Elsewhere in the
general westward movement of settlers, 'climate' was regarded as a hostile
element, a fit subject for curses and wisecracks, but, in Southern California, it becomes a major obsession. As nearly as I can discover, the miraculous qualities of the climate were invented, not by the cynical residents of

the region, but by the early tourists."[61] Likewise, before the construction of any church, Mennonites came to California in the late nineteenth century seeking restored health. Desiring an escape from the damp and cold of their homes in the East and Midwest, they saw California as a tonic for a variety of illnesses—especially tuberculosis. Moving to California for health reasons, and often only for the winter, was not just the result of overwrought imaginations; it was based on medical advice.[62]

It is not surprising, then, that during the years 1885 to 1925, Mennonites often cited health as the reason for moving to California. Health as motivator was reported on in the denominational news, such as the *Mennonite*: "Many of these [Mennonites] have gone there [Southern California] in search of climatic conditions favorable for the restoration of their health of body; others again in search of homes for themselves and their children, while this caring for their temporal welfare, it is well that they do not lose sight of those higher interests which concern not only time but eternity."[63] Similar reports occur in the *Gospel Herald*: "We are enjoying very good health since we moved here. The climate is ideal for all lung trouble and asthma."[64] Others in the *Zionsbote* claimed California's climate helped with their rheumatism.[65]

Discussions began in 1905 about building a Mennonite tubercular sanitarium. J. W. Krehbiel, who believed the climate had cured his throat problems, petitioned the governing body of the General Conference to construct a sanitarium. By 1911, the regional governing body, the Pacific District of the General Conference, was persuaded to move forward with the project. When local residents learned of the proposed sanitarium to be built in their neighborhood, they protested, and it was moved northeast to Alta Loma. It was dedicated on March 1, 1914.[66] This was a common sequence of events: mobile laity settled in a new place, and the denominational machinery followed with institutional construction. The sanitarium was immediately plagued with problems, including lack of funding and difficulty in retaining nurses and administrators. Nine years after it opened its doors, the sanitarium closed.[67]

The sanitarium represented an important fusion of religious piety and modern social trends. It was built as a "missionary" enterprise where both the body and mind received care. As such, they kept admission fees as low as possible with the goal to eventually waive fees for the indigent. When describing their care, the administration insisted, "No [dietary] fads of any kind are followed." They boasted particularly of a "pure and adequate milk supply . . . we have our own tested cows and patients are given an abundance of good milk, cream and butter." Exercise routines for patients were "carefully graduated" and, when possible, included building and grounds maintenance, which provided a "two-sided saving, for both the patient and the management."[68] Despite an appeal to fiscal responsibility, scientifically inspired "graduated" exercise, and a "pure" milk supply, the true marker of success was "souls have been born again, others spiritually revived, and many comforted."[69] The Mennonites running the sanitarium cared for people regardless of religious orientation out of a deep sense of mission. One statistical summary reported:

> Adventist 1, Baptists 9, Brethren 4, Buddhist 1, Christian 2, Congregational 4, Catholic 5, Divine Healer 1, Episcopalian 1, Holiness 2, Methodist 19, Mennonite 7, New Thought 2, Lutheran 1, Presbyterian 11, Unitarian 1, no religious preference 31, led to Christ while here 3. Total 105.[70]

Although there is little record of the type of treatment received at Alta Loma, correspondence in denominational newspapers provides clues. One Mennonite, John Hygema, reported regularly on his quest for health in California. Hygema moved from Chicago in 1907, initially to Upland, then to Long Beach and Chico. Although he spent some time in Upland, he reported on the care at a non-Mennonite facility in Chico. He wrote in the *Gospel Herald*, "I have improved some since I came to California, yet just at this time it is almost too damp and cool to improve very fast. At first when I came to Long Beach it was nice and I improved faster."[71] Many health-seeking Mennonites settled in Upland. Indeed, Upland attracted many health seekers from across the nation, and as a result, the cost of lodging, food, and utilities were high, a situation made especially acute for patients after a long and expensive journey west. The Upland Mennonites tried to help the sick arriving in their midst and for twenty years did so, even before the sanitarium became a denominational project, through a loosely organized group of volunteers.[72]

Hygema went to a sanitarium in Chico because "I have not been able to do a good day's work for over eight years." He described one procedure: "I am placed in an electric bath-cabin with 36 lights, which sweats one, then a wash-off and a good rubbing; no medicine, but dieting, which should be practiced more among healthy people so that they might remain well."

Though he was sick, and his move to California was strictly for health reasons, he still reported on the weather. He explained that "the weather is nice at present, only exceptionally dry for this time of the season, as this is about the only time they have rain." Hygema attempted to keep his readers abreast of California life despite his sickly condition, making observations about standard irrigation practice, a threatening drought, and frost damage in the lemon and orange harvests.[73]

Eventually Hygema's illness worsened. Up to a few weeks before his death, he continued to report on weather, work, real estate, and fruit harvests. He wrote, "We have had several good showers of rain of late, so the people are encouraged again," and added that cherries would be available for market in a week, with Japanese plums ripening and figs and plums arriving soon. He visited Corning, just a few miles away, and commented, "They have their trials, being somewhat alone, three families and a few single people," but they bought an "old Methodist house" and hoped to have both Sunday school and a church building when they received a minister. Among his last reports, Hygema cautioned his readers about wily Californian land agents: "They have some nice, good land, and the financial prospect is good. However, there is plenty of poor land ... People need to have their eyes open, and especially when dealing with real estate men." Hygema died in Corning on June 21, 1908.[74]

A number of returning and future church leaders came to California for health. John S. Hirschler was a minister at Home Missions in Hillsboro, Kansas. He became ill, moved to Upland, and recovered. Hirschler then spent the rest of his life, from 1907 to 1916, promoting the Mennonite tubercular sanitarium. A General Conference minister, Michael Horsch, was a foreign missionary in the Indian Territory (present-day Oklahoma). He moved to Cucamonga in 1903, for his wife's health, and became an early leader in the General Conference mission in Los Angeles. Other church leaders included H. A. Bachman, born in Illinois, who moved to Minnesota, where he served as a minister. After becoming ill in 1914, he moved to find healing in California's mild and curative climate. Bachman recovered only to die of Spanish influenza in 1920.[75]

Mennonites grappled with the conflict between maintaining their religious and their social identity through, for example, the creation of a sanitarium, where they integrated the latest in holistic health care for a religiously diverse clientele. Health concerns were an important part of early Mennonite institutional development, especially when coupled with

Plowing a Muscat vineyard, 1928. *Source:* Records of
Reedley Mennonite Brethren Church.

modern social service and evangelistic piety. Pursuit of physical health
tied them to modern trends focused on healthy bodies while maintaining
the mission of evangelical religiosity.

Basking in California's Millennium

From this examination we find that the smaller the Mennonite group in
California, the more apocalyptic their rhetoric, and the more permanent
the move, the more isolated they felt. Although Mennonites often portrayed cities negatively, members of all denominations eventually settled
in Los Angeles and in small towns and cities throughout the Central Valley. Mennonites describing California for a Mennonite audience living
elsewhere often did so in moral, spiritual, apocalyptic, and biblical terms.
Some of those terms were oriented around judgment—especially in the urban environments of Los Angeles and San Francisco; some of those terms
were oriented around pleasure and healing—especially in the wonder of
California's natural environment.

Burning vineyard brush in the Reedley area, early 1920s.
Source: Records of Reedley Mennonite Brethren Church.

Through it all, California both beckoned and repelled. A question raised by scholars is how people hold seemingly contradictory images of geographic locations: utopia and dystopia.[76] In this context, California was itself a place of contradictions, as American culture transformed from Victorian—as seen in the ornate descriptions given of the good and evil of place—to modern.[77] As this cultural transformation occurred throughout America, it was pronounced in California, where a new mass consumer economy was developing, for example, in the nascent film industry. These tensions are by no means restricted to California, but the tourism, migration, and national expansion had all been up to this point largely oriented westward—to the Pacific.

In this chapter, we saw that a clear division between the dystopic city and the pleasurable and healing climate led to florid descriptions of California life, and that the wonder of nature mixed with religious conviction led to the construction of a sanitarium. In earlier chapters, we saw social pressures that led to a school and to continuity of religious practices, which led to the creation of churches and denominational conferences. Together these developments represent an embrace not just of traditional practice, but also of a modern response to changing circumstances. The newly arrived intended to establish centers of persistent Mennonite identity while navigating the surrounding modernizing society. Through a sanitarium, they brought together their religious beliefs, life in a miraculous paradise, and an openness to mingle with people of different backgrounds—if only to evangelize—while appropriating the latest in health care therapies. By creating traditional religious structures—churches, schools, and regional conferences—the California Mennonites, while establishing a new home, drew on the familiar. The piety of early Mennonite settlers to California became concretely visible.

By the early 1930s, the sense of wonder at California's natural world receded, though it never completely departed, and a process of "colonization" was established. In that process, Mennonites—and certainly their leaders—believed it important to settle into well-defined Mennonite communities in order to strengthen and preserve their religion. The identity-forming icons soon shifted from apocalyptic and naturalistic descriptions of California to an identifiable institutional religious culture. In a process similar to other ethno-religious groups in America, many Mennonites who migrated to California focused initially on material betterment and a brighter future, and made somewhat of a break from established eastern religious structures. Soon, however, they sought familiar denominational structures and institutions for a bewildering new religious environment.[78] Yet, as we will see in the next chapter, part of that construction project was figuring out where to draw the borderlines. That is, who was in, and who was out?

CHAPTER 4

Outsiders from Within

Defining California Mennonite Identity

The church is in the world and the target of Satan's attacks.
—Mennonite congregational history

Religious Pressures

When the Reedley Mennonite Brethren Church organized as a congregation on June 12, 1905, Pentecost Monday, almost immediately they expelled a charter couple from membership. On the charter itself is a thick purple line of ink striking out the names G. G. Wiens and Margaretha Wiens. Appended to it is a statement from Otto Reimer, dated October 31, 1979: "Shortly after this charter was signed brother Wiens had an argument with someone in field work and became so angry he pursued his opponent with a pitchfork. This action disturbed the new congregation so intensely that brother and sister Wiens' names were crossed out on the charter."[1] Here is a dramatic example of early twentieth-century Mennonite principles and practice: a charter member and his wife quickly expelled for his violent actions. Though a single example, Mennonites over the next sixty years would continue working through definitions of what it meant to be inside and outside, to be Mennonite or not. Significantly, the definitions of Mennonite were numerous and changing.

Early Reedley Mennonite Brethren families meeting in a local home,
ca. 1905—probably before they built a sanctuary. *Source:* Records of
Reedley Mennonite Brethren Church.

Several challenges demanded that Mennonites reflect on who they
were, but they were not alone. California was rapidly changing and over
these decades took in millions of immigrants from the world over as well as
millions from within the United States from the Depression through the
postwar decades. In the early 1960s, California became the most populous
American state, and fissures in its social and political realms were inten-
sifying. A growing conservatism emerged out of the grassroots of Orange
County, influenced greatly by southern evangelicals moving to California,
and there were racial tensions, even rioting, as in Watts 1965. Like the society around them, California Mennonites responded to change in a variety of
ways. The postwar world was full of optimism, change, and strife, and those
challenges swept through Mennonite communities as any other.[2]

Early tests for Mennonites included the passionate latter-day rain of
Pentecostalism and the dispassionate questioning of modernism—often
called "liberalism"—which forced Mennonite congregations to react

directly to cultural and religious changes that not only surrounded them, but also threatened from within.[3] At times even insufficient support of American evangelicalism and premillennial dispensationalism was enough to arouse suspicions of liberalism.[4] As Mennonites identified more closely with Californian evangelicalism, some congregations relegated their history to the back of church bulletins. Yet there was at least one attempt in the 1960s to create a Mennonite community based on faithfulness to historical principles key to sixteenth-century Anabaptism, especially as it related to congregational church polity.

From the 1920s to the 1960s, California Mennonite identity shifted in both cultural and religious terms. The cultural aspect stressed accommodation with the surrounding California society, made explicit by the casting-off of several Mennonite traditions. The religious aspect stressed identification and approval from conservative evangelicals while remaining distinct from Pentecostalism. Mennonites attempted to maintain boundaries with the world, even as those boundaries became increasingly permeable.

Pentecostalism

Born in Canada with roots in the Salvation Army, Aimee Semple McPherson, a flamboyantly charismatic evangelist of the early twentieth century, was very popular in 1920s Los Angeles and throughout the United States. Her mix of ambition, theatrics, Pentecostal theology, anti-communist politics, and charismatic personality led to the creation of the International Church of the Foursquare Gospel in Los Angeles. Her popularity and media savvy at the time was unparalleled; she was even the first woman in America granted a radio broadcast license. McPherson was as controversial as she was popular, and for California Mennonites, it was no different.[5]

When some Reedley Mennonite Brethren went to Los Angeles to hear her preach, the resulting controversy revealed divisions in their church when many wanted them disciplined. As Otto Reimer recalled McPherson's galvanizing reputation, "Rumors had spread far beyond California that Mrs. McPherson had been in our pulpit. These rumors were totally false, as our church had absolutely no contact with that cult and as far as [we] know that woman never was in this area." In the 1920s and 1930s, Mennonites remained wary of McPherson and Pentecostalism, describing a Reedley Pentecostal church as "quite extreme in its practice of speaking in tongues and emotional demonstrations."[6]

Members of Reedley Mennonite Brethren Church in front of sanctuary,
ca. 1913–1919. *Source:* Records of Reedley Mennonite Brethren Church.

The Reedley Church Council investigated the two sisters who "attended these meetings quite often, altho [*sic*] they probably did not practice the extreme demonstrations themselves." The Church Council decided not to expel the women from their fellowship, though pressured to do so. Instead, they held a church vote on this question: "Do we encourage the Pentecostal movement or take a definite stand against it?" The result was 8 votes for the movement and 118 opposed. The result did not end the issue, however. In 1925, a group of members who considered the church's leadership spiritually lax left to form a new congregation, which they named the South Reedley Mennonite Brethren Church.[7]

Mere contact with Pentecostalism and its emphasis on charismatic religious experience—the crux of Mennonite criticism—breached enough boundaries to land on the woeful side of the cosmic drama between good and evil. Otto Reimer observed that the division caused by the Pentecostal controversy of the 1920s was a form of evil and needed to be recorded in an honest historical account: "The church is in the world and the target of Satan's attacks and so, to be entirely factual, these unpleasant sad experiences and mistakes . . . must not be left unrecorded."[8] The situation was also important enough to the larger denomination to warrant an investigation.

The General Conference of the Mennonite Brethren Churches Board of Reference and Council (BORAC), the investigative arm of the national denomination for issues of theology, discipline, and dispute resolution, came to Reedley to examine the church split. BORAC stayed for two weeks in January 1928 and listened to testimony from people of both the Reedley and the South Reedley churches. Two issues emerged from the testimony: the influence of "false religions" such as Pentecostalism, or McPhersonism, and the more serious offense of disunity.

The Mennonites who split off, later renamed the Dinuba Mennonite Brethren Church, complained about a spiritually leaderless Reedley church. They accused the Reedley Mennonite Brethren of such worldly activities as firing off guns at weddings and spiritual emptiness, exemplified by people seeking Pentecostal experiences going unpunished. Although BORAC hoped to see the two groups reunite, it was deemed impossible, and both parties were encouraged to at least respect each other.[9] Embracing Pentecostalism was a serious matter, but for BORAC disunity was worse. Where South Reedley saw themselves as more spiritually mature than the original Reedley church, BORAC saw them guilty of discord. Group cohesion, nevertheless, was important for those remaining in Reedley Mennonite Brethren. Once, for example, a choir director disciplined a female choir member for getting a short haircut, called "hair bobbing," and he caused a greater disturbance for disciplining without consent of the congregation. Regardless, in 1937, the Dinuba Mennonite Brethren apologized to the Reedley congregation for the 1925 schism, but the two groups did not reunite.[10]

Sister Aimee, as McPherson's followers knew her, was trouble for other California Mennonites. In 1922, she came to the Lodi area for a series of revival meetings and received the support of local pastors. Among the local pastors who supported her was Mennonite Brethren J. M. Schlichting. After controversy erupted in the local Mennonite Brethren community, Schlichting resigned, but he remained a staunch supporter of such Pentecostal beliefs and practices as holiness, baptism of the Holy Spirit, and "prayer healing." A group of Mennonites even came from Reedley and Shafter to educate the Lodi Mennonites about "McPherson's heresy." One McPherson supporter was dismissed as a "holy roller." However, the issue and emotion subsided after apologies were made and Schlichting resigned.[11]

Members of the Mennonite Church did not consider themselves safe from the influences of Aimee Semple McPherson either. When their Los Angeles congregation went through a series of leadership, cultural, and authority crises in the 1920s, some members attended "McPherson Temple." One of the church board members even reported that McPherson "is nearer the Bible method of baptism, they pour."[12] There were two main forms of Mennonite baptism, immersion and pouring. Immersion involved the complete submersion of the baptismal candidate under water and then the raising of the candidate from the water. Pouring involved a small amount of water poured over the head of the candidate. The Mennonite Brethren practiced immersion, and the MC practiced pouring. In a distinct twist, we have some Mennonites finding common ground with McPherson on the issue of baptism mode, though this did not translate into acceptance or approval.

The developments in Los Angeles led to calls from the laity to the denominational leadership asking for assistance in returning to doctrinal faithfulness. Despite these calls, denominational leaders such as S. C. Yoder of the Mennonite Board of Missions simply contextualized the issue of McPherson within a larger experience of denominational factionalism in Los Angeles.[13] The situation in Southern California—the exuberance, tongues, and premillennial expectation (that in the final dispensation of history, Christians would be spared a seven-year outpouring of God's wrath before a Christ-led millennium of peace ruled the world) so important to Sister Aimee—and the concern of Mennonites regarding possible satanic influence, was for Yoder all part of what made California a distinct place in the Mennonite imagination.

In 1946, conflict over Pentecostalism reached the Rosedale Mennonite Brethren. Their minister, A. B. Goossen, resigned over the controversy surrounding his belief that speaking in tongues was proof of baptism in the Holy Spirit. Unlike the situation in Reedley twenty years earlier, this congregation did not split. The Church Council held an investigation into Goossen's theological opinion, found it unscriptural, and referred the matter to BORAC, which responded that Goossen was in error. Goossen was asked to "humble himself" for making unwise and needlessly contentious statements. After submitting a written apology, dated December 6, 1946, Goossen immediately told people that the apology did not reflect a change in his thinking, that the ruling of BORAC "did not matter," and that speaking in tongues was the only evidence of Holy Spirit baptism. He resigned as pastor on December 28, 1946.[14]

Although Goossen's story in this context ended, the issue of Pentecostal influences in Mennonite Brethren congregations was much wider. Perhaps it is ironic that Goossen went on to become an assistant pastor at Bethany Mennonite Brethren Church in Fresno, under the interim pastorate of Sam Wiens. Wiens had been hired after Bethany's former pastor, Jacob D. Hofer, resigned, when the congregation there became concerned about Pentecostal influences in him. Although Hofer had won a vote of confidence by the church membership, some thought this was suspect because it had been taken before complaints about Hofer's leadership were heard; unrest grew between the two factions. Some attributed the tension to the Devil. When a charismatic faction within the church declared to the others that the "Lord is not with them," the Pacific District Conference held meetings on the issue and, by December 1946, asked Hofer to leave. Hofer and a small number of followers left the Bethany Mennonite Brethren Church and started the Chapel of the Open Bible in 1948.[15]

From the 1920s to 1940s, Mennonites in California squared off against the influence of Aimee Semple McPherson and Pentecostalism. They saw in these religious personalities and practice something heretical even possibly satanic derived from excessive charismatic experiences. Up until the mid-1940s, Pentecostal influence inside several Mennonite communities was enough for some to conclude that the Devil lurked in their midst, and for others to lose their jobs.

There remained, however, liberals to investigate. If this was a time to be alert to Pentecostalism, it was also a time to welcome a conservative evangelicalism influenced by premillennial dispensationalism, already attractive to many Mennonites for some time.

"Liberal Sympathies"

On the heels of the Pentecostalism issue, Bethany Mennonite Brethren Church in Fresno had two major disciplinary investigations in fourteen years, in 1949 to 1950 and in 1961 to 1963. The first was over the teachings and life of their pastor, H. G. Wiens; the second concerned itself with the disruptive Sunday school teaching of Roy Just.

Wiens was hired as pastor in February 1948, and within a year and a half, complaints arose concerning his "lack of spiritual preaching" and "lifestyle." After the Church Council held a series of secret meetings to discuss his case, they confronted Wiens and asked him to resign. Church members who thought Wiens was dealt with unfairly, especially since the meetings were closed, supported him.[16] While this case had the high drama of a pastor tried behind closed doors who had followers angered over a secretive church council, it also revealed something of Mennonite identity in 1940s Fresno.

Bethany Mennonite Brethren Church was distinctive among California Mennonite congregations in that they published in their congregational history the documents used in a disciplinary investigation. The Church Council claimed its authority from Acts 20:28 and 31, where the Holy Spirit charged church overseers to be alert to dangerous influences on the community. They first claimed that the pastor was fully aware of the two closed meetings, though not invited to attend, and was asked to resign because of his theology, polity, and lifestyle. Wiens needed to leave Bethany so that they could "retain [their] testimony among evangelicals, and fill that leading part in our city and in our conference which we believe God has destined for it."[17]

The Church Council found Wiens questionable because, in addition to his alleged temper and apparent use of favoritism, he held liberal attitudes toward such "worldly" amusements as ball games, ice-skating, and cosmetics. His view of church polity was questioned because he argued with the Church Council over issues of biblical standards of church discipline (Wiens was considered lax) and for failure to cooperate with the Church Council over the issue of "outside groups or individuals" being brought into the church without prior council approval.[18]

The Church Council charged that Wiens's theology was suspect because he held "liberal sympathies." The evidence rested on six points. The council noted that Wiens had a "lack of interest in the local N.A.E." (National Association of Evangelicals), read too widely in liberal theology, made "obscure" theological comments in his sermons ("often questionable"), and held a "psychological" worldview.[19] That Wiens never espoused premillennial dispensationalist theology certainly contributed to these "liberal tendencies." The final point was that "the pastor of the Church should be the individual concerning whose theology there is no question and which does not have to be defended before conservatives."[20]

His sermons did not provide "spiritual food," but "philosophy."[21] Since questions were raised, Wiens was suspect.

There were two different understandings of Mennonite identity present; both groups identified themselves as Mennonite, but they took different theological positions. One identity, represented by the Church Council, was based on cultural separation but theological integration with local conservative evangelicalism, and the other, represented by Wiens, was a relaxing of cultural separatism mixed with a breaking from conservative evangelicalism and premillennial dispensationalism.

Wiens had his supporters, and over the first half of 1950, there was much acrimony in Bethany Mennonite Brethren Church. The dispute even drew in the young Pacific Bible Institute (PBI), the Mennonite Brethren school, which had opened in Fresno in 1944. Wiens's supporters accused PBI's president, G. W. Peters, of playing a role in his downfall. Eventually, the Pacific District Conference's Board of Reference and Counsel, a regional body with similar responsibilities as BORAC, cleared Peters, and Wiens's resignation stood. In spring 1950, it was reported that the congregation experienced healing when people asked each other's forgiveness over things said and done in the previous months.[22] John Goertzen, in 1992, described the experience: "After this evening [in 1950] a sweet peace was felt in the body. Not even a semblance of this trouble has befallen Bethany since."[23] That was true, however, only if one ignored the controversial Sunday school teacher Roy Just.

In summer 1961 Roy Just, a professor at PBI, a Sunday school teacher, and a moderator at Bethany Mennonite Brethren Church's business meetings, read a statement of apology to his church. The nature of the apology was to smooth over the unrest his Sunday school class had caused. The church officially considered it a closed case, and there was little mention of it in the church record. Yet the issues surrounding Just's Sunday school class, such as the material he chose to cover and his alleged coarse language, remained topics of discussion within the congregation well into the fall. The Church Council held a meeting where Just read another statement, and the church officially considered the matter closed.[24] It remained closed until the following summer.

In 1962, Just made controversial statements regarding Mennonite Brethren piety and non-Christian religions at a Pacific District mission conference. G. W. Peters, professor of missions at Mennonite Brethren Biblical Seminary, and J. B. Toews, director of Mennonite Brethren

Missions and Services, an agency that coordinated mission work at home and abroad, noted their objections in the records of Bethany Mennonite Brethren Church, where Just was still a member. On September 25, 1962, because of persistent discussion surrounding his Sunday school class and statements made at the mission conference, the Church Council decided to hold meetings in October to collect information.[25] The Church Council had one couple testify regarding the Sunday school class, one individual on his influence as a professor, followed by testimony in support of Just, and then Just himself.

The adult Sunday school class generated controversy for three main reasons. According to student testimony, Just deviated from the adopted curriculum and led a class on topical issues of the students' choosing; he used coarse and intimidating language; and he did not provide answers for people's questions. Important testimony came from students Mr. and Mrs. Ben Giesbrecht, who were strongly opposed to Just. The Giesbrechts identified themselves as "M. B. [Mennonite Brethren] by choice not by inheritance," declaring they could leave when they wanted, thereby assuming significant political capital. The Giesbrechts' claim highlights a significant issue for California Mennonite Brethren: were they a people or an evangelical denomination? The Giesbrechts, by this simple assertion, understood the Mennonite Brethren to be both and found it empowering to navigate that tension.

Mrs. Giesbrecht was very concerned with the coarse subjects Just covered, such as "discussing a man with encephalitis of the testicles," in a class with "single kids," likely in their twenties.[26] Ben continued with the second-hand testimony of Just's neighbor, who complained that Just did not disapprove of his daughters dancing even if chaperoned. Just continued to incur their disapproval. He had a powerfully negative opinion of noncombatant military service and did not support the nondenominational evangelical ministry Youth for Christ, both of which cast suspicion on him. Ben also testified, based on second-hand accounts, that Just never even invited one of his neighbors to church. The concerns over Just's ambivalence toward evangelical organizations, dancing, and evangelism were exacerbated by Just's refusal to provide definitive answers to discussion questions at Sunday school. Both Mr. and Mrs. Giesbrecht testified that Just never took a position against attending "shows" or against what they perceived to be a permissive attitude among some Mennonites of attending shows with non-Christians in order to lead them to Christ.[27]

When the examination came to specific theological content, Mrs. Gies-brecht was upset: "We were supposed to be studying Calvinism. He ran down the grace of God—it was awful—it was terrible." Mr. Giesbrecht testified that in addition to running down the grace of God, Just made light of a song: "We're not sure which song it was, perhaps 'at the cross'[;] he made light of the cross." Just also never mentioned upcoming Billy Graham meetings, and the class never sent Mr. Giesbrecht a card when he was in the hospital. It especially disturbed Ben Giesbrecht when Just had a book discussion in class when the official curriculum required they discuss "our witness to our neighbors."[28] Although this topical and discus-sion-oriented class may have suited the college-aged crowd, it was intoler-able for some of an older generation of Mennonite Brethren, who wanted from their church leaders answers, direction, and strict interpretation of behavior codes. Meanwhile, a younger generation accepted ambiguity.

That a generation gap existed in such a context as Sunday school cur-riculum is not surprising, nor was the concern some parents had over the influence of the college professor on their children. John Friesen, unidenti-fied as to his position in the Bethany church, testified to the Church Coun-cil that Just had, at a public meeting, criticized the Mennonite Brethren position against smoking tobacco and dancing. What Just said was that if a prohibition existed against tobacco and dancing, there should be one on overeating. Friesen said that he had to "shudder" at some of Just's teach-ings. From that Friesen concluded, "A professor who questions smoking or dancing didn't have [a] close relationship to the Lord. I gathered he was looking for license [to behave immorally]."[29] Any attempt to demonstrate and critique behavior codes was selective and simply dismissed as a search for immoral license.

Friesen also considered Just overly concerned with relief work. The Mennonite Brethren, he explained, were the least concerned of Ameri-can Mennonite groups about relief work because they were interested in Christ: "I had to conclude that his main concern was not where did Christ stand but how much bread did we toss on the freeway."[30] Friesen then ad-dressed the issue of comparative religions. On the issue of non-Christian religions, someone reported that Just had said other scriptures contained truth. Friesen testified that not only was his generation taught in Bible school that all religions, other than Christianity, come short of truth, but that as a professor, Just "undermine[d]" the young minds of students. For, Friesen concluded, "the devil is not out to spare the M. B." In short,

Friesen testified that Just stood for "nothing." Friesen also claimed that he could not talk to Just directly because he did not have an education and could not "counteract [Just on] any philosophical question."[31] Two distinct Mennonitisms were revealed as stark opposites in this case, if not in actual practice: social relief at the expense of evangelism and an other-worldly cosmic drama replete with evil forces pushing social relief to the side.

In Just's defense, Carl Wohlgemuth, a member of his class, testified that he found the class important for its "spirit of inquiry" discussing topics both directly and indirectly related to Christian faith. Wohlgemuth singled out people who could not accept criticism of their own group as those offended by Just's teaching. Yet, the core issue with Just was not his alleged liberal sympathies or syncretism—he was judged as dangerously close to syncretism—but his teaching style. A student defended him on this point: "This class has caused me to think and to learn. I have finally come to understand the Christian life. There is real freedom of expression."[32]

Concern for the Christian life informed Just's defense before the Church Council. Based on scriptures regarding settling conflicts for the preservation of church order, Just did not engage the testimony of detractors who never spoke to him. Rather, he simply stated that he did not mean to cause controversy and acknowledged that he was intimidating at times when he thought people gave lazy or unreflective answers to questions. He confessed that such an approach, coupled with coarse language, was not wise. Just claimed his goal was to have a biblically based Sunday school that reflected the daily concerns of his students. In addition, one person even became a convert to Christianity in his class after attending the church for four years. In defending his position on the Holy Spirit working in non-Christian religions, Just argued, "The Holy Spirit deals with people" and was likely reflected in other scriptures. He read from the Bhagavad-Gita at the conference but declared to the council, "I am not a syncretist."[33]

After his testimony, Just left the room, and the Church Council discussed their findings. The Church Council decided that Just was neither a syncretist nor a relativist. Just's problems arose because he was not a theologian, and therefore, in a peculiar embrace of modern academic and professional specialization, Brother Wiens of the council said, "We can't allow non-theologians to strike a norm for us in theology in the church." Brother Wiebe asked if the Church Council could make any judgment if they were not theologians themselves. Brother Wiens retreated quickly to a counter-modern anti-expert position, saying they may pass judgment on theology as God excused the Apostle Paul for acting in ignorance. The real issue for the Church Council was how to ban Just from teaching. In order to pass such a sanction, they needed a reason, and according to the testimony, they did not have a compelling one. They finally settled on "unrest in the class." It was proposed that Just be suspended from teaching Sunday school for one year. The affair ended with the Church Council accepting Just's repentance for his abrasive teaching style and affirming that he was an evangelical. Just then left California for Kansas to become president of Tabor College, the only four-year liberal arts college the Mennonite Brethren ran at the time. That Just could make such a move is indicative of a larger plurality of religious thought among the Mennonite Brethren throughout the United States.[34]

These two church investigations, rich in their detail, show a congregation finding its way among Pentecostal, modernist, and conservative evangelical influences. With the exception of a few, concerns about the deleterious influences of syncretism and modernism were particularly acute. Although many Mennonites entered Californian society through conservative evangelicalism, a younger generation in the 1960s attempted to connect with the historical meaning of their religion and find a way into California society through professions and social action. These are two examples of finding moorings in times of change. One reflected the significant role of strict religious, even fundamentalist, concerns with rules of conduct, teaching, and practice, providing direction and stability in the transformations brought by modernity.[35] Proponents of the other welcomed changes, found meaning in questions sooner than answers, but needed an anchor—and looking back four centuries, they found one.

Heritage and Experiments

In 1963, the College Community Church: Mennonite Brethren (hereafter College Community) formed in Clovis, in part out of the Roy Just controversy, and in part as a church expansion project of Bethany Mennonite Brethren. Of their charter members, thirty-one were from Bethany, nine from the Butler Avenue Mennonite Brethren Church, two from Minneapolis, and one each from Oklahoma and Kansas. There was one admitted by baptism and five by their testimony of Christian faith, presumably baptized in a Mennonite Brethren church elsewhere. The rest were from Mennonite Brethren churches in the San Joaquin Valley.[36]

The new church in Clovis held their first informal meeting on October 14, 1962, and explored the idea of a new Mennonite Brethren congregation in the area. Ultimately they agreed to start one. Although there was a split with Bethany, good will existed between them. They held joint baptisms, and Clovis asked Bethany to license them a minister for the interim period as they organized. When it came time to send invitations for their charter day service, special mention was made of Bethany.[37]

College Community began their work in January 1963 and intentionally identified themselves with the historical Anabaptist and Mennonite Brethren reform movements of sixteenth-century Europe and nineteenth-century Russia. Unlike many Mennonite congregations in California, this urban, professional, and youthful congregation held their Anabaptist heritage close. Even their reasons for having services begin in January were predicated on a restorative reading of history that connected their existence to prior significant church reforms and splits. In particular, they chose January as their month because sixteenth-century Anabaptism began in January 1525, and the evangelical reforms and schism in Russia resulting in the creation of the Mennonite Brethren Church occurred in January 1860.[38] They broke from local tradition, however, regarding the order of the Sunday service by holding Sunday school after the worship service and regarding polity by encouraging greater lay participation.

By fall 1963 College Community had decided to wait to frame a constitution: "We are a young church and do not desire an iron clad constitution but would prefer to be guided by the minutes of previous meetings."[39] They desired that "spiritual leadership" come from the Church Council, not a singular leader. Their pastor was to engage specifically in the ministry of "word and prayer" and delegate responsibilities to the laity. In times of congregational stress, their organization statement advises, "The brethren of the church must never fear to speak the truth in love or to receive counsel and admonition given it the spirit of Christian love."[40] This was distinct to College Community, as most Mennonite churches held to a strong pastor and church council model of church governance. Planning to run their church in this fashion was an attempt to identify with selected sixteenth-century Anabaptist ideals.

Politics and History

Of course, Mennonite thinking on historical identity did not begin in the 1960s. Questions of historical identity in early 1950s Reedley, for example, were not always so simple. A. H. Unruh, a Mennonite Brethren church historian, was commissioned by the denomination to write a history of the Mennonite Brethren in response to perceived threats to their historical identity, in particular the influence of non-Mennonite seminaries on newly trained professional clergy. Reedley's Church Council objected to Unruh's treatment of them. On June 11, 1954, a three-member committee was formed to review the unpublished manuscript. They reported on July 8, 1954: "A great deal that should not be in there is, and many things that should be in are left out. It was moved and seconded that the Committee see to it that the chapter pertaining to our church be written as it should be."[41] A month later, on August 19, 1954, the council resolved that the committee delegated to study Unruh's manuscript "rewrite the chapter setting forth data, growth and accomplishments of our church." The self-definition as laid out by the Church Council was "growth and accomplishments," a set of standards that diverged from traditional Mennonite themes of community, discipleship, and nonresistant love.[42]

As the Mennonite Brethren adapted to the stress and changes in California from the 1920s to the 1960s, the General Conference also needed to adapt to the challenges of what it meant to be an "insider." In the pressure of 1930s California, the General Conference's First Mennonite Church of Upland began a monthly newsletter, the *Herald*. From 1937 to 1940, through a series of editorials and a feature, "The Pastor's Chat," a culturally progressive and theologically conservative Mennonitism was staked out. Lester Hostetler, editor of the *Herald* and pastor of the Upland church, positioned himself between social concerns and the retention of tradition and heritage. Over four years coverage included church music, appropriate worship service behavior, voting in elections, and pacifism. These issues, while appearing eclectic, were representative of two parallel streams in California Mennonitism: social progressivism and religio-cultural conservatism.[43]

For General Conference Mennonites in Upland, the *Herald* advocated for reverential church music, and that choirs and music directors have near equal status with the preacher. Yet, this was not without controversy, as one pastor who argued that choir gowns democratized the singers was in turn criticized for advocating "uppish, stylish, high-brow, [and] Roman-ish" trappings. Ultimately, the *Herald* encouraged Mennonites to learn their history out of "self-respect" and to explain their denomination to outsiders without being "embarrassed or apologetic."[44]

A parallel concern among the Upland Mennonites was living proper Mennonite lives as good Americans. Hostetler of the *Herald* argued that not only was American citizenship a great blessing but also that America was the greatest nation on earth. Despite its greatness, however, national improvement was necessary. Beyond simply dealing with drunkenness, divorce, kidnapping, lynching, racketeering, immoral movies, and a "sa-lacious" popular culture, America should revisit, he argued, the ban on granting citizenship for pacifists. Upland Mennonites described the call to defend one's country as hypocrisy, for it was really a call to kill. In the pages of the *Herald* patriotism was defined in the summer of 1937 as liv-ing a morally upstanding life: "quiet, peaceable, and useful."[45] Rejection of war, therefore, went beyond military exemption to include critiques of militarism in general, and pacifism went beyond religious scruple to embody patriotic expression.

In 1939, the First Mennonite Church of Upland published a list of six "principles and teachings" of Mennonites: the church as a "body" of like-minded believers baptized upon their individual confessions of faith; separation of church and state where Christian obedience to the state must not conflict with Christian "scriptures or . . . conscience"; a prohibition on secret, "oath-bound" societies; "non-violent resistance" that practices "overcoming of evil with good"; and a "congregational and democratic" polity with Christ as the "head." The final principle was to agree on "ac-cepted evangelical doctrines" that affirm the primacy given to the Bible as "infallible rule of faith and conduct."[46] This statement of principles, com-bined with the *Herald*, documents desired parameters of General Confer-ence Mennonitism as socially engaged pacifism and evangelically pious comportment.

During the summer of 1940, Hostetler concluded that a militarized so-ciety designed to protect democracy merely replaced it with a form of dic-tatorship. He encouraged his readers to consider the arguments of socialist presidential candidate Norman Thomas and hoped they would learn a political argument for peace: "On the greatest of all issues, peace and war, there is no difference between the major parties." He spared little in his social critique, even bringing it to bear on Thanksgiving Day for its focus on a lavish dinner and not the reasons for the Pilgrim Fathers' thankfulness. When the Ham and Eggs movement—a left-of-center California pension movement of the mid-to-late 1930s—enjoyed influence in the 1938 hotly contested state election, Hostetler supported them for highlighting the poverty and unemployment among older citizens. "Hamanders," as supporters were called, argued that thirty dollars be paid every Thursday to every Californian over fifty years of age. As a ballot initiative, it was narrowly defeated. Even though a strongly anti-union proposition was also defeated, the political momentum in Southern California shifted rightward. Hamstrung, the Democrats lost the governor's office in the following election, which blunted much of the New Deal's force in California. Politically, a gradual shift to Republican conservatism began for the many evangelical migrants from the mid-and southwestern states who had come to California as Democrats.[47]

These articles attempted to define appropriate Mennonite politics and practices in a time of social and political flux in California. However, the *Herald* did not reflect all General Conference concerns. In the late 1950s, General Conference Mennonites in California attempted to protect their youth in public schools from such societal influences as dancing, and they attempted to engage political leaders in their concerns as part of their "civic responsibility." In January 1957 and 1958, Pastor Ramon H. Jantz wrote letters to Shafter High School requesting that students from the First Mennonite Church be excused from a square dance "because of certain religious principles."[48] These local concerns reveal an important mixture of conservative social mores and political engagement; the one does not preclude the other.

Similar to the Mennonite Brethren, General Conference Mennonite identity shifted in the 1950s. Unlike the Mennonite Brethren, the General Conference was more concerned with historical literacy. In Winton, for example, lay members requested a Mennonite history Sunday school class.[49] Like the Mennonite Brethren, however, there was a split (although amiable) when their Reedley congregation formed a newer congregation in Fresno in the early 1950s. In fall 1952, a group of Reedley Mennonite Church congregants who lived in Fresno had been meeting locally for picnics, potluck dinners, and fellowship when it occurred to them to start a Fresno church. A year later they did so, with the support of the First Mennonite Church in Reedley.[50] Once their church was constructed in 1956, members of the new Mennonite Community Church in Fresno distributed a flyer that gave a brief historical description of who Mennonites were and of their new building.[51]

Congregations in Los Angeles, Fresno, and Winton intentionally traced their church roots to Menno Simons in the sixteenth century and provided brief surveys of Mennonite history. Such histories were given from an evangelical Anabaptist theological perspective, stressing the primacy of the Bible, salvation through Jesus Christ, and living a life characterized by discipleship and love for all humanity.[52] The Mennonite Community Church bulletins—weekly publications in which church service content, weekly activities, and congregational concerns were printed—also reflected a politically active conservative evangelicalism over such issues as Bible reading in the schools and conscription. Throughout the 1950s, they remained largely evangelical in tone, with concerns and church services oriented to the themes of sin, personal nearness to God, evangelism, and salvation.[53]

Behavior Codes and Church Authority

Furthermore, behavior codes through the late 1920s and 1930s created tension. Shafter Mennonite Brethren faced several important cultural issues: German language, worldly amusements, voluntary military enlistment, and women's hair bobbing. In the church's own historical account, the issue of hair bobbing, or short haircuts, was given the most attention. The interest in the cut of women's hair suggests something not only of the importance of individual piety for Mennonite Brethren identity, but also of its gendered expression. In 1925, the church announced that women who engaged in the practice were banned from taking communion and removed from full membership. The Shafter Mennonite Brethren softened their anti—hair-bobbing stance in 1930, declaring it the "wish" of the church that the practice be abandoned. This softening came as the congregation itself took an increasingly flexible position on various behavioral rules, among them children playing ball games and performing in school plays, and, of course, hair bobbing.[54]

Such flexibility in the 1920s and 1930s continued to evolve. Anthropologist Miriam Warner studied the Mennonite Brethren in San Jose, in particular their "dual membership" as an ethnic and religious group whose goals were sometimes at odds with each other.[55] The religious side of the Mennonite Brethren stressed modesty and not showing off success, whereas the ethnic side expected to see success. Using the idea of "enclavement," Warner describes the Mennonite Brethren as living in groups surrounded by permeable boundaries. These boundaries with the outside world were defined by ideology and theology, not physical distance. Thus, the Mennonite Brethren ease in working with groups as varied as the Gideons, the Boy Scouts, and the Red Cross was not contradictory.[56]

To maintain their identity as an ethnic group and to regulate religious belief, churches, schools, a college, a seminary, hospitals, and a residential care home were initially built. The dilemma for the Mennonite Brethren was that they had an ethnic tradition defined by a religiosity requiring expansion through missions. The contradictory forces of missions and ethno-religious identity were often addressed by dismissing ethnicity as unimportant, even dangerous. Despite a tendency to live in enclaves, accommodation continued apace.[57]

Interestingly, weddings in the 1950s provided ample opportunity for churches to regulate religious practice at the intersection of cultural adaptation and religious conviction. Several congregations created new policies governing weddings as a reaction against a process of accommodation already well under way. The Bakersfield Mennonite Brethren Church (later renamed Heritage Bible Church) passed a set of "principles" governing weddings that permitted only "sacred music," to be approved by the marrying minister, and stipulated that "dresses used by the women should be modest . . . no off-the-shoulder gowns be worn, or strapless dresses." The policy restricted brides and grooms to two attendants each, and no pictures were allowed during the wedding service or ceremony in the sanctuary.[58]

The Rosedale Mennonite Brethren Church also issued regulations for a proper Mennonite wedding. Rosedale's rule was similar to Bakersfield's: weddings were to have Bible-based sermons and a prayer delivered at a prominent place in the ceremony. As with Bakersfield, Rosedale was quite concerned about music. Music was to be "sacred," "uplifting and edifying," not "secular" or "light," and never played during the ceremony. Bride's dresses were never to be strapless or off the shoulder, and both bride and groom were permitted one attendant each. Rings could be exchanged, but not during the ceremony. Even a groom kissing his bride after the wedding was considered "worldly" and disallowed.[59]

For MC Mennonites, tensions over behavior codes and church authority dominated the 1920s and 1930s, which for Calvary Mennonite Church (then the 35th Street Mission) included the selling of tobacco as "inconsistent to our religion."[60] An early and controversial leader in Los Angeles was Mennonite bishop and pastor J. P. Bontrager. There were several sides to his controversial nature: a progressive approach to church doctrine and administration that stressed flexibility, financial incompetence, and a tendency to ignore conference authority. On December 22, 1922, H. E. Widmer, of Bakersfield, reported to Brother Loucks at the Mennonite Board of Missions that in Los Angeles, many Mennonites believed unconventional ideas. Widmer pleaded, "Where should the line be drawn!"[61]

Widmer was concerned about Mennonites who espoused the second blessing of the Holy Spirit, the necessity of immersion baptism for salvation, and the prohibition against eating pork. He observed that there was "absolute discord as to what a bonnet is so that some wear one thing and some wear another and some nothing." Some even questioned whether those "born again" were saved by grace and, therefore, never sinned again. In response to these ideas circulating through the Los Angeles mission, Bontrager, reportedly, gave "his philosophy of it and admits himself as undecided in so many things[,] and that leaves many under the impression [that] if he does not know[,] how can I know[,] and therefore so many do the way they do in the congregations they came from. You may imagine the unity is marred in such existing things."[62] Widmer continued, "I know it's hard to please everybody but as I am learning to know there are two sides to all questions and that it is easier to ask a question then to answer it. We have a member that wears a moustache without the full beard." Moustaches without beards were considered too fashionable. Although wearing the bonnet for women was in decline by 1955, the change appears to have developed along generational lines, and its decline varied throughout the United States. Moreover, the Mennonite Church used distinctive conservative dress more than either the General Conference or the Mennonite Brethren, though in the later decades of the twentieth century, they relinquished plain dress.[63] At issue was unity and discord in the fellowship manifest in diverse practices and ambiguity over proper dress, facial hair, and allegedly indecisive leadership.

The concern of the larger Mennonite Church was not Widmer's question; rather, it was the appropriate role and rule of authority from which the fellowship's unity was to follow. In January 1923, the Los Angeles mission, led by Bontrager, withdrew itself from the oversight of the

Mennonite Board of Missions and Charities (Mission Board), a national body. The Los Angeles mission wanted to be an independent congregation in the Pacific Coast Conference. They gave sensible reasons: the two boards (national and regional) that oversaw the mission were located so far away that visits from them were rare; the Los Angeles mission already owned a building; and its members found upsetting the many unspecified rumors that circulated throughout the district regarding the work in Los Angeles. In response, the Mission Board and the Pacific District Mission Board declared the withdrawal to be outside Bontrager's authority.[64] A mission it would remain.

The division between the general Mission Board and the Los Angeles mission grew more acrimonious when the General Board replaced Bontrager with a new superintendent, Frank B. Showalter, from Virginia. Showalter had an advantage over Bontrager; he did not need financial support from the local congregants. Bontrager, talented otherwise, was seemingly financially inept. As many within the Los Angeles mission did not accept Showalter, it was reasonable to expect that they would not be generous or eager in their financial support. D. H. Bender, president of Hesston College and Bible School in Kansas, astutely advised the Mission Board not to return the problem to the Pacific District Mission Board as they had sent the problem east in the first place. In 1924, as Bontrager enjoyed the support of the majority of the Los Angeles mission, leadership in the Midwest admitted the obvious direction of events and eventually transformed the mission into an independent congregation.[65]

Meanwhile, J. L. Rutt, a representative of the Los Angeles mission, provided a succinct reason to D. H. Bender for the actions they took: "If I was to state frankly what the greatest cause of the trouble in the Los Angeles congregation is; it would be the chageableness [sic] or if I may say it the deceptive way of doing things of those in charge of our mission here, perhaps the best word to use here would be double tongued." The example Rutt cited was the appointment of Showalter by the Mission Board, against the desires of, and without consulting, the mission. Rutt argued that the mission's leadership was not at fault for Bontrager's resignation or for the rise of Bontrager's local rival, Ben Swartzendruber—who was somewhat suspect for having never preached on the controversial issue of prayer coverings.[66] D. H. Bender remained concerned, however, with Swartzendruber's belief in the second blessing of the Holy Spirit, "that wild second work doctrine."[67]

Two years later, D. H. Bender asked Showalter to resign to placate the

Los Angeles mission. That attempt at pacifying the Los Angeles group did not work, however, because it coincided with Bontrager calling his local rival, Swartzendruber, "two-faced." The antagonism polarized the congregation. Any solution to the crisis taken by the mission alienated a sizable portion of the congregation. The issue that galvanized the various factions, however, was absentee denominational authority supposedly running the mission, exacerbated by power struggles within the mission involving Bontrager, Swartzendruber, and Showalter. Bontrager later confessed his wrong doing. In summer 1926, representatives of the Los Angeles congregation wrote a letter to the Mennonite Board of Missions and Charities requesting they become a fully independent congregation so that they could fix the problems themselves.[68]

Internal unity remained an issue in early 1928, when Bontrager was accused of failing to work in harmony with his superiors. Bontrager's irritation with the authority of the Mission Board resulted from their refusal to properly fund the mission, refusing to buy property necessary for expansion in the early 1920s, and insisting he follow their counsel.[69] Subsequently, Bontrager was accused of "hinder[ing] others from falling in line" and ordered by the Mission Board to "make good his promises and work in harmony with the board."[70]

By the late 1920s and early 1930s, two issues emerged that helped resolve the authority question in Los Angeles: Bontrager's financial incompetence and the question of dress. Bontrager's inability to run a fiscally sound operation was no revelation to anyone and was one important element in the case against him. His standing as local bishop (pastor) and superintendent of the mission insulated him from simple attempts to have him removed. Finally, the parties reached a compromise agreement, where Bontrager remained bishop if financial management was given to a competent, non-clerical treasurer. Bontrager agreed.

At the same time these issues of authority, independence, and leadership swirled about, the question of appropriate clerical apparel surfaced. The issue of whether clergy had to wear the "plain coat"—a plain black coat without lapels—created resentment over perceived restrictive policies of the controlling boards. Showalter, despite being unwelcome, had tried to force all church workers to wear the plain coat. The Los Angeles mission had promptly rejected that policy. Although Los Angeles was granted permission to choose their own "destiny," as an independent congregation, on the issue of the clerical plain coat and clothing prohibitions, such as on neckties, both the Mennonite Board of Missions and Charities (MBMC, sometimes called "Mission Board") and the Pacific Coast Conference expected them to follow denominational policy as a matter of unity. From the perspective of the local congregation, it was a matter of outside control and restrictive policies. Denominational leadership attributed the root of these problems to the fact that churches in the American West were made of people from many places, and therefore, many traditions vied for expression.[71]

Within a decade of becoming an independently run church, the Los Angeles Mennonites requested, in 1938, that they be returned to mission status. Life under the Pacific Coast District, where they were members as an independent congregation, was more restrictive than they had anticipated. The Pacific Coast District appointed a new bishop to Los Angeles, Brother G. D. Shenk, a cultural conservative, who raised the apparel issue again. Tensions developed once more in the Los Angeles congregation over dress codes concerning prayer coverings, clerical plain coats, and neckties. The MBMC expressed dismay over—but did not punish—the tendency in Los Angeles to ignore traditional dress codes. To the ire of Los Angeles Mennonites, the Pacific Coast Conference assigned them a bishop who attempted to enforce the dress codes with appeals to conference authority. Conference authority was an argument that held little weight in Los Angeles. Some members, however, enjoyed the cultural conservatism of Bishop Shenk, and one deacon even advocated for the forcible shaving of women's heads if they failed to wear the prayer covering, based on the biblical text 1 Corinthians 11:72.[72]

As Los Angeles was a city where the Mennonite Church desired a presence, and where many took winter vacations, it seemed prudent once again to welcome the Los Angeles congregation as a mission and not lose it entirely. This return to mission status was made to protect the Los Angeles Mennonite Church from the excesses of cultural conservatives appointed by the regional mission board in Oregon.[73] The leadership of the Mennonite Church, represented by S. C. Yoder, agreed with the request from Los Angeles, provided they stop their sartorial "quibbling" over coats, coverings, and neckties. Yoder asked the Los Angeles Mennonites to accept those who believed in the conservative dress codes and to understand that shifts in church/mission status in itself would not end the acrimony; only they could do that.[74]

Not until Glen Whitaker arrived from Oregon in 1940 was their partisan politicking and religio-cultural conservatism transcended. The transition to an intercultural church began, and new tensions emerged as they encountered Pentecostals, Catholics, Mormons, Jews, and "New Thoughters" in their neighborhood.[75] In addition to their recovered mission status, the Los Angeles congregation hoped for new leadership young enough to compete in the religious marketplace of Southern California while retaining Mennonite teachings and community.[76]

By fall 1940, Whitaker began a shop for local boys and a club for girls that operated in conjunction with the mission's Sunday school program. Within two years of the request for a new leader and mission status, in order to break the control of the cultural conservatives, the Los Angeles congregation, a homogenous Mennonite community of Swiss-German background, had a Sunday school class of sixteen African-American children and one Korean boy.[77] Racial tensions developed in Mennonite Los Angeles, and in the early 1940s, questions of Mennonite identity in the Mennonite church community were less about denominational authority or the cut of one's coat, and more about religion and race. These attempts by churches and their leaders to thread the socio-religious needle, from haircuts to wedding kisses, are part of at least two religious impulses— boundary maintenance with "the world" and evangelical engagement. A great diversity of people lived in California, where a long history of religious entrepreneurship had led many to practice their religious faith in ways they sought fit, and Mennonites were no exception. Mennonites seemingly were disappearing into the very promise that made California so attractive. The story might end here if Mennonites were not their own historical actors, but they were, and they carved out their space.

Religious and Cultural Tremors

From the 1920s to the 1960s, an evolving Mennonite identity was increasingly focused on evangelical criteria, giving primacy to individual piety and less emphasis on a traditionally understood Anabaptist Mennonite group orientation. There was a shift from outside theological influences—for example, Aimee Semple McPherson and Pentecostalism—to such cultural issues as tobacco use and higher education. All Mennonite groups struggled with Pentecostalism as a negative outside influence. However, the Mennonite Brethren, during the middle decades of the twentieth century, shifted their concerns to those influences that affected their relationship with evangelicals.

Part of the axis that the Mennonite Brethren were moving on was a rural-urban and trans-generational one; the tensions in Bethany can be understood as between rurality and urbanity, where understandings of "insider and outsider" were different. In other words, between the two factions, the challenge posed by modernity was different. Some in Bethany found modernity to be the terrible presence of ambiguity and constant questioning in the church's own education program, and relevance was sought through traditional structures of authority. Young urban professionals, however, found in modernity careers and worldviews that thrived in ambiguity, and they sought their own relevance in society. That turn to modernity was complemented with a desire to understand their Anabaptist roots.

General Conference Mennonites, perhaps the most socially progressive of the three, also most clearly described the type of Americanization they wished to experience—a love of country tempered with pacifism. Despite an inclination to social progressivism, some traditional Mennonite boundaries remained, for example, the prohibition on children attending dances. The smallest group in California, the Mennonite Church, no longer lonely and isolated, aggressively pursued a leadership that struck a balance between the fluid California social environment and their own traditional practices. They chafed against excessive cultural conservatism, especially over dress codes, and demanded that they approve local leaders as opposed to having them sent by a mission or conference board in Oregon or the Midwest.

The dynamics of group identity are seen in issues of dress codes and denominational authority in Los Angeles among Mennonite church members. Faithfulness to the group was connected to the theological principle of nonconformity to the world. Questions of neckties, moustaches, prayer coverings, and plain coats were not petty issues for those concerned; rather, they were connected to a theological and cultural idea of group identity that was also expressed in their difficulties with distant denominational authority. Though this happened among MC Mennonites across the country, as it concerned California, denominational leadership explained difficulties in Los Angeles as distinctive to California, a place where many different groups lived together.

In California, Mennonites largely accommodated the surrounding society through attempts at defining themselves as good Americans, asserting local control over their missions or churches, and relaxing dress codes. Yet, the lines between Mennonitism and society shifted. The Mennonite

Brethren, concerned with Pentecostalism in the 1920s, became concerned with such worldly influences during the 1940s and 1950s as excessive weddings and appropriate Sunday school content and teaching style.

Early twentieth-century Mennonite descriptions of California as a wonderland largely disappeared during World War II. The questions turned to "liberal sympathies," syncretism, and sufficient support of evangelicalism. Images used to understand self and society had changed. The Reedley Mennonite Brethren illustrate this change clearly. In fifty years they went from expelling G. G. and Margaretha Wiens in 1905 for a violent outburst of temper to demanding that the denomination in its official history record success in terms of statistical growth. Emerging from these early experiences began various strategies to maintain and understand Mennonitism in the face of California modernity. There was developing an already accessibly conservative evangelicalism, socially oriented "secular" orientations to social problems, and impulses toward restoring sixteenth-century Anabaptism ideals in a postwar urban context. It was all in play. As these shifts occurred, Mennonites were confronted with racial and religious diversity, and in the next chapter, we add these elements to the growing social complexity.

CHAPTER 5

New Neighbors

Confronting Racial and Religious Pluralism

The race issue looms pretty large here.
—Le Roy Bechler, Mennonite pastor in Los Angeles, 1960

Mennonites in the City of Angels

All three major Mennonite denominations—Mennonite Brethren, Mennonite Church, and General Conference Mennonites— wrestled with the ethno-religious character of their identities. Among the many factors that propelled Mennonites to migrate to California was evangelistic mission. They faced daunting challenges in their mission efforts as they sought to bridge deep cultural, religious, and racial chasms in a place where millions of immigrants were settling.

In the early twentieth century, Mennonite mission efforts in Los Angeles were primarily directed toward the needs of urban Mennonites and, as expressed in the early 1920s, "to unite the members of our churches living there."[1] Evangelism and social work aimed at non-Mennonites in the local community were secondary. After World War II, issues of race and religion grew more prominent as Mennonite mission efforts focused more directly on outsiders. Whether in relation to African-Americans in Los Angeles, migrant laborers in the San Joaquin Valley, or Catholics in both areas, the cross-currents of racial and religious pluralism became a significant challenge for the Mennonites, as for other white evangelical transplants to California.[2]

Mennonite Brethren in the Shadow of Satan

The Mennonite Brethren Pacific District's first mission project was City Terrace Mission Chapel in Los Angeles, opened in 1926 and headed by A. W. Friesen and his wife. The Friesens had decided to locate there after a local Mennonite pastor had shown them around City Terrace, a section of Los Angeles then populated by Jews and Catholics. However, they found it difficult to relate to their new neighbors: "The work in cities is difficult, especially among Jews and Catholics who have been taught to disbelieve the teachings of Jesus Christ."[3] It was a sentiment shared by many Protestant groups, including other Mennonites, who uniformly dismissed Roman Catholicism as a false religion. Perhaps the persistent anti-Catholicism was, as Jay P. Dolan described, similar to nineteenth-century American Protestant anti-Catholicism—"a leftover from the Protestant Reformation"—and the Reformation legacy was one that early California Mennonites hoped to preserve, at least in part.[4]

City Terrace was not only largely Jewish and Catholic but also near an African-American community.[5] Despite efforts by the Friesens and others, harmony among the various groups was elusive. In the late 1940s the mission reported that white and African-American children had trouble getting along, but as a result of "Released Time" (sometimes called "Release Time")—an education program developed in post–World War II California, where students were excused from class for religious instruction—the mission had become a colorful mix of "Negroes, whites, Mexicans and Filipinos."[6]

Workers at City Terrace Mission believed that God blessed their "work among the colored people."[7] They identified themselves as "evangelical Protestant[s]" engaged in a God-given "real ministry" in a neighborhood populated by Jews, Catholics, English, Germans, and Italians.[8] Just as Pentecostalism was a problem for Mennonites earlier in the twentieth century, mid-century engagements with religious pluralism also challenged them. This was a time when religious diversity was viewed as having little virtue, and Mennonites, along with much of the Protestant mainstream, considered Catholics and Jews "negligent and indifferent." In Fresno, some members of Sunset Gardens Mennonite Brethren Church, located in a Spanish-speaking Latin American neighborhood, even described the mere presence of Mormons and Jehovah's Witnesses as proof of Satan's attacks.[9]

The City Terrace Gospel Tabernacle and church bus, Los Angeles, California (undated).
Source: Vernon Friesen Collection.

The late 1940s was also a time when American evangelicalism discovered a new voice in Billy Graham, who was popularized during his 1949 Los Angeles revivals when California newspaper baron William Randolph Hearst demanded that his papers "puff" him.[10] The spirit of revival caught on at City Terrace Mission, which "point[ed] the way [to Christ] to many" and described "great spectacular meetings where scores have thronged the altar." The mission enjoyed an average weekly attendance of 500 at meetings and classes. Leaders wrote their mission reports in the revivalist evangelical language of "prayer warriors," asking, "Are you praying earnestly, fervently as we [witness] to these people in darkness," and telling stories of evangelical conversions mixed with entreaties to pray for "souls saved."[11]

Although the apocalyptic imagery explored in earlier chapters largely faded in the postwar years, Satan was still considered the culprit in 1950 when a number of mission workers took ill at the City Terrace Mission Chapel. As the Friesens exclaimed, "Last year Satan tried to hinder much as he always does."[12] However, the mission workers primarily emphasized the need for personal conversion of non-Christians and the divine help necessary for daily survival in Los Angeles: "God has proved over and over again that He protects His servants not only spiritually but also physically. One day a man looked for us with a shotgun and another drew a knife on me, but God marvelously took things in hand." On another occasion, "a gang tried to disturb our services . . . but found it impossible because we had three policemen guarding our meeting. Many more exciting experiences which also prove God's protecting care for His own, could be related."[13] Though they recorded no satanic disturbances that year, there were shotgun-wielding strangers and gangs that necessitated the protection of God and the police.

When City Terrace applied to become a formal Mennonite Brethren congregation and full member of the conference, as opposed to a fledgling mission church subsidized by the Board of Home Missions, they appealed to the ideal of denominational unity. However, they assumed that their diverse membership and geographic location in a demographically mixed place, though interesting, would pose a hurdle for acceptance into the larger denomination. The mission workers had reported on "difficulties [that] attacked us," and how witnessing in an area populated by Jews, English, Germans, Italian, and Spanish-speaking Catholics would "challenge any evangelical church." Thus their congregation could not help but be ethnically diverse. "Though these people do not come from a Mennonite background as most of you do, we are praying that you will make us feel that we are one with you," the leaders wrote to the larger Mennonite Brethren conference.[14]

The sense of battle continued into the 1950s. Gone was the violent urban dystopia, and worries about Satan faded somewhat, but a swelling population of tremendous ethnic and religious diversity pressed on Mennonite enclaves. In Southern California an older understanding of Mennonite identity was changing as a once stable and homogeneous Mennonite culture gave way to a demographically inclusive identity grounded in evangelicalism. Nonetheless, the change was slow for Mennonites who hailed from traditional moorings, as fear of youth gangs and Catholics remained close in their minds.

In 1956, Harold Schroeder, pastor of City Terrace Mennonite Brethren Church, wrote a letter to Rev. Waldo Wiebe, a Mennonite Brethren in Shafter, about the work in Los Angeles. Schroeder described two difficulties about their location: the youth gangs that made the streets seem unsafe at night, and another reason, "even more serious . . . the Roman Catholic Church." The Catholics had a church and school only three blocks away from the Mennonite Brethren congregation and had "made quite a bid on the community." Undaunted, Schroeder resolved that his neighborhood not be left to the Catholics and thus "deprived" of the Christian gospel.[15]

Although anti-Catholicism was common throughout Mennonite denominations and much of Protestantism, the blend of races, cultures, and religions—though of great concern—encouraged the Mennonite Brethren to stay and work harder than ever as missionaries. An example of this came in the late 1950s, when immigrants from Nicaragua settled in their neighborhood. Again, evangelical belief and practice energized the Mennonite Brethren with the religio-cultural resources and motivation to remain in a changing neighborhood.[16]

City Terrace, however, was only part of the Mennonite Brethren experience in Los Angeles. Demographics were changing at an increasing clip after the war. The United States Supreme Court struck down restrictive covenants in 1948, making illegal a long-standing practice of racial exclusion in selling property. Despite what some observers saw as the death of Jim Crow in Southern California, the ending of restrictive covenants did not end exclusionary practices. By the late 1950s, suburbs were mostly white, and blacks in south-central Los Angeles were largely prevented from moving and finding gainful employment. As the industrial economy shifted to advanced aerospace work, access to the necessary technical training was blocked for African-Americans because public schools were tiered by location. The Los Angeles Mennonite Brethren Church in the south-central area of the city closed in 1957, twenty-three years after it opened. As the Mennonites retreated to the suburbs of Downey and Lakewood to the southeast, they were part of a wider white migration— known by its racial impetus as "white flight"—that also included other evangelical churches.[17]

The evolving Mennonite Brethren story in Los Angeles had many complexities, as volatile race relations marked the history of the south-central sector of the city. Some Mennonites stayed as mission workers, and others dispersed. Mennonite Brethren were not the only white middle-class evangelicals wrestling with what to do in neighborhoods undergoing seismic racial and ethnic shifts in the 1950s. For example, evangelical Pepperdine College (now Pepperdine University) was initially located in Los Angeles in the 1930s. But by 1981, Pepperdine gave up on being a downtown campus and moved to Malibu. The school initially opened the Malibu branch in the early 1970s, when recruiting and fund-raising difficulties arose after the 1965 Watts riots and the 1969 shooting of a black student by a white Pepperdine security guard. What had been a safe white working-class, even middle-class, neighborhood with neighboring Watts, which by World War II was home to professional African-American workers, had in the postwar decades become a neighborhood populated by working poor blacks. Whites were leaving, and even if some of the evangelical crowd held on for a time, the Mennonite Brethren and mainstays of the evangelical old guard such as Pepperdine and the Church of the Open Door also eventually left.[18]

Facing an "Aggressively Evil Culture"

The story of the Mennonite Church, with its Swiss-German cultural roots, parallels in many ways the experience of the Mennonite Brethren denomination. When a group of Swiss-German Mennonites formed a congregation in the Los Angeles area in 1916, they gathered as a culturally homogenous congregation. Ironically, although the initial members were Swiss-German Mennonites, the only pastor they could find was an Armenian River Brethren named Mashack Krikorian. The fit made sense, as the River Brethren were a conservative Anabaptist church grounded in pietism and an offshoot of the Brethren In Christ. This initiative, originally called the 35th Street Mission, or the Los Angeles Church and Mission, was renamed Calvary Mennonite Church in 1940 after it moved to Seventy-Third Street. In 1960 Calvary divided over racial issues.

As early as 1921, Calvary Mennonite Church (then the 35th Street Mission) experienced internal tensions in relating to its non-Mennonite neighbors. At the July 24, 1921, meeting of the Los Angeles Church and Mission Committee, a resolution was passed stating that the Los Angeles congregation was a mission "worthy of our recognition" and that staff be assigned to it. Two months later, the Los Angeles mission sought a new location "on account of the Mormons buying all the lots [of land] all around the mission." The mission board agreed and resolved to begin a search for a new location within a week.[19] It was a complex undertaking for Calvary Mennonite members to redefine themselves, located as they were in a pluralistic and racially diverse urban setting.

By 1930, Calvary drew Mennonites from the Upland region for its worship services but found itself in a large urban environment wondering how to proceed in its work. The members articulated a deep sense of responsibility for their mission and asked fellow Mennonites, "Will you pray for us that the work may prosper in this large city and that many souls may find the Savior?"[20] Because of their sense of mission, the Calvary Mennonites held evangelistic meetings largely attended by co-religionists.[21] There were both conversions and "reconsecrations" at the meetings, and non-Mennonites from the community attended primarily to see their children in the mission's Christmas program. At the program, mission workers gave out food baskets to the attendees and delivered the seasonal message of Jesus' birth.[22] They deemed the event a success: "All seemed to enjoy the evening, if smiles are a criterion to gauge inner thoughts accurately."[23] Although the Mennonites found community outreach important, affirmation of their separation from the larger social world was also an objective of revival meetings. After a three-week series of meetings in 1932, "a number came forward to renew their consecration . . . As a visible result of the meetings the mark of separation from the world is clearly observable."[24]

It took until 1939 and the efforts of Glen Whitaker, a white pastor, for Mennonites to extend their mission efforts to the local black population. He began by ministering to children through a handicrafts program. The program became quite popular after he promised the children they would get a nickel if they brought a friend: "At first this activity was only for the white children but soon a number of colored children came. With an interest among the colored people, they began thinking of starting a Sunday school for them in this area."[25]

Despite these sputtering starts, only after World War II did an interracial ministry with the growing black population take root, when John Zehr, another white pastor, arrived. Many white congregants, however, resisted the interracial advances. Mennonites who had arrived in Los Angeles in the early decades of the twentieth century were a "tight homogenous group, both ethnically and religiously." On the Pacific Coast, they attempted to strictly enforce a cultural separation from the world—while still ministering to it.[26] Yet, as their conceptions of religious identity changed in California, their understandings of race and ethnicity were also stretched.

At mid-century some in the Los Angeles Mennonite Church wanted to minister to local blacks, but integrating the congregation was difficult. Whitaker worked with all groups who came to his Sunday school and military draft class and used a rural metaphor to describe the population of his mission efforts as "the field." As interest in Whitaker's Sunday school class and his children's camping ministry increased, the district mission board appointed a superintendent for them, H. E. Shoup. He was the first person chosen for this role and in fact had earlier sold the building to the congregation when they had moved to Seventy-Third Street with the understanding that "when the colored people organized a congregation they could buy it for themselves."[27] Already in 1950, however, the 35th Street Mission for the Colored in Los Angeles "requested the privilege to be a congregation independent of Calvary Mennonite Church on 73rd Street."[28] Mennonite Los Angeles was changing.

Whitaker did more than develop a Sunday school program; he was also deeply involved in running rural camps—a response to "the tyranny of modern city life."[29] In the 1940s, in Hidden Valley, near Los Angeles, Whitaker helped develop the first permanent campsite for the Mennonites. The camp's purpose was not only child evangelism, but also to teach children about their place in "God's creation."[30] During the 1950s, advocates of camping ministry increasingly used the language of rational management in place of natural retreat from urban ills. Camp ministries were increasingly described as "welfare camping," reaching underprivileged children and minority ethnic groups through "specialized programming." At mid-century, camps had become cultural sites that reflected the increasingly bureaucratic nature of religious missions while facilitating multicultural and interracial meetings.[31]

In 1955, Calvary Mennonite Church in Los Angeles expressed "gratitude" to the regional mission board for affirming plans to establish a Spanish-speaking mission in Los Angeles. Calvary did expect, however, that although they would run the mission, the national Mennonite Church body would pay for it. Calvary's support for a Spanish-language mission wavered as concerns over the financial stability of such a program emerged. In June 1956, another pastor at Calvary, John Zehr, sensed an undercurrent of "disapproval" in the congregation toward the Spanish initiative. Nevertheless, a month later, Jacob Shetler, president of South Pacific Mennonite District Mission Board, informed the secretary of home missions in Missouri that Calvary was "settled again" and could be counted on to support the Spanish outreach.[32]

Financial matters aside, in Los Angeles the Mennonite Church found the population "ever-changing."[33] Leaders of children's clubs, who believed Roman Catholic children were being prevented from attending Sunday school, reached out to local Catholics. Using rural-urban language, Zehr describes their work: "We have no plot of potatoes or corn to hoe for our missionary project. Club is our missionary project." The Sunday school had sixty to seventy children "of all races." Yet the city remained dystopic: "The culture that surrounds us is aggressively evil. The city church is immediately on the defensive against the encroachments of a wicked society." In response to their "evil" surroundings, Mennonite youth went to the beach for an annual beach party. Although an earlier generation had sought healing and divine instruction at the coast, the new generation "looks forward to this relaxation and fellowship on the shores of the Pacific Ocean."[34]

When Shetler began the process of finding a location for the mission in a Spanish-speaking area of Los Angeles, he discovered that several Protestant church groups—Methodist, Presbyterian, Baptist, Pentecostal Holiness, and Foursquare Gospel Church—were already located in the same neighborhood the Mennonites wished to settle. Shetler learned from the Foursquare pastor that work among the Spanish-speaking population was difficult because a nearby large Catholic church, which served the Latino population, opposed Protestant efforts to convert them.[35]

The Los Angeles Spanish Mission recorded similar concerns with Catholicism from 1956 to 1960. The workers at the L.A. Spanish Mission found that "communication with the whites about spiritual things is easier than the Spanish," and that Jehovah's Witnesses spoke about their religious beliefs more than "the average run of Protestants." This was a concern because Mennonites believed that the "Spanish easily fall prey" to the influence of Jehovah's Witnesses. In Los Angeles, Mennonite workers discovered that they not only had to deal with religious pluralism but also had to assert their own distinct identity because they were often confused with Jehovah's Witnesses. As one worker reported, "It has almost made me feel like putting in bold letters 'We are Mennonite Christians.'" Though Mennonites established a mission in Los Angeles to address a "great need," people in their neighborhood asked them not to hand out "information about [their] religion." In a reversal for Mennonites, they now found themselves losing out to the more aggressive Seventh-day Adventists.[36]

The concerns about Catholic influence continued with the expansion of the Mennonite Church's Spanish mission work to Montebello and Pico

Rivera in the late 1950s. When conversations with some of the children came to the topic of souls, Mennonite workers told the boys, aged twelve to fourteen years, that Catholics too could go to heaven "if they have met the conditions" and understand "sin and salvation." However, mission workers reported that difficulties arose for Catholic children at home when they "accepted Christ" at the mission. At the children's homes, "they receive no help" in their conversion and were still taken to catechism and Catholic services, which only deepened Mennonite concern.[37]

Catholics, who of course considered themselves Christians, especially frustrated the Mennonites.[38] James and Noreen Roth, in 1959, reported from the recently established Pico Rivera Spanish Mission in Los Angeles that it was difficult for them to present their gospel message to "Latin Americans who have had Catholic training from childhood up." Despite this alleged difficulty in reaching Catholics, the listeners of the Mennonite radio program *Luz y Verdad*, who wrote the station, were mostly Christians or "followed some cult or were Catholics or professed nothing at all."[39]

In addition to the African-American Sunday school program and the camps, Mennonites in the postwar era increasingly attempted interracial ministry with Spanish radio broadcasts. By the late 1950s, racial dynamics in the neighborhood had shifted from Mexican-American and Euro-white to predominantly African-American. The church divided over race, and the majority of its white members moved to the suburban Faith Mennonite Church in Downey, and Calvary became an African-American Mennonite Church congregation. In 1960, under the guidance of interim pastor James Lark, the church made the transition from Swiss-German Mennonite to African-American Mennonite. Lark was the first African-American Mennonite bishop.[40]

On April 3, 1960, Calvary Mennonite Church voted in favor of asking the South Pacific District Mission Board and the General Mission Board to take over their work as an African-American mission. Nelson Kauffman, secretary for home missions, in Hannibal, Missouri, interpreted this action as providing the opportunity for the entire South Pacific District Mission Board to develop a plan for church extension in California. For Kauffman this was an opportunity to run an African-American mission at the regional level. To ensure the church's viability, Kauffman invited Le Roy Bechler, a Swiss-German Mennonite who had trained under James Lark in Chicago and had worked among African-Americans in Michigan. After initially showing little or no interest in Los Angeles, Bechler finally came for a visit.[41]

Bechler found the situation in Los Angeles disheartening: "The [church] council seemed to have little or no interest in reaching the community . . . The group (who plan to leave) admit that they have been a failure in reaching the community, but are ready to leave it go at that." It was evangelism without integration. Bechler observed that despite reasons white congregants gave to explain their difficulties in staying at Calvary, including travel distances from home to church, "they further admit[ed] that distance is not the only factor involved since some who plan to withdraw will drive just as far. The race issue looms pretty large here." Bechler concluded that "for the sake of the Gospel," it was better that those people, who could not handle interracial neighborhoods and congregations, move away.[42]

At the time of Bechler's visit, following a series of interim pastors in the late 1950s, Calvary considered selling its property in order to move to a new neighborhood. Though the church leadership was convinced by the Home Missions Board to stay in south Los Angeles, the majority of congregants left anyway and, by 1960, had formed the Faith Mennonite Church in Downey. Calvary, now under the leadership of Bechler, adopted a more aggressive outreach to the community. Before the split, membership growth occurred primarily along family lines and Mennonite transfers. To break from these patterns, the congregation directly engaged the neighborhood. One of Bechler's first moves was to join the local parent-teacher association. Later, he credited these efforts for increased racial diversity by the 1980s.[43]

The remaining congregation at Calvary in 1961 described Le Roy and Irene Bechler's arrival as "a signal for a general [white] exodus." Bechler almost immediately issued "about 30 church letters," ostensibly for white membership transfer.[44] The African-American congregants accused the white members who departed of being ignorant and naïve. James Lark, in the January 1, 1961, church bulletin, observed, "For some time members of the Church considered that a shift in population trend demanded a change of church location . . . after much discussion and many meetings, the District and General Mission Boards agreed to take over and operate the 73rd St. plant [facility] as a Mennonite Church congregation."[45]

The changing ethnic demographics affected other ministries as well. In 1960 the president of the South Pacific Mennonite District Mission Board informed Lester Hershey, director of Spanish broadcasts in Ribonito, Puerto Rico, that the Spanish-language broadcasts to Los Angeles were to be cut because "in the last ten years or so [this has] become a colored area." He concluded that Calvary's focus will move away "from the Spanish to a more or less colored work."[46]

Thus by the early 1960s, the congregation had morphed into a "community of reconciliation" for the local African-American population. This transformation from an intentional cultural Mennonite community, rooted in its past European identity, to an African-American congregation within two generations could be viewed on one hand as a success for establishing an African-American Mennonite church in the heart of Los Angeles, but on the other hand as a failure for any hopes of birthing an interracial Mennonite church.[47]

General Conference Mennonites Join the White Flight

The Mennonite Brethren and the Mennonite Church were not alone in their struggles with racial issues. Already in 1909, the General Conference Mennonites had established a mission in a Los Angeles neighborhood they described as "Christless and churchless," populated by "Spanish and Italian Roman Catholics," and stunted by the perceived accruements of Catholicism's "superstition and its ignorance."[48] They portrayed priests as violently opposed to Christianity despite the eager hearts of the Catholic laity: "Notwithstanding the fact that the priests warn their people and even threaten them, the Lord has prospered the [Mennonite] work and graciously blessed the labors of a few."[49] There is brief mention of racial difficulty already in 1914, when the General Conference River Mission Station felt compelled to move because of the increased numbers of Asians and Italian Catholics moving into their neighborhood.

In the early 1920s, the Mennonites characterized the Italians as "indiffer[ent]," with an attitude of "get[ting] what they could without exerting themselves."[50] Despite the Mennonites' original vision of evangelizing a community that enjoyed little Protestant presence,[51] the rising number of Italians caused enough concern among the Mennonites that they moved away. In 1923, over the course of five months, the mission gave three reasons for its move. From January to March 1923, as families fled, Italian families replaced them in the neighborhood but did not attend the mission.[52] In April 1923 the mission highlighted "unruly" Italian boys who came to Sunday school, sometimes destroying property, and thus "it was thought best to discontinue as not much spiritual food could be left with the boys, they were coming more for a good time."[53] Finally, in May, the mission noted that if it moved, a Baptist mission would remain in the neighborhood and that the central L.A. location of the mission made attendance problematic for some Mennonites because of "traffic conditions" downtown.[54] In 1924, within fifteen years of opening its doors, the General Conference mission in Los Angeles—the Whosoever Will Mission— moved to another neighborhood and became the Immanuel Mennonite Church.

Los Angeles, for most Mennonites, was a bewildering bazaar of religious options and ethnic diversity, where the foreign mission field came to their doorsteps—indeed, the "heathen" were arriving from Asia and "Roman Catholic countries." Nevertheless, as Asians and Catholics moved to Los Angeles, Mennonites discovered that their other neighbors were Mexican, Italian, Greek, and Austrian. Implying a connection, a description of racial and national diversity was followed by a discussion of the violent, crime-infested city, where even police feared for their safety.[55]

People at Immanuel Mennonite Church—which eventually also moved to Downey, a more white suburb of Los Angeles at the time—found their fellow Los Angelinos so "mixed up in their minds with the teachings of Christian Science, Spiritism, Seventh-Day Adventism, Russellism, etc., that they either try to believe it all or refuse to believe anything."[56] What made these observations and actions by the Mennonites of the Whosoever Will Mission/Immanuel Mennonite Church significant was that in the 1935 *Mennonite Year Book*, they congratulated themselves as being specially equipped by God for city mission work, upholding the principles of nonresistance, and maintaining "opposition to secret societies and taking of oaths."[57]

They believed that their combination of theological purity and agrarian past resulted in "God . . . developing a class of people which He perhaps intended to use as a 'salt' among civilized nations." An idealized agrarian past made them well equipped to come from the country to save the city, because in America, the Mennonite "salt" prospered, and when combined with the "wise policies of the nation," it created "a sturdy race, a great faith and an unquestionable integrity."[58] An agrarian myth fused to American exceptionalism helped construct a sense of cultural, religious, and ethnic self-confidence, if not superiority.

Although the record falls silent, by the late 1950s, a letter written to

the Board of Home Missions in Chicago described the "adverse" population changes in Los Angeles, where increasing numbers of African-
Americans were moving in. The board wrote back, encouraging them to
sell their church property and leave. If they chose not to sell and move, the
Board of Home Missions warned, their property value would diminish
and they might have to give it away.[59]

In 1959, the Pacific District Conference of the General Conference
Mennonites, rethinking how they had handled race in their denomination, passed a resolution stating that they "have not always reflected a
Christian concern in this matter [racial discrimination]." The resolution
made other important points. First, it acknowledged the role President
Dwight D. Eisenhower had played in improving race relations in America
and pledged their support for him "in preserving the rights, dignity and
opportunities for Negroes and all minorities." Second, they pledged support for Martin Luther King and commended him and his supporters "for
their dependence on prayer and nonviolence amidst grave threats, suffering and injustice."[60]

After acknowledging the leaders' efforts to end racial discrimination
and finding common religious ground with King, the resolution encouraged members of their churches to write letters, on their own, to both
President Eisenhower and Reverend King. The resolution ended with a
declaration that the General Conference churches of the Pacific District
Conference should include minorities at all levels of service and administration.[61] But still, the congregation moved to suburban Downey.

Mennonite concerns at mid-century over the race and religions of non-
Mennonites stretched far beyond Los Angeles. Farther north, in the San
Joaquin Valley, an at-times strident anti-Catholicism was clearly present
in the mission outreach to migrant farm workers and their families.

Migrant Missions in the San Joaquin Valley

Mennonite missions to migrant laborers began in 1949. Migrant outreach
initiatives included counseling, a child nursery, evening recreational activities, educational programs, a traveling library, a nurse, a summer children's
program called Vacation Bible School, and Sunday school.[62] Although
outreach to migrant laborers emerged from local congregational initiatives, after World War II the nationally administered inter-Mennonite
relief agency Mennonite Central Committee (MCC), with its regional

offices, largely ran the migrant programs. Several religious groups were involved with migrant labor mission work, and by 1953, when the Mennonite Church's South Pacific Mission Board explored the Coalinga area for mission possibilities, they found not only Mennonites there but also "the Pentecostal Church and other similar groups" running Sunday schools.[63]

In January 1950, MCC began a Voluntary Service (VS) unit in Huron to minister to migrant workers. The VS program provided alternative service work in lieu of civil defense duties to Mennonite young people who qualified as conscientious objectors with I-W status. Although MCC assumed General Conference (GC) Mennonite support, the Mennonite Brethren initially rejected involvement in the program. The GC First Mennonite Church in Reedley began work in April that year with migrant laborers at a camp in Shafter. They believed that because the camp in Shafter was government run, it was better to work there than at the camp in Huron.[64]

A Mennonite trend toward closer working relationships with the government in the postwar decades was accompanied by the "total MCC approach," which combined social action with a presentation of the Christian faith. This combination of social and evangelical impulses caused some internal conflicts between workers and administrators, as when some signed up for the migrant program with the intention of evangelizing the laborers without addressing social concerns. Evangelism was certainly an objective of MCC but never the sole reason for engaging in its work.

With the growing association of social and evangelistic work, Mennonites used language describing migrant workers as if through an "imperialist gaze," assuming elements of Mennonite cultural superiority and authority.[65] In a letter to Ray Horst, assistant director of VS in Akron, Pennsylvania, Arlene Sitler, administrative assistant of MCC in Fresno County, discussed the future direction of the migrant program by the end of 1950: "Many of the migrants [are] becoming Christians and consequently stabilizing and elevating their standards of living. We learned much from their [migrants'] experience although our work will not be a strictly religious program."[66] The program, run by a parachurch organization, incorporated medical, recreational, and educational elements. With its mixture of evangelical religion and social action, some VS volunteers stressed evangelism; others stressed social justice. What bothered Arthur Jost, administrator of Kings View Homes (a Mennonite mental health facility in Reedley) and a member of the MCC West Coast leadership, was that Mennonites from eastern states emphasized the social program so strongly that "when they came West they perhaps even forgot their Bibles."[67]

If the absence of Bibles from the eastern states was lamented, in 1951, the influence of local agribusiness was formidable. That spring, people in migrant ministry debated moving their operation to Santa Clara Valley, near San Jose, because they found the summer temperatures in the San Joaquin Valley too hot. The large valley growers wanted the Mennonites to maintain their programs in the valley's labor camps, and so there they stayed.[68]

Endorsements by valley growers did not resolve all Mennonite insecurities. Despite the growers' acceptance of the Mennonite migrant ministry, the perception ministry workers had was that if their work was too overtly Mennonite, their attempts to convert Catholics would be ineffective.[69] This was significant because MCC discovered that the majority religion in the camps was Catholic or unnamed "radical religious cults." The presence of these other faiths defined for MCC the "need for the Church." Part of MCC's vision, beyond helping migrants transcend Catholicism and cults, was to guide the workers into permanent vocations. There was a stated urgency in this, as it appeared that mechanical pickers would soon replace human ones. Mennonites combined their concern for worker instability in the face of modernization with vocational training. The vocational training was to help laborers become "reliable Christian citizens."[70]

In the migrant labor camps of the San Joaquin Valley, Mennonite descriptions of Catholicism were largely negative.[71] Mennonite rhetoric often conflated "Mexican," "Mexican-American," "Spanish," and "Catholic" with "back-sliding," "fallen away," or "for the most part misfortunates [sic]." Mennonite camp workers described Catholics as territorial. When some Catholic Sisters from an unnamed order learned of the Mennonite mission to the children of migrant workers, they "forbade the children to come," for "they felt [this camp] was their territory." A Mennonite writer hoped that someone would present the children with the "true gospel, after the Catholics are through with their program." Using images of food and hunger to describe the desires of the laity, Mennonite language depicted Catholicism as unsatisfying. The Hispanic Catholics were "hungering after the true Bread of Life," and they "crave[d] spiritual food."[72] Accordingly, Mennonites understood that they needed to teach migrant workers the "ideals which will make [them] happier," taking up "responsibility to his fellow man and to his God."[73] In addition, an MCC interim director noted that although migrant workers had not "saved for the rainy days," the Mennonite workers must understand that the migrants did not cause all their problems "by [their own] improper financial habits."[74]

Mennonites did not confine their depictions, which reflected a certain sense of superiority over migrant workers, to religion. One example involves cleanliness, establishing a clean white child as the standard by which to judge other children. Judy (no last name given), working in a Fresno County migrant camp, wrote to her mother about a white girl. The girl was "filthier than all the brown kids put together," but after a washing she "changed from an ugly little mess to a beautiful little doll! She has blond hair and blue eyes—just adorable." Judy also characterized migrant workers as "uneducated, [possessing] no culture, so unsanitary, and so poverty stricken."[75] Judy's description of the migrant experience was more complex. She also empathetically described the migrant workers as having been taken advantage of, living in deplorable conditions of another's making. Other anecdotal reports present migrant workers and their families actively resisting their conditions, playing games, having parties, cooking, and showing gratitude to Mennonites.[76]

Despite such rhetorical confidence and having the support of the MCC, the migrant mission program was fraught with instability. The First General Conference Mennonite Church of Reedley regularly sent workers to conduct Sunday classes at the Coalinga camp mission, but in the early 1950s, they needed support from the MCC West Coast Regional Office. In 1952, the MCC West Coast Regional Office even expressed concern that the operation in Coalinga would fail during the summer due to financial and mission worker shortages. Growers in the area secured financial support, but the mission worker supply remained uncertain.[77]

By the mid-1950s, the migrant ministry, known informally as "The 'Church' on Wheels," was working with various community organizations and government departments, including Public Health Services, the American Red Cross, local adult education programs in high schools, law enforcement, and the Department of Employment. So, while evangelical in its desire to lead people to Christian salvation, the ministry was also part of a wider social reform movement that tied various groups together to make the tedium and hard labor of migrant workers tolerable.[78]

In 1959, after the Brethren In Christ and the Reedley Mennonite

Brethren Church showed interest in running the Huron migrant camp, the main MCC ministry for migrant labor in California—which began in Coalinga and moved to Huron in 1955—closed due to a lack of leadership and its geographic distance from the Mennonite constituency.

Meanwhile, in the mid-1950s, the Mennonite Brethren began work among Hispanics outside the labor camp context. In 1955 members of the Reedley church rented a dance hall in the nearby migrant farm worker village of La Colonia (now Parlier). They passed out program flyers, but no one came. In preparation for the second meeting, the Mennonite Brethren workers went to homes to pick up people in order to bring them. However, they forgot the keys to the building and instead held the meeting in their cars. Such difficulties notwithstanding, three years later, in 1958, the average attendance in Parlier was over two hundred. Mennonite Brethren preachers such as Dr. Schlichting, the first of the mission preachers, spoke through interpreters and in that process trained Hispanic leaders. In fact, "interpreting proved to be a training ground for young Hispanic preachers." Dr. Schlichting started Hispanic churches in Reedley in 1962, Orange Cove in 1965, and Traver in 1979. Hispanics eventually pastored all these churches, founded by Anglos. The Home Missions Board of the Pacific District Conference of Mennonite Brethren Churches supported these churches as they increasingly "gain[ed] more self-sufficiency."[79]

A Mennonite Brethren study by Ruby Dahl assessing their work among Spanish speakers in the Reedley-Dinuba area described three characteristics of Hispanic people: they are usually Catholic, individualistic, and migrant. In interviews with Mennonite Brethren pastors who worked with Mexicans and Mexican-Americans, the pastors described Catholicism as a religion captivated by idols and superstition, and Catholics as possessing no understanding that church and daily life were connected. Dahl described Mexican-Americans as individualistic, but not egalitarian, because the men were hard drinkers who needed to seduce women to prove their manliness, and the women were expected to remain sexually pure for the sake of the home. The study concluded that the best way to evangelize Mexican-Americans, captivated—as the argument went—by their superstitious, idolatrous, and "simple and childlike" religion, was to reach them while they were still migrants and unsettled geographically and economically. It would make conversion easier.[80]

Pluralism, Diversity, and Anxiety

However cognizant Mennonites were of their Christian obligation to be a witness of their faith to all peoples (and their experiences in Southern California and the San Joaquin Valley show that they clearly were), when racial diversity encircled them at mid-century, they made disparate responses. The Mennonite Church in Los Angeles started a new church in the suburbs and provided the option to move, resulting in a white migration to a suburban church, with the urban one becoming an African-American congregation. The Mennonite Brethren considered their urban location a "hard" place to live and work, but they stayed as a mission-based church even as the Anglo Mennonite congregation closed. Perhaps their evangelical sense of mission provided enough religious and social capital, in the context of missions, to remain when Italian Catholics and African-Americans moved in. Thus, while City Terrace remained faithful to its origins as a mission to non-Mennonites, the Los Angeles Mennonite Brethren Church closed in the face of changing demographics.

Rhetorically, Mennonites characterized the Catholicism of many of their neighbors as governed by threatening priests, "ignorance," and "indifference." Whether it was Italian Catholics in 1920s Los Angeles or Hispanic Catholics in postwar San Joaquin Valley migrant labor camps, Mennonites approached their religious, ethnic, and racial "other" neighbors with a measure of caution, purpose, and at times superiority.

Los Angeles Mennonites of European descent faced the pressures of pluralism at mid-century as population shifts in Southern California brought not only new neighbors, but new anxieties. White Mennonites of Germanic, Swiss, or Dutch-Prussian-Russian stock reacted to their African-American neighbors both by staying in inner-city communities and by moving to suburbs that aligned with their own socioeconomic and racial identities. The more "progressive" the denomination, the more likely its members were to flee.[81] The more evangelical and less attached to Mennonite sociocultural form, the more likely Mennonites were to stay in urban areas, even if with a strong sense of errand, as the demographics changed.

In postwar California, Mennonites engaged increasingly with mainstream California culture. As seen in previous chapters, if they were awed and embattled upon migrating to the garden that was California by forces beyond their control, they were nonetheless able to project a distinctive Mennonite identity by constructing new religious patterns and social institutions. They enjoyed California's healing environment and adapted certain ethno-religious characteristics, such as dress codes, to their new cultural environment.

By mid-century Mennonites enjoyed a robust confidence in their accomplishments in California's diverse and pluralistic society. Their transformation included a growing sympathy toward mainstream conservative evangelicalism. Moreover, their comfort with being Californian blossomed in the twentieth century as they navigated a pluralistic religious environment and adapted their own ethno-religious identity. Changing religious and racial demographics forced diverse responses in Los Angeles, while in the San Joaquin Valley, Mennonites, with little hesitation, employed colonialist tropes to describe migrant workers, most of whom were of Hispanic Catholic background, and displayed the white evangelical racial anxieties of the day. Ironically, Mennonites clearly saw their new neighbors as outsiders, as they—in a half-century about-face—were now working, observing, and reporting as California insiders. Change was everywhere in society and church. Although various plans and tactics were used to navigate new demographic realities along the lines of mission outreach and church location, the evolving nature of gender roles also emerged. We turn to explore part of the evolution of gendered roles in Mennonite religious practice through the example of women's missionary societies.

CHAPTER 6

From Sewing Circles to Missionary Societies

The Public Roles of Women in the Church

Lord help us to accomplish the greatest possible good in
the shortest possible time.
—Reedley MB Church Women's Missionary Society theme for 1940–1941

Sewing in Church

From the early twentieth century on, Mennonite women took the initiative in creating sewing circles in California. As with much else in life, over the course of the 1900s, there were struggles with changing roles and identities as well as jockeying with authority. In sewing circles, which became missionary societies, Mennonite women openly, creatively, and actively associated with a range of evangelical and mainstream organizations. Over the course of especially the postwar decades, they expanded their role in the church and used images resonant with American exceptionalism to identify themselves.[1] Though often denied formal leadership roles in Mennonite churches, women exercised influence through missions, which acted as "parallel organizations" to church structures.[2] The women found themselves living as insiders and outsiders in their own churches, but they were not "passive victims of religious ideologies." They negotiated "roles within the ideologies" of their churches while addressing issues of gender, evangelism, and social relief.[3] At midcentury, they recalibrated their efforts through rationalized administration, hard work, and patriotic show.

Mennonites were creating new organizations as an integral part of their response to various internal and external pressures. Organizations such as women's sewing circles show how the development of new institutions reflects a changing vision of Mennonites in society—especially as groups such as the Mennonite Central Committee (MCC), Voluntary Service (VS), women's groups, and schools interact.

Women began the first California Mennonite Brethren sewing circle in 1913 in the Reedley Mennonite Brethren Church. They gathered to raise money for missions in Russia, China, and India. That first year they collected $50 for two missionaries in China and $125 for missions in India. By 1918, they had raised $820 and, in 1919, $1,545.[4] On January 21, 1937, twenty-five years later, a second group formed in Reedley, the Christian Charity Workers. Accounting for changing dynamics for women, this was an evening group for younger women with children or jobs.[5]

Missions were an entirely suitable, and among the only, venues for women to access public roles in church. They also formed "to organize a mission society in order that they as sisters of the church would be enabled to more specifically serve to further the work of the Lord."[6] The language is a subtle and complex merging of not only gender expectations, but internal church cohesion grounded in gendered relations of "sisters"—to each other and presumably to the "brothers." At their inaugural meeting, the 1913 Reedley group acted on their convictions, fusing piety with administrative process, in reading scripture, praying, and democratically electing their officers by ballot. Thus, "with great enthusiasm the work was begun by bringing together some funds and materials with which to begin working." They began quilting and mending clothes as "a testimony to their commitment to mission work." It was a gendered, tactile, and clearly public expression of faith.[7]

In promoting their work in both spiritual and material terms, they sought the blessing of church leaders. Their pastor, Rev. John Berg, praised them "for their noble efforts and advised them to proceed without delay and agreed to bring the matter [of their organizing] to the church membership for approval." Berg did so and the church membership accepted the group with "their blessing" and regarded them "as an official service" of the church. The circle credited that support for encouraging many women to join. At their recognition service, Reverend Berg prayed; read Acts 9:35–43, a text about a woman named Dorcas who helped an invalid with garments she made; and "gave them much good advice which later proved of great value."[8]

Decades later, the sewing circle looked back over their work and wrote anniversary histories, which over time included significant though subtle changes themselves. The paragraphs describing the start of the "Women's Missionary Society" in both the 1955 and 1980 histories are nearly identical except for the insertion of a short phrase in 1980. The 1955 edition concludes: "This resulted in the formation of the Pacific District Women's Missionary Service, the object of which is to keep the missionary societies informed of the ways in which they can assist in carrying out conference projects."[9] In the 1980 edition, the corresponding sentence reads, "The main functions of the women's district conference group are to inform all missionary groups of the district about ways in which they can assist in conference projects, *and to emphasize the importance of prayer to undergird the work of the Mennonite Brethren.*"[10]

The change signals a pietistic and evangelical cultural shift from emphasizing practical affairs to individual practices. The 1955 history concludes: "God's blessing has rested upon this women's organization, and it has been used in the Master's service to help bring the Gospel 'To all the World.' His Word, as found in Isaiah 58:11, has again proved itself true. 'And the Lord shall guide thee continually . . . and thou shalt be like a watered garden and like a spring of water whose waters fail not.' "[11] The 1980 account is more succinct. It adheres to the same point of God's approval but does so with less rhetorical flourish: "God has blessed and is continuing to bless the work of the M. B. Missionary Society in bringing the Gospel 'to all the world.' "[12] Between these accounts, twenty-five years apart, their identification with evangelical piety became clearer.

As the Reedley sewing circles expanded and adapted to the needs of their membership, women in the nearby Shafter Mennonite Brethren Church had an altogether different experience. There, it took two years for the Church Council to accept the sewing circle in principle and an additional seven years to fully approve it in 1928. Although they disbanded in 1934, under the leadership of Mrs. P. P. Rempel, they reorganized into the "'Bible Class and Sewing Hour.' "[13] This does not, however, denote inactivity.

During the 1920s and 1930s, most of the clothes and money given by the Shafter church to the starving Mennonites in Russia and Canada came through the women's sewing circle. In fact, they finally overcame Church Council's reluctance to approve their sewing circle when they agreed to buy the church a piano, using the old one as a down payment. John C. Penner and Adolf I. Frantz, Shafter chroniclers, strongly disapproved of the council's terms: "What Christian condescension! From then on until the present day, except for a few war years, when on account of a gas shortage, transportation was lacking, the women of the church have sewed and quilted, conducted sales, donated of their time and money to such an extent that their work constitutes one of the brightest chapters in the history of the Mennonite Brethren relief and Missionary enterprise."[14] Sewing circle ministry spread quickly as groups formed in prewar Reedley, Shafter, and Los Angeles.

Women asserted influence by creating their own organization and making choices regarding the work they did. Moreover, their choices were consequential for everyone in the church. They were negotiating roles within religious ideologies.[15] Such conflict and negotiation did not dampen their liveliness as they developed organizations. Shafter's records begin on September 4, 1923, with thirty-one women attending, although this was their fourteenth meeting. They met in a member's home, where meetings typically opened and closed with singing, prayer, and scripture reading. Like their counterparts in Reedley, the Shafter women held annual relief sales and only missed the 1933 sale when they sewed for the Red Cross. Such was their pattern throughout the 1920s and 1930s.[16]

Shafter disbanded for five years but reorganized on March 2, 1939, and "met for the purpose of organizing a Bible Class and sewing hour. [Where] the ladies strongly desired more time to study the Bible under her [Mrs. P. P. Rempel's] able leadership."[17] Their projects remained mission oriented: visiting homes and collecting and mending clothing for missionaries. On one exceptional occasion, they even installed a bathroom for Mrs. Rempel after sending her and her daughter on a vacation. All their work was performed in a religious context that placed priority on Bible study and "able leadership," where they met needs both from within and without their group.[18]

After several years, the church deaconate—a church office devoted to spiritual and physical needs within the congregation—demonstrated its approval when the deacons approached the Bible Class for canned fruit. The deacons told the women that they hoped to bring canned fruit on visits to poor people and asked if the Bible Class was willing to can it for them. The women decided to can apricots in June and asked of themselves that everyone "visit some sick or lonely person before the next meeting."[19]

In addition to the apricots, they canned approximately 200 quarts of peaches that June.[20] By the 1940s, the Shafter women had established a stable and active mission organization, complete with an effective leadership structure, standardized meeting structure, and the authority to decide not only on which projects to work but also their level of cooperation with the deacons.

As Shafter's circle was beginning, women at the General Conference's Whosoever Will Mission (later the Immanuel Mennonite Church) in Los Angeles created the Mary-Martha Circle on September 29, 1918, under the leadership of Ina Feighner. It was one of two circles there, and its name came from the New Testament texts Luke 10:38–42 and John 11. Their purpose was "to study the life of Christ more fully in detail and to be a help in the church wherever necessary."[21] Although the details of the early years of the Mary-Martha Circle are sketchy, in early 1919 they held their first evening service for the entire church, which was praised: "What a fine organization to help make matters more attractive and blessed!"[22] At times, they also visited other Mennonite churches to deliver a missionary program.[23] Throughout the 1930s, the two circles at Immanuel focused on different forms of mission: the Mary and Martha Circle stressed the needs of their congregation and Bible study; the Missionary Sewing Society collected and mended clothing for relief in Africa, Asia, and Canada.[24]

In a Time of War

Just as it touched most everything else, World War II affected sewing circles. As migrant labor camps and Civilian Public Service (CPS) camps—camps for conscientious objectors to perform work of national importance in lieu of military service—emerged, foreign mission support declined within many circles. Within the General Conference, at the Women's Missionary Sewing Society at Immanuel Mennonite Church, both the labor camps and the CPS camps took precedence. War forced greater interdenominational work through such agencies as the Mennonite Central Committee (MCC) and CPS. Although migrant camps received baby clothes and some money, CPS received most of the attention, including food, kitchen supplies, Christmas cards, and clothing donations.[25]

In 1948, the Pacific District secretary for the Mennonite Church, Anna M. Snyder, read a paper at the district's Annual Sewing Circle Meeting titled, "Service Not a Substitute for Spirituality." It is one of the more theologically reflective statements by California women societies on the nature of their work. She outlined her understanding of the relationship between spirituality and church work in terms of evangelical and pietistic theology: "Spirituality is the result of the operation of the Spirit of God by the instrument of the Word of God upon the individual," and "the source of spirituality is Christ Himself." Snyder embraced the individual's experience of Christ in evangelical terms, where the person submits to Christ and confesses sin, thus "receiv[ing] pardon through the merits of the atoning work of Christ in the shedding of His blood on Calvary." Having experienced the "operation of the Spirit of God," then succumbing to God's voice and finally adhering to an evangelical theology of atonement, Snyder argued, she and other faithful were ready to "to prove our faith by our works . . . [understanding] that our service will be to the glory of God, that it will be the result of and not a substitute for spirituality."[26] They constructed their identity by combining piety, evangelicalism, and social action.

The sewing circle at the Bethany Mennonite Brethren Church in Fresno, for example, worked not only for their church but also the local Red Cross, representing a broad understanding of priorities and social-religious affiliation. The Bethany sewing circle began on February 15, 1940, and made two decisions that day: whether to strike out on their own or join the Reedley Mennonite Brethren Women's Missionary Society, and whether to work for the Red Cross. They decided to form their own independent group. At the following meeting, on March 21, 1940, they appointed a committee to study the possibility of doing work for the Red Cross. Three years later, on March 4, 1943, they decided to work for the Red Cross only when the organization needed help and after a special meeting was called to decide action on a case-by-case basis. Those restrictions were short-lived. On April 1, 1943, some women took Red Cross work home with them from their meeting. Red Cross work was fully embraced by June 24, 1943, when without holding a special meeting, or recording any discussion, it was their official project that day.[27]

The Bethany circle established a similar structure as the others: electing a slate of officers, opening a bank account, assessing a membership fee (twenty-five cents), and forming committees for various tasks, ranging from the Red Cross to refreshments. They organized their meetings around singing, prayer, scripture reading, and project work while dividing their attention between the Red Cross and Mennonite service projects.[28] They operated in a similar way to women in Dinuba, who split their work between Mennonites in the military—for whom they made a "service flag, on which to put the names of the boys in the service of our country"—and CPS men at Three Rivers Camp, for whom they made aprons.[29]

At the same time, the Reedley Women's Missionary Society ran very successful relief sales, averaging $4,000 a year from 1943 through 1945. The sales raised money and collected needed items for the church building fund, the mental health hospital Kings View Homes (KVH), the senior care facility Home for the Aged, and their own church.[30] As they grew, they developed a rational organizational structure. In their yearbooks, which contain the upcoming year's activities and meeting outlines, a different theme for each year was recorded. In 1940 the motto was a folksy "To serve the master is our aim, M. B. Mission Society is our name." Each year, they also elected a slate of officers to fill twelve positions: president, vice-president, treasurer, secretary, gift treasurer, sewing advisor, assistant advisor, program chairman, hostess chairman, visiting chairman, charity chairman, and decoration chairman.[31] Throughout the early 1940s, annual themes included a prayer, "Lord help us to accomplish the greatest possible good in the shortest possible time," and a slogan, "For God and Home and Everyland."[32]

In 1942, they created the office of historian, a position that had several incarnations. It began as a separate office in 1942–1943, was combined with public chairman in 1944–1945, and dropped completely in 1951 until finally paired with the publicity chairman in 1957. The duties of historian are not given, but in practice the historian kept a scrapbook of pictures, mementos such as banquet invitations, and newspaper clippings.[33] Although the historian appears to have been more a chronicler, the results of her work helped fashion and preserve women's understanding of their work, its significance, and their identity.

The Shafter sewing circle did very well through most of the 1940s. It averaged nearly twenty members a year for over sixteen years and made dozens of comforters and quilts for MCC, along with collecting thousands of pounds of used clothing. In addition, they worked on several projects for the church and on one occasion with the Boy Scouts.[34] When the *Zionsbote*, the official publication of the Mennonite Brethren Church in North America, reported a need for bedding, the sewing circles advertised the need in the local newspaper, and in response the community donated eighteen comforters, twelve blankets, and nine pillows, in addition to the ninety-eight comforters made by the circle. Its meetings also mixed work

The Reedley Mennonite Brethren Church Missionary Society, ca. 1951.
Source: Records of Reedley Mennonite Brethren Church.

with spiritual development, often simultaneously: "For our devotions we usually quoted Bible verses and sang songs, not only for devotions, but also while working."[35]

The Shafter sewing circle had to overcome some financial difficulties in the late 1940s. After running out of money in March 1947, an appeal was made to their pastor, Rev. H. D. Wiebe, who then held a special Easter offering for them, raising sixty dollars.[36] After the special offering, they were told "there would always be money in the church treasury to carry on their work."[37] Actions such as this offering, the pastor helping the circle when in need, the large amount of work the sewing circle did for the church itself, in addition to sewing clothes for the needy, demonstrates a supportive relationship between the women and the larger church. Such support changed, however, when a new pastor collided with a growing regional women's movement.

Postwar: Rationalizing the Work

In October 1948, the Mennonite Brethren Pacific District Conference asked the Reedley Missionary Society "to make a survey of the women's groups in the district, and to report on their activities, finances, and on their distribution of the money. An outcome of this survey, the conference saw the necessity for coordination." The result was the creation of the Pacific District Women's Missionary Service, with the mandate "to keep the missionary societies informed of the ways in which they can assist in carrying out conference projects."[38] The survey found that there were eighteen women's groups with approximately 380 members with a combined cash income of approximately $20,000. When the values of relief materials were added, it totaled approximately $40,000. Following the report, the conference was favorably disposed to their formally organizing in order to avoid duplication in their work as individual circles. At the Mennonite Brethren regional district level, the Women's' Missionary Service (WMS) formally organized on November 14, 1948, with the support of the conference and most of the pastors. There was some resistance, mostly from Rev. Waldo Wiebe, the new pastor in Shafter.[39]

All that was left was formal recognition of the WMS at a service in Reedley that November. Waldo Wiebe, who disapproved of the idea, wrote J. B. Toews, pastor of Reedley Mennonite Brethren Church, a letter informing him of a resolution passed by Shafter's Church Council:

> You are aware of my personal reaction as to the report at the Conference, and I wish at this time to further convey the feeling of the Church Council which is in perfect agreement and have made the following resolution which we wish that you would present to the sisters who are in charge of calling this meeting: "We, the Church council of the Shafter Mennonite Brethren Church, encourage our sisters to continue with the work but we do not wish them to organize with the intention to report to the Pacific District Conference."[40]

Toews replied, "After consulting with the brethren H. R. Wiens and B. J. Braun, we felt that it would not be a proper procedure to read your letter to the group for as much as the Conference had passed a resolution recommending that this organization be effected." Later Toews suggested, "It would be the proper procedure to register such an opinion to the Conference instead of to the sisters who have proceeded on the strength of our Conference recommendation."[41] Wiebe was effectively rebuffed, and the service went as planned.

Wiebe, however, had already hedged his position by telling Toews that the women in his church did not even want to be there. In his telling:

"We have also talked to our Sewing Circle. We have as a church no objection in their planning together and counseling together of how to carry on their work, but our Sewing Circle officers do not wish to be presented at the conference in a report that is given by their organization as an official Conference organization." Wiebe claimed, "They rather choose to work quietly under the direction of our local relief committee and Church Council who shall make it a point to report and carefully pray and support the worthy efforts of our Sewing Circle."[42]

As historian Valerie Rempel discovered, the Shafter women actually believed their ambition was ignored and experience misrepresented. In fact, their minutes show they planned to be in Reedley and were surprised when Wiebe requested they not attend.[43] The women respected his request, though not without disappointment. In the minutes of the Shafter sewing circle, the following comments were underlined—and it is only in regards to this issue that any underlining occurs anywhere in their minutes—"This is Wednesday [November 3, 1948], we met today because we expected to go to Reedley tomorrow to organize as a womens [sic] mission society [sic]." The minutes of November 18, 1948, begin with, also underlined, "We didn't go to Reedley after all." Two weeks later, on December 2, 1948, the minutes read, "For our devotional Rev. Wiebe read Exodus 35:23 to 26 and explained to us why he thinks we should not join the womens missionary soicioty [sic]."[44] Despite resistance from their church's leadership, the sewing circle found it in their interest to be a part of the larger WMS and worked to that end.[45] They joined WMS in January 1950.

The organizers of the November 1948 recognition service were prepared for some resistance: "A missionary visiting our Missionary Society, informed us of strong opposition from several pastors to such an organization. We felt that we had to expect some opposition, since any new thing, no matter how good, has usually some opposition." The WMS responded in spiritually humble fashion: "It drove us to our knees, and we prayed much for God's guidance, and that His will be done." Some of the women thought that the problem was in church leaders who feared a power struggle: "It seemed that some [church leaders] were fearful that the women wanted to be on the Conference Program and gradually would take over." After opposition subsided, and the WMS had grown to twenty-eight circles with a membership of approximately nine hundred, the leader behind its creation, Lydia Martens, reflected: "We also thank the Lord for those who were opposed, for it caused us to pray much, and search our hearts to see whether we were really seeking only the glory of God."[46] The WMS never intended to usurp authority, but their very creation worried some. They searched their hearts as good pietistic evangelicals and found that in this case, they were correct and continued on their way.[47]

However, WMS did intend to be part of the American story. In the 1948 general report of the sewing circles of the Pacific District Conference, WMS president, Lydia Martens, historicized the creation of sewing circles. She located their significance in the westward course of American settlement and domestic influence of women: "As people moved westward and new churches were organized, in time they also had their Missionary Societies, the women realizing that there were some things to be done in the kingdom of God which only women could do." She recounted a story of "an expectant mother on the verge of despair because of the adverse circumstances, not knowing how she would clothe or feed her baby, found new hope when she saw the little embroidered designs on the baby garments and the label, 'In the Name of Christ!'" Finally, linking it to their project, "Today every church in the Pacific District Conference has one or more such groups, with a total of eighteen groups, an approximate membership of three hundred and eighty."[48] It was a thematically rich tale linking gender, faith, and nation.

Martens wove together images of America's westward expansion with the strength and civilizing work of women: "It is difficult to give an accurate report of all that the women do, as women do numerous little things in the home that go unnoticed and yet mean so much in making a home pleasant, which is also true in our societies. Too, a great deal has been done of which no record has been kept." Her report helped establish a self-awareness that their work was of national importance. Their list of projects beyond the Mennonite world was impressive: "Red Cross, Release Hour, North Carolina Mission, Christian Radio Programs, Los Angeles Children's Home, Grace Children's Home, American Bible Society."[49] They fused traditional womanhood, grounded in family, with national ambition, which was reflected in the scope of their work.

Over the following year, 1949, the WMS executive located the functional place of the WMS within the larger conference. In February 1949, they adopted the tentative name Pacific Coast Women's Missionary Society and passed a series of resolutions: "To be of help and to work with the individual circles; to try and distribute the work of supplying the needs of going missionaries and those out in the field; to call for unified prayer for our missionaries and relief workers." They "divided the work into 6 phases; Prayer, Missionary Program, Missionary Sewing, M.C.C., Extension Work, and Home for aged." They drew up specific tasks for the six phases, "to avoid duplication of our work at one place, and perhaps avoid omitting some needs entirely at another field."[50] The transformation of a once grassroots network of local sewing circles into an efficient umbrella organization was well under way.

Expanding the Work

At their annual meetings, held each November, WMS invited a special speaker to deliver an address. In 1949 they invited Rev. A. E. Janzen, executive secretary of the Mennonite Brethren Board of Foreign Missions. He underscored the connection between WMS's purpose and America's ascendancy: "He stressed the fact to us how fortunate women in America are compared to the women of heathen lands. Christianity changes woman's place from slavery to a higher level of understanding."[51] Janzen's understanding of the "place" of women within the church and society was predicated on American exceptionalism and selective historical memory concerning the complex relationship between Christianity and slavery. Another Mennonite Brethren leader, J. B. Toews, always supportive of the WMS, spoke in 1956 and "stressed the important part the woman has in the motivation of the spiritual program in our conference."[52] In the former, women were acted on by the historical forces of American Christianity; in the latter, women acted on conference work.

The role of women in mid-twentieth-century Mennonite Brethren Pacific Conference work expanded dramatically through the 1950s. In that decade, at least two themes emerged: WMS continued a process of professionalizing and expanding relief work, and church leaders increasingly sought financial assistance from them while verbally embracing traditional domestic roles. WMS in its growth eventually encouraged organizational conformism as its influence in the Pacific District Conference grew.

New local groups continued to form. At the first meeting of Fresno's Butler Avenue Mennonite Brethren women's missionary society (to be named the Mary-Martha Circle), in May 1957, they read John 15, discussed their name, and filled a range of administrative offices, including president, vice-president, and secretary-treasurer, as well as work, MCC, program, and hostess committees. They agreed to hold two meetings a month in the daytime and evening, with each one beginning with a devotional led by a member. At their second meeting, they held an installation ceremony for the officers, where the president stood in the center, officers stood around her forming spokes, and the rest encircled them to form a wheel. The symbolism, as it was explained, was that for a wheel to work, all parts were important. Afterward, they had a skit "on the proper ways of visiting in Japan," and renamed the Sunshine Committee as the Cheer Committee.[53]

Over the next two years, the Mary-Martha Circle received many donations from their members, including a sewing machine, "saladizer," and forty serving trays. Butler's board of trustees authorized the Mary-Martha Circle to choose the pattern of dishes and tableware for the church. They also created a flower committee responsible for acquiring and arranging flowers for the church. The Mary-Martha Circle held a "grocery shower" for Mennonite Brethren Biblical Seminary (MBBS, now Fresno Pacific Biblical Seminary) students, raising twenty dollars in groceries and four dollars in cash from forty-two women.[54]

At the regional level, back in 1954, WMS had made several decisions to develop their structural identity, including adopting a constitution, which framed their purpose: "To promote spiritual growth. To help the various needs of our church, District Conference and General Conference with prayers, sewing, donations in kind and cash."[55] The constitution defined voting practices, membership requirements, the executive committee, and a smaller executive board. The only deference made to male leadership in the document was the automatic inclusion of pastors' wives in the WMS and in the WMS executive board. Powers within the WMS executive committee increased whereby they could bypass a two-thirds majority vote and call special meetings of the executive board. They also decided at the meeting that in the future, all money collected locally was to be forwarded to the secretary-treasurer, signaling a centralizing of power and resources.[56] The WMS membership retained final approval of which projects to support, and requests from Mennonite institutions increased through the 1950s.

Arthur Jost, who had recently established KVH in Reedley, secured the support of churches to help with furnishing KVH, but in their agreements, churches often made it a project for their sewing circles. Jost thought this "irregular" as the churches "will expect credit be given in the conference books for this expenditure," instead of to the sewing circles.[57] Yet the societies grew only as a denominational presence, and at the WMS' January 12, 1955, meeting, Jost asked them if they could provide KVH with a sewing machine. The WMS approved the request and gave the money on April 12, 1955. This appears to be the first recorded event of a representative of a denominational institution coming to the WMS asking for help. Significantly, WMS at the same meeting decided to further their rationalizing process: "The committee [executive] favored that we ask the Foreign Mission Board for a unified program for the sewing circles."[58] By the mid-1950s, WMS grew more professional, the executive committee gathered more authority, and denominational institutions recognized and understood their influence.

Furthermore, in the mid-1950s, WMS created the Missionary Rally, an all-day fund-raiser with singing, scripture readings, devotionals, and committee report presentations. WMS provided their membership with a list of project options on which they voted. At the first rally, March 15, 1956, in Fresno, they gave the offering of $154.27 to a radio broadcast ministry in Japan. KVH came again to WMS, this time requesting a piano—though the women did not record their response. That fall, WMS made two recommendations concerning relief projects: support a missionary nurse at the maternity hospital in Africa at $1000 a year and "accept an educational project [providing] groceries, clothing and baby furniture, at the Mennonite Brethren Biblical Seminary."[59] Educational projects such as MBBS dominated WMS in the 1960s and coincided with the rise of the MCC West Coast Regional Office—which also worked with migrant camps and relief centers—and its own annual mission auction. Though the circles provided a comparatively small percentage of the seminary's budget, the school's administrators greatly appreciated their assistance.

Despite the increased conference presence for WMS, some Mennonite leaders still considered them free labor. In 1959, when Pacific Bible Institute and Junior College in Fresno opened a new classroom wing, the school held a social function for its dedication, and the North American Mennonite Brethren Board of Education turned to WMS: "To make this anticipated large company of guests feel welcome and show a token of appreciation for their attendance the committee believes it would be very appropriate to serve light refreshments for the occasion." The rationale: "Since the sisters of the Womens [sic] Missionary Service are so actively engaged in the Educational program of our Conference, the committee

Members of the Reedley Mennonite Brethren Church Missionary Society
preparing to board buses to attend the Pacific District Conference Women's
Missionary Service annual meeting in Shafter, California, 1955.
Source: Records of Reedley Mennonite Brethren Church.

would like to extend a special invitation to all the sisters of the service. We would further ask whether a representation [*sic*] from each of the various circles would be willing to serve the refreshments during the open house."[60] Despite the expanding role and influence of WMS, some denominational administrators regarded them as simply eager to serve punch.[61]

By 1960, other developments signaled that WMS was modernizing. They had an official origins narrative to recite at official functions that emphasized unity, coordination in helping missionaries, and their directing of monies to projects within and outside the conference. In fall 1960, one of the original WMS committees changed its name from Missionary Sewing Committee to Missionary Supply Committee. They were about so much more than sewing.[62]

Religious Teachings

J. B. Toews, while pastor at Reedley Mennonite Brethren Church in 1950, delivered a few sermons for women's missionary societies where he spoke on the appropriate place for women. In his Mother's Day sermon, "A Godly Mother," Toews began with the premise that women were the moral engine behind family, society, and church: "Where there are godly mothers, there is a strong Church." The mother teaches child values and possesses "the communication of nature." Toews clarified the point of communication of nature with two examples: the first was found in animals, where, for example, hens raise chickens. The second example was theological: God, "not college training," endowed mothers with people skills; "psychology is natural to mothers."[63]

Toews was aware that his sympathetic position toward an active role for women in the church was not always popular: "Tradition of Mennonites held women in very insignificant place as concerns responsibility in the church and in the Kingdom of God." Not surprisingly, Toews reflected the mid-century milieu in praising the power of women as inherent in their "natural" position: "Degeneration of the dignity of woman hood [is] always prominent in spiritual and moral decline of a nation and spiritual life." In promoting WMS's position within the Pacific District, he maintained the premise of a created natural order that provided a woman with power through children and home.[64]

Rev. Waldo Wiebe, the pastor in Shafter who attempted to block WMS's formation, held a similar, though extreme, understanding of the maternal nature of female power. In January 1950, after Shafter joined the WMS, they adopted the name Mission Relief Workers. On April 6, 1950, they observed that their name "includes much and may we humbly try to fulfill what the name implies." The Mission Relief Workers filled their year with plenty of work, including a year-end banquet in May with their husbands and an approval for a $600 commitment to furnish a bedroom at KVH. Pastor Wiebe led a Bible study series on women's role in the church.[65]

Wiebe's devotional was heartfelt: "He read Math. 18, 1 to 14 [Matthew 18:1–4]. He said he had, had a longing to talk to us Mothers for quite some time, because he felt there was work to do for us Mothers, right here at home, which he thought we have neglected very much." He described their failings in generational terms: "Therefore, he first brought out these thoughts. The responsibility of the older to the younger. The value of a child. He asked have you talked and prayed with one of our church daughters lately? Our greatest sin is omission. He begged us to take this with us for the summer months and pray for grace to talk to our girls."[66]

When the Mission Relief Workers of Shafter joined the WMS, they pledged to raise $600 for KVH, made eight comforters, and embroidered the church aprons. Despite this, when Wiebe spoke on a biblical text about rank in the kingdom of God, the women described feelings of guilt: "I think we all felt our short comings and expressed it in our prayers and asked for forgiveness."[67] If Toews's understanding of gender and nature led to expanding responsibility, Wiebe's understanding led to restriction. He led other devotionals in the early 1950s. including "Do's and Don'ts of a Christian Home," "Christian atmosphere in the Home," "A Christian Home," and "What a mother can do to create a Christian atmosphere in the Home."[68] The significance of these reactions, however, came in the women forcing the issue through avenues of church ministry.

The theme of a Christian woman keeping a Christian home was not solely the province of male leadership. For the 1955–1956 year, the Dinuba Mennonite Brethren sewing circle used "The Christian Woman" as its annual theme. Under this theme, they held the following devotionals: "Her Church and Conduct," "Her Responsibility and Influence in the Home," "Her Position and Service in the Church," "Her Avenues of Witness and Service in the Community," and "Her Position on the Mission Field."[69] Meanwhile, in Reedley, themes for much of the 1950s kept to the image of church expansion, with one example connecting it to domesticity, "We Sew and Serve." Other annual themes included "Wider Horizons: The Gospel for the Whole World" and "Spread the Sail."[70] These themes connecting community and church involvement reveal the scope of their ambition.

The 1960s continued some of these themes as others began. The yearbooks of the Reedley Mennonite Brethren Church's Women's Missionary Society reflect images of modernity and cold war piety, such as rocket ships and a clock set to five minutes to twelve made subservient to a recurring image of a cross superimposed over the earth. By 1970, the apocalyptic "Behold He Cometh [to] Occupy" adorned its covers.[71]

The WMS, both in its Pacific District Conference manifestation and at the congregational level, provided not only comforters for missionaries, but also identity and autonomy for women in a denomination largely ambivalent to their role. That ambivalence, or even outright opposition, did not stop them but often strengthened them. They created a social organization, managed it professionally, and exerted influence in their religious world. The process of professionalizing through the 1940s and

1950s turned a series of unconnected sewing circles into a large umbrella organization, which in the 1950s raised over a quarter of a million dollars for relief work.[72]

Esther Brandt clearly connected WMS to the larger purpose of American progress. At a WMS executive committee meeting in April 1961, "Mrs. Brandt reviewed the work of the Women's Missionary Service. She related how the organization had begun with 18 circles twelve years ago and now has 40 in number . . . [and she] spoke of seeing the Liberty Bell and how it symbolizes freedom, and yet, through the years, so many changes have taken place in our land. So, too, many changes have taken place in the work of the Women's Missionary Service." She continued by reminding WMS of its initial purpose by quoting their founding sisters: "To promote spiritual growth. To help the various needs of our church, District conference and General Conference with our prayers, sewing, donations in kind and cash." Finally, she charged the group to forgo personal feelings and seek the good of the larger group.[73] It was a hybrid of American exceptionalism, Mennonite bureaucracy, maternal feminism, and group submission, and it called for sacrifice to WMS.[74] Through their ambition, sacrifice, evangelical piety, social concern, grassroots origin, and growing bureaucracy, Mennonite Brethren women were, as the WMS motto put it, redeeming the time.

During the stressful demographic shifts of the 1950s at Calvary Mennonite Church (MC) in Los Angeles, the Woman's Missionary Society promoted themselves by connecting their membership, womanhood, and Mennonite responsibility: "Everyone that can should try to attend this worthy endeavor. It would be too bad if such a fine thing as sewing circle should die out because no one any longer is willing to support it with their time and effort."[75] Or two years later: "Sewing circle like other Christian service requires that you prove to the Lord why you cannot come rather than having Him give you some reason why you should serve in this way. Every sister who is physically able to be at sewing surely ought to be there to contribute her part to this great service of the church."[76] The urgings continued through the decade, pricking women's consciences to keep the circle itself functioning in a time of congregational stress. In summer 1956, the sewing circle laid out their balancing act in church bulletins, where issues of identity and women's role in church and modern life coalesced: "All sisters are urged to come to this meeting [Ladies Sewing Circle]. If you can't sew this is the best place to learn. Surely we can arrange to come once a month to work a few hours for people who are less fortunate than we in spite of all the latest gadgets we must contend with."[77]

Minnie Graber, president for the denominational-wide body Women's Missionary Society Association (WMSA), instituted a process to make more efficient the delegation of work to the circles. She proposed that future planning by the national body be informed by questionnaires returned by local circles and that future communication flow both ways through district secretaries. The regional districts would ideally have more say regarding what local constituents worked on. In so doing, the WMSA's general committee agreed not to bypass district secretaries in their communications with local circles, and in return, local circles would complete their questionnaires.[78] This development rationalized efficient communications, centralized control, and linked local congregations to district secretaries and ultimately to the national body in Elkhart, Indiana.

The California circles were much smaller in number than those on the East Coast.[79] Aware of these comparisons in size, one California circle president countered the implied slight: "Here in California our work is different. So many women work and our groups are quite small at best."[80] On one occasion the secretary of the South Pacific Women's Missionary and Service Auxiliary informed Graber about the difficulty of being located so far from the head office and how it seemed that in California, they were running on "old steam," though she confessed that if it were not for the WMSA, she "would be bored."[81] Her letters indicate that such work was as much for building social networks as for performing church work, at times revealing the persistence of feeling isolated on the West Coast.

America the Beautiful

In Los Angeles, after the General Conference congregation Immanuel moved to Downey in the late 1950s, the Women's Missionary Society experienced a decline in revenue and attendance. Revenue that peaked at $872.28 in 1950 declined to under $400 by the mid-1950s. It rose to more than $500 dollars for the remainder of the decade.[82] Attendance was difficult to maintain in the 1950s, and they did three things to strengthen it: they joined the National Association of Evangelicals' Woman's Auxiliary and the United Church Women of Downey, and they made any woman who attended three consecutive meetings an automatic member. The constitution permitted the latter of these three strategies when receipts dropped below $400 and average attendance fell to fourteen in 1956. With the new policy, by 1958, they had a membership of forty-four, an average attendance of thirty, and an $80 increase in donations.[83]

North in Reedley, General Conference Mennonite women organized the Worthwhile Circle in the 1940s, with the purpose to facilitate "Christian Fellowship" and "maintain missionary interest among the women of our church."[84] Their theme verse, in 1945–1946, was Revelation 3:8, where Christ says, "Behold I have set before thee an open door." Throughout the 1940s, their yearbooks contained a picture of a globe, with the words "Committed Unto Us," emphasizing their need to evangelize.[85] Throughout the 1950s the Worthwhile Circle, like other women's groups, engaged MCC at the relief center in Reedley to support missionaries in America and overseas as well as work at KVH. The mission emphasis was shifting from foreign to American fields, concentrated in southern states from North Carolina to Arizona. Although there was always a mix of support for American and foreign missions throughout most of the 1950s, by 1957, the only foreign mission they supported was the Congo Inland Mission. In 1958, they listed no foreign mission.[86]

The Worthwhile Circle, as with many such Mennonite groups throughout California, divided their time between service projects and study sessions. They focused their meetings on the city and studying foreign countries and regions such as India, Pakistan, and Ceylon, where "darkness has turned to dawning under Christ's Church," as well as Southeast Asia and Japan.[87] For the theme of Spanish-speaking Americans, they titled the meeting, "They too Need Christ." America itself was celebrated with meetings themed "America the Beautiful," where they discussed ministry to migrant laborers. They even discussed Japan with particular attention to the "race problem" and the church's response. Creating "restaurants" in the church's social hall, the women explored cities and cultures around the world through French, Italian, and Hawaiian cuisine.[88] In 1959 they studied North America and the Middle East, which only strengthened their conviction that "the true religion of Christianity was the religion we should spread through out the world." Later that year, they studied Hawaii, "the paradise of the Pacific," Canada, and Mexico.[89]

Similarly, the Women's Missionary Society of the Mennonite Community Church in Fresno, in the late 1950s, had placed on their yearbook covers a hand-drawn globe with the theme of "The Darkness Shall Turn to Dawning."[90] In 1956, they reported a membership of twenty-five and an average attendance of eighteen. They hosted several dinners, which were their primary source of income, followed by offerings. Although they gave their funds to the General Conference Mission Society, Mennonite Biblical Seminary, American Indian missions, and Africa, the largest expenditures were for dishes and furniture in the church.[91] For the remainder of the 1950s, the primary sources of income were offerings and vaguely titled "projects," while the largest outlays were for the kitchen and social committees, followed by projects and missions.[92]

By 1960, their support for foreign missions was funneled through MCC and the MCC Clothing Center in Reedley, completing the women's circles' shift in focus to primarily domestic concerns. The Worthwhile Circle also hosted dinners for a variety of groups: their church men's group, the Reedley Christian Business Men's Committee, and the Woman's Christian Temperance Union (WCTU). They held a "Bethel banquet"— presumably for Bethel College—and a shower for the Fresno Rescue Mission, and they fund-raised for the YMCA Camp.[93] Similarly, the First Mennonite Sewing Circle in Shafter assisted MCC to raise money for KVH, and the sewing circle in Upland assisted foreign missions through their district conference and MCC, though at times their largest budget outlays went to the Upland church to support the parsonage and host fund-raiser dinners.[94]

One notable exception to the trend of hosting fund-raising dinners for men's groups occurred when the men hosted a dinner for the women. The Worthwhile Circle reported in 1958, "The Mother-Daughter banquet was also an unique experience for the guests attending. The dinner was prepared and served by the Men's Brotherhood." That year the Men's Brotherhood gave recognition "to those brave men who helped cook and serve the Mother-Daughter banquet," but also thanked "all those ladies of the Worthwhile Circle, and many others, who put forth the extra effort in the very good dinners."[95] A year later, to underscore the significance of this gendered role reversal, the Men's Brotherhood described themselves as "brave soldiers."[96]

Domestic Pietism

Scholars such as Amanda Porterfield have noticed that "idealized perceptions" of women, while possibly damaging, can carry authority. When women transformed the world by extending the ideals of "domestic

pietism" beyond the home, they extended the family and home outward. For California Mennonites, such realities were made clear by cir-
cumstance, when administrators and seminary presidents came, cup in
hand, seeking funds from women's missionary societies. These women
transformed domestic work—sewing and mending of clothing—into an
efficient set of denominational organizations that, through negotiations,
received conference recognition and grew in influence. These women
did not abandon Mennonite identity; they shaped Mennonite identity
in the context of social outreach and mission activity. They also extended
it beyond home and church, intentionally framing their understanding of
identity and work around religious, patriotic, and gender identities with
global, even apocalyptic implications.[97]

In postwar California, women in the missionary societies also identified with American exceptionalism. There were intentional connections
made between their work and westward expansion, the Liberty Bell, millennial expectation, and responsibility to spread help and hope throughout the world as in such mottos as "Redeeming the Time," or "Behold He
Cometh to Occupy." Mennonites identified with American expansion,
ideals, and freedom.[98] This atmosphere of expectation was thickening at
a time when the operations of the missionary services were modernizing,
rationalizing, and professionalizing. Clearly much changed for California
Mennonites in the twentieth century, and it was especially noticeable
during wartime—whether the war was hot or cold. Turning to war in the
next chapter, we see the complex relationship between pacifism and citizenship.

CHAPTER 7

Peaceful Patriots

California Mennonites during World War II

Our ammunition for days like these.
—Inscription on the drawing of a Bible on the cover of the *Snowliner*
(CPS camp newsletter), 1943

The Camps

If there is a single identifying marker for Mennonites, it is peace. Described variously as pacifism, peace witnessing, nonviolence, nonresistance, or conscientious objection, this theological ideal has been an integral part of historical Mennonite identity. Since Menno Simons heard of the apocalyptic disaster at Münster and at a monastery located nearby him in 1530s Netherlands, this theological impulse has been a major part of Mennonitism.[1] The Dutch-Prussian-Russian Mennonites, for example, migrated throughout early modern Europe due to a mix of economic pressures and avoidance of military service. The principle has a long history influencing Mennonite behavior throughout American history, from the American Revolution on. It has marginalized American Mennonites, even earning them a measure of persecution during World War I.[2]

In twentieth-century America, three texts dominated the articulation of Mennonite pacifism: Harold S. Bender, "The Anabaptist Vision" (1944); Guy F. Hershberger, *War, Peace, and Nonresistance* (1946); and John Howard Yoder, *The Politics of Jesus* (1972). These three scholars attempted to establish the nonviolent position as normative for American Mennonites, even if practice did not always match the ideal.[3] In fact, some Mennonites were quite ambivalent about pacifism.

World War II was not only a time of testing for Mennonites regarding pacifism, but it was a watershed experience that smoothed the way for greater modernization and integration into urban American life. For Mennonites in California, we see this in everything from the sewing circles of the previous chapter to the construction of hospitals in the next. In this chapter, we will see the effects of war in the context of national service and legal ramifications of nonresistance for citizenship—where clarity is sought in a time of ambiguity.

Many migrants came to California during the first half of the twentieth century to work in the aerospace and defense industries. In a similar vein, during World War II, many Mennonites came to California because of national defense, but of a different sort.[4] Mennonites and the federal government ran a number of Civilian Public Service (CPS) camps in California. Established in 1941, CPS was a national program established between the Historic Peace Churches (Brethren, Mennonites, and Quakers) and the American government. Its purpose was to provide conscientious objectors, in lieu of military service, work of national importance that did not violate their conscience. Participating denominations funded and ran the camps while the federal government provided oversight.[5]

To help fund the program, there was a fifty-cent assessment per member of the Mennonite churches for the first six months. Mennonites saw this as a testimony to their faith: "The responsibility of the Church is great, the opportunity unlimited to establish the Government's faith in the Church of today and to learn from the church Camps thrift industry, constructive living. etc."[6] There would be some disappointment in Mennonite involvement. At the Reedley Mennonite Church, for example, only 52 percent of the church membership participated in CPS support, and the Church Council found it necessary to remind their congregation that the opportunity for alternative service in a time of war was made possible by a generous government. Furthermore, they told the congregation, "many of our forefathers left their homes and migrated to a new country for religious freedom and many have come to this country for the same purpose. We like to sing 'Faith of our Fathers' but each one of us must answer for himself, is it a conviction that comes from the heart or is it just lip service?"[7] In the camps, young Mennonite men not only fought forest

A CPS crew at Side Camp Mosquito. *Source:* Herman E. Friesen Collection.

fires and cared for tubercular patients, they also considered what it meant to be American, Christian, and Mennonite.

Mennonite churches supported their CPS men, and when possible, subject to time off and gasoline availability, CPSers visited local Mennonite churches, to sing songs and take communion.[8] The Mennonite-run CPS camps in California included Three Rivers, North Fork, Camino, and a hospital unit in Livermore. Three Rivers Camp, eighty miles southwest of Fresno, was run from May 1943 to June 1946 by the Mennonite Central Committee (MCC) under the National Park Service. It had a capacity of 150 men. Their primary task was fire suppression and firefighting. North Fork was fifty miles northeast of Fresno, located at the base of the Sierra Nevadas; it ran from May 1942 to March 1946 on the site of a former New Deal Civilian Conservation Corps camp. They fought forest fires and engaged in fire prevention under the United States Forest Service. During its run, the camp spent 4,689 "man-days" in firefighting and 14,232 days in fire suppression. Camino, also known as Camp Snowline, was a forestry camp located east of Sacramento. The Livermore CPS unit was located at the United States Veterans' Hospital in Livermore for tubercular patients and had 117 men during its run from December 1945 to December 1946.[9]

The CPS was about national service, but it was also a context for learning. They screened educational films, hosted guest speakers, held weekly religious services, and engaged in Bible study as well as the study of "Mennonite Heritage" and tolerance for those "who do not agree with us."[10] Camps also published newsletters, which included, along with essential camp information, commentary on various issues and discussion of questions relating to Mennonitism, pacifism, and American identity. An early example of the kind of philosophical musings in these newsletters was Arthur Jost's 1943 article "Vistas." Jost, who went on to administer the Kings View Homes mental health hospital in the 1950s, used nature to comment on human maturation. He wrote of changing truths, or appearances of truth, as "vista" changes. In this, he argued, experience changes the appearance of truth, and even reveals a new truth, casting away the old.[11]

During the months of June through October 1943, CPSer Miles Eaton published a series of articles on pacifism and non-Christian religions called "In My Father's House," in the *Snowliner*, the Camino camp newspaper. These articles were descriptive and often sympathetic toward non-Christian forms of pacifism. The first was on Hinduism: "We like to think of Pacifism as a purely Christian institution. But in all fairness, if we want to acknowledge the truth of the matter, we must grant the honor of age to Hinduism." Although the author acknowledged a warrior class in Hinduism, he acknowledged the same for Christianity and connected the pacifism of the two religions through their respective minority positions in their religions. After briefly tracing Hindu pacifism, Eaton qualified himself: "It is not our place to argue whether this is true or not."[12]

Other religions Eaton dealt with included Zarathustrianism, "Egyptian Teachings," Buddhism, and Jainism. Buddhism received the most glowing treatment, described as "the one great religion which has never fought a holy war" and "the greatest of the pacifist religions." He considered too the Buddhist concept of suffering, as caused by ignorance, a "truly marvelous concept," concluding, "Buddhism is the religion of compassion."[13] For Eaton, the bond of pacifism was strong between religions. In practice, however, when the government, in spring 1944, assigned a group of Russian Molokans—sectarian Christians who broke from the Russian Orthodox Church espousing bibliocentrism and pacifism—to Camino, the Mennonite response was hardly generous.

Molokans were accused by Mennonites of drinking, carousing, and having "a different approach to the moral and ethical side of life than we have." Of particular concern for the camp director was the effect on the Mennonites: "How many non-Mennonite assignees we can absorb without seriously breaking down our philosophy of administration, without getting into difficulty through misunderstanding with our Mennonite Constituency" and then having, perhaps, the Selective Service losing faith in Mennonite camps.[14] This interreligious tension may have simply been the result of relative proximity, as there were no Buddhists recorded at the Mennonite CPS camps. Other similarly minded Protestant and Mennonite groups populated the camps, and they all lived in close quarters that could exacerbate internecine tensions over cultural differences, even on issues such as the place of head coverings and the ritual of communion.

Of particular interest for camp writers was their sense of mission, even destiny, in the protection of democracy and the advancement of American ideals. They connected themselves to America's Founding Fathers and their quest for religious freedom. It was a common sentiment in CPS that they were sacrificing for their country, calling it a "privilege" to serve both country and conscience. As such, they understood the importance of their work in national and patriotic terms. One CPSer captured this sense of mission to protect American ideals of democracy and religious freedom: "Modern war breeds a bureaucratic octopus that fattens itself on oppression and inevitably results in strangulation of both Christianity and Democracy."[15]

They acknowledged that they were fortunate to live in a country that permitted the "privilege" of CPS work, where in the previous world war, conscientious objectors walked a much "tougher road." Thus, some CPS men attempted to understand their sometimes tedious work as possessing a higher purpose. They desired to show the world "that through that particular act you are opposed to the slaughter engulfing the world today. A monotonous job can thus become the witness of a deep-seated belief."[16]

CPSers also expressed themes of pacifism, religion, and national identity through newsletter cover art. During 1942 and 1943, the *Snowliner* carried hand-drawn images of war and peace on its covers, including bombs falling with "peace on Earth" and "Good will toward men" written on banners attached to them; drawings of tanks inside destroyed cities; and a Bible with the words "Our Ammunition For Days Like These." They all made poignant editorial comment on the events of the day. One in particular depicted a sword with the words of Lieutenant General Lesley J. McNair written on sheets of paper: "We must lust for battle; our object in life must be to kill . . . kill or be killed." Next to these were the words of

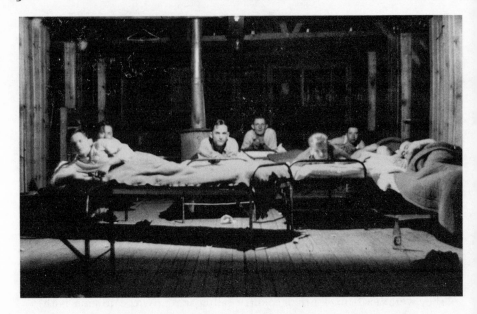

"A block at midnight": Several CPSers in their dorm room.
Source: Herman E. Friesen Collection.

Jesus written on a scroll, by a cross: "Love your enemies, do good to them which hate you."[17] The covers went beyond an implied critique of militarism to insert CPS campers into the civil-religious American holiday cycle, depicting Pilgrims and American Indians at Thanksgiving, and Abraham Lincoln accompanied with an excerpt from his second inaugural address.[18]

CPSers understood their work as preserving Christianity and democracy, but local non-Mennonite communities did not always agree. One poignant example took place in December 1942, when some men at Camino Camp No. 31 made toys for Japanese children in nearby internment camps. A local opponent of the CPS, L. J. Anderson, wrote letters to the *Placerville Times* and the Selective Service, protesting the actions of those men. Anderson's argument was that CPS was un-American and that they supported the enemy by giving toys to Japanese children.[19] In fact, the response of Mennonites to Japanese internment extended beyond CPS-made toys. Members of the Mennonite community in Reedley saw their Japanese neighbors off at the train station with cookies and punch, and at least one family purchased the land of a Japanese family to sell back upon their return.[20] Mennonite marginalization was exacerbated by their demonstrations of kindness to other outsiders. American Mennonites discovered their faith, patriotism, and embrace of American ideals to be insufficient.

In early 1943, after the issue of toys for Japanese children faded, a new controversy emerged when some CPS men refused to pick peaches for local farmers. At stake for CPS men was the unclear financial relationship between the peach harvest and the war effort. Until the government cleared the matter of where money raised from the sale of peaches went, CPS and MCC made it a matter of individual conscience. If a camp member could participate in the harvest, in good conscience, with the financial situation unresolved, that was fine by CPS. Some in the local community were upset that peach picking was even an issue; some CPS supporters were upset with what appeared to be CPS's concession to win public approval.[21]

There were debates in camps about the issue of peach picking and pruning. Those in favor cited public relations and noted that income tax goes to war, arguing that what the government does with its money is a different question than the pacifist directly participating in war. Those against cited the importance of consistency and how the issue of peaches could undermine the entire CPS program.[22] Firefighting to save forests, by contrast, was not similarly debated, despite the possible use of lumber for the war effort.

The above examples illustrate that although the creation of CPS was important for the Peace Churches, it also drew them into an intimate, complicated, and contradictory relationship with the federal government. This new relationship sharpened Mennonite desire to be identified as part of American culture, and the arguments about peaches advancing the war effort, while avoiding the larger question of whether CPS was by its very existence supporting the war effort, demonstrated this. Mennonites took pride in their work of national significance.

The question of being a good American and a good Mennonite pacifist included questions of what it meant to live in materialistic, evangelical California. In a short exchange between Erwin Goering, director of Camp No. 31, in Camino, with "Esko & Co.," the question of defining West Coast Mennonitism was discussed. Goering noted its geographic significance: "You can tell these coast guys from the rest by the philosophy of life they have. It is tremendous how much geographic location has to do with our thinking or lack of thinking. By geography of course I mean the materialism that is encountered in the location. More and more it seems that our people are succumbing to a gross materialism that is as sly as a snake in the

Group photo of the crew at CPS Camp No. 31. *Source:* Herman E. Friesen Collection.

grass." He also observed a general lack of piety: "Too many people are not aware to what is happening. Right here in Winton, Cal., the Holdeman [Mennonite] Community is a Sunday working group during irrigation and fruit picking time. Well, make of it what we may, if that isn't desecrating the Sunday, it will take a lot of rationalization to get over feeling that way for me."[23]

In California, Goering observed, "Anything that means money goes. What the next fellow doesn't know won't hurt him. So excuse yourself and go IAO [noncombatant military service]; incidentally, you get your monthly check, save your reputation, get your pension, and the door to jobs will be wide open to you after the war. Yea-a-a-a, and you belong to the (un)American Legion, you good Mennonite." At fault were overly evangelical church leaders in California: "Excuse the outburst. It is aimed at some of the so called Mennonite ministers (or should I say so called ministers) who preach good evangelism, yes, so good that you ought to go to the front as a soldier to preach to them salvation before they go into the beyond, poor fellows."[24] To which Esko Loewen replied, that if European Mennonitism was "captured" by Karl Barth, American Mennonitism was "plagued by materialism." Loewen concluded that despite having the religious conviction to take a stand against war, Mennonites on the coast wore blinders to materialism.[25]

In CPS camps Mennonite men held different opinions as to what it meant to be Mennonite, despite holding pacifism in common. The camp newsletters reveal that CPS was a place to serve America and a time to think about what that meant. Mennonites used symbols of civil religion, such as Thanksgiving Day, and ideals of the Constitution, notably freedom of religion, to stake a position as faithful Americans and Mennonites. Mennonites working in the camps believed that they served both God and country, even when that service demanded of some not to pick peaches and others to send gifts to Japanese children in internment camps. Being Mennonite and American in CPS caused friction within local communities, yet the experience of CPS was liminal—betwixt society and church, not entirely satisfying either, but creating something new. Underlying CPS was a love of country combined with a duty to serve America, but in a way respectful of their conscience, formed by religious belief and practice.[26]

Some CPS men reflected on how the wider world perceived them. When Harold Gaede, of Three Rivers Camp, met three female marines, he wrote, "Gabbed a while with 3 Marine girls . . . Pretty friendly. Wonder what they would have said if they would have known I was a CO [conscientious objector]."[27] Despite such concerns, CPS participants took pride when the military establishment described their work as truly of national importance and in their newsletters defended the significance of the camps. Fighting forest fires was one example, and Mennonites argued that preserving natural resources was vital to national defense, as cities like Los Angeles need forests to maintain water supplies.[28]

The Churches

Pluralism and Boundaries

In 1944, the minister-at-large for the Pacific District Conference of the General Conference Mennonite Church reported at the annual conference on his visits with CPS men in California, Oregon, and Idaho. Men in CPS camps were pessimistic about what home, church, and government could really do to make the world better. These men, in addition to their pessimism of the future world order, and their special service to their country, also encountered different forms of Christianity. One CPS man discussed Christian pluralism by thinking of it as a family with God as the "heavenly Parent" and the humans as children. In this manner, he kept his faith intact in face of competing beliefs.[29] This was not just a concern with non-Mennonites, as there were also inter-Mennonite tensions in the camps.

In the case of the Mennonite Brethren, in a report to its Pacific District Conference, pluralism was welcomed: "We appreciate the spiritual care and the ministry of our own conference brethren as they come to us, and we would certainly appreciate to fellowship in larger groups as Mennonite Brethren, but in being separated, out among the other groups of Mennonites, we have learned to love and appreciate very many of them."[30] This harmony was more difficult to create in reality. Some CPS men "privately" said they preferred church services among their own group. Harold Gaede, at Three Rivers Camp, wrote in his diary, "The Mennonite Brethren and the (Old) Mennonites tended to argue."[31]

One such argument in camp life was over such religious practices as communion. The Mennonite Church historically practiced closed communion—administered by a local bishop or minister, in which only members of the Mennonite Church could partake. When other CPS men requested a communion service at the Camino Camp, the director, Leland Bachman, of the Mennonite Church, wrote Orie Miller, MCC executive secretary, for advice. Bachman wanted to know how to hold communion when church policy required closed communion. Miller responded that since communion could be so divisive, camps were not to hold communion, but groups within a camp could hold their own communion with their own church leaders.[32]

Major disagreements continued among different groups of Mennonites. Roger Frantz, for example, asked his pastor for advice on how to deal with Mennonite diversity: "The Mennonite boys [MC] believe quite differently on certain things than we [MB] do but we get along very well. I would like very much to have some information on how our church interprets First Corinthians eleven, verse one to sixteen, concerning the prayer head covering. The Mennonite boys are all ardent believers in the prayer head-covering."[33] The markers of Mennonitism in these examples were less about nonresistance and more about interdenominational boundary maintenance, as found in the issues of communion and head coverings. If pacifism promised a commonality to their experience in the camps, Mennonites established boundaries in other ways, as in debating communion and head coverings.

The Armed Forces

The Kern County Christian Fellowship, a group formed from the Bakersfield, Rosedale, and Shafter Mennonite Brethren congregations to hold annual youth revivals, incorporated CPS in some of their meetings during the 1940s. At the Annual Kern County Christian Fellowship Conference, on September 5–7, 1942, the message was "Christian youth need not despair, resort to Epicureanism or Stoicism, as does the world but rather it can use the crisis as stepping stones to improve spirituality by repentance and going deeper." This spiritual improvement was biblical and mission oriented: "Using the method of Esther [in the Old Testament], youth should fast and pray. Preparing for the peace and the great missionary era which will follow demands the best physical, intellectual and spiritual equipment." At the same conference, a singing group from the North Fork CPS camp performed songs, and a speaker described CPS life. Following the conference, organizers discussed where to send the offering money; suggestions included CPS or war bonds, though they did not record their final decision.[34]

Not only were Mennonite churches supportive of their men serving in CPS, they were also supportive of their men serving in the military. The two groups seemed to co-exist in the same congregations with little tension. As anthropologist Dan Forsyth discovered, in some cases congregations were evenly divided in their convictions regarding nonresistance yet maintained friendly relationships.[35]

Jacob J. Toews, pastor of the Shafter Mennonite Brethren Church, wrote Roger Frantz, a congregant in the CPS Smokejumper unit in Oregon, to apologize for missing him during his furlough home. Toews wrote, "If our brothers come from the CPS Camps it is always harder for me to notice them than it is for boys who come back out of the armed forces. The latter wearing a uniform, while the first do not."[36] Men from CPS and the armed forces co-existed in the same church, and uniforms worn in church created no officially recorded tension. Another CPS participant from Shafter confirmed this position when he wrote back, "My, it will really be a pleasure to work with you and the church again with all the boys back from the C.P.S. and Armed Forces."[37] Similarly, the Reedley Mennonite Church discussed how to integrate the men who served through welcome committees and agreements to assist them "financial or otherwise" and to deliberately combat intolerant attitudes that may exist against them.[38]

Regardless of denomination, churches respected and welcomed home those who served in the armed services and those who served in the CPS. First Mennonite Church in Paso Robles (GC) published the addresses of men in service for congregants to write them letters. In the address list, men in the armed services were included alongside those in CPS.[39] The First Mennonite Church in Upland, in 1943, observed Memorial Day by honoring all those who made America strong. In addition to the soldiers who died in past wars, they sought to honor honest, hardworking Americans from all lines of work. They supported CPS through such activities as canning food for the men as a way of "binding the camps and churches" together.[40] Similarly, in Reedley, First Mennonite Church agreed to a measure to purchase American and Christian flags for the pulpit and support the community in V-Day celebrations.[41]

Other Mennonite congregations took similar actions as Paso Robles and Upland. The Dinuba Mennonite Brethren Church passed a resolution to give each man an official farewell in their leaving for either the army or CPS. The First Mennonite Church of Upland (GC) congregation was committed to providing pastoral visits for CPS participants. In addition to supporting CPS, Rosedale Mennonite Brethren officially replaced German with English after the Pearl Harbor bombing, as did the Reedley First Mennonite Brethren Church and Reedley Mennonite Church, though they were already an English-speaking congregation.[42] In the case of Reedley Mennonite Church, the week following Pearl Harbor, Paul Eymann reported on a meeting he had with city councilmen, where it was suggested that the church discontinue speaking German in public, accommodate evacuees as necessary, and cooperate with blackouts.[43]

Churches often decided to compensate their CPS members upon their return at the equivalent rate the armed forces paid.[44] The Shafter Mennonite Brethren Church immediately passed a set of resolutions after the Pearl Harbor bombing, including a declaration of appreciation for Congress, recognizing them as a Historic Peace Church. One resolution said in part, "We fully pledge our individual as well as collective support in matters of blackouts, should they ever occur again." Shafter Mennonite Brethren also pledged support for the English language and were committed to using English as much as possible while not criticizing the American government. They concluded that they would help, as far as their consciences permitted, the afflicted and their own members who of their own accord strayed from these resolutions and found themselves in unnamed "entanglements."[45]

The only California congregation to pass a decision against members serving in the military was the Reedley Mennonite Brethren Church. On August 31, 1944, "A motion was made and seconded to recommend to the church that all members who serve in the Armed Forces as combatant soldiers, be taken off the membership record. Motion carried."[46] This motion specifies combatant soldiers, not those in noncombatant roles. Reedley Mennonite Brethren was the only Californian Mennonite congregation to pass a resolution forbidding church members who served in the armed forces to join the American Legion. They based their decision on 2 Corinthians 6:14–18, which demanded that the Christian remain separate from the world and avoid partnerships with non-Christians.[47]

In 1952 Dr. Menno S. Gaede, a Mennonite Brethren, was elected to the Reedley city council, becoming mayor in 1954 for two years. Born in Kansas, educated at Tabor College and the Kansas University Medical School, Gaede was known for his work in starting the hospital project in Reedley in 1938, later named the Sierra-Kings District Hospital. Gaede was also a past president of the Kiwanis.[48] He had always been active in Reedley's community life. In addition to Kiwanis, he was a member of and in leadership roles for the chamber of commerce, YMCA, Scouts, Reedley High School and college athletic teams, PTA, church activities, and the Kings Canyon Republican Assembly. While mayor, one of the more difficult and time-consuming tasks was establishing Reedley's Civil Defense Plan. "It [public service] is an experience one can only get by being here, just as one experiences the grim realities of war by serving on the front line! They are all experiences that widen a man's horizons of living and make one realize that 'God's mercies are new every morning, God's grace is born fresh with the day, God's good gifts are all freely given to us every step of the way.' "[49] Of war, he knew much.

Gaede came from Jerome, Arizona, to Reedley in September 1936 "to establish a medical practice." He made his first visit to Reedley in 1930, taking a Model A Ford Roadster over the "grapevine" road from Los Angeles. During World War II, 1944 to 1945, Gaede served as Lt. Commander in the U.S. Navy Medical Corps. As one of four doctors, he was in the Pacific Ocean Theatre aboard the USS *Warren*, an attack transport with 500 crewmen and 2,000 "fighting men," and on active duty during six invasions (Marshall Islands, Leyte, Saipan, Guam, Pellilu, Okinawa). They took in wounded from other ships during those battles. Many died, and Gaede, also an identification officer, had to ensure that each casualty was properly recorded.[50] The realities of Mennonite wartime participation and rejection were complex. Though our understanding of Mennonite military participation remains thin, it is part of the larger story of social and cultural engagement with society.

Citizens of Two Kingdoms

Wartime brought the values of pacifists and the state into direct confrontation, and CPS provided a negotiated compromise between them. An individual applying for American citizenship foregrounded the antagonistic relationship between pacifist church and secular state.

Arthur Jost was a Canadian citizen, born in Flowing Well, Saskatchewan. During World War II, he worked briefly in a California CPS camp before being transferred to a mental health hospital in Provo, Utah. In Provo, Jost developed an interest in mental health and after the war played a pivotal role in starting and running a hospital in Reedley. During the 1950s, Jost sought American citizenship, triggering a decade-long odyssey through the court system all the way to the Supreme Court of the United States. His journey highlighted some complexities of American Mennonite identity.

Silas Langley's treatment of Jost's citizenship case remains the standard account, in which he observes that American attitudes were in a continuous tension between security and liberty, characterized in part by progressive and restrictive understandings of the rights of conscientious objectors. His study framed the social tension as "internal security vs. individual rights . . . in a democratic and pluralistic defense-oriented society." In this analysis, progressives advocated individual rights, including freedom of religion, and restrictives advocated "security and responsibility." For Jost, American jurisprudence was dominated by restrictives.[51]

In a broader analysis of pacifism and the Supreme Court, Joel Balzer argues that Jost's naturalization case represents a fundamental shift in the Supreme Court's position regarding the acceptance of pacifist aliens as American citizens. Under the McCarran Act (1950), Congress shifted from nonacceptance to acceptance with the provision of an alternate citizenship oath for conscientious objectors. Jost was the first test of the McCarran Act to make it to the Supreme Court. Though the Court never heard the case, Balzer argues that Jost nevertheless represents the end of that shift.[52] The case was withdrawn by the Immigration and Naturalization Service (INS) just prior to its hearing.

Jost's citizenship difficulties can also be traced to his church, the Reedley Mennonite Brethren Church, and the Pacific District Conference. In 1948, his church adopted a statement that approved noncombatant military service but without taking the required oath. The Pacific District Conference accepted Reedley's statement, leading to a Mennonite Brethren interpretive trend of leniency toward noncombatant service. That leniency negatively affected Jost's citizenship application. Jost pointed out in a letter written July 15, 1954, to B. J. Braun, chair of the Committee of Reference and Counsel (a denominational office that at the time handled theological issues and questions of church practice), that the Pacific District Conference's position was impossible, if not illegal, because all noncombatants must take the oath.[53]

Naturalization examiner Judah S. Hemmer initially denied Jost's citizenship petition because he thought Jost did not provide "clear and convincing" evidence that his nonresistance was the result of "religious training and belief." Hemmer reached his conclusion based on an investigation he undertook in the Reedley area, where some Mennonite Brethren church leaders said noncombatant service was a viable option for the Mennonite Brethren. Jost's task was to demonstrate "clear and convincing evidence" of "religious training and belief" that his pacifism was sincere in order to be eligible to take the 1940 oath of citizenship, which did not require the bearing of arms for national defense. Thus, while Jost worked to demonstrate his religious training and belief, he accepted the help of the American Civil Liberties Union (ACLU). Out of a concern with being "unequally yoked" with non-Christians, he kept them at arm's length. Some Mennonites nonetheless criticized him for his fervent pursuit of such an "earthly prize" as American citizenship, but he mostly enjoyed support from Mennonites and non-Mennonites alike.[54]

There was evidence against Jost's claim that the Mennonite Brethren taught the principle of nonresistance, or at least a refusal to accept noncombatancy, especially as found in the Pacific District Conference's 1948 statement, which unrealistically permitted noncombatant service without taking the oath. Moreover, Rev. Dan Friesen, a Mennonite Brethren pastor from Fresno, testified, "There is nothing in the Mennonite creed or teaching to prevent one from wearing the uniform of the Armed Forces, and . . . the Mennonites as an organization does not teach its members that they should refrain from performing noncombatant service in the Armed Forces."[55] Additional similar testimony confirmed that the Mennonite Brethren did not clearly oppose noncombatant service, which Jost acknowledged.[56]

At the appeal of Hemmer's ruling, held at the court of appeal in the Fourth Appellate District of California, Jost faced several challenges. First, it was difficult for him to argue against such testimony from local Mennonite ministers as "the Mennonite religion not only does not train or teach that its members should refuse to wear the uniform of the Armed Services, but instructions were that they should register for non-combatant duty."[57] Whereas, in his "Appellant's Reply Brief," Jost argued, "The only conflict which appellee (and *amicus*) grasp at are as to the interpretation to be given to the Mennonite creed, a theological question."[58] In fact, Jost outlined what he argued were two errors made by the court: one was that "the religious faith to which one belongs *must require* the non-combatant stand," and the example he gave was of vice-president-elect Richard Nixon, member of Society of Friends, who was also a World War II lieutenant commander in the navy. The second error, he argued, was that the appellee "overlooked . . . that the law is that one *can* defend and support the Constitution without the use of force."[59] At this stage, however, Jost faced down the testimony from pastors and the legal objections with little success.

The Fourth Appellate District Court of Appeal upheld the opinion of the Superior Court of Fresno. Despite this setback, Jost enjoyed broad support, as seen by the list of churches and organizations that filed as Friend of the Court: the ACLU–Southern California Branch; American Friends Service Committee, Pacific Southwest Regional Executive Committee; Brethren Service Commission of the General Brotherhood Board; Church of the Brethren; Congregational Conference of Southern California; Southwest Fellowship of Reconciliation; Mennonite Central Committee; and Richard W. Petherbridge of the National Service Board for Religious Objectors.[60]

Buoyed by his support, Jost continued his citizenship quest and moved to have his case reheard. Jost's primary argument rested on the point that "Congress defined the term 'Religious Training and Belief' as meaning 'an individual's belief in relation to a Supreme Being involving duties superior to those arising from any human relation, but does not include essentially politically sociological or philosophical views or a merely personal code.'"[61] In his "Petition for Rehearing," Jost argued that in the earlier ruling, there had been an erroneous application of the law, which would require a church to have as a tenet that all members must take the noncombatant oath before any could be naturalized with the alternate oath. Therefore, no Mennonite could take the oath. Moreover, the trial court exercised personal discretion, not legal discretion, in its ruling, as Congress had in mind individual belief, not an organization's belief, as derived from the Selective Draft Act of 1947. The court established, incorrectly, that one cannot learn a position from a religious organization unless all adherents apply the position as an official tenet. Jost testified that the greatest influence in his life came from his parents and the Krimmer Mennonite Brethren Church he had grown up in.[62] Thus, when he moved to the West Coast, he was pleased to find Mennonite Brethren leaders that agreed with him.

The Fourth District Court of Appeal reheard his case, accepting the evidence originally rejected—though not coming strictly from a church, it pertained to his religious training, including publications by MCC, John Horsch, and the *Yearbook of the 44th General Conference of the Mennonite Brethren*, as well as testimony of his family. Furthermore, the theory that Jost had acted out of fear for his personal safety did not fit with Jost's testimony of his willingness to go to the war front as a civilian medic.[63] In Jost's appeal, he reminded the court that the Mennonites were a Historic Peace Church, as determined by the U.S. government, and as such ran CPS units during World War II.[64]

In the "Brief Amici Curiae," filed by the Southern California Branch of the ACLU on Jost's behalf, the ACLU argued "that 'religious belief' as a general principle, and as pertinent here, is an individual matter, involving a direct relationship between a given individual and certain comprehensive forces and values that are operative in the universe . . . there are a great many views represented among religious groups; but there is general agreement that 'religious belief' requires individual participation and experience."[65] It is significant that a Mennonite, belonging to a religious group that held as a basic teaching the primacy of the faith community, retained the assistance of the ACLU—Southern California Branch, a modern, liberal, and secular group, as Friend of the Court, whose argument was based on individualism. Both were interested, however, in the issue of freedom of religion and the individual's right to that freedom.

Jost petitioned the Supreme Court of California to "prevent the continuation of a great injustice involving the free exercise of religious conscience and the right of such person to become a citizen of the United States." Underlying Jost's case was the argument that this was an individual matter, not an organizational one; that some Mennonites chose noncombatant service did not nullify the teaching the petitioner, as an individual, received.[66] Ruling that citizenship was a "high privilege," and that if any doubt existed in the petition for naturalization, the petition must be rejected, the California Supreme Court concluded that since Jost's petition had been rejected twice, his petition for a hearing was also rejected.[67]

Fellow Mennonites were mostly supportive of Jost's pursuit of American citizenship and the lengths he went to get it. Some, however, tempered their support. P. C. Hiebert, chairman of the Mennonite Brethren Board of General Welfare and Public Relations, in a letter dated March 28, 1955, stated, "I regret to hear that your citizenship has not been acquired . . . As important as it is to have citizenship in a good country, nevertheless that is far out-weighed by the citizenship we have in the kingdom of God."[68] Nevertheless, support for Jost was broad, and when his case arrived next at the Supreme Court of the United States, Dean Acheson, the former secretary of state, under President Harry Truman, became his legal representation. Acheson's involvement in the case was certainly significant. Not only had Jost tirelessly navigated his way to the Supreme Court, but now he had the "architect" of the cold war, a man whose fingerprints were all over the Truman Doctrine, who was hounded by Joseph McCarthy Republicans for being "soft on Communism," arguing his case out of general consideration for the Mennonite record working against injustice and misery. Acheson made his argument for Mennonite exemption for both combatant and noncombatant service based on Mennonite history.[69]

None of the drama of having Acheson on Jost's side came to the public square because the case before the Supreme Court was withdrawn by the Justice Department, with consent of the INS, in the final moments before its hearing.[70] It was a long and difficult process, but after several years and the government's ultimate withdrawal of the case, the way to citizenship had been cleared. Jost finally became an American.

Jost's difficulty in acquiring American citizenship is traceable to various issues: the temper of the time, conflicting messages given by Mennonite

Brethren leaders as to their official position, and the brief acceptance of an idiosyncratic understanding of noncombatant service by the Pacific District Conference in 1948. This case study of an individual's quest for American citizenship asks clear questions of what it means to be a good American and a good Mennonite as issues of defense, duties of citizenship, and religious practice intersect. Jost's experience in CPS not only led to the creation of Kings View Homes in Reedley, but was also used as evidence of his religious convictions before the naturalization court. CPS existed as an expression of Mennonite nonresistance. The Mennonites who worked in the camps were of similar conviction regarding pacifism, but there were certainly many differences as to what it meant to be a Mennonite.

Pacifism and Patriotism

By the end of the 1950s, the Mennonite Brethren, as evidenced by the difficulties experienced by Arthur Jost in his citizenship application, struggled with what nonresistance meant within the matrix of American identity. Part of the problem was the relationship of fundamentalist and liberal Christians within the denomination on the question of pacifism. J. B. Toews, pastor of Reedley Mennonite Brethren Church, returned from a Peace Conference at Winona Lake, Indiana, and reported that some there thought that pacifism and biblical nonresistance had no common ground. At the conference, he found a plurality of opinions among Mennonites from across America as to the meaning of nonresistance and its relationship to the government and social order. Toews argued before the Board of Welfare and Public Relations that the Mennonite Brethren had to clarify their terminology and theology.[71]

Yet the social-theological climate made it a complex endeavor for the Mennonite Brethren in California: "If most liberal groups come out with an expression of nonresistance, then who is against it? The fundamentalist groups. We as M.B.s are fundamental but believe in nonresistance. Could we have discussion on this problem?"[72] Mennonite Brethren wanted to be "fundamental" in their beliefs, as fundamentalists were, but unlike fundamentalists, they retained nonresistance as a theological ideal, if not evenly practiced. The crux of the issue for the Mennonite Brethren was that fundamentalists rejected pacifism and theological liberals embraced it, and they did not want to be associated with liberals. Caught between these theological polarities, Mennonite Brethren seemingly defaulted to

an inconsistent application of pacifism, which proved difficult for individuals like Jost.

Toews continued to explain the weaknesses in the Mennonite Brethren
position and highlighted three concerns: nonresistance was part of an oral
tradition and not a set of beliefs written down; confessions of faith apparently notwithstanding, the topic was largely avoided by the conference;
and CPS was criticized by some as "not a full and complete expression of
our nonresistance." The Board vote was "almost unanimous" in its agreement with Toews's comments.[73]

Civilian Public Service did not satisfy the extremes of opinion: fundamentalists rejected pacifism, and liberals rejected pragmatic accommodation. Thus the Mennonite Brethren appeared ambiguous regarding
nonresistance. In response to postwar civil defense pressures, the MCC
Voluntary Service (VS) program began, which ultimately helped administer the government mandated I-W service for conscientious objectors,
where in lieu of twenty-four months' military service, they gave equivalent time to service of national importance—as in mental health care. I-W
was similar to CPS in that participating churches bore the cost of administration and program delivery while the government provided oversight.
VS and the I-W requirement were used effectively by Kings View Homes
and migrant worker programs in California to keep staff levels full.

There was another reason for VS, however. An undated document,
likely from the early 1950s, acknowledges the peculiar experience of
conscientious objectors along the West Coast and the need for a service
organization to deal directly with the possibility of a draft. Reflecting on
earlier experiences during World War I, Mennonite Brethren in the West
experienced little of the wartime persecution co-religionists had endured
in places like Kansas: "It is difficult to understand how we have escaped
persecution here on the West Coast even in a small measure."[74] Grateful
for avoiding the persecution experienced in places like Kansas, they hoped
the VS program would set a precedent of service and commitment satisfying to Americans before Congress instituted a future draft.

Ideally, the national service requirement would be met not deep in the
woods isolated from society, but in a hospital—the example they gave—
where Mennonites could directly meet the needs of human suffering.[75]
The Mennonite Brethren produced a list of New Testament verses from
three Gospels and various epistles to clarify general Mennonite theology behind nonresistant pacifism.[76] In a letter to Mennonite Brethren

pastors in the Pacific District Conference, written in spring 1951, O. B. Reimer, chairman of the Board of Welfare and Public Relations Committee, stressed that Mennonites must be prepared to sacrifice for their country as others do. To this end, Reimer highlighted the civilian program they had created, with service units working in hospitals, as appropriate testimony for nonresistant people if a shooting war ever erupted.[77]

There were varieties of pacifisms in California as there were varieties of Mennonites. Mennonites expressed themselves as much with nonresistant communitarian ideals as with conservative evangelical pietism and American patriotism. World War II and the CPS experience was, as one historian put it, "the transforming event of the twentieth century" for American Mennonites, where "issues that had dominated the life of the church before the war receded and new ones came to define its life and character."[78] Mennonites associated with American Civil Religion as part of their pacifism while enjoying the approval of military leaders regarding their work of national importance. They lived in society and wished to influence it through their faith and actions, which was itself influenced by evangelical Protestantism.

Mennonite Brethren ministers did not agree on the official church position regarding noncombatant military service. No unified understanding of pacifism or Mennonitism existed within CPS camps. Despite CPS effectively marking Mennonites as outside the American mainstream, there were disagreements over whether the program compromised too much with the government, such as in the issue of peach picking. CPS was also a cultural site where older church issues came to the surface. There were significant inter-Mennonite tensions over the practice of communion and, in one case, the Mennonite Church practice of wearing head coverings. The CPS was successful in that Mennonites, along with other denominations, negotiated a compromise over the issue of conscription with the federal government. It is ironic that in protecting and exercising the principles of separation of church and state, and freedom of religion, a deeper relationship with a wartime government was necessary. Part of their service to America involved work in mental health facilities. As we will see in the next chapter, the success of those experiences was directly responsible for the creation of a network of five Mennonite mental health hospitals across the country. Two of them were in the San Joaquin Valley. The new venture began with Arthur Jost and his work in CPS.[79]

CHAPTER 8

Socially Active Mennonitism and Mental Health

The Origins of Kings View Homes

You people have unique care.
—Dr. Jackson Dillon, psychiatrist, on Mennonites, 1951

Beginnings

Immediately in postwar California, flush with the success of the Civilian Public Service (CPS), there was an expanding array of social relief efforts through the local Mennonite Central Committee (MCC) and churches. The institutional presence of Mennonites was growing at a rapid rate. As with CPS, the institutional expansion of California Mennonites articulated a sense of identity and drew them nearer to society's political structures. An especially poignant example of this development is the creation of Kings View Homes (KVH), a mental health hospital in Reedley. Although California health care in the early twentieth century was, in part, defined by curative sunshine, soon the application of scientific principles dominated health care delivery, and we see both in the early sanitarium. As the twentieth century advanced, health care, by necessity, became a professional activity, and despite the compassionate and religious motivation behind KVH, religion seemingly disappeared.

The flurry of Mennonite activity in the first postwar decade was part

of a larger Californian response to changing times. Related directly to a
rapid expansion of suburban developments, Californians were building
at a quick pace. As the state's population continued to rise quickly, communities were built with schools, houses of worship, and other religious
institutions anchoring them along with parks and shopping malls. The
1950s was also a decade of tremendous expansion for religious infrastructure, with many seminaries, houses of worship, and social services built.
Within California, all this building, including massive school, community college, and university construction—coinciding with expanding
networks of highways—was supporting old-time residents and the vast
number of newcomers.[1] Within this swirl of optimism and activity the
Mennonites too established a significant presence in churches, schools,
and community service organizations.

Emerging directly from the CPS experience was an ambitious undertaking to establish Mennonite mental health hospitals throughout the
country. In California, Arthur Jost headed this project, and it signaled a
larger irony: the rise of a "secularized" Mennonitism.[2] Henry Schmidt,
Mennonite Brethren seminary professor and president, observed that the
twentieth-century experience was largely one of "reluctant involvement,"
where tensions between "continuity" and "discontinuity" were typical.
These tensions were found in attempts to maintain Mennonites' particular
ethical religious expression, geographic isolation, and cultural separation.
However, they accepted such citizenship demands as voting and, increasingly, military service, or at least lost some compulsion to avoid them. In
so doing, Mennonites grew in their acceptance of "patriotic nationalism,"
and we see this in such projects as KVH and its social, religious, and cultural motivations.[3]

As early as 1937, the Mennonite Brethren Pacific District Conference
(PDC) discussed mental health care. They believed that mental health
care was necessary for some, but as a medical practice, it was largely biased
against religion. Despite this concern, when they visited the state hospital
in Stockton in 1938, they felt welcomed and were encouraged to sing and
preach to fellow Mennonites.[4]

The real momentum to establish a center for mental health care developed from CPS, when many Mennonite CPSers were stationed in mental
health hospitals. Scholars have linked CPS involvement in mental hospitals during World War II with postwar Mennonite socio-religious activism. During World War II, approximately 1,500 Mennonite men served

in mental hospitals, and many reported that the mentally ill lived in deplorable conditions.[5]

In the mid-1940s, MCC studied mental illness among Mennonites and
discovered that more than one thousand American Mennonites suffered
some form of it. Mennonite leaders, such as Arthur Jost, considered the
general apathetic attitude toward the mentally ill an indictment against
the Mennonites. As West Coast Mennonites took initiative on this issue,
the significance of people like Jost grew.[6]

The PDC made recommendations in 1946: "We see a very definite
need for a mental institution. We feel that we are not equipped to receive
such cases; also, our license of operation is for a Home for the Aged only.
Therefore we recommend that the conference take some definite action
toward the establishment of such [an] institution in connection with
MCC."[7] The PDC added and approved a clarification in the original minutes that the Home for the Aged (a Mennonite Brethren senior care facility created in 1942) and the future mental institution remain separate.[8]

By the following summer, the Mennonite Brethren Committee of the
Home for the Aged, voted unanimously to support the mental hospital and
"co-operate to the fullest extent possible."[9] After exploring the possibility
of opening a mental hospital in California, Elmer Ediger of the planning
committee reported that a psychiatrist in Los Angeles supported the project:
"He feels that the psychiatrically validated 'spiritual' ministry should distinguish the Mennonite institutions for [the] emotionally ill." Furthermore, "Discussion regarding the philosophy of a Mennonite institution
was helpful, however, he, not having had first hand institutional experience but only clinical office work, could not help too much in the field of
suggestions regarding the nature of the institution policies and staff."[10]
That fell to a proven Mennonite Brethren administrator, Arthur Jost.

Before his involvement in mental health, Jost had been the administrator of the Home for the Aged in Reedley, which he left in 1953 to de-
vote more time to KVH.[11] When Jost filed the first report of the "M.C.C.
Mental Hospital Project," his narrative framed the mental health issue
in terms of the secularization of mental health care, mistreatment of patients, Mennonite inaction, and specific Mennonites suffering at mental
health institutions. Jost introduced his report with a telling statement:
"Our modern day of secularization and strife seemingly has led many of
us [Mennonites] into a deeper appreciation of our Christian privileges."
By this statement, Jost indicated that secularization, while creating a host

of problems in society, provided a place to enact religious convictions. He then listed various groups in the Mennonite constituency that had institutions built to serve them. These institutions included schools and senior care facilities. Those who suffered from mental illness, however, went to state institutions, where standards of care were questionable.[12]

No longer, argued Jost, could Mennonites claim innocence regarding the treatment of the mentally ill or that mental illness did not afflict their own people: "Today we know that there is nothing magic about mental illness; it is largely a cause and effect relationship which is no respecter of persons. Today we know that medical care together with kindly treatment and intercessory prayer, which is possible only in Christian institutions, can restore many of them to mental and spiritual health."[13] Jost tied the de-mythologizing of mental illness as nothing "magical" to the spiritualizing of its care as "kindly" and "intercessory prayer" which only "Christian" institutions could provide. He navigated between two sets of concern: the spiritual concerns of Mennonites and the medical concerns of professional health care.

Jost took care to highlight the problems of the secular institutions: "There is no segregation from the evil influences often rampant in these [state] institutions." Furthermore, he reported that the treatment of patients was often deplorable if not violent. Finally, Jost described, albeit anecdotally, the treatment of Mennonite sufferers of mental illness in state or other private facilities in tones that suggested dark malevolence: "I have seen a Mennonite sister . . .who was imprisoned in a cage like a beast and her agony was indescribable. A Mennonite brother, who with his religious utterings incensed the attendants, was choked until unconscious. Recently I was shown the ward where our own brother, a minister to whom our conference owes a great debt, was kept in an unusually clean room yet where he was crowded into a godless, lonely environment."[14]

The language Jost used depicted men and women, leaders and laity, as suffering mental illness exacerbated by facilities that caged them like beasts, persecuted them for religious utterances, or at least kept them in a lonely godless environment. Jost reminded his audience of the evangelistic possibilities and suggested that such ministry was a "fuller Christian service" necessary for earning the church respect in the local community: "Although this work is directed particularly to those who are of the household of faith, we want to consider this as a type of missionary service which we can be rendering in a very special way."[15]

Construction

On May 3, 1947, MCC authorized the construction of KVH, with Jost as its administrator, and the creation of a committee, made of representatives of the West Coast Mennonite constituency, to run it. In fall 1949, construction began on a forty-three-acre plot, and in March 1951, KVH opened its doors. Patient activities included music and farming, which generated income for KVH.[16] Kings View Homes, though planned as a long-term care facility before its opening, set aside four beds for acutely mentally ill patients. Thus, Kings View Homes was also known as Kings View Hospital.[17]

The KVH program enjoyed the support of the Mennonite Brethren Church, whose Board of General Welfare and Public Relations in January 1950 passed the following resolution: "Kings View Homes. Work on this project has been started. The Churches on the West Coast are making special drives to finance the building of these homes. We are pleased to hear that the work is progressing and are thankful for the efforts of the Pacific District Conference in this regard. We are urging our churches to support this worthy cause."[18] Not only churches supported the cause, but other Mennonite Brethren agencies, such as the Committee for Bible Camps, saw potential in working with KVH.[19]

Support from the local community, however, was not as readily forthcoming. In two letters to Elmer Ediger, of MCC in Akron, Pennsylvania, Jost described local resistance. Initially, he characterized local concerns as typical: "The community here around our property just like thousands of other American communities has many questions regarding the mental hospital." Jost assured Ediger that "neighbors with Mennonite American or German backgrounds have responded well," and that opposition was essentially the orchestration of one couple, Mr. and Mrs. Peloin. Mr. Peloin, an apparently influential man in Reedley, worked to persuade people to vote against KVH. He offered as a compromise that KVH reconstitute itself as an "Old People's Home." Though accurate in the short term, as KVH began treating chronically ill patients, many of whom were elderly, Jost argued it was dishonest to have promoted the facility to the State of California and the Mennonite constituency as a mental health hospital and then proceed as an elder care facility.[20]

Of particular concern for Jost was the local Armenian population: "It is unfortunate that the Armenian people, who band together just like Mennonites on an issue, do not favor the project." Jost thought that Armenians were planning to attend the local meetings with "an unnecessary number [of participants]." He also believed that Peloin's motivation was influenced by his own desire to buy the same plot of land. Peloin, however, attributed his opposition to the hospital to his wife's fears: "She is afraid of all mentally ill, except those that cannot walk." If the vote went against KVH, Jost had a second option: find land in an area populated primarily by Mennonites in a school district with few, if any, Armenians.[21]

In a letter dated April 8, 1948, on the eve of the vote, Jost informed Elmer Ediger that, despite some struggle to win local approval, it would be forthcoming: "[It's] utterly preposterous that people make so much ado about nothing." He hinted that part of the problem was their pacifist background: "the price to pay for our stand during the last war."[22] Three years later, H. R. Martens, on the KVH Advisory Committee, concluded that "hostile opposition" to the hospital was shifting to "acceptance" as local uncertainties regarding KVH subsided.[23]

Throughout 1948, the struggle to generate Mennonite support continued, and responsibility to educate local Mennonite congregations fell to the MCC Peace Committee. Throughout the experience, Jost linked evangelical piety and social action. For himself, the challenges in moving KVH forward were also a spiritual matter: "The project as a whole is moving slowly and with great difficulties at some points. With the expression of interest which I contact continually and with the way in which developments have taken place we feel the Lord is definitely leading, but we have also experienced a greater dependence on Him leaving the whole matter in His hand."[24] He concluded that church support came largely from educational visits, not fund-raising visits, with particularly large turnouts in Upland and Reedley.[25] To demonstrate the project's fiscal viability, Jost proposed that KVH be built primarily with voluntary Mennonite labor. Demonstrating the project's social responsibility, Jost explained that KVH was a response to society's tendency to cast the mentally ill aside.[26] Thus, Jost wove together evangelicalism and social activism into whole cloth.

At the ground breaking, on November 20, 1949, Jost had mixed feelings. Though he had some success promoting KVH to Mennonites, non-Mennonites were less enthused: "We were somewhat disappointed that not more members of the community (non-Mennonite) were present."[27] There was a measure of success on another front, as MCC had always hoped that the hospital would be a venue of inter-Mennonite cooperation.[28] By 1952, KVH reported that "only three churches were uninterested" and that Mennonites were asking more questions about mental health care and considering KVH "their mental hospital."[29] Nonetheless, Jost acknowledged, "we realize that this project does not inherently register the sense of urgency that foreign relief and refugee projects do."[30] Working to bring mental health into the same realm of Mennonite consciousness as foreign missions and refugee work, supporters of KVH were most frustrated with fund-raising. They complained as late as 1950, "we as yet have not received enough contributions to assure completion of the Kings View Homes building."[31]

Despite these frustrations, KVH served an important symbolic function of inter-Mennonite ecumenism, though run almost entirely by the Mennonite Brethren. Their geographic isolation from the main anchors of American Mennonitism in the eastern states made the symbolic function of inter-Mennonite cooperation possible. Jost observed, "In the past we have frequently stressed the importance of the [Mennonite Central Committee West Coast Regional Office] center on the West Coast as a symbol of our combined effort. The mental hospital is entering into that same function and I continue to believe that it is important particularly because of our distance to Akron."[32]

Kings View Homes was also important in mediating a growing relationship between the Mennonites and California society. At the opening ceremony, Dr. Frank Tallman, of the California Department of Health, representing the governor, thanked the Mennonites and encouraged them "to go forward in their program for the mentally ill."[33] KVH was a church-run institution but not overtly religious in its presentation. Even the name was symbolic of this, for despite its apparent Christian imagery, Jost explained, KVH was named after the Kings River.[34]

The county commissioner found KVH's location acceptable: "The selected site was a bit isolated although only two and half miles from town on the edge of a thickly populated Mennonite community." The site encompassed forty-three acres with fruit trees and fertile soil: "The soil is some of the best in the San Joaquin Valley and is capable of producing any of the crops native to central California." Modernist architecture, simple, practical, and prebuilt, became common in 1945 as Californian suburbs and housing construction ballooned, and here this architecture was a point of pride for Mennonites: "The building is strictly modernistic in design and yet every effort has been made in both design and construction to keep costs on the lowest possible plane."[35] Construction lasted from January 29, 1950, to February 1, 1951, using prefabricated materials and donated labor, both of which kept costs down for a church organization on a tight budget. The industry journal *Mental Hospitals* praised KVH as a model for low-cost construction, and denominational leaders such as P. C. Hiebert recognized Jost's administration of KVH as "efficient administrative work."[36] Now it was time to hire a doctor.

Religion and Health Care

Following World War II, when the plan to create a Mennonite mental health program emerged, no Mennonite psychiatrists existed. From the start, Jost and Ediger pursued "active treatment rather than merely custodial care" and the best of progressive mental health treatment.[37] Staff initially came from the wider community, though "great care was used to secure a staff sympathetic to Mennonite Christian concerns."[38] KVH, therefore, employed non-Mennonite psychiatrists, who naturally enough wielded considerable influence on the hospital's early development, posing some challenges and interesting recommendations.

The first KVH psychiatrist, Dr. Jackson Dillon, encouraged the hospital to adopt a Mennonite religious element: "Our hospital doctor is of the very best and understands our Mennonite faith. Recently Dr. Dillon was asked to appear before the Executive Board as to future guidance for the Hospital Staff. Dr. Dillon gave us a very encouraging report stating that others give good medical care. But you people have unique care, and something that I call extra which is a healing ministry in itself. We should have been pleased had he used the word Christian instead of the word unique, but doctors like to use more of a medical term."[39] According to Jost, non-Mennonite doctors were perceived by some Mennonites to "approach all problems with an experimental eye," which "debunk[ed] old customs."[40] The "old customs," likely of a religious nature, were also replaced by Mennonites with a concern for efficient, rational, and modern administrative practices.

In its first twenty years of operation, KVH grew from a small psychiatric hospital to a mental health center serving a population of more than 400,000 in five counties. It established a reputation for its efficiency and rational delivery of service, as in the following praise found in *Hospital and*

Kings View Hospital, Reedley. *Source:* Records of
Reedley Mennonite Brethren Church.

Community Psychiatry: "Its [KVH] experience demonstrates that a private
organization can effectively deliver services usually provided by government agencies."[41]

From the beginning, Jost worked closely with state officials in the creation and running of the facility. In a conference Jost, Dr. Frank Tallman,
director of the California Department of Mental Hygiene, concluded that
he wanted to start a National Mental Health Foundation (NMHF) chapter in California in order to include MCC in the establishment of an "attendant training program." Tallman explained that an NMHF chapter in
California would "unify the uncoordinated Californian agencies" and that
NMHF was more oriented to mental health than existing general health
agencies and therefore had better resources and funding for mental health.
MCC's contribution to the training curriculum, through Jost, "would not
be on the technical level but in terms of attendant attitudes and experience
on the level of 'personal relationships.' "[42]

In his relationship with Tallman, Jost worked to build closer relationships with the California government. Jost wrote to Tallman, "We would like to discuss further with you the possibility of such units and the part we might have in the development of such as well as in reaping the benefits such a program might have toward our own mental health activities."[43] It became a fruitful relationship. By the mid-1950s, Jost's administrative team situated KVH on an increasingly vague boundary between Mennonite religiosity and California society.[44]

Jost had his start in mental health work while in a CPS unit in Provo, Utah. In a 1943 letter to the *Christian Leader*, the official publication of the United States Conference of Mennonite Brethren Churches, he wrote, "In this field we saw avenues of unlimited service to humanity; we saw in it a similarity to the kind of service Jesus had in mind when He commands us to serve 'the least of these.' . . . We realize that we are dealing with souls, although sick and irresponsible, they are and deserve to be treated as such."[45] By the time Jost took the reins of KVH, he had undergone his own shift in focus. A decade later, he described KVH for the *Mennonite Encyclopedia* in clearly less religious terms: "The present services include full psychiatric care, medical workup in conjunction with local general medical facilities, outpatient care, and foster home care. All types of mental patients are admitted."[46]

Jost was not alone. Jim S. Gaede, chair of the Board of General Welfare and Public Relations, also navigated this boundary in accepting the position of psychiatric social worker at KVH for two reasons: "to be true to Christ and to be true to myself." Gaede worked in his denomination's psychiatric hospital as a trained psychiatric social worker in a fashion that was authentic to himself—as an individual.[47]

Moreover, hospital administrators gauged their growing success by local and professional acceptance, especially as their workers increasingly spoke at professional meetings. By 1962, however, Mennonite leaders expressed concern over the decline in the number of Mennonite nurses. They feared the Mennonite constituency at the hospital might be completely replaced by secular outsiders.[48] Ironically, the increased success of efforts to reach out to the wider community, so enthusiastically embraced and pursued by hospital administration, threatened to alienate the very constituency that sponsored them.

In the early 1960s, when plans were established to build a second Mennonite mental health hospital in Bakersfield, significant changes in the Mennonite social position in central California made development possible. In the case of Bakersfield, local experts invited the Mennonites to construct a hospital ward near the Greater Bakersfield Memorial Hospital. The invitation even came with government funding and a rent of one dollar a year for fifty years. These planners of the Bakersfield hospital stressed that no money, only personnel and expertise, were required of the Mennonite constituency. The Bakersfield medical community considered such a hospital necessary, and the Mennonites considered it an opportunity to provide services in a California region with a large Mennonite population; they could "enlarge their witness."[49] The new facility in Bakersfield was located "on grounds adjacent" to the Memorial Hospital of Greater Bakersfield. Mennonites quickly seized the opportunity to purchase the land out "of fear that one of the other hospitals in the area, particularly the Catholic hospital, will 'beat them to the punch.' "[50]

When the Mennonite Mental Health Services Board approved the expansion of KVH into Bakersfield, in 1963, the language used in the announcement was more generic than specifically Mennonite. The new hospital was to be "love centered." The citizens of the State of California had accepted the work at KVH and its "effectiveness of a psychiatric treatment program, which is motivated by a philosophy of life with love as its central theme." One patient wrote, "The Mennonites and their way of love is what we all need." In the context of mental health care, Mennonitism seems to have been understood often enough as "love-centered psychiatric therapy," or more generally, "the therapeutic effect of Christian love."[51] Christian faith and an ethereal, generic-sounding "love" were considered efficacious.

In summer 1963, the builders of the Bakersfield Hospital waited for approval from state and federal government grants. The denominational Board of General Welfare and Public Relations announced that this new hospital "will be owned and operated by the Mennonite churches, [though] the identification with the larger community general hospital will be very close."[52] Ultimately, this project, by which Mennonites served society and their own constituency, would not clearly mark Christian and Mennonite identity, but would work comfortably with "secular" society. On the cover of the October 16, 1966, Kern View Hospital dedication bulletin was an American Flag and a Christian Flag with crossed staffs alongside a picture of the United States Capitol in the lower left corner; the entanglement with American Civil Religion seemed complete.[53]

Mennonite engagement with mainstream culture and society, as exemplified by the mental health program, was clearly articulated in the Bakersfield hospital proposal. The proposal stated, "It is difficult for any-one outside California to understand why a fifth hospital should be lo-cated to so unbalance the Mennonite Mental Health program in relation to Mennonite constituency."[54] The fifth hospital being in California was a result of local Central Valley needs and recognition of the good work done in KVH in Reedley. Mennonites established mental health hospitals in the rest of the country according to Mennonite demographics; in Califor-nia, however, the Mennonite presence, while important, was not the sole determinant of location.

Considering Mennonite demographics, California was the least pop-ulated American region and the only region at the time planning a branch hospital. The board of the Greater Bakersfield Memorial Hospital also did not consider the Mennonite initiative and presence to be that of "out-siders"; they saw the Mennonites and general hospital to be two groups "thinking together and working together on a common problem." The Kings View Homes Board of Directors, in compiling their report on the feasibility of the Bakersfield project, made considerable effort to dem-onstrate that Mennonites were not considered "foreign elements," that Bakersfield understood their emphasis on "Christian love" in health care. This proposal, unlike the proposal for Kings View, rarely used the word Mennonite. Instead, Kern View relied on the more generic terms of "Christian," "Christian love," and "Christian service."[55]

Perhaps it was ironic that Jost and KVH helped draw California Men-nonites into the mainstream of California life by acting on principles born out of CPS. As the religious and denominational impulses that initially governed the creation of KVH were replaced by more "secular," or generi-cally Christian-appearing, ideals, the process of mediating between Cali-fornia and Mennonite culture gave way to religious and cultural assimila-tion. Aspects of American Mennonitism secularized in central California in part through its socially active care for the mentally ill.

Government and Mennonite Care

Part of the legacy of Arthur Jost and KVH was their growing reliance on government funding: "Of all the MMHS [Mennonite Mental Health Services] centers and hospitals, Kings View has been the most heavily in-volved in public funding in terms of dollars received." When KVH closed briefly, in 1957–1958, due to financial difficulties, Jost found that MCC "curiously" placed the needs of Mennonites over the needs of others, suggesting that Jost understood his constituency to be much larger than the Mennonites.[56] The reopening of Kings View in 1958, under greater local Mennonite control, was part of a larger MCC strategy to relinquish control of the mental health centers to local Mennonite constituencies. In KVH's case, this coincided with other difficulties.[57] In evaluating this relationship with local, state, and federal governments, Jost concluded, "One of the obvious results of public funding was the rapid growth of Kings View over a relatively short period of time." Rapid growth came with problems, and Jost listed the primary difficulties as staff recruitment and a strain on the "spirit of unity" at KVH.

Jost believed that taking government funding and contracts exacerbated tension with Mennonite churches that had initially raised funds and built the hospital. By the late 1950s, the Mennonite perception was that KVH had been "'taken over' by government." Finally, in his analysis of government funding and Mennonite hospitals, Jost observed: "We have noted that leaning on government for funds coincided with a diminishing sense of responsibility on the part of the churches, that in some centers there seemed to be a tendency to downplay the Christian/Mennonite identity, that there was some drifting of the constituency from the centers (or vice versa) over a period of time." However, as he argued, coincidence is not causation: "But it would be difficult to demonstrate a direct tie between these developments and receiving government funding."[58] Certainly, the receipt of government funding was a reality shared by all Mennonite hospitals, but Kings View depended the most, by dollar amount, on government grants. The hospital and constituency were nonetheless drifting apart.

In his report to the advisory committee in December 1952, Jost described the religious and therapeutic mix at Kings View in decidedly individualistic terms. Without reference to any particular Christian or Mennonite teaching, he wrote: "In spite of the fact that we have conducted morning devotionals each week day and Sunday school each Sunday morning plus devotional services every other Thursday, I feel that we need to expand in terms of individualized spiritual service."[59] Jost thought that an expansion of religious service would be helpful if it included local ministers. Jackson Dillon, their psychiatrist, suggested that KVH "should continue to do this work within the institution."[60] This was certainly a Christian-influenced hospital, but the Mennonite connection was seemingly weakening as Jost worked hard to keep the hospitals in front of mental health developments.

In 1953 he reported to MCC that "the term and concept of mental health is with us to stay and that we are bound to relate many of the problems which are common to us to the mental health concept."[61] One of the more peculiar developments at Kings View was the avoidance of hiring a chaplain or holding religious services. There were early attempts at morning devotional services and allowing patients to listen to church services on the radio. Yet, attempts to organize a devotional program were confined to the creation of a committee, "perhaps," to coordinate it.[62] The result was a virtual absence of Mennonite religious expression in the hospital.

Despite problems that eventually emerged with their psychiatrist, Dr. Jackson Dillon, he was consistently supportive of the Mennonite religion and the most surprised at the lack of religious services at KVH. He was encouraged by the ability of Kings View to help and place patients of different religions in the hospital. Dillon appreciated not only the "Christian influence" of the staff as an important addition to the psychiatric community, but also the ideas of holding devotional services in the morning and assisting patients to attend church services at the staff's own expense. Of particular significance was that as medical director, Dillon stressed the importance of Mennonite Christianity.[63]

The relationship between administration, medical staff, and their "Christian Witness" was examined in a Kings View Homes Study Committee report in 1955. It concluded that professional training was not enough to define the work at KVH; it needed Christianity to use science for its own ends. The report recommended that KVH build a chapel "as a symbol of the spiritual objectives of the Church in her hospital program" to demonstrate "that there is perfect harmony between true science and the laws of God." The report stated that it was congruent with Christian principles to have non-Christian psychiatrists treating patients in a Christian hospital because God created the laws of medical science for everyone. What was needed, however, was a governing structure cognizant of the "responsibility of the church to maintain that [Christian] witness."[64] Within five years, Jost referred to the position of chaplain "as a parallel role to the psychiatrist." Jost believed that the final say in a psychiatric hospital was not necessarily that of the psychiatrist, but of this parallel chaplain, though one was never hired.[65]

With the planned closing and reorganization of KVH in late 1957, Jost continued to speak of the desirability of having a chaplain for the needs of patients. However, he placed priority on the prestige of the hospital in the psychiatric community. Research conducted at Kings View gave it "considerable prominence" along with changes to California law through the Short-Doyle Program, which opened up government contracts to private hospitals to provide community mental health services for indigent patients. Jost was excited by the prospect of a closer working relationship with the state government in such a program.[66]

In what appears to be a swift reversal of priorities, on May 3, 1957, Jost reported, "A chaplain should be considered for our staff." Two weeks later, on May 18, 1957, Jost presented a "partial condensation of brochure material" that included text describing the role of the chaplain and how patients may attend local Protestant or Catholic services.[67] By December 1958, the Chaplaincy Program was given "careful consideration," though it lacked funding.[68]

The question of having a Chaplaincy Program continued. In spring 1959, after the hospital reopened, Jost reported: "From time to time, the patients have asked and wondered why the hospital doesn't make use of its Christian symbol. Very often the question comes why did a church engage in a mental hospital program. Without the presence of a chaplain, these questions are sometimes difficult to answer and at best are answered superficially."[69] Jost was certainly a Mennonite Christian, but the trend at KVH was increasingly ambiguous, at the administrative level, concerning religious identity. Other Mennonite mental health centers throughout the United States did not create a chaplaincy until the 1950s, but even then, this trend did not spread to all.[70]

The religious question was more complex for Jost than simply professional reputation. He questioned the direction of KVH, "Are we consciously and conscientiously rendering a service in the name of Christ?" He found the process of "developing our churchwide goals" to be "discouragingly slow," and he felt responsibility for that slow pace: "I often feel guilty and selfish when patients and their families commend the Mennonite church for offering such an important and appreciated service to this area to realize how little the church, outside of staff, Board and M.M.H.S. is involved." The hospital, according to Jost, exhibited a "lack of . . . religious counsel." As standards of professional society led psychiatry, he hoped the chaplain, as "the church's counterpart to medical science's agent, the psychiatrist, will take his place around the discussion table in our hospital."[71] These rueful ruminations about the spiritual and Mennonite character of KVH, while significant, were not common. The KVH leadership soon returned to pressing issues of hospital administration, and religious questions had to wait.

In the early 1960s, KVH began pursuing accreditation by the American Psychiatry Association in order to access insurance monies as well as "prestige and status."[72] At the same time, a committee was also struck to study the issue of a Chaplaincy Program and to recommend one if the budget allowed.[73] It remained difficult to establish a chaplaincy position. In the 1960 report, Dr. Charles A. Davis, medical director, simply stated on the chaplaincy issue: "This remains to be developed. We recognize that there are several factors which have caused this aspect of our program to go so slowly ... This is such an important position that much study should be given it—to feel out the duties of a chaplain, see how his world will integrate with the existing program, and to find the special individual who could fill the role."[74] They clearly took seriously the idea of a chaplaincy; finding a qualified Mennonite or the will to create the position was more complicated.

The First Psychiatrist

The relationship between Dr. Jackson Dillon, the first psychiatrist and medical director of KVH, with the Mennonite administration of KVH is revealing, on issues of health care and religion. Dillon was a strong supporter of KVH's continued expansion.[75] In particular, he highlighted the "personalized, interested care" provided by KVH and was sympathetic to the Mennonite emphasis on involving the family in a patient's recovery, a new concept at the time.[76] Orie Miller, of the advisory committee, asked him what he thought of non-Christian psychiatrists: "Dr. Dillon pointed out that the main consideration as far as he was concerned was that the psychiatrist on the staff be properly qualified. He felt that Christian or non-Christian psychiatrists could be integrated into our staff if they were well trained doctors."[77] Dillon, an influential non-Mennonite psychiatrist at KVH, held to the professional goals of training first and integration second. He believed that where differences of religious opinion occurred, they would simply smooth themselves out.

In early 1957, Dr. Dillon wrote a letter to Orie Miller, describing his desire, and that of his colleague Dr. Ludwig, to elevate the psychiatric care to the highest standards while working with the church. Dillon, despite his support, faulted Mennonites for not taking psychiatric care seriously enough as a religious or theological issue: "It is imperative to eliminate as many conflicting feelings [regarding psychiatry and religion] in ideology and in other matters as it is humanly possible."[78]

Though the religious element was muted at KVH, Dillon persistently questioned its absence in a church hospital. In a June 8, 1957, memo to Delmar Stahly, Jost described Dillon's confusion regarding Mennonites:

> It is significant and has been a mystery to Dr. Dillon from the beginning, why a church psychiatric hospital is interested in competent psychiatry and is blind about competent theological staff. He has consistently urged a competent chaplain or at least pastoral assistance so that the patients' needs are met more adequately in various ways, i.e. devotional program, staff counseling, and working with patient's minister. He has been fur-ther baffled by the distance of Mennonite pastors of the area. This lack of interest is understandable generally, but hardly on the part of pastors who have gotten their churches to build a mental hospital.[79]

Dillon encouraged the administrators to recruit young Mennonites into psychiatry. However, administrative reports include little, if any, com-ment on the devotional or religious implications of their work, including the contribution and experience of Voluntary Service (VS) workers. Non-Mennonite medical staff also encouraged administrators to recruit Men-nonites.[80]

Nevertheless, the administration had problems with Dillon and his apparently strained relationships with some area psychiatrists. Some al-leged that Dillon often refused to work with psychiatrists who disagreed with his therapeutic opinion, and they in turn would not refer patients to KVH. Jost reported that any attempt to broach the topic with Dillon re-sulted in threats to resign, causing KVH administrators to back away from any discussion. Though Dillon apparently repaired at least one relation-ship with a prominent Fresno psychiatrist in 1957, tensions persisted.[81]

Regardless, by December 1957, KVH closed in order to reorganize. Since Jost had defended Dillon and his ideas the longest, he was in an awkward position when required to choose between sponsors and doc-tors. Jost supported the doctors. When KVH closed, one board member observed, "How the patron Saint Dillon has led him [Jost] down a blind alley—the same alley that H. R. [Martens, a KVH sponsor] warned him about and Art [Jost] is forced to close the institution."[82] Finally, on the eve of KVH's temporary closing, Jost made one last defense of Drs. Dillon and Ludwig: "We were led in a direction which is quite standard in contemporary psychiatry. [Milieu therapy, where there is no lock-down of patients, emphasizing warm staff and patient relationships and pleasant surroundings] . . . The direction was right and proper, and in my opinion, irreversible." Jost continued to argue that in reorganization, KVH should build on the existing foundation: "We have little choice to do otherwise if we want to have a progressive program and one which will accomplish the purpose of the church in this area."[83] Jost, however, was willing to let go of the builders of that foundation.

Jost wrote that Dillon had caused several problems in his relationships with Fresno psychiatrists and that local professional perceptions of KVH had dimmed.[84] As KVH sat at the crossroads, Dillon departed and observed that these Mennonites needed to clarify for themselves what they thought about psychiatric care, because even though they wanted a Mennonite psychiatrist, none seemed to exist.[85]

Despite questions about the appropriate mix of religion and science in California Mennonite health care, issues of government funding, dependency on non-Mennonite specialists, and a lack of religious symbols, the larger Mennonite community read in their denominational history that KVH was an example of "exemplary cooperation of all Mennonite groups."[86] As early as March 17, 1950, however, Jost reported that closer ties between KVH and the Mental Health Services section of MCC was possible if one of their directors, or assistant directors, actually made a visit to the West Coast.[87]

Civic Mennonitism

Health care service was a conduit for Mennonite accommodation with society, and it went beyond KVH. It even included providing ambulance service for a number of years at mid-century. By the early 1950s, Cairns Funeral Home had provided ambulance service in Reedley for many years. Over time the costs of running the service grew too far out of proportion to the revenues it generated, and Cairns Funeral Home pulled out. A single small business simply could not sustain the operation. Simultaneously, in

1953, due to the high accident rate on highways in Fresno County, the California Highway Patrol was pressuring the Reedley Chamber of Commerce to create a safety council, as other valley towns had done. Reedley followed the trend, and the first order of business for their new safety council was to organize ambulance service. It organized a fund-raising drive known as the "Green Cross," where people who donated a dollar or more received a green cross sticker for their car. The safety council raised enough money, together with a fee schedule of seven dollars a call plus fifty cents per mile, to restart ambulance service in Reedley and the surrounding area.[88]

To keep costs down, the safety council decided that the ambulance be operated by trained reliable volunteers. At the suggestion of Marden Habegger, local physician and member of the First Mennonite Church, the volunteer aspect of the service was handed over to the MCC under the leadership of Arthur Jost, who was working with Mennonite volunteers at KVH, fulfilling their I-W service requirements to the government. Jost was on board and saw the opportunity as a way to show Reedley that local Mennonites were willing to serve their community twenty-four hours a day. Trained in driving by the California Highway Patrol and first aid by the high school nurse, twelve single young MCC men took to the task of operating the local ambulance, for service and excitement.[89]

The service began on August 8, 1953, and in a 1947 six-cylinder Chevrolet, young Mennonite men worked the valley and hills as far as there was paved road in their district. Within two years, they replaced the Chevrolet with a newer, more reliable vehicle, and more men from local car dealerships and the lumberyard began donating their time to run the service. A point of pride for Reedley was the low cost of the service to the taxpayer, as local police and fire departments tended to provide ambulance services in the valley. In Reedley the police had a significant role in training and keeping records and schedules of drivers, but the costs of administration were kept low on account of the volunteer nature, community support, and reasonable rates charged to users. In fact, the Reedley ambulance service did not add anything to the tax bill.[90]

Mennonite civic engagement through health care also involved the Home for the Aged in Reedley. Significantly, Jost was the administrator at Home for the Aged before moving to KVH. By the late 1950s, KVH was moving increasingly toward a medical and professional model of service described in generic Christian terms without any particularly Mennonite content. The Home for the Aged, in contrast, dealt with moral discipline issues as problems of "evil," as was the case when a misunderstanding between a married man and another women found in the basement alone had an "appearance of evil."[91] While understanding discipline problems morally, the Home for the Aged also refused to join a rest home association: "Since ours was a church home and we were getting along well, we would not want to join any organization of this kind."[92]

The same principle of not joining with the "world" applied to asking oil companies for funds. A second Home for the Aged was opened in 1960 in the Shafter area, where there were wealthy oil and land companies that could have been solicited. The General Board made a decision on funding for the Home for the Aged that stood in contrast to the increasing closeness between KVH and the state and federal governments. Their 1960 decision stated, "With regard to soliciting money for the Shafter Home from the big oil companies and the Kern County Land Company, it was felt that we did not feel like soliciting the world."[93] The question was not who was right or wrong; rather, there were two distinct trajectories in two institutions, intimately connected, that both cared for people. One kept to a model of Mennonite suspicion of the world and dealt with discipline issues in moral terms like "evil." The other, under the leadership of Jost, moved to a more mainstream model of professional accreditation, association, and government funding. It moved from being an institution created in the Mennonite idealism of CPS to one where explicitly traditional Mennonite identifying markers were virtually absent.

The trajectory of KVH, as demonstrated by its relationship with the professional medical staff and its ambiguity regarding a chaplaincy and religious services, came from an administration that in its early years articulated a clear case of working in the will of God to engage a peculiarly Mennonite form of ministry, providing care to the mentally ill. As Jost wrote in 1950: "We feel that the Lord has directed in a very special way to make possible the steps which have been taken and we seek further guidance and direction in order to be of service to those who are unfortunate in becoming ill in mind and spirit." Furthermore, "We feel a deep conviction that the Lord has also placed the sufferers in our midst for a purpose and yet we must humbly admit that they have received the least consideration and appreciation among all in the school of suffering."[94] KVH was an important facet of Californian Mennonite institutional self-identification. Through the delivery of mental health care, ambulance service, and a

Home for the Aged, Mennonites were increasingly a part of mainstream California life, engaging the culture as quietly religious and socially active members.

Kings View Homes was a successful mental health facility in California's San Joaquin Valley, which at the time had no such facility. The Mennonites involved with KVH entered into a strategy of influencing their surroundings through the sincere expression of religious conviction through caring for the mentally ill. That expression, while distinguishing them in California society, ironically helped bring them into the mainstream, as compassionate, though increasingly secularized, religious people.

When KVH reopened in March 1958, the administration boasted ten new patients, with only two coming from the Mennonite constituency. The remaining eight were referred by, among others, local physicians, psychiatrists, and district attorneys. KVH's administration considered this proof that the aggressive promotional efforts during the shutdown period were effective and that KVH was further integrated into California society.[95] Early in his career, when writing or speaking for Mennonite groups, Jost had included religious elements in his presentations.[96] Already by the mid-1950s, however, he was rarely drawing attention to any religious or spiritual aspect of work at KVH. Though he refuted such extreme religious claims that mental illness was "demon possession," he did not completely ignore spirituality in mental health, acknowledging, "prayer can contribute . . . as it helps to straighten out the crooked paths of unhealthy human relationships."[97]

Jost and KVH played an important role in the overall expansion of Mennonite identity in mid-twentieth century California. Created out of the success of the CPS, KVH, as administrated by Jost, represents a stream of Mennonitism in California characterized by social, cultural, and ideological integration. For example, under Jost's leadership, KVH received more government funding than any other American Mennonite hospital.

The religious program of KVH involved some devotional time and assistance for patients to attend local churches; however, despite the advocacy of non-Mennonite staff, no substantial Mennonite religious presence developed. Jost certainly was not anti-religious, or even a-religious. As a health care administrator, he took his lead from the larger psychiatric community and government grant programs. Looking at the KVH records, we can see that religion played a very minor role, and in government testimony, virtually none.[98] KVH embodied Mennonite ideals of social relief, yet in this case, barely connected with those ideals religiously. Though Jost was not representative of all Mennonites, he was a go-between Mennonites and California society. He represented a socially active Mennonitism increasingly comfortable with Sacramento. Service to the community born of a religious imperative was also a strategy of accommodation along the lines of service, here healthcare. We saw this in the sanitariums in the early 1900s, and in the postwar years in large projects such as KVH and local ones such as the Reedley ambulance. Professionalization and modernization reached most aspects of Mennonite experience, including service ministries of food and clothing distribution, to which we turn in the next chapter.

CHAPTER 9

Feeding the Hungry

A Story of Piety and Professionalization

Many people in Europe will be hungry and cold this winter.
—Relief worker, 1947

Grapes and Raisins

In addition to pacifism and healthcare, concern with helping the materially less fortunate was another important religious marker for Mennonites. Even in describing their success at modern agriculture in citrus and grapes, Mennonites in California turned to religious language. In the 1940s and 1950s, articles in *Mennonite Life* depicted agriculture as spiritualized and mechanized. On a settlement near Upland, the hardships in their early years were told as a story of how citrus farmers came into their own once trees bore fruit, yet their success did not overshadow their faith: "These pioneers maintained their interest in the church . . . the early Mennonite settlers in Upland were more than farmers and tenders of trees. They were Christians and church members . . . Mennonite life was and is physically nurtured here by a particular and unique industry [and] spiritual sustenance came from the source of all blessings everywhere— God, our eternal Strength and Refuge."[1] Even when reporters gave very detailed descriptions of soil types, income, pruning, or chemical applications, religious idioms were used: "No matter how hard man may labor, no matter how developed his technological processes become, it still remains true that 'only God can make a tree.'"[2]

The Mennonite embrace of modernized agriculture included an ever-present socio-religious piety: "The people of these churches have given to relief a portion of what they raised in answer to the challenge: 'The hungry people of Europe must be fed!'"[3] Prosperity in California came with a challenge—feed the hungry. This too was a story of piety and pro-fessionalization.

Beginnings

During and after World War I, Mennonites in Russia wrote letters to co-religionists throughout America asking for help. General Conference Mennonites in Reedley, for example, moved to encourage their denomina-tion to join with the Mennonite Church and Quakers who were already responding to the need in Russia. They proposed to work through the Emergency Relief Commission and send a delegation.[4] California Men-nonites, led by three men from Reedley—M. B. Fast, W. P. Neufeld, and B. B. Reimer—responded by gathering clothing. Of these three, Fast, later joined by Neufeld, went to Russia with the shipment.[5] These two pastors distributed the clothing and learned that many Russian Mennonites had contacts in California.[6] Upon their return, Fast tried to educate Menno-nites in the western and midwestern states about conditions in Siberia: "The reports and the agitation of Bro. Fast led to the first general organiza-tion of Mennonites for relief."[7] When Fast visited Immanuel Mennonite Church in Los Angeles, he made quite an impression: "[Fast] related many striking incidences of his travels amongst our Mennonites. As a result, rich gifts were donated to help the sufferers. How grateful ought we to be on the one hand and on the other willing to help. Reports from eye-witnesses strike the respective cords much quicker than articles in the papers and magazines."[8]

Their successful visit to Russia helped contribute to the creation of the Mennonite Central Committee (MCC) to coordinate relief efforts. In the Pacific District, William Neufeld became its representative.[9] In 1922, the need for clothing and relief continued, and an auction sale was held on John K. Warkentin's farm near Reedley. It was run by three Reedley Mennonite Brethren: auctioneers Georg Knaak and J. P. Siebert and clerk Phil E. Thiessen. Despite little publicity, they raised more than seventeen hundred dollars for Mennonites in Ukraine, Crimea, and Siberia.[10]

There was also a one-time effort in 1924 by California Mennonites in the Reedley area to ship raisins to alleviate starvation in Germany, their

first relief effort for non-Russian Mennonites.[11] The relief sale was the first
of its kind and became an annual event in various regions throughout North
America, beginning in the 1940s, and an annual West Coast event, beginning in 1968. By the 1960s, important differences from the earlier relief
sales were apparent. No longer were these efforts limited to co-religionists
in ad hoc response to particular needs; they now annually raised funds for
projects helping people throughout the world from many religions.[12]

Early Programs

When the Reedley MCC Relief Office opened in 1946, with its primary
purpose of running the Reedley Clothing Center (hereafter Clothing Center), relief work in the area became "a year-around job."[13] After three years
of operation, in June 1949, the Clothing Center became the West Coast
Office of MCC (MCC-WCO), with Arthur Jost as its administrator.[14]
Despite its focus as a clothing center, it engaged in several major projects:
food distribution, the mental health hospital Kings View Homes (KVH)
in Reedley, assistance for World War II refugees, a camp experience for
disabled children, and a raisins-for-the-hungry program. An early report
written for John A. Hostetter, material aid director of MCC, described the
new Clothing Center as getting off to a slow but stable start: "The work
here is not as large as at some of the other Centers but the interest and
cooperation is very good."[15]

The report stressed that local Mennonites supported the Clothing
Center with healthy donations as women volunteers guided its early success. Clothing needed to be mended before shipment overseas, and it was
"groups of women from the local churches who [were] faithful in coming
in to help with the mending." A "class of girls" from a local school also came
to sew during class period, which contributed to its success. The sewing
lessons were presented to the schoolgirls as an opportunity to "stimulate
interest in helping others."[16] Furthermore, sewing circles, from various
churches, contributed a significant amount of clothing.[17] In 1946, special
blessings and commendation were given to the women volunteers at the
Clothing Center: "May God bless the many busy mothers and others who
have given of their time and energy to help feed and cloth[e] the needy
families in war torn countries."[18]

When, in 1947, similar gratitude was expressed, it emphasized a gendered division of labor: "Women's groups are organized to come regularly

to keep the mending pile from toppling over. Other[s] come to help pack fruit and soap. Men come to burlap the bales and transfer them to storage. They use their trucks to haul our shipments to the docks."[19] Alternatively, "Men did the heavy work and women and girls cut the peaches and put them on trays."[20] Women in MCC and the sewing circles clearly understood and reinforced these divisions of labor. Nevertheless, it is a mistake to conclude from this a lack of agency.

Agency was clear in 1948, when young mothers "organized themselves at the beginning of the year to sew for missions and relief." They worked together one evening a week at first, then every other week, to sew for the Clothing Center. At the end of the year, they held an open display "to show what can be accomplished by willingness and consecration and, perhaps, a sacrifice of time and physical effort and to encourage others to become interested also." The day after the display, approximately 200 pounds of "mostly new clothing" was donated to the center, which succeeded largely because of women's mission societies.[21]

Women volunteers and efficient organization were the keys to success for the Clothing Center as they were for the mission societies. In 1946, the first year of its operation, the center demonstrated "what an organized effort can accomplish."[22] In this case, concerning potato canning: "Four Mennonite churches were organized into groups of about 8–12 women and 2 men for each day's canning. They were allowed the use of a high school cannery and also the services of one or two women experienced in commercial canning. About 1200–1400 No. 2.5 tins of potatoes and 550 tins of meat were processed in a day. This same group is canning tomatoes and corn to be delivered to the Center as soon as possible after the work is finished."[23] Although voluntary labor was significant, they attributed the resulting success of canning so many tins of potatoes to their specialized equipment and their organization—not to a specifically communal canning experience, or even to religious motivation.

Men from the Civilian Public Service (CPS) also played important roles as packers of food, clothing, and household items, though their involvement ended in 1947, when the CPS program ended. In the course of its first year, the center shipped "a carload of canned foods," seven and a half tons of dried fruit, eight tons of clothing, and a ton of soap. Despite such early success, the CPS labor supply soon disappeared. In preparation for the inevitable departure of CPS men, the Clothing Center looked "forward to having another sister here to help soon."[24] Despite the helpful and necessary labor the men provided, their replacements were expected to be women.

The speed of the Clothing Center's expansion was impressive. Within two years of its creation, they shipped food and clothing to people in at least four countries: Paraguay, China, Germany, and Italy. Despite working quickly to help people on three continents, the initial purpose was to help the suffering of Europe: "Many people in Europe will be hungry and cold this winter. This is our opportunity to share with them of such things as we have received from the Lord. Can we meet the challenge?"[25] Some in Europe certainly thought they had. A Dutch Mennonite minister from Holland commended them: "The clothing you gave will wear out; the soap will disappear; the food will be eaten; the spirit and love that prompted the giving in the name of Christ will be of lasting benefit."[26]

Despite early success, there remained tensions. In the early years, MCC-WCO's most common complaint was the scattered nature of the West Coast Mennonite population. This demographic reality resulted in delayed receipt of donations from the other western states of Oregon, Washington, Arizona, and Idaho, and in its operations, California's interests naturally dominated due to its size. A second tension was the low quality of clothing donations. Staff attempted to educate their constituency as to the importance of sending wearable clothing and not articles so soiled or worn that they would be discarded anyways. Despite such entreaties, people sent clothing in need of repairs, and volunteers did the mending and called it "Christian fellowship."[27]

Even with the stress of working with western congregations "scattered over a large area," the Clothing Center understood the relationship between its constituent parts as being "a link in the chain . . . [reaching] the far corners of the earth. It is through such images that people in MCC-WCO sought a common identity across the vast western region: May that chain not be broken by unfaithfulness or neglect on the part of any of us."[28]

Raisins and Refugees

In the late 1940s, MCC-WCO was also involved in collecting raisins for relief export. In a letter to Charles Brannan, secretary of agriculture in Washington, DC, Arthur Jost, MCC-WCO administrator, requested that the Raisin Administrative Committee make raisins available for relief purposes. As MCC was part of the President's Council of Voluntary

Relief Agencies, Jost made the case for obtaining government surplus raisins by arguing that over the past several years, they had sent 100 tons of raisins annually to Europe and South America that never "enter[ed] channels competitive with or prejudicial to exportable commodities." Jost also expected, as in the past, that they would handle the raisins under "our own supervision," ensuring a measure of separation with the federal government. Since they already raised the funds for purchasing those raisins, however, Jost was ready to move them.[29]

Jost applied political pressure: "It might interest you to know that our California constituency supporting this raisin program numbers about 2,500 to 3,000 of whom the majority are growers or have a definite interest in the raisin industry."[30] In December 1949, still waiting for the Department of Agriculture's response, Jost wrote Paul Goering of the National Service Board for Religious Objectors (NSBRO) in Washington, DC, to explain that the raisin program was a subsidy program. The raisin program purchased surplus raisins only after harvests were divided into three pools: free tonnage (for regular markets), reserve tonnage (for need and surplus), and surplus tonnage (for livestock feed).[31]

Lobbying was important because the Agriculture Department, while aware of the Mennonites, was unfamiliar with the details of their work. Jost worked through NSBRO to "jar the authorization loose," but as the request was part of a larger authorization from the Agriculture Department, NSBRO informed Jost that they would have to wait until regular channels dealt with their request.[32] Finally, Jost got the raisins needed for their relief work from the Raisin Administrative Committee. Due to the cost of transport ($150 a ton) to Paraguay, they decided to ship only to Europe, which cost $75 a ton. The raisins left for Vienna from San Francisco in the early summer of 1950.[33]

At the same time, in the wake of World War II, they worked with refugee assistance. Although MCC-WCO's work with war refugees did not constitute a large portion of their activity, they worked in conjunction with MCC to bring refugees to the United States.[34] At one point, there was discussion in MCC about whether California would pick up more refugees if more refugees would choose to go there. As the cost of a trip from Europe through the Panama Canal was twice that of bringing someone to the eastern seaboard, however, it was a hard sell to the Mennonite constituency. Jost commented: "It was pointed out that California had only taken relatively few D.P.s [Displaced Persons] across. Pettice

Reedley area Mennonites packing raisins for European relief, 1948.
Source: Otto B. Reimer Papers.

[International Refugee Organization representative Susan Pettice] argued that a ship could bring 2 loads from Europe to the east coast in the time it would take to cross the Panama to California. She also argued the additional cost of $1000.00 a day would make it impractical," and since sponsors had to absorb costs, additional charges would simply dampen West Coast enthusiasm.[35]

Discussion about coordinating relief efforts among voluntary agencies, state commissions, and local services inspired Jost: "I received a great deal of help in seeing the larger possibilities of helping the several families which we have received here at Reedley."[36] Jost was also heavily involved in securing funding for Kings View Hospital, now under construction. He pointed to an important aspect of how he understood Mennonite service—governmental and nonreligious organizations could oversee it, even mainstream it, provided the cause was congruent with Mennonite convictions.

As the question of displaced persons subsided, the Advisory Committee on Resettlement of Displaced Persons in California observed that the primary concern in local communities for refugee intake was depressed wages. The advisory committee defended those they brought in as people who "proved to be desirable as future citizens," who obeyed the law, held down jobs, owned homes, caused no disturbances, nor made any "injury to our own citizens."[37]

The latter half of the 1940s was characterized by a conviction that organizational efficiency was the best means of production for compassionate ends. MCC-WCO created the Clothing Center at this time, which stressed the principle of efficient organization and provided leadership opportunities for women. In addition, MCC-WCO lobbied government for surplus raisins and worked with broad international organizations for the benefit of European war refugees. Unlike clothing, food, and raisin distribution, the refugee benefit program was directed to co-religionists specifically, and California's geographic location was seen as a liability because of transportation costs.

Summer Camp

As part of its activities, MCC ran Voluntary Service (VS), to which people signed up for service projects that ranged in length from a few months to a few years, as already seen in relation to migrant labor. On the West Coast, however, the first VS unit was administered in conjunction with the Crippled Children's Society summer camp in San Bernardino, California. The Los Angeles–based society helped people who had a range of disabilities. VS administrators were impressed initially with the "mountainous environment," which had the net effect of producing "an inspirational atmosphere."[38] Although the environment may have been inspirational for the children, in camp reports, two themes dominated: how happy everyone in their care was and tensions between Mennonite and non-Mennonite workers.

One volunteer, Gladys Buller, wrote that while working at Camp Paivika for the Crippled Children was "a thrilling experience," some of the non-Mennonites found "the hardest task for any person or organization is living up to principles with which they are not acquainted." Some of the volunteers who came for camp work experience "had hardly heard of the group called Mennonites" and were frustrated with having to keep to religious principles "which are difficult for them." Buller understood the difficulties of those who would "smoke, dance and play cards" and, therefore, "cannot together give the Christian testimony."[39] This concern ran through the group, where some thought that mixing Mennonites and non-Mennonites made for unclear expectations and a "lack of spiritual emphasis."[40]

The Mennonites cooperated with the Crippled Children's Camp by providing volunteer workers at the height of the polio outbreaks in the United States, just before a vaccine was developed. When Helen Tieszen submitted her evaluation of the summer VS unit, she reflected on being out of contact with Mennonites for over a year. From her camp experience, Tieszen learned that, despite some disagreements, she was still "truly a Mennonite in attitude and belief."[41]

Despite this reaffirmation of her religious identity, she revealed that non-Mennonites thought Mennonites possessed a "seeming unfriendliness" and that "some uncomfortable situations arose, and it wasn't always pleasant to be making excuses." Within the group, tensions centered on how the Mennonites defined worldliness for everyone. As Tieszen described the Mennonite attitude: "[The world is] very bad and evil while we were good—and weren't we wonderful for coming all this distance to help crippled children!" Mennonites tended to indulge in what she described as a "self-praise attitude . . . which I think is wide-spread among us and needs to be brought to our attention." The internecine stress complicated the spiritual aspect of the program, but Tieszen concluded, "Although I feel that our unit has not been the reservoir of spiritual strength which it might have been, it has, provided, at least in part, the power for action . . . In a way, the split in our [Mennonite] group seemed inevitable, unfortunate though it was."[42]

In this effort to work within society, they found themselves in tension with co-workers, as their efforts went beyond volunteerism to compelling the moral commitment of others, thus alienating themselves. After a visit to the camp in June 1950, however, Arlene Sitler enthused about its religious diversity. The organization had people of several different religions, including fifteen from MCC as well as Catholics and Seventh-day Adventists. Sitler found this especially appealing because the Crippled Children's Society served all faiths, where no one religion should dominate.[43]

An anonymous evaluation of the camp, from August 1950, concluded on a positive note: "Camp Paivika meets the basic requirement of the V.S. unit in that it exists at a place where there exists a real human need which can be met in the name of Christ." This report described the work of the camp as important but not "urgent" in the sense that if they did not do it, someone would have. In the Los Angeles vicinity, the report singled out the "university area," where many people would be willing to help the children. The difference was believed to be in the Christian nature of their help, for "if the unit were not here our positions would be filled by non-Christians." Without reference to the internal strife between Mennonites and non-Mennonites, this report concluded that although non-Christians could do a good job, the program would miss the advantages of a "Christian 'plus' which is vital."[44]

Where Tieszen and worker reports underscored the struggles between groups in the camp, the August 1950 report described the unit's relationship as "cordial." In this report, the differences between the workers were downplayed: "The individual unit members very easily assumed their places in the camp program." In fact, the only noticeable difference between Mennonites and non-Mennonites was that Mennonites largely excused themselves from participating in camp dances. This evaluation concluded, "The matter of dancing was really the only place where unit members stood out from the rest of the staff in the camp program. In all evaluations, one felt that the staff appreciated the presence of the unit. A Christian life can not but be attractive to others." Although workers in the unit were of different religious backgrounds, there were in this account only slight tensions among a few individuals and an overall positive Christian presence modeled for the campers.[45]

By early 1951, in discussing the composition of the VS unit for the upcoming camping season, Sitler suggested to Ray Horst in Akron, Pennsylvania, that because there were already forty non-Mennonites in the service, "it may be well to confine ourselves to Mennonites as much as possible." To underscore the desirability of Mennonites, Sitler reported that the camp director, who also worked for UCLA's Physical Education Department, said "our personnel were best suited for counselor positions."[46] Although Sitler was unclear about whether the director referred to the VS unit in general or to Mennonites in particular, the praise was used to promote her conclusion that from this time forward, only Mennonites should be assigned.

The MCC decided, in April 1951, that members of the Crippled Children's Camp unit would mostly be Mennonites to "remit a more consistent witness to the other workers at the Camp." They were attracting only female applicants and wondered about their inability to attract males.[47] Since spring 1950, it had been difficult to recruit men to the camp.

VS attracted twelve volunteers, but men were mostly volunteering for construction labor at Kings View Homes (KVH).[48] What made the situation especially complicated was MCC's commitment to make their VS units gender balanced. Thus, having committed themselves in this way, their unit for the Crippled Children's Camps would remain half-full. Because MCC had promised the camp eight workers, they now had to go back and make sure the camp was flexible on the issue of gender balance, which the MCC did not want to do.[49]

Reorganization

Glenn Esh, acting director of MCC in Akron, Pennsylvania, wrote Jost in spring 1952 concerned about the administration of the Reedley Clothing Center. Although the main office in Akron calculated that clothing should be processed at eight cents a pound, in Reedley it cost eleven cents a pound. Therefore, lending support through a VS placement was out of the question, as the cost per pound would increase too much. As it stood, Ada King in Reedley was doing most of the work at the center, including heavy lifting and baling the clothing, which was more "than a woman should be asked to undertake." For King personally, the "strain of this physical work . . . cannot be expected to continue under such circumstances for any length of time." As Reedley had too few workers yet high operational costs, Akron had reason to close it down and shift its work to Newton, Kansas. There was also vague mention of the "attitude of the [Mennonite] people" of California, suggesting that closing the Reedley center was the best option for everyone.[50]

In response, Allen Linscheid, administrative assistant of MCC-WCO, wrote that they had reorganized staff schedules to relieve King of some of the physical demands. Linscheid also informed Akron that they were searching for a way to have the expense of VS workers locally underwritten. Regardless, Linscheid insisted that local Mennonite congregations support MCC and give funds as a percentage of their own budgets, even though churches also ran their own relief programs.[51]

Before MCC took these drastic measures, the parties engaged in much conversation. In 1953, MCC's main office instituted a new system of handling and shipping clothing at the centers based on a system of labeling codes. They made the decision based on the experiences at centers in Ephrata, Pennsylvania, and in Akron without as much knowledge of the situation in Reedley. In a letter to Ada King, Clothing Center supervisor in Reedley, Wendell Metzler, relief administrative assistant in Akron, admitted his ignorance of the California work: "I hope that I'm not assuming too much on operations at Reedley because I don't know what it is exactly like."[52] The sense of distance between California and Pennsylvania became especially acute by the end of the decade, and efficiency and communication did little to slow the continued demise of the Clothing Center.

Yet, in the Clothing Center itself, things seemed to be going very well. In spring 1954, MCC-WCO discussed establishing a dried fruit and raisin distribution program alongside soap making and meat, vegetable, and other fruit projects. The Clothing Center's success in a variety of endeavors resulted in understandable optimism; with the Clothing Center filled, they now needed more space.[53] They had expanded operations such that by 1954, they were shipping thirty-eight tons of raisins annually to such countries as Korea, Germany, Austria, Jordan, and France. In May 1954, they purchased their raisins at $127.50 a ton, down from $175.00 a ton in January, after raising money through various drives. At the same time, the Clothing Center was overflowing, and construction began on a new MCC Clothing Center in Reedley. The building project raised money through the church, especially the Reedley Mennonite Brethren, First Mennonite Church in Reedley, and Dinuba Mennonite Brethren.[54] Difficulties, however, were gathering on the horizon.

By 1957, securing funding for the Clothing Center had become increasingly difficult. MCC in Akron said that funds had to be raised locally. Meanwhile, the Mennonite conferences on the West Coast "felt that this was not feasible," because they had no budgetary room for it.[55] Administrators at MCC decided that the Clothing Center should become a collection depot, with volunteers processing the clothing at fixed times throughout the year: November, April, and July. A woman would supervise those processing times, with Ada King serving as cook and giving general advice. The lack of financial support from the Californian Mennonites, however, was not lost on Robert Miller, associate director of MCC Foreign Relief and Services: "I enjoyed becoming acquainted with California Mennonites. We have not been receiving a great deal of financial support from your churches but I have the impression that most people are really interested in the relief program."[56] This acquaintance with California Mennonites did not last long or spread far in MCC.

Meanwhile, Jost saw that MCC-WCO's greatest period of activity had

passed. He commented: "The route obviously is long between the Reedley office to West Coast churches via Conference headquarters. However,
there is still some advantages in the West Coast office awareness and direction of West Coast interest and needs. On closer analysis, however,
it became apparent that the developing duplication between Akron and
Reedley was not justified; Akron was going more and more directly to the
Conference headquarters on West Coast interests." Jost acknowledged the
reality: "I regard this as a natural and maturing development."[57]

By the late 1950s, other differences between MCC and California had
emerged. Jost wrote the associate executive secretary of MCC, William
Snyder, on June 26, 1957, to register a complaint. He noted the problem of geography: "The obvious problem of MCC meetings being spread
over the calendar instead of being grouped. For persons spending only the
night traveling or a few hours and dollars in the air, single or conveniently
grouped meetings are desirable. For those traveling from the West Coast it
would seem desirable to group meetings even to the point of some incon-
venience in order to save travel time and expense." Jost understood that in
relation to the rest of the country, the West was growing in importance: "It
is important for MCC to cultivate Western interest . . . The West will continue to grow and take on significance in terms of Mennonite interests."[58]
Snyder responded that West Coast concerns were real enough, but they
simply were not a majority: "Even though grouping meetings would be
a good thing in the case [of a few] from the West Coast, it does not help
many others." Snyder suggested a possible travel allowance from MCC,
but for the time being, different agencies within MCC's umbrella held
their meetings spread out over the year.[59] Regardless, in winter 1958,
Snyder informed Jost, who was now associated exclusively with Kings
View Homes (KVH), that the regional office in Reedley would have to
decrease its services but continue to receive clothing donations.[60]

In 1959, Snyder conceded: "I agree that we have not been tied into the
West Coast too well . . . we should do something to strengthen our representation there."[61] All this led to a closing of regional offices. Following
the Kansas model, West Coast Mennonites formed a regional relief committee. This came a day after Snyder sent a memo to Orie Miller, also in
the executive office of MCC, stating that they needed "to think clearly on
activating West Coast constituency" and develop "a formula that would
tie the West Coast into our program a bit better than it has been since Arthur [Jost] has not been able to give as much attention to the work because

of his growing program and responsibilities at Kings View Hospital."[62]
With this reorganization of the mental health program, Jost and MCC
separated, which allowed him to run KVH.[63]

Jost summarized the issues in a letter dated July 25, 1960: "Over a
considerable period, we have discussed future plans for the West Coast
Clothing Center in Reedley. The Mennonite Central Committee in Akron have felt for some time that they would like to see more local direction
and planning in the clothing and relief contribution planning and it seems
that a number of West Coast representatives have been thinking in this
direction." Jost also brought together two principle issues into the struggle
of continuing work in California: "The news which reaches us daily is
ample witness to the fact that we will be continually challenged to provide
material assistance to the millions of hungry and unclothed. We should
also give further thought to the discipline of giving as Christians as we
approach this problem of our future West Coast action."[64]

Thus, by the late 1950s, with sharp declines in donations, the Clothing
Center in Reedley was in trouble and would close. As the cost of processing a pound of clothing was more expensive in Reedley than in the other
centers in the United States, MCC suggested some cost-cutting options:
close down completely and ship all donated items to Newton, Kansas, or
run the center entirely by volunteers. They chose the latter. In September
1960, Mennonites formed the West Coast Relief Committee (WCRC)
to replace the regional office in order to streamline the clothing center and
make it cost effective while generally promoting MCC. As the Reedley
center reorganized into WCRC, the committee hoped that responsibility
for the Clothing Center would shift to the women's missionary societies.
They held discussions on convincing women within driving distance to
voluntarily mend and sort clothes.[65] WCRC, composed only of Californians, now had jurisdiction over the entire West Coast. Early on, they
suggested that the women in the missionary societies pay a fee, an idea
they quickly discarded. They sought assistance from Selma Linschied,
who ran the center in Newton, Kansas, but changes from above were on
their way.[66]

A year later, the transition was complete, and the WCRC was in full
operation, with a membership made entirely of Californians from Chino,
Atwater, Reedley, Bakersfield, and Dinuba. In December 1961, WCRC
appealed for help from MCC headquarters in Akron regarding blankets
for Vietnam. Although directed by MCC, the WCRC, which ostensibly

represented the entire West Coast, made its appeal only to California churches.[67] This was, perhaps, a sign of California's increasing dominance in the Pacific Coast region by the 1960s.

On May 25, 1962, WCRC agreed to incorporate itself in California for tax purposes. Drives continued for raisins, dried peaches, beans, and rice. Late that year, as movement toward incorporation went forward, frustration in California's relationship with Akron developed over the deed to the Reedley property. As MCC in Akron was the owner of the Clothing Center property, purchased on April 29, 1954, they had to deed the land back to Reedley for incorporation in California.[68] This legal maneuver was not intended to alter the relationship between Reedley and Akron; however, there was a growing sense of alienation in Reedley: "It is a feeling of the committee that already we feel a lack of interest in our Committee and the Center on the part of Akron as exemplified by the fact that no one has visited the Center from the main office in nearly two years."[69] This belief in growing apathy or ambivalence on behalf of Akron increased, so that by the mid-1960s, Akron suggested that Reedley develop a plan and budget to become more independent of the main office in Pennsylvania.[70]

Strategies for promotion became important because in 1964, West Coast Mennonites were ambivalent about the center itself as the "the percentage of our constituent churches participating is not particularly good," and "one-half of the contributed amount came from one congregation alone."[71] WCRC developed other strategies for improvement over the next few years. They hoped to increase membership by including, for example, a woman from each of the Mennonite conferences. John Hostetler, material aid director of MCC, suggested further that "the lady members of the WCRC be responsible to publish your newsletter" and that WCRC appoint a "Contact Sister" for each of the sewing circles.[72]

Then in 1966, plans began for MCC to resurrect the relief sale in California, which they did in 1968. The WCRC promoted the sale through nostalgic memories of a rural midwestern past in Kansas, not the actual events of the first sale in 1920, and lobbied the Reedley Chamber of Commerce. With a calculated marketing strategy, WCRC observed, "Many West Coasters who brought with them the memory of the old-fashioned farm sales in the East and would support this kind of appeal."[73] Two years later, in Chicago, at an inter-Mennonite meeting about relief sales held around the country, it was the West Coast Mennonites who impressed the national group with their self-promotion and marketing of raisins as a peculiar California contribution. They concluded: "It appears as though WCRC has become a pacesetter!"[74]

Compassion and Bureaucracy

In the mid-1960s the WCRC took over the administration of a program called Project Bridgebuilding. MCC had created Project Bridgebuilding to generate goodwill between Japan and the United States. It was the idea of missionaries to Japan and Dr. Gan Sakakibara, the president of Tokyo English Center, at the encouragement of Orie Miller of MCC. Emma Schlichting, of Akron, Pennsylvania, was to implement the project, but on March 16, 1965, the program was handed over to the WCRC. This project brought Japanese students to the United States to live for a few weeks in an American home as a way of mediating cultural differences and misunderstandings.[75] Project Bridgebuilding was an example of Mennonites' increasing awareness of and interaction with racial and ethnic pluralism at home.

As Mennonites continued to establish themselves as good Americans in the postwar decades, through the creation of various charitable and social justice—oriented institutions, they projected a distinct identity through their activism. They thoroughly entered California society, and religious markers of justice and peace helped facilitate their assimilation into postwar California; yet in doing so, they maintained a particular sense of their Mennonite identity—so much so that when Mennonites, led by Jost, created a mental health hospital to meet needs they had been unaware of until their CPS experiences, they navigated the concerns and expectations of their respective denominations, the local community, and state government. Beginning with CPS during World War II, Mennonites became increasingly comfortable working with all levels of government.

As Donald Kraybill demonstrates, the shift from ethnic markers of identity to ones of service and peacemaking, through the cultural efficacy of MCC, had taken place.[76] In California, Jost exemplified that aspect of Mennonitism in the role he played as mediator between Mennonites and broader society, both in his citizenship trials and in his work as an administrator. Mennonites were creating a presence in California that was religious, active, and institutional. Peace and social justice were the solvents that dissolved any lingering deposits of resistance Mennonites had about becoming full and good members of American society. Through the

Henry and Elizabeth Peters cutting peaches for a Mennonite Central Committee
fruit-drying project, ca. 1970s. *Source:* Records of Reedley Mennonite Brethren Church.

postwar decades, Mennonites constructed a variety of missions and services for people often at society's margins, including displaced persons,
Kings View Homes, and migrant labor ministry. The creation of the Clothing Center contributed to California Mennonite identity by its pursuit of
professionalism, efficiency, and political integration. Having set about the
task of transforming California society, they soon needed schools to protect the group and smooth out any remaining rough edges with the world
around them. In particular, Mennonites pursued liberal arts and seminary
education to this end, as we will see, in the next chapter, among the Mennonite Brethren in Fresno.

CHAPTER 10

Protect and Assimilate

Evangelical Education in California

We are, as a denomination headed toward disintegration.
—B. J. Braun, president of Mennonite Brethren Biblical Seminary, 1959

Cultural Ferment

By the mid-1960s, the evangelically inclined Mennonite Brethren sought their own historical identity while navigating California society. Considering the array of social services they established, Mennonites made their mark on life in central California. From the non-religious trends of some social programs and an enlarged world of pacifism and pluralism that resulted from the CPS experiences, there was also an attempt to reconstitute evangelical Anabaptism in the California context through higher education. All these streams of activity combined to create an expanded religious identity that blended progressive and conservative streams of evangelical theology with Mennonite historical identity.

By World War II and in the immediate postwar decades, Mennonite Brethren were expanding and establishing several new congregations, reflecting a numerical and institutional construction boom. In Fresno, the largest city in the San Joaquin Valley, Fresno Mennonite Brethren Church, also known as Bethany Mennonite Brethren Church, organized in 1942 with thirty-four members who had been meeting for several years. They purchased a building site in 1946 and "erected a spacious church building which was greatly enlarged in 1954."[1] The Mennonite Brethren went on a building spree during the 1940s and 1950s in the Fresno-Reedley area, building churches, the Home for the Aged in Reedley, a Bible institute, a mental health hospital, and a seminary, among other institutions.[2] From 1952 to 1962, for example, they established five churches in urban centers, with three in Fresno. All were amiable breaks from larger churches in Shafter, Reedley, and Fresno.

In fall 1955, the Heinrichses, a Fresno couple from Bethany Mennonite Brethren Church, held Sunday school classes in their home on the corner of Butler and Chestnut. The Heinrichses advertised their Sunday school to children on Halloween when they gave out invitations to the children who came trick-or-treating. Down the block from their home, the Mennonite Brethren Biblical Seminary (MBBS) had recently opened, and, in January 1956, the Heinrichses moved the Sunday school from their home into the seminary. During the early years, new members to the Sunday school came from "the Mother Church"—as Bethany was called—and from smaller towns in central California (Dinuba, Orland, Shafter) as well as from larger centers, such as Bakersfield, Reedley, and Los Angeles. From outside California, the congregation drew members from British Columbia, Nebraska, Kansas, and Oklahoma.[3] The Heinrichses' efforts led to the creation of the Butler Avenue Mennonite Brethren Church on April 4, 1957.[4]

This expansion of the number of congregations was part of a Pacific District Conference (PDC) vision to create new churches in the Fresno area. In the 1950s, the neighborhood around Butler experienced a housing boom, created in part by the federal government allowance assisting veterans in buying homes. One result of this government program was that many lower-income and minority families moved into southeast Fresno, as noted in one study undertaken by a seminary student at MBBS: "The result [of the government housing program] is an inter-racial neighborhood with a high percentage of Blacks and Hispanics. Consequently, most of the church families have moved to different locations."[5] Although some Mennonite families left as racial demographics changed, the Butler church continued its community outreach programs, including evangelism, support for a Billy Graham crusade, Campus Crusade, neighborhood Bible Clubs, and the Small World Preschool. They discovered that children's programs "drew the church and community closer together."[6]

In the early 1960s, an additional two congregations formed as exten-

sions of larger churches with the intention to create more flexible structures of church governance. Kingsburg Mennonite Brethren Church
formed as an extension of both the Dinuba and the Reedley Mennonite
Brethren churches. The Kingsburg congregation intended to form a flexible organizational structure in order to make changes easily as needed.[7]
The Wasco Bible Church (MB) was formed out of the Shafter Mennonite
Brethren to accommodate several people who had to travel long distances
to church.[8] In 1959, Wasco's pastor, Werner Kroeker, reported that "the
formation of a simple yet functional structure has given us a smoothly operating Church with responsibility delegated to many yet not so decen-
tralized as to permit duplication or neglect."[9]

Among the various transformations and Mennonite expansion under
way in postwar California, higher education brought various tensions and
trends into clear focus. Mennonites sought a religious identity congruent
with urban developments, an emerging sense of historical identity, and
closer relations with California evangelicals. Evangelical Anabaptism was
the faith to accomplish all three goals. Although urbanization was a process under way throughout the country, California represents the earliest
and largest urban settlements of American Mennonites. Not until the early
1940s, however, did Mennonites begin to live in substantial numbers in
such cities as Fresno. Urbanization for Mennonites was swifter in California than elsewhere in the country.[10] As Reedley already had the largest
Mennonite Brethren congregation in the country, the attraction to both
Reedley and nearby Fresno was natural. Within eleven years, Fresno became a significant Mennonite Brethren center with the creation of Pacific
Bible Institute (PBI, now Fresno Pacific University) in 1944, and MBBS
(now Fresno Pacific Biblical Seminary) in 1955. The story of Mennonite
education in California is largely a Mennonite Brethren one.

Institutional development and the increasing rationalization of Mennonite participation in Californian society were as much about resilience
as accommodation. As Mennonites urbanized, the role of education in the
creation and protection of identity deepened. Gone were issues of German
language retention important to Mennonite schools earlier in the twentieth century; new on the pedagogical front were religious influences of
Southern Californian fundamentalism and Kansas Mennonite liberalism.

In postwar California, Mennonites attempted to navigate the stormy
seas of fundamentalism as an exterior threat and liberalism as an inte-
rior threat through church-based education. Three schools in particular

concerned Mennonite Brethren leadership, the dispensationalist Dallas Theological Seminary, the Bible Institute of Los Angeles (BIOLA)— places where many Mennonite Brethren pastors were trained—and the Training School for Christian Works (now Azusa Pacific University), with its "strong emphasis on the charismatic."[11]

Piety without Fundamentalism and Liberalism

Among the reasons for starting PBI, and placing it in California, were pietistic influences in Mennonite culture. As historian Paul Toews observed, pietism has been part of the Mennonite Brethren theological matrix since their origins in 1860 Russia. Pietism emphasizes personal religious experience, personal spiritual discipline, and individual religious expression. Thus, it exists in some tension with the more communally based ideals of Anabaptism. In higher education, the linking of Anabaptism with evangelicalism was an attempt to retain the religious energy of pietism without collapsing into fundamentalism. The Mennonite Brethren hoped that a Bible institute would train their young people in both pietistic spiritual disciplines and nonresistance.[12]

Furthermore, Mennonite Brethren needed not only to respond to concerns of fundamentalist influences and liberal challenges, but also to prepare their young people for increased participation in the professional world. Thus, the development of Mennonite undergraduate education in Fresno in the 1940s was in the context historian Paul Toews describes: "[There was] in the West a high degree of cultural and institutional ferment. The repeated efforts to begin a school between 1916 and 1944 and the subsequent changes of the school reflect the uncertainty." Moreover, he argues, "The story of schooling among western MBs (Mennonite Brethren) is the story of the search for both intellectual and institutional coherence. It is the story of the church's enduring quest to center and identify itself. It is the search for shelter in a world of strong cross currents."[13] The images of ferment, changes, uncertainty, coherence, center, identity, and shelter suggest that the school was about more than the pursuit of knowledge; it was to create "intellectual and institutional coherence," as a shelter for young Mennonites in a storm-tossed world.

Church-related education had been a part of the California Mennonite experience since the creation of the Bible Academy in Reedley earlier in the century. In 1940, postsecondary education became increasingly important when the Pacific District Conference formed a committee to explore the issue of a Bible institute in Fresno. They approved the school in 1941 as a place "where the young people might avail themselves of a sound Biblical training in an institution organically related to their own conference."[14]

A key issue in creating PBI was the modernist-fundamentalist conflict. When the oldest American Mennonite Brethren School, Kansas's Tabor College, found itself in the 1940s in the midst of the modernist-fundamentalist controversy, perceptions eclipsed reality.[15] West Coast Mennonite Brethren believed Tabor was influenced by liberal modernism. This perception developed in part through a particular interpretation of Tabor's 1942 hiring of Peter E. Schellenberg as president. Schellenberg, a psychologist, was one of the first American Mennonite Brethren to earn a Ph.D. and remain in the church. President for over ten years, he eventually resigned, and John N. C. Hiebert replaced him. Hiebert was a missionary and hired to "affirm and protect the 'faith of the fathers.'"[16] Other issues in Kansas also contributed to concerns of modernism at Tabor. Many of the Tabor faculty at mid-century attended Central Baptist Seminary in Kansas City, and as historian Paul Toews describes, "Such persons wanted more clear cut statements of MB theology and were quick to see signs of modernism."[17]

Additionally, in 1943, the Mennonite Brethren general conference asked Schellenberg to explain the orthodoxy of his religious life and the college, and to "declare publicly the limits of psychology."[18] Nonetheless, the school kept him until he resigned in 1951. In California, the tension in Kansas was part of the reason to open PBI in 1944. At mid-century, the Mennonite Brethren in central California were concerned with the absence of nonresistance teachings in the dispensationalist fundamentalist schools in Southern California and Texas as well as with a perceived liberal advance from the east, which could easily alienate students—who may then attend non–Mennonite Brethren schools.[19]

Pacific Bible Institute opened on September 18, 1944, with twenty-seven students, six faculty members, and five objectives: "(1) To give young people thorough knowledge of the Bible; (2) To train them in the highest type of Christian living in whatever walk of life they may find themselves; (3) To prepare them for Christian service, at home or abroad; (4) To fortify them against the various unscriptural philosophies of life; (5) To send forth sanctified Christlike personalities, yielded and obedient to the Master."[20] Initially PBI offered a three-year Bible program, which was the forerunner of their four-year degree programs: bachelor of arts and bachelor of theology. In order to "safeguard the Institute against liberal trends," faculty was accountable to the Pacific Bible Institute Committee, which both reported to the district and had authority over hiring and firings.[21]

In the early years of the school, its purpose was to "implant" Mennonite spiritual principles in the students, led by an administration retaining a traditional identity, which originated among rural Mennonites "in relative isolation [who] felt no need for new theological precision."[22] At the beginning, however, PBI was influenced by fundamentalism. The first PBI catalog described the rationale for the school's existence: "The reasons for this urge for a school here in the west are many . . . The first, of course, was the realization for the great need of Christian workers in our churches who would be able to meet the intellectual progress of our time." It continued, "Secondly, the horror on the part of parents and churches for the hazards that students confront today in some theological schools, and thirdly, the unmistakable but simple fact that a church body cannot long continue in its true channel unless its doctrinal principles and church policy are definitely and squarely implanted in its coming generation."[23]

The tripartite basis for PBI's existence in the West reveals further its fundamentalist origins when read against "An Abridged Statement of Faith," which says in part, "The Pacific Bible Institute holds and teaches . . . that the Bible is the verbally inspired and infallible Word of God." It affirms other tenets of fundamentalist Christianity, including a literal reading of the Bible, especially as it concerns Jesus' virgin birth, death on a cross, and bodily resurrection.[24] Moreover, listed first among PBI's educational aims was "to uphold a positive interpretation of the Scriptures which shall lead the student to become firmly grounded in the great doctrines of the Bible." Other aims included a deepening of spirituality, "to uphold the principles of peace, separation from the world, simplicity of life, sanctity of the home, and diligent habits of industry." Some of these were certainly Mennonite distinctives—peace and simplicity—while others suited well general sympathies across many religious lines—sanctity of home and diligence.[25]

In its second catalog, PBI expanded its presentation to include course descriptions. Among them was a course called "Dispensations," which, when considered alongside the statement of faith, purpose, and aims of

The Pacific Bible Institute building at Tuolomne and L Streets (c. 1946–1959).
Source: Records of Fresno Pacific University.

PBI, locates the school solidly in a Christian context influenced heavily by fundamentalism and dispensationalism, two traditions not organically Anabaptist.[26] Although PBI did not list "Dispensations" for the 1950–1951 school year, the aforementioned theological principles, educational aims, and historical accounting of its purpose remained their published self-description through at least the 1950s.[27]

Throughout the 1940s and 1950s, Mennonites in California increasingly worked outside the farm and church. Many became business owners or joined professions previously ignored. The cultural world of the Mennonites broadened at mid-century as the professional and business worlds drew Mennonites into such organizations as the Christian Businessmen's Committee and the National Association of Evangelicals.[28]

By the end of the 1950s, the Pacific District Conference decided that the liberal arts model should replace the Bible institute model to address changes in society and students. PBI would offer courses other than Bible, theology, German, and church history, in order to train young people to live and work in the professional world. In these evolving trends co-existed an education and an evolving sense of identity: protect and assimilate.

In 1959, B. J. Braun, president of both MBBS and PBI, which shared their administration until the early 1960s, reiterated the need for a

The most iconic photo of Pacific Bible Institute at Tuolumne and L Streets.
Source: Records of Fresno Pacific University.

denominational Bible institute and college. Braun reported to the United States Conference of the Mennonite Brethren Church, "I hope that we have enough spiritual discernment to recognize that when we send our children into the state schools, we are sending them into enemy territory from the standpoint that their view of life is diametrically opposed to the Christian way of life." The children, therefore, must be "rooted" in their faith.[29] Braun continued his report by explaining that parents of potential Mennonite students needed to know that without the type of higher education the church provided, their children could be successful but secularized. This explanation came with a warning:

I predict that within 10 years many Mennonite Brethren parents may have opportunity to brag of the achievements of their sons and daughters in the areas that concern themselves primarily with bigger and better productions for an even higher standard of living, supersonic travel to the moon, transcontinental missiles of destruction, and radar walls of defense, etc. In brief—unless we can bring our churches to a sudden halt and induce them to preach to our parents that Christian education alone is able to give their children a Christian view of life—we are, as a denomination headed toward disintegration—either through secularizing of their minds, or through a weakening of a sense of loyalty by sending them to Christian schools of other denominations.[30]

He considered it a "long felt need on the West Coast" to have a denominational institute so their students did not have to go to schools with "interpretations and emphasis which were foreign to M.B. views." When churches called in pastors trained outside the Mennonite Brethren world, these pastors brought those foreign ideas with them. MB needed a denominational seminary so that pastors could be trained in-house, and with their professional credentials, gain respect: "Whether or not it [was] a symptom of an ill state of spiritual affairs that people do not desire to listen to the preaching of someone, of whom they feel, that he his less qualified then they, is beside the point."[31]

The development of the school seemed to come quickly. To the chagrin of Tabor College, events in California moved "too fast to understand." Tabor College stated their dislike of PBI's ambitions and argued that a second liberal arts college created unnecessary competition for students. They saw PBI violating the spirit of the "unification" program of the mid-1950s: "Your proposal [to become a liberal arts school] violates the original agreement, that we would give up our seminary and you would relinquish the liberal arts."[32] Nevertheless, PBI was not about to relinquish the liberal arts.

Under the "unified" plan formed in 1954, the Mennonite Brethren schools of higher education in the United States would operate under a single board, with both schools owned by national denominational conferences instead of regional ones. The schools and their roles included Tabor College as the "senior college," PBI as the Bible institute and junior college, and MBBS as the seminary (to be opened in 1955). Shortly after unification, under President Braun, PBI began its move to liberal arts education, which we see in the 1959–1960 catalog, with a variety of courses listed in several liberal arts disciplines. In 1961, this shift was made official, and the name of the school changed to Pacific College. However, as early as 1955, Frank C. Peters, president of Tabor College, wrote B. J. Braun to respond to the plan to develop a liberal arts program in Fresno: "We know that we cannot set the policies for P.B.I., nor would we attempt to curtail its program. This decision belongs to the Board. They set the policies and then we must operate within their wishes. If the Board ratifies your proposal, we will recognize it. However, as long as they do not, we wish to register our disapproval."[33]

Furthermore, Peters underscored that if PBI went ahead with its curriculum change, the two schools would compete for the same students: "To me, however, this seems ridiculous. This is what we were trying to avoid when we 'unified.'" Peters's main concern was not just the protection of his school, but that the denomination could not support two liberal arts colleges, and he even suggested that if need be, build in California, but keep only one school. That did not happen, and the two schools continue to operate as liberal arts schools.[34]

Location gave PBI an advantage: in Fresno 30 percent of the American Mennonite Brethren population lived within fifty miles of the campus, and nearly 50 percent lived in the Pacific states of Washington, Oregon, and California.[35] Mennonites promoted Fresno in terms of weather: winter was "crisp and conducive to school life," and racial diversity helpful for students to "learn both the manner and customs" of people they might evangelize.[36] In 1961, Joel Wiebe, interim director of the Bible institute, justified Mennonite Brethren liberal arts education as a part of the "Great Commission," attributed to Jesus just before the end of his ministry, when he said, "go out into all the world and preach the Gospel,—teaching them . . . [especially] with life becoming more complex and involved."[37]

In the late 1950s, PBI transformed itself after a period of declining enrollments and financial difficulty. Apparently, some of the financial difficulty resulted from confusion in the "unified budget," an experiment to have all Mennonite Brethren postsecondary schools operate under one budget. In a special report as part of the unified budget experiment, the financial problems at PBI were considered the result of unnamed, vague "insidious forces." Determined to make the school a success, PBI embarked on an aggressive recruitment program in 1957 and saw its enrollments slowly increase. Despite the alleged presence of "insidious forces," PBI representatives reasserted the religious and geographic significance of the school: "Within the domain of God's good pleasure that there should be a significant place for our schools in this rich valley."[38]

In California, Mennonites thought the enrollment declines of the late 1950s were due to a changing educational need. On the West Coast there seemed to be a demand for a new type of school, different from the Bible institute model. They designed this new school on a liberal arts model, making it responsive to shifting social trends, including a growing involvement in professional careers, as well as growing comfort among Mennonite Brethren with the larger society.[39]

Some individuals recruited by PBI noted the religious significance of locating the school in California. Lando Hiebert of Grace Bible Institute in Omaha, Nebraska, declined a job offer at PBI because he associated California with the temptation of spiritual dullness. He considered life and work in the Midwest to be the equivalent of a willingness "to take up my cross, and deny myself," whereas California was a siren call to be resisted. In his words, "for me, it became the 'California Call' when it becomes easy to leave the disagreeable here and travel to the land of Glory and ease."[40] California, the land of ease, continued in its role as arcadian garden, luring people from the seriousness of the Midwest. Even if California Mennonites largely abandoned these images, others, like Hiebert, were tempted by their seductive quality.

The California Mennonite Brethren, by the early 1960s, made various cultural moves to integrate with a broader evangelical culture. In the case of education, the decision to create a liberal arts college was another strategy of cultural engagement. Tensions between an insular Mennonite piety and a growing comfort with American society characterized mid-twentieth-century Mennonite education in California.[41] Some at the conference perceived the Mennonite embrace of a liberal arts college, instead of a Bible school, as a "trend among our people today, especially on the West Coast."[42] Considering Tabor College already existed, these comments indicate a shift in the larger American Mennonite Brethren experience now finding its center of gravity by the Pacific.

Avoiding Theological Demise

Eleven years after the founding of PBI, in 1955, similar issues influenced the creation of MBBS, in Fresno. MB need for a seminary increased as the changes brought by urbanization and professionalization at mid-century affected the Mennonites. The Mennonite Brethren were concerned that both professional trends and dispensationalist fundamentalism negatively influenced their pastors trained at non-Mennonite seminaries. Their concern, as expressed by J. B. Toews, was the very survival of Mennonitism. They designed the seminary to prevent the "systematic destruction of the theological distinctives which brought the Mennonite Brethren fellowship into being."[43]

Beyond the sociological, historical, and theological reasons for constructing a seminary, there was the additional question of where to locate the school. The locations deemed most suitable were Winnipeg, Manitoba; Hillsboro, Kansas; and Fresno. All three locations had sizable Mennonite Brethren populations and an existing postsecondary Mennonite school. The Canadian Conference voted for Hillsboro, Kansas, the clear frontrunner, and the Pacific District Churches invited the seminary to the West Coast, but only "if [the] General Conference sees fit to put it there."[44] The debate over location continued. In addition to other factors such as available faculty, land, and buildings, one document in the 1950s bluntly stated, "Climatic conditions in California are conducive to good work."[45]

At the January 1949 meeting, the Seminary Commission—a denominational committee formed to deal with the establishment of a seminary —asked Tabor College to raise their Bible school "to seminary standing." At the same meeting, the Pacific District Conference submitted that they would not insist that the seminary be located in Fresno.[46] Later that month, however, the commission chose Fresno. The factors that swung the decision included a desire to "decentralize conference activities" and, in light of the faithfulness of West Coast Mennonite Brethren to support conference activities, some thought it fair "to have at least one General Conference project on the West Coast."[47]

On September 8, 1955, MBBS opened its doors. It was created "to consolidate leadership and peoplehood theologically," especially with the rise of professional and paid pastorate growing gradually throughout the denomination. Henry Schmidt connected the creation of the MBBS ultimately to urbanization, theological diversity, and individualism.[48] Moreover, the Mennonite Brethren's largely middle-class status, which Schmidt attributed to frugality and hard work, signaled a growing political conservatism. This conservatism was the result of "their own tradition

An early photo of the Mennonite Brethren Biblical Seminary administrative building, ca. 1950s.
Source: Records of Mennonite Brethren Biblical Seminary.

of theological conservatism; their admiration of Eisenhower's political and religious leadership; their affiliation with the National Association of Evangelicals; and their support of Billy Graham as God's prophet to America." During the presidential election of 1960, the political conservatism of some leading Mennonite Brethren was clear. With the very real possibility of a Roman Catholic president, Orlando Harms, editor of the Mennonite Brethren denominational magazine *Christian Leader*, urged his readers to vote Republican.[49] Throughout the 1960s, suburban middle-class California in general turned conservative, and many Mennonites there did too.[50]

The question of Mennonite identity was an important one for the young seminary. In 1957, President Braun of PBI and MBBS reported to the United States Mennonite Brethren Board of Education that although the seminary was "one in spirit with the great historic evangelical movement, we are still a denominational school seeking to uphold and sharpen Mennonite brethren distinctives." The question remained, what were these distinctives? President Braun summarized the distinctives into ten points that emphasized a church defined by those with a "personal experimental aspect of regeneration"; "the separated life" from the world; church discipline; "home training" oriented to church involvement; biblical theology; "thrift, industry, neighborliness"; pacifism; "Church-sponsored education"; a "mission consciousness"; and finally, one's entire life subordinated to Christ's entire "program."[51] Many wanted it to be explicitly Anabaptist, with a biblical focus highlighting the Mennonite Brethren tradition. This desire was countered by a concern that Anabaptist identity would mark the seminary as "merely" a Mennonite school, only superficially evangelical.[52]

In the early 1960s, the administration and faculty, influenced by dispensationalist fundamentalism, challenged traditional Mennonite distinctives. By the mid-1960s, a new administration, focused on orienting the seminary into an evangelical Anabaptist school, challenged the dispensationalism of the mid-to-late 1950s.

In 1960, the seminary issued "A Statement of Philosophy and Purpose of Mennonite Brethren Biblical Seminary," which affirmed "the doctrinal position of historic orthodoxy, and unhesitatingly declares its affinity, in doctrine, to the broader stream of evangelical Christianity." Within this broad stream of evangelical theology, there was an affirmation of a Mennonite identity "oriented in the Bible."[53] By 1961, it was already clear to some influential and young faculty members that the people running the school advocated a narrow dispensationalism derived from Dallas Theological Seminary. A. J. Klassen, a theology professor, reflected on the differences in the statements of purpose in 1957 and 1960, and noted, "Each of these statements underlines the importance of [Mennonite Brethren] denominational distincitves. However, a careful review of the course offerings indicates scant attention to this area in a single two-hour course." That course, "Anabaptist Theology," Klassen observed, was offered as early as 1956 but was never taught in the school's first ten years.[54] Thus, the school had two factions, one from the school's inception that included the administration and some faculty who wanted the seminary to be similar to Dallas Theological Seminary, and a younger, more recently hired faculty that wanted it to be an Anabaptist Mennonite school grounded in evangelicalism.

An example of this tension was the name of the seminary. At issue was whether Mennonites should overlay whatever historical, cultural, or theological value the Mennonite Brethren brought with explicit reference to evangelicalism. Thus, to attract students from beyond the Mennonite Brethren constituency, R. M. Baerg proposed in a document prepared for the executive committee of the MB Board of Education that the board consider changing the seminary name. The rationale for the suggestion was "to remove the cultural implication reflected from their history of Mennonitism [Mennonite Brethren] in general thus opening the way for wider inter-relationships with other groups of Mennonite orientation as well as non-Mennonite backgrounds."[55]

Baerg proposed the name change, ostensibly to remove the Mennonite Brethren designation, to placate concerns in the wider evangelical community that the seminary was fatally limited by its apparently "very narrow cultural frame of reference, which in large circles of the evangelical world overshadows the recognition of our spiritual and theological frame of reference."[56] This argument expressed a desire by some for an evangelical seminary run by Mennonites, not a Mennonite seminary. For the Mennonite Brethren to succeed in California, the reasoning went, they must first disappear into it. To have history was to have unnecessary cultural freight.

One young faculty person at neighboring Pacific College, John E. Toews, wrote his father, the future seminary president J. B. Toews, on several occasions regarding MBBS's intellectual climate, where he himself had been a recent student. John Toews judged its leadership, such as R. M. Baerg, as too dependent on the dispensationalism and dogmatic conservatism found at Dallas Theological Seminary, which Baerg and other faculty had attended. Appealing to the evangelical Anabaptist tradition, John E. Toews argued that if the school adopted the theological stance of Dallas, there was no reason for MBBS to exist; one could simply go to Texas. John Toews was also concerned with issues of academic integrity, such as grade inflation, poor lecturing skills, and faculty teaching courses simply from their Dallas Theological Seminary student notebooks. He sought a way between the narrow dogmatism of Dallas influence and what appeared to many as the alternative of mainline Protestant liberalism. John Toews' solution was to turn the school toward Anabaptism and embrace the Mennonite Brethren heritage as a legitimate contribution to evangelical Christianity on the West Coast.[57]

Though MBBS had been founded in the theological tradition of fundamentalist dispensationalism, in the mid-1960s J. B. Toews attempted to shift it toward an evangelical Anabaptist Mennonite identity. J. B. Toews became president in 1964 and made significant advances on the question of the school's evangelical Mennonite identity. First, he argued, the seminary needed to comply with accepted American standards of theological education.[58] Second, Toews was clear at the start of his presidency that MBBS would be an evangelical Anabaptist seminary, grounded in a biblical evangelical theology made distinctly Anabaptist. That biblical evangelical Anabaptist theology, for Toews, was reminiscent of Harold Bender's trilateral definition of Anabaptism, which stressed Mennonite identity and history through nonresistance in a voluntarily established community of believers bonded together by love and "separated from the world." Toews understood that the community, separated from the world, was a witness of Mennonite Brethren convictions to society. The character of the seminary, under Toews, was Mennonite Brethren and evangelically Anabaptist in nature.[59]

Under Toews's presidency, the seminary catalog for the first time published a "purpose and philosophy" statement that clarified and expanded the idealistic claim to history as found in the first catalog: "It remains a fact of history that no religious movement can preserve its God-entrusted distinctives without its own proper institution and literature."[60] In the 1965 catalog, a five-part statement of "purpose and philosophy" described the seminary as graduate school, school of biblical theology, Christian experience, churchmanship, and missions. Further, the seminary's purpose was the pursuit of "academic excellence" focused on a biblio-centric curriculum, grounded in "the Anabaptist view of the church." The Anabaptist view of the church for the seminary was the church as a "called out" community of Christians advocating a "corporate witness to the society of which it is a part." Within that witness, one was to live "the life of love and peace with all men" in order to "exemplify the life of the true New Testament Church."[61] This statement was a departure from the fundamentalist leanings of previous years, and it presented a clear intention to situate the seminary in a historical faith system. The statement also took seriously the social context of the school, serious scholarship, and spiritual development in a biblical, evangelical, and Anabaptist fashion.[62]

Shelters from the Storms

As historian Paul Toews observed, the history of both Fresno Pacific College (formerly PBI) and MBBS was a tale of the Mennonite Brethren at-

President J. B. Toews of Mennonite Brethren Biblical Seminary. *Source:* Records of
Mennonite Brethren Biblical Seminary.

tempting to preserve their history.[63] Pacific College hired Peter Klassen in
1962. He was the first Mennonite Brethren scholar trained in Mennonite
Anabaptist history hired by a Mennonite Brethren institution since 1948.
At Pacific College, a Mennonite Brethren historical renaissance emerged.
The increased awareness of Mennonite Brethren historical identity included Pacific College giving Anabaptist-themed names to their buildings, starting in 1958 with Sattler Hall. Much of this activity occurred in
the late 1960s and early 1970s, however, when the school gave buildings
and quads such Anabaptist monikers as Marpeck, Strasbourg, and Wit-
marsum. The naming of buildings and quads was only part of the historical
recovery.[64]

The historical recovery also swept the MBBS campus in the mid-1960s. Within ten years of the seminary opening, J. B. Toews, pastor of the Reedley Mennonite Brethren Church in the late 1940s and early 1950s, was hired as president, and he turned the seminary toward historic evangelical Anabaptism. J. B. Toews's vision to recapture the evangelical Anabaptist roots of Mennonite Brethrenism led to academic courses in Anabaptist history, and within five years, a near complete turnover in faculty took place. In the late 1960s, to preserve their history, the Mennonite Brethren created the Historical Commission, which ran the newly created archives and historical library in Fresno. It was "the most extensive set of commitments to nurturing memory ever made by an MB conference." This occurred in California, where the Mennonites were "more urbanized, occupationally diversified and theologically fractured" than the Mennonite Church was when they experienced a historical flowering in the wake of Harold Bender's 1944 "Anabaptist Vision."[65]

For the Mennonite Brethren, historical recovery came from the pressures of California society. Peter Klassen, who was college present at the start of the Mennonite Brethren historical renaissance, reflected: "To many of us involved in that endeavor in the 1960s, it seemed that the 'Anabaptist Vision' had grown dim, at least in the Mennonite Brethren Churches of California. We are grateful that God in His providence used the [California Mennonite Historical] Society to renew that vision and bear witness to His grace among us."[66] The California Mennonite Historical Society, historical library, archives run by Pacific College, and MBBS's Hiebert Library, Bible institute, and seminary shared the same campus. It was an integrated and collaborative effort.

After World War II, Mennonites in California largely assimilated to California's religious and secular culture and bore many resemblances to their evangelical conservative Protestant neighbors. Their assimilation was hastened, perhaps, by the dominance of the Mennonite Brethren, who, from their formation in Russia in 1860, were more evangelical, pietistic, individualistic, and professional by occupation than other Mennonite groups. That fundamentalist institutions, such as BIOLA and Dallas Theological Seminary, attracted California Mennonites is not a surprise. The growing influence of Southern California evangelicalism, the result largely of mass migrations from the central and southern states, also involved Mennonites. In the context of education, the creation of schools designed to promote Mennonite Brethren identity smoothed the process

of integration within a broad evangelical culture. In fact, even the schools'
campuses symbolically connected them with a broader American culture.
Both PBI and MBBS took shape in architecturally impressive buildings.
PBI purchased a building designed by famous American architect Julia
Morgan, which they left for the Chestnut campus in 1960 and finally sold
in 1962. The move to the outskirts of Fresno in the mid-1950s coincided
with the construction of MBBS in the striking Giffen Mansion, built by
Wylie M. Giffen, an early twentieth-century agricultural leader.[67]

The historical recovery was part of a process that made formal societies and official archives possible. At the same time, these schools, while
preparing students for the modern work world, also promoted theological
education that did not alienate either evangelical Anabaptists or conservative evangelicals. As agricultural activity had initially lured Mennonites
at the turn of the century, it again became a focus of intense attention in
the early 1970s. Questions of faith, race, economics, and geographic region melted together in the fruit and vegetable fields of the valley. This
time, however, as we will see in chapter 11, many Mennonites were the
socioeconomic insiders.

CHAPTER 11

Labor Tensions

Mennonite Growers, the United Farm Workers, and the Farm Labor Problem

People in Akron heard Calif[ornia] Mennonites carry guns
—Mennonite leader Guy F. Hershberger, 1974

Transforming Pacifism

In the 1930s, several hundred Mennonites fled Communist Russia through Harbin, China, and settled in the Reedley area. One of these migrants, H. P. Isaak, wrote his memoirs in 1976 and introduced the story of his flight from Communism with his troubled feelings about the recent farm labor activism of Cesar Chávez. Isaak argued that Chávez's actions, emphasizing workers over employers, too closely resembled the values of Communist Russia; these values would only harm America.[1]

The organization of California farm workers, and the subsequent strikes and boycotts, were part of a tense socio-political atmosphere in the state. Many Mennonites across the country followed the events in California and saw, not disturbing threats to America, but hopeful social protest. These differing Mennonite responses to the California farm labor tensions revealed significant fissures within American Mennonitism.

The role of Mennonites in American religious historiography is well known: Mennonites are Germanic rural agrarian pacifists. Whether one considers ethnic, economic, theological, or activist themes, this stereotype is not without merit. The tropes almost appear settled. Mennonites are counted among the Historic Peace Churches, a designation with much significance, especially in times of war. They are largely pacifist in their ideology, with many attempting to practice it in times of war, and until the last-third of the twentieth century, they were mainly agriculturists. In the decades following World War II, the pressures of modernity were tremendous, and Mennonites largely responded by moving to cities, entering professions, and developing efficient rationalized church bureaucracies. In California, these transitions began earlier, during the 1930s, when Mennonite religious identity was increasingly influenced by the conservative evangelicalism that was gaining prominence in California— also a result of Depression-era southern migration to California.[2]

Having settled primarily in the San Joaquin Valley, Mennonites entered many and varied professions, as exemplified by the Eymann family of Reedley in the early 1900s, as noted in chapter 1. Naturally, many were in agribusiness. In 1951, *LIFE* magazine published a photo essay of a new generation of American millionaires located in the agriculturally rich San Joaquin Valley. Among those featured was Mennonite farmer, businessman, and inventor Ed Peters. Casting the story of successful Central Valley agriculturalists in the mythology of "new millionaires, who have become rich by turning the earth with their muscle and watering it as well with their sweat," an inspiriting introduction enraptured by the rugged individual, *LIFE* overlooked the hydraulic history of Central Valley farming. By the end of the essay, agricultural practice was defined as "scientific" with its application of fertilizers, deep-well pumping, and "vast mechanization."[3]

Although Mennonites worked hard and built large enterprises as first- or second-generation entrepreneurs and farmers in California, already in the 1930s, federal assistance was needed to bring water to the fertile yet parched earth. Peters came to California from Saskatchewan, Canada, in the 1930s when he was a boy. After a try at grapes, the Peters family switched to potatoes, where Ed Peters would make his name by 1951.[4] Successful as a potato, grain, and cotton farmer and businessman, he ran a potato-washing and packing outfit for neighboring farmers. Later, his ambition and success led him to become president of the National Potato Council, opposing federal farm subsidies for potatoes. *LIFE* presented Peters as a symbol of the successful immigrant farmer to California, pictured relaxing by his pool, shirtsleeves rolled-up, eating grapes.[5]

By the 1970s, however, the mythic agrarian pacifist identity of American Mennonites had undergone significant transformation in California. Though such transformations occurred elsewhere, what drew the California experience into relief was its confluence of social, political, and economic tensions. When California farm labor politics became national in scale, due largely to a widely publicized boycott of Californian grapes handpicked by migrant labor, some Mennonites questioned their socioeconomic location in American society. The primacy of the agrarian pacifist myth as the template for American Mennonite identity also came under scrutiny.

United Farm Workers

The United Farm Workers (UFW), an agriculture labor union, formed in the 1960s under the leadership of Cesar Chávez.[6] He was born in Arizona, where during the 1930s, his family lost their farm. His family joined with others and moved to California to pick fruit. A formative moment in this westward move occurred when, as a child, Chávez was refused service at a restaurant in Brawley, California, because they did not serve Mexicans. Later, after spending time in the barrios of San Jose, in 1962 he went to work with farm workers in Delano, just north of Bakersfield, in Kern County. In only a few years, his concern over local farm labor practices became a national phenomenon through the well-publicized grape boycott and strikes against growers. In its first decade, under the leadership of Cesar Chávez and Dolores Huerta, the UFW enjoyed several successes, including acquiring collective bargaining for agriculture laborers, signing contracts with growers, and securing better wages.[7]

There were several Mennonite growers in California who employed migrant labor. Curious how California Mennonites were dealing with the labor-grower tensions in California in the 1960s and 1970s, along with the rise of Cesar Chávez and the UFW, two groups of Mennonites from eastern states came as observers and investigators for the larger denomination. The first came from the inter-Mennonite relief agency Mennonite Central Committee (MCC) Peace Section, which advised, educated, and studied on issues of peace and government, and the second were students from the Mennonite Church school, Indiana's Goshen College. These two groups, distinct from each other, came to California to better understand the farm labor situation and are examined respectively in the next two sections of this chapter.

The eastern visitors described their experiences in California and revealed how, despite similar religious backgrounds, not understanding California made it difficult to find common cause. That difficulty revealed cracks in their common religious heritage regarding assumptions of Mennonite identity, Anabaptist theology and religion, economic class, and race—all exacerbated by geographic distance. The fault lines between western and eastern Mennonites appeared at times both surprising and insurmountable.

The reports and diary of these eastern Mennonites are more than just a chronicles of events. As Melanie Springer Mock insightfully demonstrates in the context of male conscientious objectors during World War II: "The language of a diary therefore reflects not only the self in a certain place and time, but also the self constructed by that place and time. The diary's language reveals, as well, the writer's desire to use what he understands and knows as a means of representing what at the moment remains outside this realm of knowing." In other words, such writing reveals assumptions individuals bring to group identity, and what the group expects of the individual, and a "symbolic identity" is mutually constructed.[8]

Enter Peace Section

The delegation of Mennonites from the MCC Peace Section, located in Indiana and Pennsylvania, was formed in spring 1974 in response to news of labor tensions in California, tensions that involved Mennonite growers. The delegates were to visit California and report on their findings. In a letter to fellow delegate Guy F. Hershberger, dated March 29, 1974, Paul Kraybill, general secretary of the Mennonite Church General Board, reflected on the delegation's visit to California earlier that month: "The concern regarding the farm labor problem in California has been mentioned frequently in the Council and it was felt that here is an area where the brotherhood should be better informed about the issues." Hershberger was asked to lead this assignment because of his good reputation in the church and lengthy experience on issues of peace and justice. Leaders like Hershberger and Kraybill thought it possible that the California labor problem was simply a passing event from which they could gain experience: "This is not necessarily a continuing program concern of the Council but served to stimulate thought and develop new conviction and understanding."[9]

After spending a week in California in March 1974, Ted Koontz, associate executive secretary of the Peace Section, produced a summary of possible actions. He proposed that the Peace Section "not identify ... with any organizational position in the dispute but that it seek to serve the purposes of justice and reconciliation among the various parties." Koontz also took into consideration for his report suggestions given by unnamed West Coast Mennonite leaders. He advised them to hold to four points: keep Mennonites informed of any legislative developments, place volunteers in California to help farm workers with the assistance of West Coast Mennonites, respond to requests for help from the West as opposed to moving ahead without such an indication, and lead seminars on farm issues and labor management relations. Koontz underscored the importance of waiting for the West Coast to ask for help first.[10]

Despite overtures made to the ideal of local control, friction developed. After the Peace Section made their report, Guy Hershberger wrote Daniel Hertzler of the Mennonite Publishing House: "I should report that all this [a seemingly pro–Cesar Chávez, UFW, and UFW boycott article in the *Mennonite*] is well known in the Fresno-Reedley area, as well as at Goshen and other parts of the brotherhood and that some people do not feel very happy about it. Indeed we have a real problem to remain on good terms— that is the eastern section of the church on good terms with the San Joaquin Valley section."[11] The article in question, likely Robert M. Herhold's "To be a Man," described a visit to a UFW meeting where Chávez spoke. Herhold focused his text on the religious nature of Chávez's work, his Catholic identity, and the significance of Christianity to his nonviolent principles. Growers were described simply as sincere but misguided people struggling to cope and adjust to social change.[12]

Harold R. Regier, secretary for Peace and Social Concerns for Home Ministries in the General Conference Mennonite Church, also a member of the fact-finding mission to the San Joaquin Valley, reflected on the situation in California and attempted to find a way between the main factions of farmers, UFW, and the Teamsters. He suggested that justice could be found, for all sides had legitimate concerns and all sides used dubious methods to attain their goals.[13]

In Hershberger's notes, taken on the spring 1974 visit to California, he revealed important differences between the MCC and Mennonite farmers. He recorded that on a visit with Alvin Peters, a Mennonite farmer in Reedley, Peters gave the following opinions: "Sermon on mount doesn't work in business [.] It must have been written 20 yrs or more after the time. Isn't meant to be obeyed." Concerning the biblical passage of Matthew 25, where Jesus describes the path to heaven incorporating service to the poor and oppressed, "Re matt 25 and getting to heaven for having clothed the naked etc. salvation only by the blood of Xt. [Christ]— these social Problems not our job." Hershberger noted that the place and assumptions of eastern Mennonites must be kept in check: "Peace and Soc. Concerns people must be careful not to go on the bandwagon for everyone who shouts peace[.] This thing will have to be settled politically and the church should leave hands off matters they don't know anything about," and besides, "People in Akron heard Calif[.] Mennonites carry guns[.]"[14] As Hershberger observed, everyone was guilty of stereotypes and failures to understand; therefore, he attempted to treat everyone cautiously.

Hershberger concluded that while being slow to criticize when facts are unknown, MCC Peace Section acted commendably by not identifying with the farmers, UFW, or Teamsters. Hershberger also opposed any boycotts, however, for "in the case of the UFW it would be promoting a lost cause," and it would be divisive in the Mennonite community. He recommended that "Mennonites should avoid the extravagant view that this is a communist conspiracy bent on ceding the Southwest United States to Mexico," and "that while Chávez is a sincere idealist, with the welfare of farm workers at heart he also seems unable to achieve these goals." He continued, "Mennonites affected by the UFW in any way should not hesitate to enter into sympathetic conversation with it in an effort to achieve understanding and reconciliation."[15] In other words, California Mennonites should reject the UFW for its unattainable idealism and reject the extravagant claim of Mexican reconquest made by some. The irony was not lost on other church leaders, as the recommendations seemed to contradict historical Mennonite appeals to idealism.

Hubert Schwartzentruber, associate secretary of the Mennonite Board of Congregational Ministries, responded, "To end war is also a lost cause but our tradition calls for us to continually promote peace. Most issues that we work at are divisive. I see us not relinquishing our effort because of the possibility of being divisive, but be redemptive as we work at them." In fact, not supporting the boycott would simply align the church with "the system that is destroying justice." Rather, Schwartzentruber argued, like Martin Luther King, Jr., and his efforts to keep the civil rights movement Christian, Mennonites should "surround Chávez with a new kind of justice and power to develop the movement"—that is, take a strong position on the side of the farm worker grounded in Mennonite Christianity and expressed through joining the UFW boycott. Schwartzentruber continued, "It seems to me that to come out in strong support for the Mennonite growers would also be hazardous."[16]

According to Schwartzentruber's critique, Hershberger, in his attempt to find a way through the tension, tacitly supported a justice-destroying system that would through nonparticipation in the boycott alienate Latino Mennonites. Schwartzentruber saw the churchly component of the issue as both class and race based, between rich white Mennonites and poor Latino Mennonites. The church, he argued, should make a clear decision to support workers over growers to overcome the impasse. Hershberger saw in California all sides claiming the moral high ground, employing suspect tactics at times, and argued that increased dialogue in Mennonite circles could break the deadlock.

If there was a place where California Mennonites were given a voice by an eastern-based denominational leadership, it was in these reports. During their week in California, Regier, Hershberger, and Koontz met with several individuals, including many Mennonite Brethren and General Conference farmers; Harry Kubo, president of the Nisei Farmers League; Arthur Jost, administrator of Kings View Hospital; farm workers for Mennonite farmers; the president of the Central California Farmers Association; two UFW staff persons; one Mexican-American farmer who started as a laborer; two Mexican-American students at Fresno Pacific College (FPC, now Fresno Pacific University) who had been workers; a Teamsters organizer; Mexican-American Mennonite Brethren workers; and Dr. A. W. Schlichting, a MB chiropractor who was instrumental in starting five Mexican-American Mennonite Brethren churches in the Fresno-Reedley area. Alvin Peters and Arnold Reimer, Mennonite farmers, arranged most contacts for the Peace Section.[17]

The confluence of racial, religious, economic, and national identities made such ambitions to "brotherhood" difficult to achieve. According to Koontz's report, growers (he does not distinguish between Mennonite and non-Mennonite), whether they were large or small, generally believed, "that the UFW is a part of a Communist conspiracy for world revolution or a part of a plan to reclaim the Southwest for Mexico or to form a new nation. They believe that the UFW is determined to destroy the free-enterprise system and take the land away from the farmers who

are there." Despite the swirling of conspiracies laden with the imagina-
tive power of Communist-led reconquest, it was also common to understand migrant worker poverty as the result of their own "mismanaging
money or unwillingness to work when work is available." Growers also
dismissed accusations of exploitative child labor practices as misguided,
because young child labor "is in keeping with Mexican culture and is seen
as a good, wholesome learning experience for children."[18] Therefore, problems of migrant labor poverty were the result of a laziness and financial
mismanagement; the problem of exploitative child labor resulted from a
strong family and work ethic in the laborers' culture.

Mennonite growers insisted that their quarrel was with the UFW and
that their relationship with most workers was healthy. These growers
leveled two significant criticisms against the UFW: it did not represent
the majority of workers; and its seniority-based hiring system, the "hiring hall," took the power of hiring away from the farmer and placed it in
union hands, meaning that seniority rules could split families because time
spent on a particular farm counted less than time spent as a union worker.
Due to their perception of the unreasonableness of the UFW and lower
worker productivity within the UFW, some of the larger growers began to
work with the Teamsters. Growers were also critical of the government's
management of the union situation. They expected there to be laws enacted requiring secret ballots for union elections and bans on both harvest
strikes and secondary boycotts.[19]

Despite grower desire for government action, preferably federal action,
in dealing with the labor situation, Mennonite growers also expected the
church to reflect their concerns regarding social order and evangelical mission. One observed, "Mennonite farmers were unanimous in their view
that the church should not take the side of UFW. They indicated that this
action on behalf of some other denominations had split those denominations. Some felt that the church should not become involved at all, but
should rather preach the gospel." The role of the church, to some farmers,
was to spread information to help "counter some of the misinformation
being disseminated by the UFW and its supporters." Some local churches
even saw UFW as incompatible with Christianity, "They [the churches]
feel that the cause of the UFW is close[d] to the New Testament gospel
with its concern for the poor and oppressed."[20]

Predictably, the responses of the UFW to similar questions by the Peace
Section were quite different. Workers from the UFW denied any plot

to return the Southwest to Mexico, any connection to communism, and any attempt to start a new Mexican-American country. Rather, they saw their efforts as bringing "social changes needed for the betterment of the workers which are not always part of a typical union's program." This betterment was understood as advancing Mexican-American involvement in education, economics, and politics. Health care and preventive medicine were also described as germane to their program. UFW representatives claimed that worker opposition to UFW did not come from the majority who made California their permanent home, but came from transient workers. To counter some farmers' claims, the UFW pointed to changes in the hiring hall where seniority was redefined as length of time on a particular farm, not as a union worker.[21]

United Farm Workers opposed a ban on harvest strikes and found the legislative climate cool toward new unions. The Teamsters were not sympathetic to the UFW and concurred with many observations made by farmers: UFW workers mismanaged money, the hiring hall divided families, and the UFW and Chávez caused an increase in the Mexican-American high school dropout rate. Although the Teamsters added a layer of complexity to the tensions, they were a minor presence in these reports, despite their claim to having increased support from workers since 1973, when many contracts between growers and the UFW expired, including about 4,000 signatures on a petition asking Teamsters to represent them.[22] Meanwhile, the UFW had 50,000 dues-paying members in 1970.[23] Cooperation between growers and Teamsters in 1973 strained the UFW, which called for more strikes, boycotts, and secondary boycotts, and who at times encountered violence on the fields. It was in this context, nearly a decade into the grower–UFW tensions itself, that the eastern Mennonites found themselves exploring the responses of Mennonite growers.

Workers on Mennonite farms generally reported that they were "happy with their situation of employment" and registered opposition to UFW, especially when they desired to work and UFW desired to strike. Two Mexican-American farm workers, who were also FPC students, disagreed on their views of UFW. One who had been a UFW worker did not like Chávez, while the other, who was never a member of the UFW, did. Mexican-American Mennonites also expressed a range of opinions and varying degrees of support for the UFW, which were tied into wage and piecework preferences. The more difficulty one had collecting union benefits, the greater the dislike for the union.[24]

Individual workers interviewed could agree on motives: "With the exception of one person, they had no doubt that Chávez was seeking the welfare of the farm workers and that the UFW was not attempting to take over the land for Mexico." They scoffed at the idea that workers chose not to work when work existed even at too low wages. Illegal immigration created conflict for some workers, who expressed concern over the immigrants' plight and yet understood the need for higher American wages for themselves.[25]

These workers believed that the federal government should do more to enforce immigration laws. The report's author concluded that the worker interviews revealed two main points: first, there is no monolithic farm worker, as their opinions cover a broad range of likes and dislikes for unions and farmers; and second, though Mennonite farmers were quiet on actual worker experience, they were genuine in relating to labor. The report concluded: "I am convinced that the Mennonite farmers we spoke to sincerely want to do the right thing in this situation and that they do, in general, have good relationship with their workers. As far as we were able to determine, Mennonites have also responded in a nonviolent way in this situation."[26] In the delegates' final analysis, at the risk of political equivocation due to the complexity of the issue, they thought that because they were a North American agency, they needed to work on this problem without alienating the parties involved; it was a difficult task, as the fence to sit on was thin and rickety. Furthermore, there was also the question of Mennonite identity, established along the racial/ethnic lines on which their congregations formed: "There are four MB Mexican-American churches, which have developed as missions from the MB churches in the area. Members of these churches are primarily farm workers."[27]

Mennonites made many attempts to understand their identity in modern America, and at mid-century, Harold Bender's "Anabaptist Vision" dominated the discussion. His vision had three points: true practice of Christianity happens in community, the community is maintained through mutual discipleship (training and accountability), and the principle of love and nonresistance are to govern all relationships.[28] Bender's vision reigned over Mennonite self-identification for much of the middle decades of the twentieth century, and it had an institutional home: Goshen College.

Student Visitors Provoke Debate

Students from Indiana's Goshen College were the second Mennonite group to visit California from eastern states specifically to study farm labor issues. In her diary, Beth Sutter described and commented on her experiences over about thirteen days in the Fresno-Reedley area in late May and early June 1974, providing an interpretation of events from a college student's perspective. Sutter was apparently not as supportive of and less willing to understand Mennonite farmer concerns in California as the MCC Peace Section was. Sutter's experience in California began with a visit to a chapel service at FPC, where she began to observe not only the labor issue, but also a different Anabaptism that at first glance was notable for its informality: "It was strange. Before we went to chapel, Paul Toews suggested that we go because Anabaptism is this guy's 'thing.' The [chapel] speaker was a history prof. And in his talk he said he couldn't get through the speech without mentioning Anabaptist heritage. The audience laughed. This continued throughout the talk. Is Anabaptism here a joke, a novelty, a hobby?"[29]

Later in the day, she received an important, albeit brief, summary of California Mennonitism. On a visit to the college library, the student delegates met, coincidentally, an earlier acquaintance and had a lengthy conversation, which revealed to Sutter some of the nuances of California Mennonite thought and life steeped in conservative evangelicalism:

Alden [Ewert, public relations at FPC] talked a lot about the MB church. He told us how the MBs moved there and for a long time (until recently) had no seminaries so their preachers went to Wheaton [College], Moody Bible [Institute] etc. This produced a God and Country theology. Churches have flags, and little emphasis is placed on nonresistance in many of the churches. Alden wished the church would be more involved in social action issues. He sees the gospel as more than saved souls—he sees total need of people. He is criticized by other MB for his involvement in such issues as the Viet Nam War, questioning civil religion in the MB church, war tax issues etc.[30]

Sutter documented more of Ewert's thoughts on California Mennonitism, and she agreed with his criticisms and concerns about its evangelical nature: "Anabaptist teachings are lacking in the MB church, Alden feels. He said he thinks many of the preachers would just as soon leave it alone. Alden stays with the MB Church in hopes of keeping alive some of his and others concerns on Anabaptism and justice for the oppressed, hopefully bringing the church into a fuller awareness of its mission."[31] For the students, however, such friendly encounters with like-minded Mennonites were not typical, and various Mennonitisms clashed.

The students had an early visit with Leo Miller, a General Conference Mennonite pastor in Reedley, who described the issue as "touchy." Though there were not many farmers in his church, he arranged for visits with two (unnamed). According to Sutter's diary, after the visit with Pastor Miller, they met with Arnold Reimer, a General Conference farmer whose fruit farm consisted of thirty acres and a packing shed. After some conversation and questions from the students, Miller asked the visitors from Indiana some questions, and the differences in these American Mennonitisms began to come through. As Beth Sutter recalled,

> His questions were loaded ... The first question was, "Why did you come to CA when its labor laws and wages are better than other states?" He said there are worse problems in Appalachia, Ohio, Georgia, and other countries. He really has to question our sincerity, he says. We explained that Alvin Peters [Mennonite farmer] had invited us and that CA was the central location of the UFW, which we wanted to study. Ruth [Sutter, another member on the student trip] said that CA was of interest to us because of the Mennonite farmers involved. Arnold asked how many people Chávez has had on our campus trying to organize us. He was getting excited, and his wife said she thought we'd talked enough, because he had a heart condition and shouldn't get too upset. Boy, I felt terrible! Arnold took everything so personally—but why am I so shocked? Of course he'll take it personally."[32]

Perhaps even more surprising for the students was their visit with Henry Janzen, pastor of Reedley Mennonite Brethren Church. Janzen identified the problem as being primarily one between two unions, where "the Teamsters is an <u>American union</u> ... whereas the United Farm Workers is <u>social reform</u>."[33] The pastor of Reedley Mennonite Brethren echoed many of the concerns of Mennonite farmers, as Beth Sutter notes, "Henry questions why people are concerned about CA when its farmworkers are paid the highest wages for farmwork in the nation." Beyond differences between unions, Janzen surprised Sutter with his reflection on the religious chasm between parties in the labor issue, asking, "How can Christians talk reason, or deal with non-Christians?"[34]

In defense of Mennonite growers, Janzen pointed out that his son, who had an eighty-acre farm, often received gifts from workers who visited Mexico. Sutter commented, "We heard that story over and over at different farms." Janzen continued to defend the interethnic relations in the local Mennonite Brethren world:

> After talking about the "non-Christian workers" which the MB farmers couldn't deal with, Janzen said, "But we're real concerned people because we have four mission churches." These churches are separate from the big 1500 member MB church, but "we even invite them into our church one Sunday night a year to give their testimonies and sing." He went on to say that these people don't know how to budget their money, and how they could have nice houses if they wanted them. He kept saying that if the people "had a Mennonite background" they'd be successful and know how to save. As far as what Christians can do, Janzen said, "Until these people get the gospel, there's nothing we can do." After these people "get the gospel" they'll move up economically.[35]

He described the boycott as, "'the most vicious tool ever implemented.' It hurts the farmer that is 'using the income on his ranch to further missions,' so when we boycott, we are 'boycotting missions.'" The meeting ended with Janzen asking each of the visitors if they were "born-again Christians."[36] Beth Sutter was surprised to find that the issue for Mennonite Brethren leaders like Henry Janzen was not social inequity or possible oppressive labor practices on Mennonite farms, but rather who believed the gospel and how proof lay in money management skills; it was a critique that underscored the evangelical nature of much California Mennonitism.

Sutter describes several other encounters with Mennonite farmers who echoed Janzen. Attempting to understand Mennonites in this struggle, Sutter concludes: "It's much harder for me to be identified as a Mennonite along with the Mennonites here who are exploiting and cutting down people . . . The conflict comes when I do not want to be identified with the MB growers here. 'We're a different kind of Mennonite,' I (or we) quickly add now when we say we're Mennonites. It just doesn't seem like it's the same gospel. The things Mennonites here say about 'the gospel' really frustrate me, and hearing people that I should have an identity with as Christians saying these things tears me up . . . The things that bother me most are the racist slurs and the interpretation of the gospel."[37]

On a visit to the Ray Ewy farm, Sutter encountered the conspiracy theory that UFW was working to return California to Mexico and that it was inherently violent. She was especially surprised by Ewy's conclusion that "Mexicans have to learn to laugh at themselves because 'until they can laugh at themselves, they can never fully arrive.' He said the Mexicans should be able to laugh at themselves like the Japs—anese [sic] did about their internment. Well they did not laugh then and they are not laughing now!"[38]

On a visit with Alvin Peters, they met up with a pick-up truck of his workers. Peters told Sutter, "O.K. Here I've got any type of Mexican you'd want—wetbacks, green carders, any type you'd want. Ask 'em if they want to join the Union!" On the same occasion she noted, "Somehow Alvin got on the subject about trash. He was talking about a certain type of people that are so low they aren't worth anything—they're just trash! They 'don't have any morals and they continually live in sin.' " When challenged, Peters added, "Trash wasn't just Mexicans, it was any low class of people." On a visit to Ken Reimer's farm, Sutter found similar stereotypes: the Mexican inability to budget money and that poverty was relative. "Later in the conversation Ken said that when farmworkers become Christians, a funny thing happens—they 'get goals and don't want to be farmworkers anymore'. . . . Mrs. Reimer said that in this area 'you're lucky if you can get your kids through high school having them marry a white.' "[39]

Between the more muted and nuanced tones of the Peace Section report and the surprise and indignation in Sutter's diary, Mennonites from the east clearly saw a different Mennonitism at work in central California. This can be attributed in part to interactions of Mennonites from different regions, but also to different denominations. California Mennonites are largely Mennonite Brethren. From their beginnings in nineteenth-century Russia, they have been more open to pietistic, evangelical, and fundamentalist theologies. The intersection of Mennonitisms—socially activist Goshen students, the inter-Mennonite MCC anchored in the east, and a population of California Mennonites largely conservative and evangelical—revealed the power of assumptions. Differing pedigrees of American Mennonitism found each other in the fields of the San Joaquin

Valley, and like long-forgotten relatives, they found each other strange. It turned out they read their Bibles differently, understood the relationship of labor and capital differently, and both found it aggravating that questions of class, race, and political views at this time trumped theology and religious practice.

Mennonite Brethren farmers were alleged to have engaged in such practices as using child and illegal immigrant labor, providing unsafe working conditions, and paying low wages. Yet, as Bob Buxman discovered, the situation was more complex, as growers resisted the allegations as caricatures and asserted that they acted more responsibly than they were given credit for. Concerning child labor, for example, they explained that they permitted parents to take their children, who were not hired directly by the farmer, with them to pick raisin grapes; they tried to avoid hiring illegal labor—though the measures allegedly taken were not always the most strenuous to ensure a legal labor force. Yet differences in perception between farmer and worker persisted. Mennonite Brethren farmers saw their priorities in proper order as Christian faith, their laborers, and farming; their laborers saw those same priorities practiced in the exact opposite order. Both, however, agreed that the Mennonite Brethren farmer was most alike the popular image of the California farmer in terms of antiunionism.[40]

The MCC authors, maintaining a moderate posture in their labor politics, favorably represented Mennonite Peter Enns, who owned a large farm, as he brought to their attention a layer of tension not previously addressed—as growers and labor struggled with each other, the small farmer was being squeezed out by large corporate farms. Enns "talked very favorably about opportunities for Christian Mennonite businessmen to sit together and talk about Christian ethics in relation to their business management and labor problems." He would like the Christian community to actually discuss what a fair wage is. Enns reiterated that many socially concerned Mennonites unfairly singled out California, and that some of the California Mennonite growers were seriously annoyed with their eastern co-religionists, especially when growers of all sizes were largely treated the same.[41]

On July 30, 1974, concerned Mennonites met at Goshen College for a forum on the United Farm Workers and grower issues, sponsored by the Mennonite Board of Congregational Ministries. The discussion was based on the reports of Hershberger, Koontz, and Regier; the Lupe DeLeon and

Neftali Torres report; and the report by students Beth Sutter, Ruth Sutter, and Dan Hertzler.[42] The discussions dealt with how to categorize UFW: some claimed it was a social movement, which Mennonites could "tie into the U.F.W. with our servanthood concept providing health, educational and other services"; others said it was an ethnic identity and Chicano movement, not a union. In a peculiar understanding of ethnic identity, the forum concluded that because the UFW also existed in the eastern United States, it was not part of an ethnic identity. One participant, Dan Hertzler, even suggested, without explanation, that the problem for Mennonites was "our middle America concept of Christian faith. Mennonites tend to be supportive of the status quo."[43] From the appearance of these tensions, the status quo was either unknown or different for everyone.

Anabaptist Visions Clash

The Goshen students came from a liberal arts college in Indiana that in its leadership was known for melding Mennonite identity and social activism. Through the late 1940s and 1950s, there was questioning in some Mennonite circles about what the "peace witness" should consist of. For much of American Mennonite experience, pacifism was characterized as a reluctance to perform military service and a mandate to live peacefully, to themselves, to be "still in the land" as some put it. Yet, after World War II, the discussion turned increasingly toward a more active, politically engaged, and less quiet "peace witness." This conversation was happening as the civil rights movement was growing, and the nonviolent example set by the Baptist Martin Luther King, Jr., and Roman Catholic Chávez were particularly persuasive. Within the Mennonite Church, the denomination to which Goshen College belonged, the shift to a socially active peace witness was well under way.[44]

The Anabaptist vision, described earlier, was a religious call for Mennonites to be peaceful followers of Jesus, living in community accountable to each other. J. Lawrence Burkholder articulated another important "vision" in the late 1950s. Burkholder argued for a view of justice whereby Mennonites became engaged with society and therefore needed to make some necessary concessions for the larger ideal of justice. In 1960, after a very cool reception by Goshen College leaders, he left to teach at Harvard Divinity School. Burkholder returned to Goshen in 1971 to become its president, signifying an important shift in the school's identity, and he was president in 1974 when issues in California led to student visits and conferences held on campus. He described Mennonites who were not social activists and draft resisters as part of a "drift into comfortable membership in American society."[45]

Although the tensions in California were often framed in singular terms in these reports, they reflected a degree of antipathy between regional Mennonitisms defined by rurality and urbanization and between religiosities progressive and conservative evangelical, exacerbated by geographic distance and economic convictions. In a gathering of General Conference Mennonite farmers, they thought the solution to labor problems resided with lawmakers and that the church could offer more than the overly simplistic three-choice set of siding with workers, siding with farmers, or neutrality. At the very least, some farmers suggested, the church could offer reconciliation and "simply present the facts."[46]

The MCC Peace Section also noted that despite attitudes attributed to Alvin Peters, his workers opposed the union and felt that negotiating with the farmer directly was advantageous. In other words, although real differences existed between the perceptions of Peters and those of his workers, both sides considered their arrangement workable and mutually agreeable.[47] Some California Mennonite hosts and workers expressed interest in having a meeting of informal discussions with Mennonite farmers. The Mennonite Brethren were in a unique situation to facilitate this, because they possessed a sizable population of both workers and farmers.

By the mid-1970s, it was clear, demonstrated through this convulsive issue, that American Mennonitism was a plurality. It always had been, but in the early 1970s, assumptions regarding "peace" and "justice" were made that simply assumed something to be solid when in actuality it was fluid. In fact, the fissures were more than theological; they were racial, economic, and geographic. Rural and urban cultures formed to exacerbate existing fault lines in a small set of denominations already prone to schism. Moreover, an amalgam of conservative politics and evangelicalism, which emerged as a considerable force in Ronald Reagan's California, appealed to many Golden State Mennonites. Eastern Mennonites, working from an intellectual milieu energized by Burkholder and the recent success of John Howard Yoder's *The Politics of Jesus* (1972), found their western coreligionists unrecognizable.

In central California, eastern-based Mennonites scrambled to map out the scope of American Mennonitism through the language of a liberal-protestant social activism available to them, refracted through a particular Anabaptist lens. What they found to their surprise, however, was that the map was already creased along the folds of race, labor-intensive capitalist agriculture, and conservative evangelical religion.

The reaction of eastern Mennonites to California is as instructive as the California Mennonite response to labor issues. As the opening quote to this chapter indicates, there was a perception that Mennonites in California were qualitatively different than Mennonites elsewhere. The reflection of some eastern Mennonites to the distinctive Mennonite experience and culture in California implies a divergence from historical norms; this was the case when California Mennonites sided with large economic interests against labor. In California, the Mennonite story is dominated more by a Russian Mennonite past than the Swiss-German one that forms much Mennonite church history. In the Russian context, Mennonites had much experience over centuries as wealthy landowners hiring Russian peasants to work for them and, in some cases, had been targets of peasant resistance and a Communist government.[48]

Moreover, Mennonites from eastern states had a longer tradition of coupling a perceived bucolic agrarianism with Mennonite values than with industrialized capitalist agriculture, which was the practice in California.[49] The family farm may still have been the more common agricultural arrangement in Indiana at this time; if not, it was certainly part of the recent past. California would have seemed like a different world to such observers. A culture of political conservatism and evangelical fundamentalism embraced by California Mennonites startled those from Pennsylvania and Indiana just as they in turn irritated some of their co-religionists by the Pacific.[50]

CHAPTER 12

From Digging Gold to Saving Souls

The Transformation of California Mennonite Identity

Modernity has left its mark.
—J. B. Toews, Mennonite Brethren pastor, seminary president, historian, 1993

Fluid Identities

California, despite its secular and decadent image in the popular imagination, was not a place so secularized as to be conventionally irreligious.[1] Evangelical Mennonites flourished in California, and they responded to modernity in a fashion that transformed hope and ambition from its initial apocalyptic enthusiasm into an engagement with society via healing ministries and services. The California experience produced an ambivalent pacifism and softened sectarian impulses with urban evangelical realities.[2]

In California religious historiography, scholars have usually described alternatives to Anglo-Protestantism in utopian or even mystical terms.[3] Here, the Mennonite story is a counter-narrative, where a small group of conservative evangelicals found, within a generation, a home in California's religious environment without recourse to utopian separatism or individualistic mysticism. They combined the language of paradise and dystopia with markers of institutional Mennonite culture and proceeded to both influence society and retain a particular sense of religio-cultural identity—through health care and educational facilities as well as churches and social relief organizations.

One of the ironies of the Mennonite experience in California, however, was secularization. If secularism is understood as adaptation to the larger society, taking cues from the outside world in the organization and administration of even religious activities, then the Mennonites held seemingly contradictory religious and secular impulses in their relationship to California society.[4] As effortless as all this may sound, it was filled with multiple negotiations—sometimes with one other, sometimes with the wider society.

To practice nonresistance at mid-century, for example, the Mennonites participated, along with several other religious groups and the federal government, in the creation of the Civilian Public Service (CPS), and then debated among themselves (within the CPS camps) what pacifism, Mennonitism, and Americanism meant, as well as how the concepts related to one other. When Arthur Jost applied for U.S. citizenship, local Mennonite pastors did not necessarily share his religiously informed pacifism. Yet the same Arthur Jost administered the Kings View Homes (KVH) mental health hospital, born out of his and others' CPS experiences. KVH was created out of socially concerned Mennonite Christian commitments. Nevertheless, it also played a key role in developing a "secular Mennonitism," where a socially progressive position regarding mental health administered by the Mennonite Central Committee (MCC) was eventually separated from its Mennonite religious convictions despite the protestation of non-Mennonites.

Mennonites were also evangelicals.[5] When the Mennonite Brethren built a Bible institute and seminary in Fresno in the decade of 1944–1955, the intention was to train church leaders in a decidedly conservative evangelical, even dispensational fundamentalist, fashion. This lasted until the 1960s, when a turn was made to strengthen, or restore, an evangelical Anabaptist identity that had been diluted, some thought, by an overreliance on the dispensational fundamentalism of the Bible Institute of Los Angeles (BIOLA) and Dallas Theological Seminary.

Despite a burgeoning confidence born out of World War II, the success of CPS, and the development of KVH, there were nevertheless contradictions in being Mennonite in California. These occurred in church heresy investigations focused on suspect relationships to local conservative evangelicals, in the seminary where there was a desire to become literally a "little Dallas [seminary]," and in the discussions to erase the "Mennonite Brethren" label from the names of local churches. Even at KVH, despite encouragement from non-Mennonite psychiatrists, a deliberate and obvious integration of Mennonite religion and psychiatry did not occur.

The institutionally constructed sense of social identity and activism was drawn and energized from both their evangelical Christian faith and their cultural location in California. At times California Mennonites wrote and acted in a millennially inspired manner, seeking protection from the changes that larger forces, such as modernism, pluralism, and immigration, brought to their communities—even when congregants resisted the efforts of denominational leaders. Mennonites found much success in California, yet when they engaged society, they often sought to cover that which distinguished them from mainstream evangelical California. Religious identity for Mennonites in California was always fluid, and the postwar decades were no different. What changed was the nature of Mennonites' cultural negotiations.

Church splits from 1925 to 1963 were also negotiations of Mennonite identity. In the 1920s, one such negotiation was made over the hazard posed by Pentecostalism, which exposed not only a charismatic crisis among the Mennonite Brethren but also already existing fissures in group unity and notions of faithfulness. The problem was disunity, not speaking in tongues. Yet, there was more than Pentecostalism at stake for the splinter group. South Reedley Mennonite Brethren (renamed Dinuba Mennonite Brethren in the 1930s) was also concerned with a perceived laxity of spiritual leadership in Reedley that permitted the firing of guns at weddings and did not punish people for going to hear Pentecostal preacher Aimee Semple McPherson.

Locally, the concerns about Pentecostal influence, or the degree of spiritual discipline in churches, were not simply issues of orthodoxy versus heresy; they were also cases of religious and cultural integration versus religious and cultural separation—where group unity was paramount. For denominational leaders, issues that threatened group unity were the most important. The integrity of the group trumped individual concerns. This was expressed clearly within the local membership itself when, for example, a choir director disciplined a female choir member without first taking the problem to the church body.

By the end of the 1950s, the Mennonite Brethren in Fresno experienced church splits that ran along fissures of age and education level, pitting young educated professionals against older, more traditionally deferential Mennonites. When Roy Just's "trial" in Bethany took place in the early 1960s, the case against him was made on the grounds of his inappropriate language, lack of respect for church leaders, and lack of respect for local evangelical culture. Just's defense was based on the ideals of a liberal arts education, the value of questioning authority, the acknowledgment of ambiguity even on religious questions, and respect for non-Christian religions. Although the split in Bethany was not directly precipitated by Just, it was a group of educated professionals in their twenties and early thirties who left in order to have flexibility in church worship, something more difficult in a tradition-bound congregation, even as they went on to identify themselves with historical Anabaptism.

The irony in this series of events is that the tradition-bound generation sought identification with the local conservative evangelical culture, and the professional iconoclastic generation sought identification with historical Anabaptism. Both groups integrated into California society but in different ways, on different conservative paths. None of this was effortless, as they all negotiated specific claims to specific religious visions.

The General Conference Mennonites apparently moved along a cultural axis defined by social progressivism. When MCC planned to build a regional clothing center and office in Reedley, the support of the General Conference Mennonites was assumed, whereas support from the Reedley Mennonite Brethren was not. The Mennonite Church moved along a different cultural axis that, in the California context, prompted internal conflict on the appropriate role of such traditional cultural markers as dress codes. Some of these Mennonites in Los Angeles and in the larger denomination expressed concern over a perceived lack of respect for traditional sartorial mores. They also raised questions of authority. In Los Angeles, problems for the denomination arose from a vain hope that leadership struggles in the mission and persistent tensions over dress codes would be resolved by shifting their status from mission to church and then back to mission. What came out in the available evidence was the denomination's willingness to accommodate the idiosyncrasies of the Los Angeles cohort because so many Mennonite Church members took vacations to Southern California.

The Mennonite response to both racial and religious diversity was as important. On the issue of racial diversity, a scale of tolerance developed that on the surface appeared to be ironic: the more socially progressive the group, the less likely its members were to stay in neighborhoods with a sizable influx of African-Americans. The General Conference Mennonites moved their church from Los Angeles to the suburbs in Downey, and the Mennonite Church opened a second church in Downey. White Mennonites left Los Angeles for Downey, and the Los Angeles church was transformed into an African-American congregation in the early 1960s. The Mennonite Brethren acknowledged unease with the changing demographics in their Los Angeles neighborhood of City Terrace, but this mission-formed church remained even as the Los Angeles Mennonite Brethren Church dissolved. Thus, the church, which emerged from an evangelical mission impulse, provided the Mennonite Brethren with the cultural and religious resources to stay in that particular context, but some members nonetheless participated in the "white flight" of the day from their nonmission congregation in Los Angeles.

When the three Mennonite denominations began to colonize and settle California, the evangelically oriented Mennonite Brethren came in such large numbers that their sense of geographic isolation was short-lived, and they rarely expressed the apocalyptic intensity of the smaller Mennonite Church. In short, the Mennonite Brethren were very much at home in California. Members of the Mennonite Church, the largest Mennonite group in America but the smallest in California, described the greatest degree of isolation and loneliness. They also used apocalyptic rhetoric more than the other Mennonite groups in California. That sense of loneliness was expressed not only in geographic distance from co-religionists, but also in spiritual distance from their California neighbors.

In the Cross-Currents of Modernity

The story of Mennonites in California, the accommodation of a conservative religious group to the larger culture under the impulses of modernity, is a story repeated in many places. Another telling of this story is found in a survey study of Mennonites and modernization in which the authors conclude, "While modernization tends to seduce people toward secularization, individualism, and materialism, this tendency is, for the most part, counteracted by strong religious, family, community and institutional identity that provides a sense of peoplehood."[6] The California Mennonites experienced the powerful forces of modernization sooner than those elsewhere, and their evangelical Christianity helped greatly to smooth the friction on their path into California's diversity. Mennonite identity in California was not a matter of persistent cultural traits or practices. The tradition-observant Mennonite Church members, for example, as early as the 1920s, questioned the necessity of the "plain coat," while their leaders apparently tolerated moustaches without beards and women without bonnets.

The friction Mennonites experienced early on in California was also made smoother by shifting images of identity and place, at times infused with a millennial content that mixed tropes of an Edenic and hellish world often shaped by urban-rural contexts. As the century wore on, that millennial friction drew the Mennonites closer into what has been called American Civil Religion, which on the evangelical side found warmth in dispensationalism and fundamentalism. Of course, not all California Mennonites joined this ride into history's ending at America's Pacific Coast. A younger generation coming of age in the 1960s embraced evangelical Anabaptism as an antidote to the fundamentalist influences of dispensationalism. They made this clear by taking part in a significant theological change at the seminary, led by the visionary leader of an older generation, J. B. Toews. At Pacific College in the early 1970s, a historical renaissance emerged to recover historical memory, resulting in an archive, a historical society, and renamed buildings.

In the early 1970s, eastern Mennonites visited California inspired by the labor struggles of migrant farm workers led primarily by the UFW, bringing with them a contrasting view of Mennonite identity and political sympathies. The visiting and local Mennonites discovered that they did not entirely agree on their visions of Mennonite identity in practice. The California story carried national implications—the hard reality that, in the United States, Mennonite identity was pluralistic and localized. In modernizing, Mennonites developed professionally trained pastors, strove for efficiency and rational organization in their service ministries, and developed, in the postwar decades, an increasingly intimate relationship with government.

Despite these intersections with modern society, California Mennonites had little interest in embracing theological liberalism. Their choices tended to be conservative evangelicalism cast in the Billy Graham mold, fundamentalist anti-modernism, or a made-in-California evangelical Anabaptism. Issues of group unity, masked by conflicts over doctrinal fidelity, usually drove the concerns expressed in various church splits and heresy trials, as in the case of H. G. Wiens, the pastor accused of liberalism, in the Bethany Mennonite Brethren Church in Fresno. These issues were mostly about insider/outsider religio-cultural borders and Mennonite relationships with local evangelicals. California Mennonites entered an evangelical culture where pastoral training at BIOLA carried more influence than studying Menno Simons, their sixteenth-century Reformation namesake, though, that would be challenged by J. B. Toews and others beginning in the mid-1960s.

The traditional Mennonite historical tale moves from Europe westward to North America, leaving the western half of the continent largely ignored. Although some local histories make perfunctory mention of California, most Mennonite histories and larger surveys of American religious history were content to cast them no farther west than Kansas. What this study has shown is that the California experience is more than a confection at the historical dinner; it is a significant part of the American Mennonite feast.[7]

The Mennonite Brethren prominence in the California story is the most obvious difference from the wider American Mennonite experience. When J. B. Toews studied the American Mennonite Brethren experience, he argued that modernity was the villain of the twentieth century, as it slackened traditional and historical moorings. He concluded his narrative with a two-chapter jeremiad that the Mennonite Brethren had conceded to modernity.[8] Modernity's mark—a long time in the making—was not always discouraged. Part of the Mennonite Brethren historical mooring in its Russian past was their close collaboration with government as well as their deep experience as wealthy landowners.[9]

Anthropologist James Urry has provided helpful clues to explain the Mennonite Brethren openness to modernity. He argues persuasively that to understand the Mennonite Brethren, one needs to appreciate their roots in nineteenth-century pietism, a form of Christian belief stressing personal experience and individual communion with God.[10] Those attracted to it "were entrepreneurs, men with vision and skilled with dealing with the wider world; individualists used to running their own affairs and not dependent upon others." These factors were present in the 1860 secession of the Mennonite Brethren from the larger Russian Mennonite community.[11] As Urry observed, Mennonite Brethren were individualists in their work and religion, where salvation was an individual pursuit.[12] The Mennonite Brethren from their beginnings were a pietistic, evangelical, professional, and business-oriented group, and they were the ones who came to California in the largest numbers.

Vital to the Mennonite experience in California were the changing

Present-day sanctuary and 1919 sanctuary standing together as they did from 1953 to 1965. *Source:* Records of Reedley Mennonite Brethren Church.

The south tower of the 1919 Reedley Mennonite Brethren Church falling during demolition to make room for a new Sunday school and fellowship hall wing, July 1965. *Source:* Otto B. Reimer Papers.

Reedley Mennonite Brethren Church after construction of fellowship hall (to the right)—taken after 1965. *Source:* Records of Reedley Mennonite Brethren Church.

symbols that Mennonites used to articulate their experiences and identity. Three threads in the Mennonite experience in California reflect what Kerwin Klein has called "articles of American faith: History runs East to West, California is the future, and Christ will come again."[13] If history has made its way to the Pacific Coast, and millions await Christ's return at the sandy edge of California's millennial destiny, the Mennonites too found this beach. From early twentieth-century descriptions of California to mid-century Women's Missionary Service handbook covers emblazoned with their "Redeeming the Time" motto, and from frontier imagery connected to nation building to CPSers' inserting themselves into American Civil Religion, and ultimately to seminary intellectuals eventually battling back the Bermuda grass of dispensationalism, the twentieth century drew Mennonites into not only tropes of American exceptionalism, but also California's peculiar millennial role therein.[14]

Although early Mennonite consideration of California society was mostly made in their reflections written for co-religionists elsewhere, that concern eventually turned outward. This outward turn is most easily seen with the institutional construction of the postwar decades to transform California into a healthier place. During World War II, and in the decades that followed, the turn outward was made through a mix of cultural anxiety and élan. Mennonites would create, grow, rationalize, and modernize their identity through the construction of schools, hospitals, relief agencies, women's societies, and CPS. All of these contributed to the modern

California Mennonite experience as they also did throughout the United States. Moreover, as Mennonites integrated American Civil Religion and patriotism with their religious tradition, they moved deeper into California's evangelical and cultural substrata and politically further down the halls of influence in Sacramento. Thus, California Mennonites emerged from the postwar decades modernized and Americanized.

Historian Paul Toews has observed that such institutional responses to the "acids of modernity" were an "antidote" to its corrosiveness on group particularities.[15] The antidote here was a cocktail of Mennonite activism and a range of evangelicalisms from Anabaptism to fundamentalism. Modifying Martin Marty's images of canopy and cocoon, Mennonite institutions became marquees, covering Mennonites from the threatening rains above, permitting them to step off the curb and into the street unmolested, as winds swirled about them. It was pacifism that helped draw Mennonites deeper into society. The Mennonite "peace witness" was transformed from an isolationist avoiding military service to an activist engaging with society. In this transformation, nonresistance became social service. Yet, the two were not disconnected, as the CPS experience propelled participants directly into mental health centers throughout the United States, including the seemingly secular Kings View Homes in Reedley. It was at KVH where non-Mennonites argued that Mennonite faith had much to offer in health care.

If institution building was an outer projection of a modern Mennonitism that took root in the soils of California, there were inner projects undertaken so as not to lose both their tradition and history in the historical renaissance centered in Fresno. By the 1960s, then, what was left?

Hybrid Mennonites

California Mennonites held together a set of contradictions that signaled, paradoxically, accommodation and resistance, which modified culture for their own ends. Most of their resistance to the world around them, however, was religious. It was initially directed toward urban evils and lurking devils, and then, when the cities were less demonic dens, it was directed toward new threats, which were increasingly neighbors—Catholics, Pentecostals, and even other Mennonites who were insufficiently evangelical, modernist, or, by the middle of the 1960s, fundamentalist and dispensationalist.

In California, religious symbols of meaning had shifted. Gone was the millennial energy of newly minted Mennonite settlers interpreting their new location through the lens of natural utopia and urban dystopia. New was the promise of a secular millennium, as death, misery, and pain were mediated through expanding religious bureaucracies both modern and rational. Meanwhile, as scholars at MBBS and PBI embarked on recovering Mennonite Brethren history in the late 1960s and early 1970s, the overt presence of Dallas Theological Seminary dispensationalism was discarded. While this was happening, in the mid-1970s, agricultural growers and organized labor were embroiled in conflict, and Mennonite growers encountered curious Mennonites from the east. Scholars turned to history, tradition, and heritage, as Mennonite higher education, purposed to extract and protect heritage, became increasingly the equivalent of Mennonite middle-class finishing schools, prepping the next generation to live and work in modern society. The negotiations seemed all but settled. The layers of mid-twentieth-century California Mennonite activity and involvement, both as partner to national trends and local particularities, including women's societies, schools, CPS, KVH, identity issues, heresy investigations, mission work, racial issues, and questions of religious practice, can be pulled back to see the three threads noted above knotted together in the center.

When eastern Mennonites visited in 1974, what they found were Mennonites appearing as hybrids, where pieces of Republican politics, fundamentalist virtues, West Coast informalities, and capitalist labor-intensive orchard practices were grafted together and called Mennonite. In this interesting time, 1974, eastern and western Mennonitedoms newly discovered each other.

Although California was a faraway place, it was powerfully present in the American imagination. The state was an ethno-religious greenhouse where, free from any dominant religious hegemony, myriad religious groups, both new and bizarre, traditional and transformed, could germinate and grow in its rich soil. Mennonites were drawn here for health, prosperity, and good farmland. In the process, their religious identity cast a distinctive evangelical and pietistic hue—a regional distinction reflecting in many respects the kind of Mennonites that were attracted to California. Those Mennonites, largely Mennonite Brethren already evangelical and pietistic in their religion, found California to be a welcoming home. It was here that Mennonites far away from the Mennonite centers of influence to the east faced the promises of California. It was here that Mennonites from eastern states saw exaggerated fictional Mennonites making empty gestures to a noble and instructive history while allegedly owning guns—as noted by Guy F. Hershberger in the opening quote for chapter 11.

Throughout the early decades of the twentieth century, when the initial burst of institutional construction took place, Mennonites experienced much that was new. They focused on the challenges of religious pluralism and evangelistic outreach as the theme of "latter days" surrounded them. Even when the Promised Land became a malarial swamp, California was understood as part of their biblical journey.

By World War II, Mennonites considered the size of their facilities and membership numbers as marks of success. Having embraced modern measures of achievement, what remained was to adapt to and appropriate the values and fruits of modernity, including rationalizing of services, professionalizing of ministry, and modernization of education. Within a few decades, Mennonites had traveled into the Californian apocalypse, where the new "millennium," once beckoned by natural wonder and urban dystopia, soon bathed in the glistening sheen of modernity, mediated ironically through traditional religious institutions. These sets of images must be held together. Mennonite correspondents wrote of loneliness, isolation, and the presence of evil in California's dystopic cityscapes. As well, we saw others who wrote that the natural landscape was a spiritual teacher filled with Christian apocalyptic hope. In both, California was Edenic and forbidden. As those visions were recycled continuously for their frostbitten co-religionists elsewhere, however, the machinery of denominational colonization and expansion was under way, fusing together climate, piety, and modernity.

In the process of settling California, Mennonites used several strategies to maintain a separate cultural and theological identity within and against the larger culture. In the post–World War II era, such strategies resulted in cultural assimilation, so that by the mid-twentieth century, the Mennonite story in California had developed into an interesting tale of religious conservatives—traditional agrarians—finding their way in an increasingly urban and religiously pluralist California.

California Mennonites in varying degrees responded to the pressures of modernity in ways that were not always simple but that often mixed deepening commitments to evangelicalism, Anabaptism, and even secularism. These responses—evangelical, Anabaptist, and secular—covered a broad spectrum yet represented a selective retaining and discarding of Mennonite religious practices, identities, and expressions. All these reactions to modernity with its urbanity, cultural diversity, changing economy, and shifting mores produced Mennonite forms of accommodation and resistance that reflected creative responses even if they at first appeared reactive. In short, Mennonites in California were a dynamic people who did not simply become modern, but who actively shaped their experience to engage modernity on their own terms.

A New Breed of Mennonites

The primary narrative of this book closes in the mid-1970s. In this brief epilogue, I note some of the more significant changes in the Mennonite landscape since 1975. The 1980s and 1990s were challenging times for California, especially urban California, as a confluence of influences put the brakes on over a century of effusive boosterism and gilded mythologizing. The end of the cold war, the shuttering of defense factories, and dramatic decrease in federal defense monies; demographic pressures of increased legal and illegal immigration; and overly strained public services brought about a slow reversal of fortune. Even Orange County—after a mixture of investment failure leading to a criminal conviction and voters voting down a tax increase—went bankrupt, leading to massive budget cuts and the loss of thousands of jobs. On the evangelical front, an exodus eastward had begun as some religious leaders, parachurch organizations, and folks in the pews returned to Texas and Colorado. California found itself in the rare position of having more people leave than move in. Of course, as Carey McWilliams asked so many decades ago, if the existence of California is nothing but swagger, California did have reason to boast. For the seeming implosion of the California dream in the early 1990s, by the late 1990s it returned to dizzying heights with its already diversified economy supercharged in the tech industry, though the Central Valley's own economic recovery lagged behind the rest of the state.[1]

About thirty years after Daniel Hertzler's 1970 drive from Fresno to Reedley, amid the Edenic binary of paradise and sin described in chapter 2, the arcadian image of the Central Valley turned sour. The *San Francisco*

Chronicle ran a series on California in 1999 that read more like Dante's *Inferno* than the opening chapters of Genesis, and Fresno was cast as the "cautionary tale." Providing a snapshot of the city, the article on Fresno characterized the raisin capital as wracked by perpetual unemployment, violent crime, political corruption, dead strip malls, and abandoned discount stores, all softened by a thriving literary scene and the coffee shops of the Tower District.[2] Fresno was Bay Area tragedy and Hollywood comedy. Fresno was packaged and broadcast to CBS viewers in the 1986 miniseries *Fresno*—a parody of such prime-time dramas as *Dallas* and *Falcon Crest*, where wealthy oil tycoons and vintners were replaced with a raisin empire skewering refinement. That Fresno could be a comic location spoke to public perception, however deserved or not.[3]

In these difficult decades for the Golden State, and inordinate stress on the San Joaquin Valley and Fresno in particular, Mennonites continued to work, flourish, and adapt. As Kevin Starr described the mid-1990s, the Central Valley had a population of 5 million and a robust $16-billion agricultural economy to maintain. As northern portions of the valley were becoming extensions of the Bay Area's daily commute, the Central Valley as a whole was the fastest growing region in the fast-growing state. This agricultural region, with Highway 99 running the north-south course as a knotted rope, was urbanizing at a rapid clip, and its largest city, Fresno, was experiencing the strains of rapid growth, as other nearby cities were. Pollution, gang activity, and tagging—urban vandalism and graffiti—were drawing the attention of media and government officials alike. Agriculture towns such as Huron, a key center for Mennonite mission work earlier in the century, had now become some of the poorest places in California. Huron lacked print media and schools, but with four labor camps, it did not lack razor-sharp lettuce knives for harvest, meth to numb the backbreaking pain, and a reputation for fighting. It was not just Huron, but the Central Valley was suffering. Methamphetamines were in large-scale production, so that by 2001, a million pounds of byproduct waste was seeping into the ground with an annual environmental clean-up cost to taxpayers of $10 million to mop up labs busted by law enforcement at a rate of nearly one every day and a half. The arcadia of a century ago seemed in fact like a Paradise Lost. In October 2001 the Environmental Protection Agency described the San Joaquin Valley as a "severely polluted ozone region," one of the seven worst in the country. Placed under order to comply with federal standards in five years, it did. Despite the problems rapid growth brought, the Central Valley remained attractive to people the world over. California, in the words of Kevin Starr, was a "world commonwealth," and that global diversity was soon reflected among the Mennonites.[4]

A century and a half after Johannes Dietrich Dyck and Joseph Summers arrived in California to dig for gold, two other Mennonites, at the edge of the new millennium, reflected on what California meant for their future. They framed their future around urban development. Mennonite Church USA leader Ruth Suter explained that Mennonites with "traditional" roots had two options: "hunker down in our glorious Anabaptist history and slowly die out" or "embrace the new realities of our diverse communities and celebrate our new emerging identity as an Anabaptist 'priesthood of believers.'" Suter continued, "For those of us in Arizona and California, the 'hunkering down' option just isn't viable—there are too few of us 'traditional ethnic Mennos' to remain a critical mass." As she pointed out, in 2000, Anglos were an ethnic minority among Southern California Mennonites amid the swelling groups of African, African-American, Hispanic, Hispanic American, Taiwanese, and Indonesian people.[5]

Suter noted that in the Bay Area, a "new breed" of Mennonites worked in the computer and tech industries, often with hour-long commutes to their jobs. These Mennonites often engaged in a virtual online community because they were so widely separated by work, commuting, and other involvements. Unlike those in their agrarian past, these folks lived in communities distant from each other, with little face-to-face interaction during the week. Thus, the church (online and gathered) served as a focal point for their own engagement.[6]

Chuwang Pam, born in Nigeria, moved to America in 1994 and in 1996 started the Mennonite-related Los Angeles Faith Chapel. Pam described the ethnic diversity of California Mennonites in these words: "If our search for a new identity is simply to support the existing structures, we will have questions to answer. If our search for identity is simply to reinforce our glory, we will be missing the mark. Look at what's happening right now in Los Angeles. Right now as I talk to you, we are on the march for full realization of the new Mennonite church. Today the pure 'Anglo' churches in southern California are a minority. Today the majority are people of color—Africans, African-Americans, Hispanics, and Asians. That to me is just a glimpse into what God in this millennium expects the Mennonite church to look like."[7] A glimpse of the future, perhaps; however, these late twentieth-century observations were at least a century in the making, as Mennonites in California wrestled with and adapted to changing demographics, social trends, and mission goals.

Embracing changing demographics was to come through making vital choices on how to expend resources, as demonstrated by Mennonite Community Church in Fresno. This small church, as described by Rod Janzen, rejected the siren call of building a large theater-style church with evangelical pop-rock worship music in order to plant a church in Clovis (Peace Community, 1989–1997), which became the Hmong Mennonite Church in Fresno.[8]

The first two waves of Mennonite migration came at the turn of the twentieth century and again in the 1940s for reasons including health, agriculture, and adventure. As Jeff Wright, Mennonite Urban Ministry director for Southern California, observed, there was also a third wave of immigrants who joined Mennonite churches. These immigrants did not arrive in California with a Mennonite heritage, nor were they of Euro-American ancestry. This new wave was so numerous that by the end of the twentieth century, ethnic Mennonites—descendants of white European immigrants—were a distinct minority. As late as 1978, there were fewer than twenty Mennonite churches in Southern California. Bakersfield for some was the southern border of the Mennonite domain and Southern California just a "wasteland."[9]

The makers of the Mennonite renaissance arrived from across oceans. Some of these diverse peoples had been denounced by Mennonites for their beliefs in earlier times or were cited for a host of churchly problems. Immigrants from Africa, Latin America, and Asia had long-established communities in Southern California, and by the 1980s, Mennonites made a concerted effort to plant churches among them. Progressive thinkers on issues of evangelism and church expansion realized that change was rapidly happening around them, and now Mennonites themselves needed to change.

Churches were started in numerous communities in order to meet the needs of Nigerians, Ghanaians, Mexicans, Taiwanese, Japanese, Koreans, and others. The results were encouraging: the few Mennonite congregations in Southern California in 1978 nearly tripled to fifty-six by 1998 and mostly comprised members of numerous ethnic groups speaking a variety of languages. By the end of the twentieth century, according to Jeff Wright, the multiracial mix in Southern California had reduced the number of Euro-American members in the twenty-nine churches of the

Pacific Southwest Mennonite Conference approximately to a mere 11 percent![10]

Although the numbers are difficult to track, a simple tally of church names in 2000 shows that nearly half of MCUSA churches in California were Spanish, Hmong, Indonesian, Ethiopian, and Taiwanese congregations and that their members made up nearly one-third of the total MCUSA membership in the state. For the Mennonite Brethren, just over half of churches in 2000 were Spanish, Japanese, Russian, Slavic, Korean, Ukrainian, Ethiopian, Indian, and Chinese congregations, composing about one-fifth of the total MB membership.[11] By 2012, 44 of the 105 Mennonite churches in California were ethnic minority churches (or "churches serving ethnic minority populations"). These congregations combined had approximately 3,000 members, which was nearly one-quarter of the total Mennonite membership (12,567) in California that year.[12] The numbers for ethnic and racial minority church membership are extremely rough and unarguably low as congregations throughout California were racially mixed, indicating that the number of ethnic groups and their membership was much higher.

Mennonite work among refugees coming to California has a long history too, as we have seen in MCC work. It continued in the post-1960s era as the "boat people" exodus from Cambodia to North America took place in the late 1970s and early 1980s. Though California was not a major destination, those who came were welcomed, cared for, and given assistance to start life again through the efforts of the West Coast MCC, local churches, and FPC. Combined, these Mennonite institutions had the resources necessary to respond to human tragedy in Southeast Asia. Here was one of many intersections of California Mennonites understanding their place in society as markedly Anabaptist, with the cultural and religious capital at hand to help new "outsiders" navigate new surroundings.[13]

Mennonites had joined the westward migration to California in the earlier decades of the twentieth century, but now at the century's end, their role reversed as they turned their attention to assisting other newcomers. Over the course of the 1900s, Mennonite attitudes changed on many fronts, including their views of immigration and ethnic minorities. In 1984, West Coast MCC helped establish an office in Glendale at the request of the Greater Los Angeles Mennonite Council to work with immigration concerns. This service was expanded in 1992 to include refugee issues.[14]

As we saw earlier, Mennonites engaged in missions with Hispanics who were often employed in migrant labor in the valley's fields and with those attending the City Terrace Mission in Los Angeles as early as 1926. Eventually, numerous Hispanic churches were started; most were in the Reedley-Dinuba area, but some were in San Jose, Fresno, and Los Angeles. Hispanic Mennonite Brethren churches typically emerged from a mission outreach or as an extension of an existing congregation. Regardless of their origin, the established Anglo Mennonite leaders sought to train Hispanic leadership from within the fledgling congregations. It was a challenge well into the 1980s for these new churches to survive, especially economically. Until 1978 they were not listed separately as Pacific District Conference (PDC) churches, but were counted under the wing of their "mother" churches. Even when the Hispanic churches were counted as full-fledged conference congregations, many still did not have the title to their property and received subsidies from their parent churches into the late 1980s. Thus, some local Hispanic leaders experienced the ambiguity of being suspended between independent congregation and mission church.[15]

It was not just in Southern California that new churches were planted. The PDC of Mennonite Brethren churches in the 1970s and 1980s started churches or ministries in places such as Bakersfield, Fremont, San Jose, Sacramento, and Firebaugh. This activity coincided with encouragement from the conference for individual church member participation in missions of a Mennonite or an evangelical nature—including Youth for Christ, Campus Crusade, Inter-Varsity Fellowship, and Christian Social Concerns.[16]

Part of the Mennonite success with these new church communities resulted from developing economic programs to serve and empower them. Economic empowerment for both new arrivals and those living in longer-term poverty was a challenge, and Mennonites decided to take it on. Furthermore, as the embrace of racial and ethnic diversity developed, so too did a Mennonite acceptance of charismatic Christianity. The once-condemned Pentecostalism of the early twentieth century became the celebrated neo-Pentecostal influence of the 1980s, which blended charismaticism with Anabaptism.[17]

As the 1970s and 1980s rolled on, other Mennonite ministries, such as Home Missions, continued to expand, starting churches throughout the state, from the Bay Area through the Central Valley and beyond. Shifting from a funding practice of grants and subsidies for new congregations, Home Missions began to focus on what it called "tent-making" ministries, where church ministry is supported by the labor of the worker. That is, Home Missions trained people in the skills needed for various aspects of church planting and sent them out to evangelize and start churches. Through the 1980s, the work expanded to include Spanish-language training and ministry.[18]

As Mennonite Brethren had gathered in Reedley in 1960 to work at unity among various groups and make apologies for an old fracture in Russia (1860), so they met again in 1995 in Fresno, but this meeting was more divisive. The Canadian and American constituencies found themselves more and more estranged, the delegates divided over how to even spend their time together: worship and spiritual exercises or discussions around conference structures. Furthermore, 1995 in Fresno was a significant year for American Mennonite Brethren education. The Mennonite Brethren Biblical Seminary (MBBS) was celebrating its fortieth anniversary as it and the denomination were set to decentralize their operations to points in British Columbia, Manitoba, and Kansas, while attempting to retain their "head" in California.

In 2010, MBBS changed its name to Fresno Pacific Biblical Seminary and was a separate administrative unit of Fresno Pacific University (FPU). Mennonite Brethren theological education continued in the various regional centers, and by 2012, online instruction reached a global audience from its perch at FPU in the Central Valley. As late as the mid-1990s, the majority of students at the seminary were from Canada, but within fifteen years, Canadian students virtually disappeared from the California location because they could receive a theological education in British Columbia or Manitoba. As with many other California-based evangelical enterprises, the Mennonite trend was also dispersion. Decentralizing the seminary's outreach, yet keeping its administrative head under the FPU umbrella, was a pragmatic response to changing times.

During the 1980s and 1990s, the seminary developed a highly regarded marriage and family counseling program in addition to its already established programs in biblical studies and ministry training. Over the decades, biblical scholars did not simply contribute to their scholarly disciplines, but readily engaged the issues and struggles in the MB churches throughout North America. Though the MBs delayed dealing with the issue of women as senior pastors longer than some other Mennonite denominations, it was not for a lack of thoughtful reflection, theological examination, and careful biblical exegesis. Already in the 1960s and

1970s, professors such as Alan Guenther wrote serious articles for the *MB Herald* on the issue of gender and church work. Through the 1980s, the study papers and denominationally oriented publishing continued, with some of the academics cast as "liberal" and others as "conservative" on the issue, many of whom were working at the same small seminary in the valley. The culmination of this gender work for the denomination was the publication of *Your Daughters Shall Prophecy* (1992), which provided a range of perspectives, grounded in biblical scholarship, for churches to use in their own study groups as congregations wrestled with the issue of gender and pastoral leadership.

Meanwhile, Pacific Bible Institute, founded at the end of World War II, becoming Pacific College in 1960, then Fresno Pacific College in 1976, was renamed Fresno Pacific University in 1997. The first, and only, solely Mennonite Brethren–sponsored university in North America boasted expanding enrollments, programs, and graduate studies in the last quarter of the twentieth century.

During its institutional journey, the college went through several iterations of Mennonite identity—changes significant enough to warrant revisiting the first "Fresno Pacific College Idea" of 1965. That identity statement defined the essence of FPC and served as a landmark for institutional decision making with seven descriptors: Christian, community, liberal arts, experimental, Anabaptist Mennonite, nonsectarian, and prophetic. During the 1970s, FPC benefited from federal Title III funding to expand its professional programs and graduate studies. Furthermore, the Pacific District Conference (PDC) took ownership of the college from the national denomination, localizing its administration and governance. These developments led to higher enrollments, increased hiring, and questions about the continuing relevance of the 1965 "Idea."[19]

President Edmund Janzen, in the late 1970s, motivated in part by a looming accreditation visit, initiated a process to review the "Idea" and propose any needed changes. After much deliberation and debate, a revised identity statement adopted in 1982 reduced the descriptors to three: Christian, liberal arts, and community. Most striking was the dropping of Anabaptist Mennonite. Much of the debate surrounding FPC's identity, future orientation, and mission was about the meaning of Anabaptism, Mennonitism, and evangelicalism. While a number of faculty argued for carrying the Anabaptist torch, others at the college, including board members, Mennonite Brethren pastors, and general constituents, wanted FPC to go the route of Wheaton College (Illinois) or BIOLA (the Los Angeles educational bastion of evangelicalism) and be an inclusive evangelical college and not a restrictive Mennonite college that relied on denominational identity. This debate had roots in the creation of Pacific Bible Institute in 1944, but with the ownership of the college now transferred to the regional PDC, the time was ripe to revisit it again. The 1982 statement effectively made Anabaptism and Mennonite identity invisible. Those arguing for a clear evangelical identity won the day by associating Anabaptist ideas that were embedded in the 1960s "Idea" with the hippie-style, unpatriotic pacifism of the 1960s counterculture heyday.[20]

In 1995, however, the "Idea" was once again revised with the reinsertion of "Anabaptist-Mennonite" into the text, although not as a separately highlighted distinctive of FPC's identity. In the opening decade of the twenty-first century, Fresno Pacific University established centers in North Fresno, Merced, Visalia, and Bakersfield and revised the "Idea" a fourth time as the "Fresno Pacific University Idea," which mentions not only the Anabaptist Mennonite roots of the school, but an active relationship with the Mennonite Brethren denomination.[21] These iterations of theological identity since 1944 flag the contested ground between evangelical and Anabaptist currents swirling about in the MB churches since the mid-twentieth century.

The 1990s also saw California Mennonites become more active in the arts. For one example, nationally recognized poet Jean Janzen wrote elegantly and poignantly about her Mennonite heritage. Janzen, who lived in Fresno and attended the College Community Mennonite Brethren Church, linked her spirituality to significant places in her own experience and those of her ancestors. While her Mennonite Brethren heritage informed much of her writing positively, though not without the critical eye of the poet, other Mennonite writers spoke with more of an edge. North in the Bay Area, Sheri Hostetler of Oakland, a member of a progressive Mennonite church in San Francisco, founded the magazine *Mennonot* (1993–2003) with Steve Mullet of Elkhart, Indiana. *Mennonot* was a magazine for "Mennonites on the Margins," and its pages were filled with interviews, poetry, satire, essays, and jokes.[22] Here a social justice–informed spirituality was resiliently Mennonite, if not post-modernist iconoclastic, and coming from California, it helped to stir a vital conversation among disaffected younger Mennonites.

Even as transportation and communication technology expanded exponentially in the post-1960s world, it did not close the geographic gap between California and the eastern Mennonite centers of power. In early 1975, MCC created a new separate regional body—West Coast MCC— because the former regional California office at times had strained relationships with the MCC headquarters in Pennsylvania due to geographic distance and cultural differences. The new body made official the independence that in reality had existed for decades. Nonetheless, some leaders worried that this development might break apart the national agency. That did not happen; rather, regional administration increased support for MCC generally. West Coast MCC was also the first regional office to register as a corporation, in 1979, and it went on to expand its work with the disabled, including developing residential programs in Oregon and California.[23]

Other service ministries were transformed even more dramatically. At KVH a Chaplaincy Program was eventually started, and by 1975, the hospital had opened day centers for developmentally challenged persons in Atwater and Los Banos. Despite establishing an addictions treatment center in Fresno in the late 1980s, KVH's time in Reedley was about to end. In 1990 the hospital portion of KVH closed for economic reasons and was transformed into a home for troubled adolescents. The adolescent home in turn closed and was sold in 2001. Though the brand Kings View continues today, headquartered in Fresno and with some Mennonite connections remaining, the Reedley enterprise founded by Jost had finished.[24]

Other changes at the regional conference level included women increasingly sitting on PDC boards, including the executive committee in 1985. At the local level, churches began sending more women delegates to regional conferences. In 1975, 1.6 percent of the delegates were women, but women made up 12.5 percent of the delegates in 1985. By the mid-1980s, most churches included women in their delegations, with a number regularly sending delegations of at least 25 percent women.[25]

The fragmentation and frenzy of the urban milieu did not necessarily negate neighborhood community building. Mennonites in Fresno, for example, formed a community on Kerkhoff Avenue. It was a regular grassroots neighborhood gathering started by members of College Community Church in Clovis. They hosted refugees, held potlucks, observed Christmas and Easter, and even set up a swimming pool for community use. They prided themselves on nurturing a relational "urban community" to such an extent that on the twentieth anniversary in 1992, more than 230 people from across the country came for a weekend of events.[26]

As they entered the twenty-first century, Mennonites, now diverse in ethnicity and in their understandings of Christian faith and Mennonite identity, continued to articulate a sense of place and identity as they encountered and responded to California's urban and natural environments. They now hailed not only from the Canadian prairies, American Midwest, and Russia but from Korea, Japan, Central America, and dozens of other cultural homes. This astonishing cultural diversity within the Mennonite world, which had mostly emerged since 1975, forever changed the Mennonite experience in California. Added to the changes in the first three quarters of the twentieth century—involving religious pluralism, race, gender, pacifism, institutional building, and higher education—the new diversity will leave a lasting mark on the Mennonite experience in California. Moreover, it raises the question of whether any kind of common Mennonite identity in California will be possible, if desired, in the future.

Notes

Abbreviations

CMBS-F	Center of Mennonite Brethren Studies, Fresno Pacific University, Fresno, California
CMBS-H	Center of Mennonite Brethren Studies, Tabor College, Hillsboro, Kansas
CMHSB	*California Mennonite Historical Society Bulletin*
FMCA	First Mennonite Church in Reedley Archives
GAMEO	*Global Anabaptist Mennonite Encyclopedia Online*
GH	*Gospel Herald*
MB	Mennonite Brethren
MBBS	Mennonite Brethren Biblical Seminary
MBHSWCB	*Mennonite Brethren Historical Society of the West Coast Bulletin*
MCA-G	Mennonite Church USA Archives, Goshen College, Goshen, Indiana
MCA-N	Mennonite Church USA Archives, Bethel College, North Newton, Kansas
MCC-WCO	Mennonite Central Committee, West Coast Office
ME	*Mennonite Encyclopedia*
NASB	New American Standard Bible
PBI	Pacific Bible Institute
RE	*Reedley Exponent*
TMenn	*The Mennonite*

Preface

1. McWilliams, *California*, 3.

2. McWilliams, *Southern California*, parts 4 and 13.

3. Starr, *Americans*, 415.

4. There are numerous accounts of this history of the Mennonites, though the standard survey histories remain C. Henry Smith, *Smith's Story of the Mennonites*, and Dyck, *An Introduction to Mennonite History*.

5. Ernst, "The Emergence of California."

6. Janzen, "Back to the City," 2.

7. For examples, see Ahlstrom, *A Religious History*, 231—34, 236, 753; Marty, *Pilgrims*, 365; Marty, *Under God*, 21—24; Gaustad and Schmidt, *The Religious History*, 86, 89.

8. Bellah, "Civil Religion," 1—21. See also Tuveson, *Redeemer Nation*, for his compelling analysis of the "redeemer nation" motif through American millennialism, national destiny, and the mythic quality of westward migration.

I use George Marsden's and David Bebbington's definition of evangelical. For Marsden, evangelicalism is broadly defined as a group of Christians, usually Protestant, who believe and proclaim such biblical teachings: divinity of Jesus, virgin birth, death, resurrection, and Second Coming to establish his perfect kingdom. Bebbington provides a "quadrilateral of priorities" that marks evangelicalism: biblicism (the Bible is the only acceptable guide to Christian belief), conversionism (one must have experienced a moment of conversion to Christ), crucicentrism (centrality of Christ's redemptive death on the cross), and activism (evangelism or social action).

Marsden, "The Evangelical Denomination," vii—xix. In particular, see viii—xvi and his specific mention of Mennonites, viii, xv. Helpful introductions to American evangelicalism include Marsden, *Understanding Fundamentalism and Evangelicalism*; Marsden, *Fundamentalism and American Culture*; Dayton and Johnston, *The Variety of American Evangelicalism*; Noll, *American Evangelical Christianity*; Hart, *Deconstructing Evangelicalism*; and Bebbington, *Evangelicalism in Modern Britain*, 2—3.

9. Loewen, *Diaspora*, 8. To see the larger Protestant social and religious environment in twentieth-century California, see Ernst with Anderson, *Pilgrim Progression*, chapters 5 and 6, and Ernst, "The Emergence of California," 11—52.

10. I am indebted to the following essay for the success and evangelical modification thesis: Gauvreau, "Protestantism Transformed," 61—63.

11. Sweet, "The Modernization of Protestant Religion," 31.

12. van der Veer, "Introduction," 18—20.

13. The Mennonite Church in the nineteenth century and early twentieth century was sometime referred to as the "Old Mennonite Church." In the early 2000s the Mennonite Church and the General Conference Mennonites merged to form Mennonite Church USA (MCUSA). However, that story is outside the scope of this project.

14. Luthy, *The Amish in America*, 41—45. The category of denomination remains useful in historical terms for the people, place, and time I am writing on. The category also makes sense for Mennonites, where both leaders and laity self-identified and organized mostly along denominational lines.

15. Dyck, *An Introduction to Mennonite History*, 214—35; Juhnke, *Vision, Doctrine, War*, 40—43.

16. Juhnke, *Vision, Doctrine, War*, 49—50. See chapter 1 for the late nineteenth-century context. For General Conference history, see Pannabecker, *Open Doors*. Kevin Enns-Rempel also provided assistance with this paragraph.

17. For survey histories of Mennonite Brethren history, see Toews, *A History of the Mennonite Brethren Church*, and Toews, *A Pilgrimage of Faith*.

18. Marty, *The Irony*, chapters 8, 9, and 11; Marty, *The Noise of Conflict*; and Marty, *Under God*, 2—14.

19. Marty, *The Irony*, 93—95, 150—56.

20. Ibid., 208.

21. For example, see Loewen, *Diaspora*, 3—7.

22. Ernst, "Religion in California," 43—51.

Chapter 1. Going to California

1. Haslam, *The Other California*, 3, 8; Starr, *Endangered Dreams*, 309—10; Hundley, *The Great Thirst*, 235.

2. Enns-Rempel, "A New Life in the West," 12; Enns-Rempel, "They Came From Many Places," 1—2; Enns-Rempel, "Many Roads to the San Joaquin Valley," 3; Nachtigall, "Mennonite Migration," 80. There are some minor discrepancies between the numbers of Enns-Rempel and Nachtigall due to methodology and scope of their studies. For a table of their comparisons and a satisfactory explanation of the small differences (between 1.0—2.1 percent), see Enns-Rempel, "They Came From Many Places," 7.

3. Enns-Rempel, "Mennonites in California."

4. Enns-Rempel, "Health, Wealth, and Ministry."

5. Dyck, "In the California," 25—28; "Joseph Summers," obituary.

6. Dyck, "In the California," 25—28; Smith, *Smith's Story*, 434—35. Cornelius J. Dyck quoted liberally from his elder's diary. Johannes's diary, which ended in Oregon, just before his crossing into California, concluded with the foreboding "there was trouble ahead." Cornelius commented, "Here ends the diary of my great grandfather which begins again ten years later in Russia . . . He did keep a diary during his stay in America, but on his death bed my father, his grandson, had to take those diaries and burn them before his eyes." The diary, in the end, was shorn of American content, though in the beginning it never contained Californian content. Dyck, "In the California," 27.

7. "Joseph Summers," obituary. Summers appeared to be a popular individual, heavily involved with the Mennonite Church in Elkhart, Indiana.

8. This omission of California, or the American West in general, in American religious history is a complaint of western historians: Maffly-Kipp, "Eastward Ho!," 127—48; Ernst, "The Emergence of California," 31—32.

9. P. R. Aeschliman, "The Pacific District Conference," *Mennonite Year Book*, 1930, 23.

10. Engh, *Frontier Faiths*, 55—67.

11. Ibid., xii—xiii, 12, 182, 188, 190, 206.

12. Bergman and Toevs, *History of the Mennonites in the Paso Robles Area*, 2—3. This history was also adapted in the brief article "A Centennial History," 1—4.

13. "A Centennial History," 2.

14. Ibid., 3—4; L. R. Just, "California," *ME*, vol. 1, 491—93; Harold D. Burkholder, "San Marcos Mennonite Church (Paso Robles, California, USA)," *GAMEO*, 1959, www.gameo .org/encyclopedia/contents/S2506.html.

15. Harold D. Burkholder, "San Marcos Mennonite Church (GCM)," *ME*, vol. 4, 414; "Paso Robles (CA) Second Mennonite Church (GCM)," *ME*, vol. 4, 122; Phyllis Claassen, "The Mennonite Churches in California: General Conference Mennonite Churches," n.d., pp. 2—3, 9—10, SA 296 Phyllis Claassen, MCA-N. Although there is no date on Claassen's historical account, in the same collection is correspondence from Mennonite pastors to Claassen answering her request for historical information for her project. The letters are all dated in the year 1937. P. R. Aeschliman, "History of the Pacific District Conference," *Mennonite Year Book*, 1932, 34; Cornelius Krahn, "Paso Robles First Mennonite Church, Cal," *ME*, vol. 4, 122; Cornelius Krahn, "Paso Robles First Mennonite Church (Paso Robles, California, USA)," *GAMEO*, 1959, www.gameo.org/encyclopedia/contents/P3802.html. Hege later returned and was a deacon from 1915 to 1919.

16. Burkholder, "San Marcos Mennonite Church (GCM)," 414; and, Phyllis Claassen,

"The Mennonite Churches in California," 2–3, 9–10; Menno Galle, "Mennonites in the Paso Robles Vicinity," MS.93, Menno Galle Collection, box 2, Messages: General Conference and Ministers' Conference, MCA-N.

17. P. R. Aeschliman, "History of the Pacific District Conference," *Mennonite Year Book,* 1932, 34–35; "Report of J. B. Baer to the Board of Home Missions of the General Conference," *TMenn,* March 1898; *History of the First Mennonite Church, Upland,* 1–15. The author of this report mistakenly put Upland in San Luis Obispo County. Lester Hostetler, "Upland First Mennonite Church (GCM)," *ME,* vol. 4, 788. For a history of General Conference home missions, see Barrett, *The Vision and the Reality.*

18. Ella Schmidt, "Supplement to History of First Mennonite Church," Jan. 15, 1978, vertical file, First Mennonite Church (Upland, CA), MCA-N; Phyllis Claassen, "The Mennonite Churches in California," 5–6; "First Mennonite Church Shafter, California," *Mennonite Year Book and Almanac,* 1938, 41.

19. "Brief Historical Data of Immanuel Mennonite Church," *Thirtieth Anniversary, 1910–1940,* Los Angeles, Immanuel Mennonite Church, 1940, MLA.CONG.84, Immanuel Mennonite Church, Downey, CA, box 1, Calendars, Programs, Reports, Directories, MCA-N.

20. "Our Church History 1910–1960," *Golden Anniversary 1910–1960 Immanuel Mennonite Church,* first and last page, MLA.CONG.84, box 1, Calendars, Programs, Reports, Directories, MCA-N.

21. "Brief Historical Data of Immanuel Mennonite Church," *Thirtieth Anniversary, 1910–1940;* "Our Church History 1902–1955," *50th Anniversary,* p. 2, and "Our Church History 1910–1960," *Golden Anniversary, 1910–1960, Immanuel Mennonite Church,* first and last page, MLA.CONG.84, box 1, Calendars, Programs, Reports, Directories, MCA-N.

Several documents describe this series of events, and there are some discrepancies regarding dates and names. The oldest, a 1925 constitution, reports that mission work began in 1908 at the "Riverside Mission," and the Whosoever Will Mission, which opened in 1914, was called the "Mennonite Mission Church." "Introduction and Preamble," *Constitution and Declaration of Faith of Immanuel Mennonite Church of Los Angeles,"* adopted April 19, 1925, p. 1, CB553 Living Hope Church Records (Downey, CA), box 4, Constitutions 1925–1976 file, CMBS-F. Although the 1925 constitution is the oldest document, it is the only one to make these claims. Minor differences in the other documents include the start of mission work, which in "Our Church History 1902–1955" occurred on May 4, 1909, and in February 1909 in the membership directories of 1947 and 1948. See "A Brief History of the Immanuel Mennonite Church," *Immanuel Mennonite Church Membership List 1910–1947,* back page, and, "A Brief History of the Immanuel Mennonite Church," *Immanuel Mennonite Church Membership List 1910–1948,* back page, CB553 Living Hope Church Records (Downey, CA), box 4, Membership Directories 1936–1960 file, CMBS-F.

Another difference: the River Station Mission (only called this in the membership directories of 1947 and 1948) opened in 1910. The constitution of 1944 listed the opening of what was called the River Station Mission as May 4, 1910 (*Our Church: Its History and Constitution,* adopted Jan. 9, 1944, p. 3, CB553 Living Hope Church Records (Downey, CA), box 4, Constitutions 1925–1976 file, CMBS-F). In "Our Church History 1910–1960," *Golden Anniversary, 1910–1960, Immanuel Mennonite Church,* first and last page, the opening is listed as happening on May 8, 1910.

See also Phyllis Claassen, "The Mennonite Churches in California," 6–7. For a brief history of the General Conference Pacific District Conference and its churches, see Burkholder, *The Story of Our Conference,* 1–5, 37–57.

22. This was a common enough practice among Protestants. See Dochuk, *From Bible Belt to Sunbelt*, chapters 1—2.

23. "Our Church History 1902—1955," 50th Anniversary, pp. 7—8.

24. Rev. M. J. Galle, Pastor, First Mennonite Church Paso Robles, California, "Why Was the Pacific District Conference Organized?" *Pacific District Conference of the General Conference Mennonite Church 60th Anniversary 1896—1956*, June 13—17, 1956, pp. 2—3, MLA.II.5.e, GC-Pacific District, General Conference Districts to 1969 Pacific, MCA-N; Campbell, "Seventy-Five Years on the Shores," 7—11.

25. Harold D. Burkholder, "Pacific District Conference (GCM)," ME, vol. 4, 103—104; Burkholder, "The Pacific District Conference," 24—27; Galle, "Why Was the Pacific District Conference Organized?" 1; P. R. Aeschliman, "History of the Pacific District Conference," *Mennonite Year Book*, 1932, 32.

26. *A Treasury of Historical Accounts*, 231—32, 235—36; "German Mennonites," 3B; Eymann, "Eymanns Here for nearly a Century," 9A; "Germans: Americans of the Mennonite Heritage," RE, 27 Oct. 1988, pp. 6S—7S. For a detailed account, see Enns-Rempel, "The Eymanns," 6—8.

27. Smith, *Garden of the Sun*, 437; "A Brief History of the First Mennonite Church of Reedley, California—1906—1946," *Dedication: Fortieth Anniversary Program and a Brief History of the Church*, 1946, pp. 1—2, MLA.CONG.88 First MC, Reedley, CA, box 2, Misc. file, MCA-N; and P. R. Aeschliman, "History of the Pacific District Conference," *Mennonite Year Book*, 1932, 35.

28. *Reedley: A Study of Ethnic Heritage*, 102—103; Enns-Rempel, "The Eymanns," 7—8; Zech, *Historic Reedley*, 3—4.

29. P. K. Regier, "Reedley First Mennonite Church (GCM)," ME, vol. 4, 265; "A Brief History of the First Mennonite Church of Reedley, California—1906—1946," 1—2; Phyllis Claassen, "The Mennonite Churches in California," 2—3; "Reedley, California, Mennonite Church," *Mennonite Year Book and Almanac*, 1915, 30; *The First Mennonite Church, 1906—1956, Reedley*, 1—2; Loewen, *Reedley First Mennonite Church*, 1—5; Frodsham, "A Study of the Russian-Germans," 36; and "First Mennonite Church Organized 1903," RE, 27 Oct. 1988, 4K.

30. RE, 12 May 1904, 5.

31. Zech, *Historic Reedley*, 4; Cha, *Koreans in Central California*, 50, 76.

32. Ruth, "Early Families," 70—85; Enns-Rempel, "The Eymanns," 7—8.

33. *Reedley: A Study of Ethnic Heritage*, 105.

34. Reimer, "Banking Was, Still is Bustling," 10B.

35. *A Treasury of Historical Accounts*, 241—43, quote from p. 243; *Reedley: A Study of Ethnic Heritage*, 104.

36. "Germans: Americans of the Mennonite Heritage," RE, 27 Oct. 1988, pp. 6S—7S.

37. Peters, "The Coming of the Mennonite Brethren," 159—66; Arthur J. Wiebe, "Immanuel Academy," ME, vol. 3, 1957, 13; Enns-Rempel, "From Russia," 1—2, 6—10; Reimer, "The Story of the Mennonite Brethren," paragraph 12.

38. *50th Jubilee, 1905—1955*, 57—58; *The Church Alive in its 75th Year*; 63—64, Zech, *Historic Reedley*, 74—75; Nancy Neufeld, "Immanuel began in '25 as Bible School," RE, Oct. 27, 1988, 8L.

39. *Reedley: A Study of Ethnic Heritage*, 103—104; Harold S. Bender, "Pacific District Conference (MB)," ME, vol. 4, 104; Lohrenz, "History of the Mennonite Brethren Church," 107—108; Esther Jost, "MB Church Organized in Harms' Home," RE, Oct. 27, 1988, 5K; Jacob J. Toews, "Reedley Mennonite Brethren Church," ME, vol. 4, 265; Reimer, "The Story

of the Mennonite Brethren," paragraphs 5−7. Anniversary histories of the church follow this same narrative pattern; see *50th Jubilee, 1905–1955*, 3−6, and *The Church Alive in its 75th Year*, 1−29.

40. *50th Jubilee, 1905–1955*, 63.

41. Henry H. Dick, "Lodi (CA) Mennonite Brethren Church," *ME*, vol. 3, 385; Reimche, "A History of the Woodrow Gospel Chapel," 1, 6; Engel, "History of the Church 1920s–1940s," 7−9; L. R. Just, "Lodi (California, USA)," *GAMEO*, 1957, www.gameo.org/encyclopedia /contents/lodi_california_usa. For an analysis of the cultural tensions between Volga Germans who converted to the Mennonite Brethren Church and Low German–South Russian Mennonite Brethren in a Kansas congregation, see Ollenburger, *Ebenfeld*.

42. This episode is covered in more detail in chapter 2. However, the most thorough coverage of this event remains Harder and Enns-Rempel, "The Henry J. Martens Land Scheme."

43. "The Mennonite Brethren Church of Bakersfield, California," n.d.; "Historical Sketch," *Our 50th Anniversary, Church of the Mennonite Brethren, Bakersfield, California*, 1960, 1; David Buller, "History of Mennonite Church Bakersfield," p. 1; Otto and Lydia Boese, "Early History of the Bakersfield Mennonite Brethren Church," p. 1, all in CB503 Heritage Bible Church, Bakersfield, California, box 3, Historical Accounts, CMBS-F. Some Mennonites returned to Oklahoma. See Iorio, *Faith's Harvest*, 179.

44. P. N. Hiebert, "Rosedale Mennonite Brethren Church," *ME*, vol. 4, 359.

45. Earnest Siemens, "Shafter (CA) Mennonite Brethren Church," *ME*, vol. 4, 509; Penner and Frantz, "Through the Years," 6−7.

46. Enns-Rempel, "Origins of the Pacific District," 1−3. Enns-Rempel argues persuasively that Mennonite Brethren needed increasingly complex structures as they spread over an increasingly large geographic area.

47. Smith, "Religion and Ethnicity in America," 1179.

48. Ibid., 1165−66.

49. Emanuel Stahly, correspondence, Sept. 5, and M. A., correspondence, *GH*, Sept. 12, 1908, Upland. Other letters from Upland stressing the need for visitors and ministers include H. L. Denlinger, correspondence, *GH*, Oct. 10, 1908.

50. Enns-Rempel, "Churches that Died on the Vine," 2; E. C. and L. A. Weaver, correspondence, *GH*, May 30, 1908, Dinuba.

51. Dinuba correspondent, correspondence, *GH*, April 22, 1909; and field notes, *GH*, Sept. 2, 1909.

52. Dinuba correspondent, correspondence, *GH*, April 22, 1909.

53. M. B. Weaver, correspondence, *GH*, May 27, 1909, Porterville.

54. Emanuel Stahly, correspondence, *GH*, Nov. 11, 1909, Corning.

55. Los Angeles correspondent, correspondence, *GH*, Jan. 24, 1929; Esther Kreider, correspondence, *GH*, March 27, 1913, Pasadena.

56. Los Angeles correspondent, correspondence, *GH*, Jan. 24, 1929.

57. Winton correspondent, correspondence, *GH*, Sept. 25, 1930; April 9 and Sept. 31, 1931; and Jan. 28, 1932.

58. Ibid.

59. J. J. Reber, correspondence, *GH*, Feb. 25, 1932, Turlock.

60. Wenger, *The Mennonite Church in America*, 121; Harold S. Bender, "Pacific Coast Conference (MC)," *ME*, vol. 4, 103; and John D. Leatherman, Untitled [History of Mennonite Church in Southern California], p. 4, II-15-8 SWMC History Committee, Southwest MC History, MCA-G.

61. Leatherman, Untitled, p. 5, MCA-G.

62. Shetler, *Church History of the Pacific Coast*, 45—51.

63. Enns-Rempel, "Mennonites in the Escondido Valley," 3—4; I. G. Neufeld, "Escondido Mennonite Brethren Church (Escondido, California, USA)," GAMEO, 1956, www.gameo.org/index.php?title=Escondido_Mennonite_Brethren_Church(Escondido, _California,_USA)&oldid=80572.

64. Barrett, *The Vision and the Reality*, 120.

65. P. R. Aeschliman, "History of the Pacific District Conference," *Mennonite Year Book*, 1932, 36; Enns-Rempel, "Mennonites in the Escondido Valley," 3—4. The Mennonite Brethren had a nearly identical experience in Escondido. Minutes, congregational meetings, April 7, 1909, and Sept. 19, 1915, CB542 Bethania MB Church Records (Escondido, CA), Translation of Church Book, CMBS-F; P. R. Aeschliman, "The Pacific District Conference," *Mennonite Year Book*, 1930, 23; Phyllis Claassen, "The Mennonite Churches in California," 1—2.

66. Reisner, *Cadillac Desert*, 9—10, 152, 336; Hundley, *The Great Thirst*, 234—76; Worster, *Rivers of Empire*, 233—56; Starr, *Endangered Dreams*, 309—16.

67. Harold S. Bender, "Dos Palos Mennonite Church (GCM)," *ME Supplement*, 1077. Wallace Smith, in his 1939 history of the San Joaquin Valley, mentions Mennonite "colonies" in Rosedale, Dos Palos, Lodi, and Shafter; *Garden of the Sun*, 438; P. R. Aeschliman, "The Pacific District Conference," *Mennonite Year Book*, 1930, 23.

68. Dos Palos correspondent, *Mennonite Weekly Review*, April 6, 1932.

69. Enns-Rempel, "The Mennonite Settlement of Dos Palos," 3—4.

70. Worster, *Rivers of Empire*, 4—7. Quote from p. 7.

71. Enns-Rempel, "The Mennonite Settlement of Dos Palos," 3—4; A. J. Neuenschwander, "Visiting our California Churches," *TMenn*, June 9, 1932, 5.

72. D. D. Eitzen, Pastor Immanuel Mennonite Church, to Phyllis Claassen, Bethel College, North Newton, Kansas, Feb. 24, 1937, MLA.SA 296 Phyllis Claassen, MCA-N; "Report of the Pastor," *The Immanuel Mennonite Church of Los Angeles Reports for the Annual Meeting*, Jan. 10, 1937, MLA.CONG.84, box 1, Bulletins—1952, Annual Reports—1938, 54 and 60, MCA-N. For coordinated work with BIOLA, see, in the same annual report, "Report of the Euodia Bible Club and Women's Bible Class," *The Immanuel Mennonite Church of Los Angeles Reports for the Annual Meeting*, Jan. 9, 1938.

73. Marty, *The Irony*, 93—95, 150—55.

74. Kaufman, *General Conference Mennonite Pioneers*, 278—83.

75. P. R. Aeschliman, "History of the Pacific District Conference," *Mennonite Year Book*, 1932, 37; John Bartel, "Shafter (CA) First Mennonite Church (GCM)," *ME*, vol. 4, 509.

76. Smith, "Religion and Ethnicity in America," 1158.

77. Ibid., 1181.

78. Heinz Janzen, "The Mennonites in the San Joaquin Valley," research paper (Bethel College, 1952), p. 17, Student Papers, MCA-N; Nash, *The American West*, 5—9, 22—26.

Chapter 2. Alone in the Garden

1. Hertzler, *From Germantown to Steinbach*, 145.

2. Davis, *City of Quartz*, 15—97; Starr, *Americans and the California Dream*. A popular novel from the 1930s that mixed the dream and nightmare of Hollywood, for example, is West, *The Day of the Locust*.

3. Dochuk, *From Bible Belt to Sunbelt*, 79.

4. Gasset, *Phenomenology and Art*, 70–71; Bingham, "American Wests Through Autobiography," 23–24.

5. Maffly-Kipp, "Eastward Ho!," 132.

6. Smith, *Smith's Story*, 434.

7. Smith, *Mennonites in Illinois*, 52–53. These themes were not peculiar to Mennonites. See, for example, Fjellstrom, *Swedish-American Colonization*, 11–12, 59–60, 81, 143.

8. Examples of "confessional" histories include Dyck, *An Introduction to Mennonite History*; Loewen and Nolt, *Through Fire and Water*; Smith, *Smith's Story*; Toews, *A History of the Mennonite Brethren Church*; and Toews, *A Pilgrimage of Faith*.

9. Bender, "Foreword," vii. He qualifies the statement on page x, noting that others "have had to live 'for Conscious sake,'" but adds, Mennonites at least have tried to do so "by the Holy Scriptures and the Spirit of God."

10. Kern County Land Co., *Californien als ein geeigneter Staat zur Etablirung von deutschen Kolonien: Kern County mit seinem fruchtbaren Ebenen und grossen Ansiedlung splatzen: die Kern County Land-Gesellschaft als Besitzerin von bewasserten Landereien, welche sie an deutsche Ansiedler zu verkaufen wunscht.* [California as a Suitable State for the Establishment of German Colonies: Kern County with its Fruitful Flats and Large Settlement Places: The Kern County Land Company, as owner of irrigated estates, which wants to sell them to a German Settler] Bakersfield, CA, 1895, pp. 4–5, Bancroft Library, University of California, Berkeley.

11. Ibid., 15.

12. David Goerz, "A Trip to Southern California to Investigate Lands Offered for Settlements," *TMenn*, July 1896, 74–75.

13. Ibid.

14. Ibid.

15. Worster, *Rivers of Empire*, 96–99. See John David Zehr, "Building a Church Community In the City," *Mennonite Community* (Feb. 1953): 19–20.

16. Starr, *Golden Dreams*, 32.

17. Agnes Albrecht, "A Trip to the West," *GH*, Nov. 4, 1909; Agnes Albrecht Gunden, diary, July 12, 1909. Hist. Mss. 1-332, MCA-G.

18. Agnes Albrecht Gunden, diary, July 26–27, July 29–Aug. 2, 1909. Hist. Mss. 1-332, MCA-G; Agnes Albrecht, "A Trip to the West," *GH*, Nov. 4, 1909. Oswald H. Goering also took the glass-bottomed boat to Catalina Island; Oswald H. Goering, "Trip to California: Compiled and Edited by Oswald H. Goering," Aug. 6, 1935 (compiled and edited, 1988), SA 1258, MCA-N.

19. C. Z. Yoder, "On Our Way to the Pacific Coast II," *GH*, Oct. 3, 1908.

20. Ibid.

21. Helen C. Stoesz, "My Life Experiences 1905–1936," M70 Helen C. Stoesz Papers, CMBS-F.

22. Anna B. Nissley, "A Visit to a Canyon," *GH*, March 19, 1914.

23. Anna B. Nissley, "On the Coast," *GH*, April 30, 1914.

24. Anna B. Nissley, "Observations in the Far West," *GH*, June 25, 1914.

25. Frank and Mary Smucker, correspondence, *GH*, Dec. 22, 1910, Upland.

26. Peter Neufeld, "A Trip to the Pacific Coast," *TMenn*, Jan. 25, 1938, 7, and Feb. 1, 1938, 15.

27. Oswald H. Goering, "Trip to California," Aug. 3, 1935.

28. S. B. Zook, "A Letter from S. B. Zook," *GH*, Sept. 25, 1913. See also Peter Unzicker and wife, "From Texas to California," *GH*, Dec. 14, 1916, 684.

29. S. B. Zook, "A Letter from Los Angeles, Calif.," *GH*, Aug. 13, 1913.

30. J. C. Mehl, "To the Pacific Conference," *TMenn*, Oct. 27, 1910, 4.

31. Dora Shantz Gehman, diary, Aug. 29–Sept. 5, 1930, Hist. Mss. 1–883, MCA-G.

32. Rawlings Land Company, advertisement, *Steinbach Post*, Jan. 5, 1915.

33. Karl Pohl, advertisement, *Steinbach Post*, June 6, 1923; June 13, 1923; June 20, 1923; and June 27, 1923.

34. Enns-Rempel, "In Search of the 'Greatest Mennonite Settlement,'" 2, 6–7.

35. J. D. Sherwood, President of Los Molinos Land Co., to Julius Siemens, M239 Julius and Anna Siemens Papers, box 2, Los Molinos Settlement 1910 file, CMBS-F.

36. A. Friesen to Julius Siemens, M239 Julius and Anna Siemens Papers, box 2, Russian Study Commission 1920, CMBS-F.

37. Julius Siemens, "Etliche Allgemeine _ _ _ Rkungen Ueber Unsre Mennoniten Ansiedlung Bei Fairmead, Kalifornien," pp. 1–3, M239 Julius and Anna Siemens Papers, box 1, Fairmead, California—Promotion, ca. 1913 CMBS-F. Julius Siemens, "Tatsachen über das Land bei Firebaugh, California," n.d., M239, Julius and Anna Siemens Papers, box 2, CMBS-F.

38. Siemens, "Etliche Allgemeine"; Siemens, "Tatsachen über das Land."

39. Siemens, "Etliche Allgemeine," 3.

40. J. M. Brunk, "The Mennonites in Colonizing," GH, April 8, 1909, 27–28. Although Brunk's identity is not given, looking at obituaries in GH in years recent to 1909 reveals a J. M. Brunk officiating at a funeral in Colorado. Brenneman, GH, June 27, 1908, p. 207, www.mcusa-archives.org/MennObits/1908GH/jun08.html.

41. J. M. Brunk, "The Mennonites in Colonizing," GH, April 8, 1909, 27–28.

42. Harder and Enns-Rempel, "The Henry J. Martens Land Scheme," 202. Some of the research materials for the article can be found at box 2, Martens, Henry J., 1867, CMBS-H.

43. Harder and Enns-Rempel, "The Henry J. Martens Land Scheme," 210; McClure, "The Challenge of Yesterday," 2.

44. P. B. Harms [Peter B. Harms], name on Mennonite Land Co. Henry J. Martens letterhead, to D. J. Claassen [signatory to Board of Directors agreement document], June 21, 1909, and "Articles of Agreement," Martensdale, CA, June 12, 1909, M295 Dietrich J. and Lena Claassen Papers, box 1, Documents re: Henry J. Martens and Martensdale 1907–1909, CMBS-F.

45. J. E. Bergen, "Martensdale," *Our Heritage*, compiled by Regina M. Becker (Shafter, CA: photocopy of typewritten manuscript, 1981), 30. For similar firsthand accounts, see *A History of the Mennonite Brethren Church of Rosedale*.

46. *A History of the Mennonite Brethren Church of Rosedale*, 3, 6. All Bible quotations are taken from the New American Standard Bible (Nashville: Thomas Nelson Publishers, 1977), hereafter NASB.

47. Corinna Siebert Ruth, "The Rempel Family's Escape from Death by Famine," *CMHSB* 54 (Fall 2011): 5.

48. John J. Gerbrandt, "Destination California," photocopy of a typewritten manuscript, n.d., 8–9.

49. Ibid., 11–15.

50. Two Mennonites described in memoirs their move to California from the North American plains without using sacred imagery. For one the motivation to move was to work as a teacher in a Mennonite community, and for the other, it was the presence of "good land." Parsons, *Exiles of the Steppes*, 13; Jantzen, *Frank F. Jantzen*, 9.

51. Ernest A. Eymann, "Historical Account," *A Treasury of Historical Accounts*, 1961, 231.

52. Marie Eymann-Marlar, "Marie Eymann-Marlar," *A Treasury of Historical Accounts*,

235. See also the reflections of C. P. Harms, "C. P. Harms, 241—42, and Katerine Enns-Dyck, "D.T. Enns," 242—43, both in *A Treasury of Historical Accounts*.

53. Becker, *Our Heritage Memoirs*, 3—17, 19.

54. Ruth, " 'From the Dust Bowl to California,' " 122, 126—27.

55. Ibid., 127—28.

56. The standard treatment of Russian migration to California is Hardwick, *Russian Refuge*.

57. H. S. Bender, "Harbin Refugees." *ME*, vol. 2, 657; Frodsham, "A Study of the Russian-Germans," 26; Prieb, *Peter C. Hiebert*, 88—91.

58. Prieb, *Peter C. Hiebert*, 90—91. P. C. Hiebert wrote the letter and President Hoover replied. Hoover's letter is now deposited in the Mennonite Historical Library at Bethel College, North Newton, Kansas. H. J. Krehbiel, "Reception of the Harbin Refugees at San Francisco, CA, on August 13, 1930," *TMenn*, Sept. 4, 1930, 2—3; and J. M. Regier, "Mennonite Fugitives in California," *TMenn*, Sept. 11, 1930.

59. Isaak, *Our Life Story and Escape*, 120, 122, 124.

60. Ibid., 128.

61. Neufeld, *Jacob's Journey*, 46—47, 71—85, 92. There are no details as to how she raised the money. This book is not a memoir but a story of his parents. Herb was born in Shafter, California.

62. Ibid., 100, 108.

63. Ibid., 108—14.

64. H. J. Krehbiel, "The Splendid Co-Operation of the Mennonites of Central California," *TMenn*, Nov. 13, 1930, 6. Krehbiel was the General Conference Mennonite pastor in Reedley.

65. Neufeld, *Jacob's Journey*, 113, 116. The story of the Mennonite flight to America, from Russia through China, was fictionalized in Martens, *River of Glass*.

66. Rempel, *Memories*, 3, 36. Quote from 44.

67. Ibid., 45ff.

68. Ruth, "The Stories of First Mennonite Church Members," 86.

69. Thielmann, *Escape to Freedom*; Sylvester, *From Despair to Deliverance*; Block, *Escape*; Frantz, *Water from the Well*; Becker, *A Bundle of Living*; Toews, *JB*; Auernheimer, *Memories of a Farm Boy*; Hofer, *Accepting the Challenge*.

70. Froese, " 'Where the People Tell no Lies,' " 1—3.

71. Enns-Rempel, "A New Life in the West," 12.

Chapter 3. Urban Dystopia and Divine Nature

1. John Ratzlaff, correspondence, *Zionsbote*, July 3, 1895.

2. G. G. and Marg. Wiens, correspondence, *Zionsbote*, May 3, 1905.

3. Goodykoontz, *Home Missions*, 36.

4. E. C. and L. A. Weaver, correspondence, *Gospel Witness*, Jan. 1, 1908, Dinuba; L. A. Weaver, correspondence, "Wahtoke, Calif," *GH*, July 18, 1908.

5. E. C. Weaver and L. A. Weaver, correspondence, *GH*, Dec. 23, 1909, Dinuba.

6. L. A. Weaver, correspondence, *GH*, Aug. 22, 1908; E. C. Weaver and L. A. Weaver, correspondence, *GH*, Oct. 31, 1908, and Feb. 20, 1909.

7. L. A. Weaver, correspondence, *GH*, July 22, 1909, Dinuba.

8. Emanuel Stahly, correspondence, *GH*, Sept. 5, 1908, Corning.

9. B. P. Swartzendruber, field notes, *GH*, Sept. 5, 1908; M. A., correspondence, *GH*,

Sept. 12, 1908, Upland; John D. Leatherman, Untitled [History of Mennonite Church in Southern California], p. 2, II-15-8 SWMC History Committee, Southwest MC History, MCA-G.

10. Mary Schrock, correspondence, GH, Jan. 23, 1909, Corning.

11. "The Heathen Invasion of America," GH, June 3, 1909.

12. Elmer T. Isgrigg, correspondence, GH, June 10, 1909, Dinuba.

13. Elmer T. Isgrigg, correspondence, GH, Jan. 20, 1910, Dinuba; E. C. and L. A. Weaver, correspondence, GH, Oct. 20, 1910, Dinuba; W. H. Benner, correspondence, GH, July 27, 1911, Dinuba.

14. Orva Kilmer, correspondence, GH, May 26, 1910, Portersville.

15. Orva Kilmer, correspondence, GH, March 3, 1910, Portersville.

16. J. R. Miller, correspondence, GH, Oct. 24, 1912; Dec. 19, 1912; June 19, 1913; Oct. 1, 1914, Portersville.

17. Mollie Hartzler, correspondence, GH, May 10, 1917, Terra Bella.

18. John and Maria Braun, correspondence, Zionsbote, Feb. 18, 1914, Lodi.

19. Tjne Friesen, correspondence, Zionsbote, Jan. 17, 1912, East Bakersfield; B. H. Nikkel, Church Reporter [Schreiber der Gemeinde], Zionsbote, correspondence, Nov. 5, 1913, East Bakersfield.

20. Cornelius and Maria Fiedler, correspondence, Zionsbote, April 24, 1912, Atwater.

21. Dueck, "Images of the City," 179–97.

22. For an example of the connection between moralism and labor issues, see Anderson, "'A True Revival of Religion,'" 25–49. For Progressive Era Protestantism in the Bay Area, see Anderson, "Through Fire and Fair."

23. There was a Mennonite bishop named M. S. Steiner in Ohio who lived from 1866 to 1911; this may be him. Harold S. Bender and Beulah Stauffer Hostetler, "Mennonite Church (MC)," GAMEO, 1989, www.gameo.org/encyclopedia/contents/M46610ME.html.

24. M. S. Steiner, "The Naked Truth as to San Francisco," Gospel Witness, May 16, 1906.

25. Ibid. This attitude was not peculiar to the Mennonites. See, for example, the reflection by a Methodist author at mid-century on the treatment of Chinese workers in late nineteenth-century California society: Loofbourow, In Search of God's Gold, 203–207. There is much scholarly work on Chinese experiences in turn-of-the-century California. See, for example, Saxton, The Indispensable Enemy; Chan, This Bitter-Sweet Soil; Yung, Unbound Feet; and Woo, "Protestant Work."

26. M. S. Steiner, "The Naked Truth as to San Francisco."

27. Ibid.

28. Advocate of Peace, "A Lesson of the Earthquake," TMenn, May 10, 1906; George R. Scott, "Saloons Banished from San Francisco," TMenn, May 24, 1906.

29. "Items and Comments," GH, May 23, 1908.

30. "Pacific Coast has Floods," "Items of the Week," TMenn, March 7, 1911; "Items and Comments," GH, Jan. 2, 1909; "Items and Comments," GH, Jan. 9, 1909.

31. Aldus Brackbill, "From S. California," GH, March 25, 1915. The Bible verses referenced read in part "[2:3] The chariots are enveloped in flashing steel / . . . / [2:4] The chariots race madly in the streets, / They rush wildly in the squares, / Their appearance is like torches, / They dash to and fro like lightning flashes" (NASB).

32. Dueck, "Images of the City," 187.

33. Brackbill, "From S. California."

34. C. U. Widmer, correspondence, TMenn, March 7, 1912, Reedley.

35. RH, Feb. 1913 to April 1914, passim.

36. Krehbiel, *A Trip Through Europe*, quotes from, 29–30, 23–24, 34–35, 51–52.

37. Ibid., quotes from, 55–56, 65–67.

38. Ibid., 85–88; Sir Walter Scott, "Patriotism," lines 1–6, in Arthur Quiller-Couch, ed., *The Oxford Book of English Verse: 1250–1900*, 1919, www.bartleby.com/101/547.html; John Howard Payne, "Home, Sweet Home," lines 3–4, in Thomas R. Lounsbury, ed., *Yale Book of American Verse*, 1912, www.bartleby.com/102/14.html.

39. A. R. Kurtz, correspondence, Nov. 3, 1910, and Feb. 2, 1911, GH, Los Angeles.

40. R. A. Torrey, "The Menace of the Movies," GH, Dec. 9, 1920, 734; A. R. Kurtz, "Earthquakes in Los Angeles," GH, Sept. 2, 1920, 443.

41. "Items and Comments," GH, March 16, 1933.

42. A. R. Kurtz, correspondence, July 24, 1924, GH, Los Angeles.

43. Aldus Brackbill, "From Southern California," GH, April 1, 1915; A. R. Kurtz, correspondence, July 24, 1924, GH, Los Angeles.

44. D. H. Bender, "Our Pacific Coast Missions," GH, Sept. 20, 1923, 515.

45. A. R. Kurtz, correspondence, GH, Dec. 30, 1909, El Centro; I. A. Sommer, correspondence, *TMenn*, June 10, 1920, Reedley. The General Conference Mennonites, though noting the absence of Sunday laws, did not apologize.

46. A. D. Rosenberger, correspondence, GH, Feb. 20, 1909, Montrose; J. L. Charles, correspondence, GH, April 29, 1909, Upland; Elmer T. Isgrigg, correspondence, GH, Aug. 4, 1909, Dinuba; Odessa Kilmer and Orva Kilmer, correspondence, GH, Oct. 7, 1909, Portersville; Luke E. and Mary Weaver, correspondence, GH, April 10, 1930, Winton.

47. John D. Leatherman, Untitled [History of Mennonite Church in Southern California], p. 1; and Dyck, *An Introduction to Mennonite History*, 220.

48. David Garber, "An Open Letter," *Gospel Witness*, June 7, 1905, Hesperia.

49. Ibid.

50. Ibid.

51. "California Mennonites on a Picnic," *Mennonite Yearbook and Almanac 1905*, 39.

52. Upland correspondent, correspondence, *TMenn*, Feb. 25, 1904.

53. *TMenn*, 1904–1936, passim.

54. Correspondent, correspondence, *TMenn*, Jan. 14, 1904; Jno. C. Mehl, correspondence, *TMenn*, April 30, 1908, Upland.

55. Sara C. Sprunger, correspondence, *TMenn*, Jan. 26, 1905, Cucamonga.

56. *TMenn*, correspondence, 1904–1936, passim. Specific examples include D. T. Eymann, March 10, 1904; May 13, 1909; M. J. W., April 9, 1914.

57. J. J. Wiens, correspondence, *Zionsbote*, Nov. 25, 1908; A. C. Neufeld, correspondence, *Zionsbote*, Dec. 23, 1908, and May 5, 1909.

58. Johann Ripkau, correspondence, *Zionsbote*, Nov. 1, 1911, Lodi; Ludwig Seibel, correspondence, *Zionsbote*, Dec. 2, 1914, Lodi; Jacob and Christina Knoll, correspondence, *Zionsbote*, Jan. 21, 1914, Lodi; F. J. Becker, correspondence, *Zionsbote*, April 10, 1912, El Modena.

59. Mrs. Jacob Shetler, correspondence, GH, July 30, 1936, Pasadena; Upland correspondent, correspondence, GH, May 7, 1936.

60. Mrs. Jacob Shetler, correspondence, GH, July 30, 1936, Pasadena.

61. McWilliams, *Southern California*, 98.

62. Enns-Rempel, "The Mennonite Sanitarium," 1.

63. No author, *TMenn*, Sept. 1898.

64. A. D. Rosenberger, correspondence, GH, Feb. 20, 1909, Montrose.

65. Peter and Maria Wall, correspondence, *Zionsbote*, Oct. 1, 1902, Azusa.

66. Enns-Rempel, "The Mennonite Sanitarium," 2, 7–8; Melvin Gingerich, "Menno-

nite Sanitarium (GCM)," *ME Supplement*, 1108; *The Mennonite Sanitarium*, promotional material, n.d., 3. vertical file, Mennonite Sanitarium, Alta Loma, CA, MCA-N.

67. Enns-Rempel, "The Mennonite Sanitarium," 9–10; Pannabecker, *Open Doors*, 249–50; Kaufman, *Development of the Missionary*, 120; A. S. Shelly, "Our Tuberculosis Sanatorium in Southern California," *Mennonite Yearbook and Almanac 1920*, 37.

68. Shelly, "Our Tuberculosis Sanatorium in Southern California," 35–36.

69. Ibid., 37; "Mennonite Sanatorium," promotional material, n.d., 1, 3, 7; *The Mennonite Sanitarium*, promotional material, n.d., 1, 3, 5, 9, vertical file, Mennonite Sanitarium, Alta Loma, CA, MCA-N.

70. D. J. Dahlem, Secretary, "A Triennial Report of the Sanitarium Committee," *Minutes, Reports and Papers of the Twenty-Second Session of the General Conference of the Mennonites of North America, Aug. 29–Sept. 5, 1920*, 96. The sanitarium reports from 1920 and 1923 are reprinted in Krehbiel, *The History of the General Conference*, 257–71.

71. John Hygema, letter, *Herald of Truth* (12 March 1908), 86. See also Enns-Rempel, "California in their Own Words," 7–8.

72. Enns-Rempel, "The Mennonite Sanitarium," 1–2, 7–10.

73. John Hygema, correspondence, GH, April 18, 1908, Chico.

74. John Hygema, correspondence, GH, June 13, 1908, Chico; "Minister Passes Away," GH, July 4, 1908, 216.

75. "Biographical Sketches, Rev. John S. Hirschler," *Mennonite Yearbook and Almanac 1916*, 31; "Rev. Michael Horsch," *Mennonite Yearbook, 1942*, 32–33; "Rev. H. A. Bachman," *Mennonite Yearbook and Almanac, 1921*, 22; Kaufman, *General Conference Mennonite Pioneers*, 227. The nature of the illnesses these men had was not given.

76. Dueck, "Images of the City," 192. Dueck calls this a "puzzle."

77. May, *Screening Out the Past*, 3–21.

78. Smith, "Religion and Ethnicity in America," 1174–76.

Chapter 4. Outsiders from Within

1. Otto Reimer, appended note, Oct. 31, 1979, CB525 Reedley MB Church Records, box 1, Charter 1905 file, CMBS-F. The charter was written on a piece of torn, lined notepaper, complete with jagged edges and unlabeled calculations on the back.

2. Perhaps the most accessible entry into California society and its ethos is Kevin Starr's multivolume series on California history. In particular, see *Endangered Dreams, The Dream Endures, Embattled Dreams*, and *Golden Dreams*. See also Dochuk, *From Bible Belt to Sunbelt*, and McGirr, *Suburban Warriors*.

3. Wacker, *Heaven Below*, is an excellent introduction to American Pentecostalism, a charismatic form of conservative Protestantism often accompanied with such signs of faith as "speaking in tongues" and healing.

4. Dispensationalism argues that in the last days, Christians will be raptured before seven years of tribulation, after which Christ will return, establishing a millennium of peace. Central to dispensationalism is the idea that all history is divided into seven dispensations of time, each governed by a particular covenant with God, and that the global tribulation followed by a millennium with Jesus as King is the final dispensation. See Marsden, *Fundamentalism and American Culture*, chapters 4–7; and Boyer, *When Time Shall Be No More*, chapters 1–3.

5. Blumhofer, *Aimee Semple McPherson*; Wacker, *Heaven Below*; Sutton, *Aimee Semple McPherson*.

6. Reimer, "The Story of the Mennonite Brethren," paragraphs 28–29.

7. Ibid.

8. Ibid., paragraphs 24−26; Toews, A History of the Mennonite Brethren Church, 146.

9. Minutes, "Meetings Between BORAC and the Reedley and South Reedley Mennonite Brethren Congregations," passim, A220 Board of Reference and Council Records, box 1, Minutes (translation) 1928 file, CMBS-F.

10. Reimer, The Story of the Mennonite Brethren, paragraphs 32−35.

11. Minutes, congregational meetings, March 30, April 6, June 11, Oct. 31, and Dec. 28, 1922, CB516 Vinewood Community Church Records (Lodi, CA), box 1, Congregational Meetings: 1915−1925, trans., file, CMBS-F; and The History of Vinewood Community Church, 2.

12. H. F. Lehman to S. C. Yoder, Jan. 8, 1930, IV-7-1 Executive Office—Mennonite Board of Missions, Correspondence 1908−1945, Los Angeles Mission 1927−1930, MCA-G.

13. Ibid.

14. Minutes, Nov. 22, Dec. 6 and 28, 1946, congregational meeting, CB504 Rosedale Bible Church Records (Bakersfield, CA), box 1, Congregational Meetings (bound) Sept. 1944−Oct. 1953 file, CMBS-F.

15. Goertzen, Bethany Church, 5, 12−13; Janzen, "Jacob D. Hofer," 7. For additional evidence of Hofer's and Goossen's involvement with Pentecostalism, see minutes, Dec. 3, 1946−Oct. 29, 1947, passim, CB220 Board of Reference and Council Records, box 1, series 1, Minutes/Reports 1946−1949, CMBS-F.

16. Goertzen, Bethany Church, 14−16.

17. Ibid., 16−17.

18. Ibid., 17. This apparently refers to bringing outsiders into the church building, not membership. No specific individuals or groups were named.

19. No examples of "obscure" references or "psychological" worldview are given.

20. Goertzen, Bethany Church, 18−19. These charges are also found in "Report of the Church Council on the Ministerial Aspect and Development of the Church," The Ministry of Brother H. G. Wiens, CB510 Bethany MB Church Records (Fresno, CA), box 9, H. G. Wiens Resignation 1949−1950 file, CMBS-F. These documents are not dated, but their placement in this file and their content indicate that they likely date to these events.

21. Minutes, Church Council, Dec. 6, 1949, and Feb. 13, 1950, CB510 Bethany MB Church Records (Fresno, CA), box 2, Church Council 1949 and Church Council 1950 files, CMBS-F.

22. Goertzen, Bethany Church, 19−20, 23; "A Brief Report of the Committee of Reference and Counsel of the Pacific District Submitted to the Church Council of the Bethany Mennonite Brethren Church of Fresno, California," CB510 Bethany MB Church Records (Fresno, CA), box 9, H. G. Wiens Resignation 1949−1950 file, CMBS-F.

23. Goertzen, Bethany Church, 23.

24. Minutes, Church Council, Sept. 20, 1961, CB510 Bethany MB Church Records (Fresno, CA), box 2, Council 1961−1963; minutes, Sept. 7, 1961, CB510 Bethany MB Church Records (Fresno, CA), box 1, Congregational Mtgs 1953−1961 file, CMBS-F.

25. Minutes, Church Council, Sept. 25, 1962, CB510 Bethany MB Church Records (Fresno, CA), box 2, Council 1961−1963, CMBS-F.

26. Report by Mr. & Mrs. Ben Giesbrecht, Church Council, Oct. 8, 1962, pp. 136−37, quote from p. 137, CB510 Bethany MB Church Records (Fresno, CA), box 2, Council 1961−1963, CMBS-F.

27. Ibid., 137−39.

28. Ibid., 140−42.

29. Ibid., 140–43. Quote from p. 143.

30. Ibid., 144.

31. Ibid., 144–45.

32. Ibid., Oct. 9, 1962, 149–50, 153. Quote from p. 160.

33. Ibid., 171–80. Quote from 179.

34. Minutes, Church Council, Nov. 1, 1962, p. 188–89; Jan. 31, 1963, p. 214; Feb. 6, 1963, CB510 Bethany MB Church Records (Fresno, CA), box 1, Congregational Meetings 1961–1963 file, CMBS-F; Toews, A History of the Mennonite Brethren Church, 274.

35. Toews, "Fundamentalist Conflict," 256.

36. Charter members, CB506 College Community Church: MB Records (Clovis, CA) Records, box 4, Membership & Attendance Statistics 1963–1976 file, CMBS-F. Beyond Fresno, charter members came from Rosedale and Reedley—two each.

37. Minutes, Oct. 14, Dec. 2, 1962; Jan. 25, Feb. 24, and March 25, 1963, CB506 College Community Church: MB Records (Clovis, CA), box 1, Church Council/Coordinating Council/Church Meetings 1962–1965 file, CMBS-F.

38. Joel and Lucille Wiebe, correspondence, n.d., and Werner Kroeker, correspondence, n.d., CB506 College Community Church: MB Records (Clovis, CA), box 4, Tenth Anniversary 1973 file; Untitled document [Jan. 1963], CB506 College Community Church: MB Records (Clovis, CA), box 4, Documents re: Early Events, 1963–1966, CMBS-F.

39. Minutes, Sept. 12, 1963, CB506 College Community Church: MB Records (Clovis, CA), box 1, Church Council/Coordinating Council/Church Meetings 1962–1965 file, CMBS-F.

40. "Church Organization," Minutes, Jan. 9, 1964, CB506 College Community Church: MB Records (Clovis, CA), box 1, Church Council/Coordinating Council/Church Meetings 1962–1965 file, CMBS-F.

41. Minutes, Church Council, June 11 and July 8, 1954, CB 525 Reedley MB Church Records, box 3, Church Council 1953–1954 file, CMBS-F.

42. Minutes, Church Council, Aug. 19, 1954, CB 525 Reedley MB Church Records, box 3, Church Council 1953–1954 file, CMBS-F. This is the only complaint I found against the manuscript from California.

43. "Who Are the Mennonites?" Herald of the First Mennonite Church of Upland, May 10, 1937; "The Pastor's Chat," Herald of the First Mennonite Church of Upland, May 10, 1937, 2, Upland, California, First Mennonite Church (Unprocessed), "The Herald" Newsletter of Upland, CA First Mennonite Church, 1937–44, 45 file, MCA-N.

44. "Who Are the Mennonites?"; "The Pastor's Chat."

45. "Who Are the Mennonites?"; "The Pastor's Chat"; "We Are Proud," editorial, Herald of the First Mennonite Church of Upland, Aug. 1, 1937, 1, Upland, California, First Mennonite Church (Unprocessed), "The Herald" Newsletter of Upland, CA First Mennonite Church, 1937–44, 45 file, MCA-N.

46. "The Mennonites: Principles and Teachings," Directory 1939 First Mennonite Church of Upland, p. 3, vertical file, First Mennonite Church (Upland, CA), MCA-N.

47. "The Pastor's Chat," Herald of the First Mennonite Church of Upland, Nov. 12, 1937, 3; "Ham and Eggs," and "The Fellowship," editorial, Herald of the First Mennonite Church of Upland, Nov. 18, 1938, 1; "The Pastor's Chat," Herald of the First Mennonite Church of Upland, Nov. 18, 1938, 2; "Politics and War," and "In November," editorial, 1, and "The Pastor's Chat," 2, Herald of the First Mennonite Church of Upland, Aug. 10, 1940, Upland, California, First Mennonite Church (Unprocessed), "The Herald" Newsletter of Upland, CA First Mennonite Church, 1937–44, 45 rile, MCA-N. See also Dochuk, From Bible Belt to Sunbelt, 88–92, and Starr, Endangered Dreams, chapter 7.

48. Ramon H. Jantz to Shafter High School, Jan. 17, 1957, and Jan. 18, 1958, Cong. Shafter [unprocessed], Correspondence, First Mennonite Church Shafter, MCA-N.

49. Minutes, special meeting, May 14, 1954, Bethel Mennonite Church, Winton, California, MLA.CONG.4a. Bethel Mennonite Church, Winton, CA, box 1, Council Minutes Book, MCA-N.

50. Orlando Schmidt, "A Brief History of the Mennonite Community Church Fresno, California," n.d.; G. F. Schmidt, "Early History of the Mennonite Community Church of Fresno," vertical file, Mennonite Community Church (Fresno, CA), MCA-N.

51. "Who Are the Mennonites?" A New Church in Your Community, promotional flyer, p. 2, MLA.CONG.85, Mennonite Community Church (Fresno, CA), box 3, Misc. file, MCA-N. See also Janzen, "Back to the City," 1–15.

52. "Who Are the Mennonites?"

53. Church bulletins, MLA.CONG.85, Mennonite Community Church (Fresno, CA), box 1, Bulletins 1953–56 and Bulletins 1960–1962, MCA-N.

54. Penner and Frantz, "Through the Years," 9–10. After difficulties during World War I concerning the use of German, they suspended its use, 21–22.

55. Warner, "Mennonite Brethren," 99–107.

56. Ibid.

57. All quotes ibid., 174, 197–99, 202; Warner, "Social Science," 17–23.

58. Minutes, church business meeting, Sept. 26, 1956, CB503 Heritage Bible Church Records (Bakersfield, CA), box 1, Congregational Meetings Sept. 1956–1959, CMBS-F.

59. "Rosedale M. B. Church Code for Weddings," CB504 Rosedale Bible Church Records (Bakersfield, CA), box 2, Miscellaneous file, CMBS-F. See similar regulations at Shafter Mennonite Brethren, with additional bans on weddings in dark rooms illuminated by candles and on humorous receptions. "Regulations to be Observed During Wedding Ceremonies," [approx. 1949, based on placement in file], undated document, CB530 Shafter MB Church Records, box 2, Church Council Minutes, 1940–1949, file, CMBS-F. Issues in Shafter included hair bobbing in the 1930s, weddings in the 1940s, and alcohol in the 1950s. See CB530 Shafter MB Church Records, box 2, Church Council 1931–1959 files, passim, CMBS-F.

60. Minutes, Los Angeles Church and Mission, Aug. 7, 1926, III-5-2 Calvary Mennonite Church, Secretary Book, 1921–30, MCA-G.

61. H. E. Widmer, Bakersfield, California, to Brother Loucks, Dec. 22, 1922, IV-7-1 Executive Office—Mennonite Board of Missions, Correspondence 1908–1945 Los Angeles Mission 1921–1924, MCA-G.

62. Ibid.

63. Ibid; John C. Wenger and Robert S. Kreider, "Dress," GAMEO, 1989, www.gameo .org/index.php?title=Dress&oldid=113327.

64. [S. C. Yoder] Secretary, Mennonite Board of Missions and Charities, to J. P. Bontrager, Jan. 24, 1923; J. B. Mishler, Secretary, Pacific Coast Mission Board, to S. C. Yoder, Secretary, Mennonite Board of Missions and Charities Kalena, Iowa, Jan. 31, 1923; Anonymous to D. D. Miller, Middlebury, Indiana, Jan. 24, 1923; [S. C. Yoder] Secretary, Mennonite Board of Missions and Charities, to Edward Yoder, Hubbard, Oregon, Jan. 24, 1923; Anonymous to J. B. Mishler, March 12, 1923; [S. C. Yoder] Secretary, Mennonite Board of Missions and Charities, to J. P. Bontrager, March 12, 1923; D. H. Bender, President, Hesston College and Bible School, to S. C. Yoder, Secretary, Mennonite Board of Missions and Charities Kalona, Iowa, Nov. 5, 1923, IV-7-1 Executive Office—Mennonite Board of Missions, Correspondence 1908–1945 Los Angeles Mission 1921–1924, MCA-G.

65. J. L. Rutt, Secretary, Local Mission Board of Los Angeles, to "Brother," Dec. 25, 1923; H. R. Schertz, Treasurer, Metamora, Illinois, Mennonite Board of Missions and Charities, to Brother Yoder, Jan. 6, 1924; D. H. Bender, President, Hesston College and Bible School, to S. C. Yoder, Secretary, Mennonite Board of Missions and Charities Kalona, Iowa, Jan. 10, 1924, IV-7-1 Executive Office—Mennonite Board of Missions, Correspondence 1908–1945 Los Angeles Mission 1921–1924, MCA-G.

66. J. L. Rutt to "Brother" [likely D. H. Bender], Jan. 14, 1924, IV-7-1 Executive Office—Mennonite Board of Missions, Correspondence 1908–1945 Los Angeles Mission 1921–1924, MCA-G.

67. D. H. Bender, President, Hesston College and Bible School, to S. C. Yoder, Kalona, Iowa, Jan. 28, 1924, IV-7-1 Executive Office—Mennonite Board of Missions, Correspondence 1908–1945 Los Angeles Mission 1921–1924, MCA-G.

68. S. C. Yoder to Chris Snyder, Aurora, Oregon, Oct. 30, 1925; D. H. Bender to S. C. Yoder, Goshen College, Jan. 11, 1926; J. P. Bontrager to "Brethren," Jan. 29, 1926; D. H. Bender to S. C. Yoder, Feb. 8, 1926; and J. J. Reber et al., Los Angeles congregation, to Mennonite Board of Missions and Charities, Aug. 25, 1926, IV-7-1 Executive Office—Mennonite Board of Missions, Correspondence 1908–1945 Los Angeles Mission 1925–1926, MCA-G.

69. For a detailed account see Leichty, " 'Not Going to be a Kicker,' " 3.

70. Minutes, Los Angeles Church and Mission, Jan. 1, 1927, III-5-2 Calvary Mennonite Church, Secretary Book, 1921–30, MCA-G.

71. S. C. Yoder, Secretary, Mennonite Board of Missions and Charities, to Fred Gingerich [Yoder's Cousin], Jan. 7, 1927; [Fred Gingerich] to Sanford [Yoder's Cousin], Jan. 13, 1927; S. C. Yoder, Secretary, to Executive Committees of Mennonite Board of Missions and Charities and Pacific Coast Conference, and Statement of Proposition, Feb. 24, 1927; A. J. Steiner to S. C. Yoder, Goshen, Indiana, Jan. 27, 1930, IV-7-1 Executive Office—Mennonite Board of Missions, Correspondence 1908–1945 Los Angeles Mission 1927–1930, MCA-G.

72. Jacob K. Bixler, Elkhart, Indiana [visited Los Angeles for six months then wrote these letters], to S. C. Yoder, June 15 and July 7, 1938, IV-7-1 Executive Office—Mennonite Board of Missions, Correspondence 1908–1945 Los Angeles Mission 1931–1942, MCA-G.

73. Ibid.

74. S. C. Yoder to C. I. Kroph, Hubbard, Oregon, Aug. 31, 1938, IV-7-1 Executive Office—Mennonite Board of Missions, Correspondence 1908–1945 Los Angeles Mission 1931–1942, MCA-G.

75. "Report of the Committee Appointed to Consider the Los Angeles Mission Problems," Aug. 27, 1929; S.C. Yoder, Secretary, to H. K. Stoner, Oakland, California, March 3, 1930; B. P. Swartzendruber to F. J. Gingerich, Sept. 9, 1930, IV-7-1 Executive Office—Mennonite Board of Missions, Correspondence 1908–1945 Los Angeles Mission 1931–1942, MCA-G.

76. Bixler to Yoder, June 15, 1938.

77. Glen Whitaker to S. C. Yoder, Nov. 19, 1940, IV-7-1 Executive Office—Mennonite Board of Missions, Correspondence 1908–1945 Los Angeles Mission 1931–1942, MCA-G.

Chapter 5. New Neighbors

1. Klassen, *Resolutions of the Pacific District*, 136.

2. "Home Mission," minutes of the First Pacific District Conference of the Mennonite

Brethren Church, Oct. 14–15, 1912; "Report of the Home Mission Committee," Nov. 12, 1922, *Year Book of the Pacific District Conference of the Mennonite Brethren Church, November 11–14, 1922*, trans. J. C. Penner; Schmidt, "Continuity and Change," 138; Dochuk, *From Bible Belt to Sunbelt*, 82–83, 104.There is a sizable literature on race and religion in California. Some examples include the following essays in *Religion and Society in the American West*: Burns, "The Mexican-American Catholic," 255–73, and Almirol, "Church Life Among Filipinos," 299–316. Significant monographs include Matsumoto, *Farming the Home Place*; Gregory, *American Exodus*; Johnson, *The Second Gold Rush*; and Sánchez, *Becoming Mexican American*.

3. Esau, *First Sixty Years of M. B. Missions*, 15–16, 498–502, quote from pp. 499–500; A. W. Margaret and Kenneth Friesen, *Christian Leader*, July 1943, 1, 6; "City Terrace Mission Chapel," n.d., CB517 City Terrace MB Church Records (Los Angeles, CA), History of the City Terrace Mennonite Brethren Church, CMBS-F.

4. Dolan, *The American Catholic Experience*, 201.

5. "Report on Los Angeles City Mission," *Year Book of the General Conference of the Mennonite Brethren Church of North America*, Oct. 1933, trans. J. C. Penner; A. W. and Margaret Friesen, "City Terrace Mission," *Year Book of the 41st Pacific District Conference of the Mennonite Brethren Church of North America*, Oct. 28–Nov. 2, 1950, 24.

6. Esau, *First Sixty Years of M. B. Missions*, 500. No more detail than this. Minutes, joint mission board, Sept. 11, 1947, CB260 Board of Home Missions Records, box 1 [Minutes] 1940–1949 file, CMBS-F; "Our History," California Released Time Bible Education, http://www.careleasedtime.org/Our-History.html.

7. Minutes, Board for Home Missions of the Pacific District of the Mennonite Brethren Church of North America, Oct. 24, 1947, CB260 Board of Home Missions Records, box 1 [Minutes] 1940–1949, CMBS-F.

8. Wesley Gunther, pastor, "City Terrace Mission," *Year Book of the 43rd Pacific District Conference of the Mennonite Brethren Church of North America*, Nov. 15–19, 1952, 23; Wesley Gunther and Beverly Gunther, "City Terrace Mennonite Brethren Mission," *Year Book of the 45th Pacific District Conference of the Mennonite Brethren Church of North America*, Nov. 13–17, 1954, 19.

9. Marvin Friesen and Betty Friesen, "Testimonies of Workers," *Home Missions of the Pacific District Conference* (Joint Committee for Home Missions Pacific District Conference, July 31, 1949), 7. These Friesens were not the ones who started the mission in 1926. George Sanchez, "Sunset Gardens M. B. Church," *Year Book of the 46th Pacific District Conference of the Mennonite Brethren Church of North America*, Nov. 12–16, 1955, 22; Harry Neufeld, "Sunset Gardens M. B. Church," *Year Book of the 51st Pacific District Conference of the Mennonite Brethren Church of North America*, Oct. 29–31, 1960, 27.

10. Hart, *That Old-Time Religion*, 80–82.

11. A. W. Friesen and Margaret Friesen, "City Terrace Mission," *Yearbook of the 41st Pacific District Conference of the Mennonite Brethren Church of North America*, November 1950, 24–25.

12. Ibid., 25.

13. A. W. Friesen and Margaret Friesen, "City Terrace Mission," *Yearbook of the 42nd Pacific District Conference of the Mennonite Brethren Church of North America*, November 1951, 31–32.

14. Wesley Gunther and Beverly Gunther, "City Terrace Mennonite Brethren Church," *Yearbook of the 45th Pacific District Conference of the Mennonite Brethren Church of North America*, November 1954, 19–20.

15. Harold Schroeder, Pastor, City Terrace Mennonite Brethren Church, to Rev. Waldo Wiebe, June 18, 1956. CB260 Board of Home Missions Records, box 3, Correspondence 1956, CMBS-F.

16. Harold Schroeder, Pastor, to Rev. Wiebe, Chairman, M. B. Home Mission Board, Jan. 15, 1957, CB260 Board of Home Missions Records, box 3, Correspondence 1957, CMBS-F.

17. Enns-Rempel, "Making a Home in the City," 225–26; Dochuk, *From Bible Belt to Sunbelt*, 108–10, 172–73; Starr, *Embattled Dreams*, 97.

18. Dochuk, *From Bible Belt to Sunbelt*, 51–52, 293–95, 401; Starr, *The Dream Endures*, 176–77, 181.

19. Minutes, Los Angeles Church and Mission, July 24 and Sept. 25, 1921, III-5-2 Calvary Mennonite Church, Secretary Book, 1921–30, MCA-G. For River Brethren, see Dyck, *An Introduction to Mennonite History*, 313–14.

20. Los Angeles Mission, "From Our Mission Stations," GH, Aug. 7, 1930.

21. "From our Mission Stations," GH, Nov. 20, 1930, Los Angeles.

22. Ibid.; "From Our Mission Stations," GH, Jan. 15, 1931, Los Angeles; F. B. Showalter, "From Our Mission Stations," GH, Dec. 10, 1931, Los Angeles; "From Our Mission Stations," GH, Jan. 12, 1933, Los Angeles.

23. "From Our Mission Stations," GH, Jan. 12, 1933, Los Angeles.

24. "From Our Mission Stations," GH, Dec. 8, 1932, Los Angeles.

25. Le Roy Bechler, "History of Colored Evangelism in the Mennonite Church," 1950, 35–36, Hist. Mss. 1-723, Le Roy Bechler Collection, MCA-G; Schlabach, *Gospel Versus Gospel*, 244.

26. Bechler, *The Black Mennonite Church*, 110.

27. Minutes, South Pacific Mennonite District Mission Board, Nov. 6, 1948, II-15-4 SWMC—Mission Board, Minutes 1948–60, MCA-G; and Bechler, "History of Colored Evangelism in the Mennonite Church," 35–36.

28. Minutes, Second Annual Session of the South Pacific Mennonite Conference, Nov. 24, 1950, p. 3, II-15-1 Southwest Mennonite Conference (SWMC) box 1, Minutes 1949–70, MCA-G.

29. Kauffman, *A Vision and a Legacy*, 3.

30. Ibid., 31–32.

31. Ibid., 119–20, quote from 52.

32. John D. Zehr, Pastor, Calvary Mennonite Church, to Jake Shetler, President, South Pacific Mennonite District Mission Board, June 22, 1956, II-15-4 SWMC—Mission Board, Corr. Pres.: Jacob Shetler 1955–60, MCA-G; John D. Zehr, Acting Secretary, South Pacific District Mission Board and Pastor Calvary Mennonite Church, to Nelson Kauffman, Secretary for Home Missions, Hannibal, Missouri, Dec. 6, 1955, IX-54 MCC-WCO, Corr. Secretary: Ezra Kennel 1955–67, MCA-G; Jacob Shetler, President, South Pacific Mennonite District Mission Board, to Nelson Kauffman, Secretary for Home Missions, July 26, 1956, II-15-4 SWMC—Mission Board, Corr. Pres.: Shetler 1956–60 Nelson Kaufman Outgoing, MCA-G.

33. John David Zehr, "Building a Church Community in the City," *Mennonite Community* (Feb. 1953): 18.

34. Ibid., 19–20.

35. Jacob Shetler, President, South Pacific Mennonite District Mission Board, to Nelson Kauffman, Secretary for Home Missions, Aug. 10 and Sept. 7, 1956, II-15-4 SWMC—Mission Board Collection, Corr. Pres.: Shetler 1956–60 Nelson Kaufman Outgoing, MCA-G.

36. No author, "Activities Report," from L. A. Spanish Mission to Mennonite Board of Missions and Charities, Oct. 1956; Bernhard Kroeker, "Activities Report," from L. A. Spanish Mission to Mennonite Board of Missions and Charities, May 1957; Bernhard Kroeker, "Ac-

tivities Report," from L. A. Spanish Mission to Mennonite Board of Missions and Charities, June 1958, II-15-19 Southwest Mennonite Conference—Congregations, LA Spanish Mission Activities Reports 1956—60, MCA-G.

37. Noreen and James Roth, "Activities Report," from Montebello Spanish Mission to Mennonite Board of Missions and Charities, Nov. 1958; Richard Fahndrich, "Activities Report," from Pico Rivera Spanish Mission to Mennonite Board of Missions and Charities, Nov. 8, 1959; Richard Fahndrich, "Activities Report," from Pico Rivera Spanish Mission to Mennonite Board of Missions and Charities, Jan. 1960, II-15-19 Southwest Mennonite Conference—Congregations, LA Spanish Mission Activities Reports 1956—60, MCA-G.

38. Jacob Shetler, "Work Among Latins to Open in Los Angeles Area Soon," *South West Messenger* 5, no. 1 (Sept. 1956): 1—2; Jacob Shetler, "A Blood Transfusion Needed," *South West Messenger* 2, no. 3 (May 1957): 1; minutes, South Pacific District Mission Board, Nov. 26, 1955, II-15-4 SWMC—Mission Board, Minutes 1948—60, MCA-G.

39. James and Noreen Roth, "Report of the Pico Rivera Spanish Mission in Los Angeles, California," II-13-3 Pacific Coast Conference, box 3, Mission Board Reports 1959, MCA-G.

40. Douglas D. H. Kaufman, "We've Come This Far By Faith," GH, Jan. 7, 1992, 6—7; Le Roy Bechler, "An Accurate Picture of Calvary Mennonite Church," Dec. 1, 1976, 2; Le Roy Bechler, "Calvary Mennonite Church in a Changing Community," May 15, 1978, 1—3 III-5-2 Calvary Mennonite Church, Papers, MCA-G; Le Roy Bechler, "A Statistical History of Blacks in the Mennonite Church 1898—1980," 1981, p. 70, Hist. Mss. 1-723, Le Roy Bechler Collection, MCA-G; Erb, *Studies in Mennonite City Missions*, 132—34.

41. Nelson Kauffman to Ernest Bennett, Memorandum, July 20, 1960; Nelson Kauffman to South Pacific District Mission Board Executive Committee, Sherman Maust Bishop, Calvary Mennonite and Upland Mennonite Church, Memorandum, July 20, 1960; D. J. Mishler, Personnel Secretary, Mennonite Board of Missions and Charities, Elkhart, Indiana, to Jacob Shetler, Ontario, California, Aug. 15, 1960, II-15-19 Southwest Mennonite Conferences—Congregations, Calvary Mennonite Church: Corr. 1955—64, MCA-G.

42. Jacob Shetler to Board Members of the South Pacific District Mission Board, July 30, 1969, II-15-3.6 SWMC Secretary 1950, 54, 1959—85 Collection, box 2, Conference 1960, MCA-G; Bechler, "History of Colored Evangelism in the Mennonite Church," 35—36; Le Roy Bechler and Irene Bechler, "Report of Trip to Los Angeles, Calif.," Sept. 14—18 [1960], II-15-19 Southwest Mennonite Conferences—Congregations, Calvary Mennonite Church Data, MCA-G.

43. Bechler, *The Black Mennonite Church*, 111—14; Wright, "Mennonites in Southern California," 9.

44. Hertzler, *From Germantown to Steinbach*, 123.

45. James H. Lark, "For the Record," minutes of special business meeting, Dec. 26, 1960, Church Bulletin, Jan. 1, 1961, III-5-2 Calvary Mennonite Church, Bulletins 1961, MCA-G.

46. Jacob Shetler, President, South Pacific Mennonite District Mission Board, to Lester Hershey, Director of Spanish Broadcasts in Ribonito, Puerto Rico, Aug. 19, 1960, II-15-4 SWMC—Mission Board, Corr. Pres.: Shetler 1956—60 Luz y Verdad, MCA-G.

47. Kaufman, "We've Come This Far By Faith," 6—7; Bechler, "An Accurate Picture of Calvary Mennonite Church," and "Calvary Mennonite Church in a Changing Community"; Erb, *Studies in Mennonite City Missions*, 132—34.

48. "Report of the Board of Home Missions," *TMenn Supplement*, Jan. 18, 1912, 45—49; Jacob J. Balzer, Secretary, "Report of the Board of Home Missions," *TMenn Supplement*, April 22, 1915, 51—52.

49. Balzer, "Report of the Board of Home Missions," 52.

50. Anna G. Stauffer, "The Whosoever-Will Mission Los Angeles, California," *Mennonite Year Book and Almanac, 1920*, 31; A. J. Richert, "Immanuel Mennonite Church Los Angeles, California," *Mennonite Year Book, 1935*, 31.

51. "River Station Mission 1909–1914," *Sketch Book*, 2, CB553 Living Hope Church Records (Downey, CA), box 5, "Sketch Book" [1] file, CMBS-F.

52. Church Record Book, Jan. to March 1923, CB553 Living Hope Church Records (Downey, CA), box 1, Church Record Book 1914–1924, CMBS-F.

53. Church Record Book, April 1923, CB553 Living Hope Church Records (Downey, CA), box 1, Church Record Book 1914–1924, CMBS-F. Italian Catholics had a "sizeable presence" in the Pacific coastal region; Dolan, *The American Catholic Experience*, 138.

54. Albert Claassen, mission superintendent, to Members and Friends of the Mennonite Mission Church, Los Angeles, Church Record Book [May 1923], CB553 Living Hope Church Records (Downey, CA), box 1, Church Record Book 1914–1924, CMBS-F.

55. E. F. Grubb, "Sketch and History of the Mennonite City Mission of Los Angeles, Cal.," *Mennonite Year Book and Almanac, 1914*, 22–23.

56. A. J. Richert, "Immanuel Mennonite Church Los Angeles, California," 31.

57. E. F. Grubb, "Sketch and History," 21.

58. Ibid.

59. Anonymous to Board of Home Missions, Nov. 26, 1950, and A. N. Neuenschwander, Board of Home Missions, to Rev. Alfred Regier, Pastor, Immanuel Mennonite Church, Dec. 20, 1950, CB553 Living Hope Church Records (Downey, CA), box 1, Church Council 1950–1952, CMBS-F; and "1951," *Sketch Book*, CB553 Living Hope Church Records (Downey, CA), box 5, "Sketch Book" [2] file, CMBS-F.

60. Minutes, executive session, Pacific District Conference [General Conference Mennonites], June 10–14, 1959, MLA.II.5.j Pacific District Conference File, Pacific District Conference Executive Committee 1949–66, MCA-N.

61. Ibid.

62. Elmer Ediger, "Migrant Work" ME, vol. 3, 684.

63. Minutes, South Pacific Mission Board, March 15, 1953. II-15-4 SWMC–Mission Board, Minutes 1948–60, MCA-G; Hasegawa, "The Story of Hispanic Ministries," 247–48.

64. Arthur Jost, West Coast MCC Area Administrator, Reedley, California, to Ray Horst, J. N. Byler, and Wm. T. Snyder, MCC, Akron, Pennsylvania, Jan. 7, 1950, MCC-WCO, box 2, MCC–West Coast: Correspondence Jan.–Feb. 1950–Arthur Jost, CMBS-F; Arlene Sitler, Administrative Assistant, MCC, to Ray Horst, Assistant Director, Voluntary Service Section, MCC, Akron, Pennsylvania, April 12, 1950, MCC-WCO, box 2, MCC–West Coast: Correspondence March–April 1950–Arthur Jost, CMBS-F.

65. Anderson, *Imagined Communities*, 149; Bhabha, *The Location of Culture*, 355–60.

66. Ray Horst, Assistant Director, Voluntary Service Section, MCC, Akron, Pennsylvania, to Arlene Sitler, Administrative Assistant, MCC, Aug. 16, 1950; Arlene Sitler to Ray Horst, Aug. 18, 1950, and Sept. 29, 1950, MCC-WCO, box 2, MCC–West Coast: Correspondence July–Aug. 1950–Arthur Jost and MCC–West Coast: Correspondence Sept.–Oct. 1950–Arthur Jost, CMBS-F.

67. Arthur Jost, Administrator West Coast Regional Office (MCC), to William Wiebe, Chairman, Home Mission Board, Reedley, California, Feb. 1, 1951, MCC-WCO, box 2, MCC–West Coast: Correspondence Jan. to March 1951–Arthur Jost, CMBS-F.

68. Arlene Sitler to Ray Horst, March 7, 1951, and Arlene Sitler to Mary Brown, Home

Mission Council of North America, Inc., Fresno, March 7, 1951, MCC-WCO, box 2, MCC–West Coast: Correspondence Jan. to March 1951–Arthur Jost, CMBS-F.

69. Arlene Sitler, MCC Administrative Assistant, west side of Fresno County, to Ray Horst and Orlo Kauffman, VS Section MCC, Akron, Pennsylvania, March 20, 1951, MCC-WCO, box 2, MCC–West Coast: Correspondence Jan. to March 1951–Arthur Jost, CMBS-F.

70. Arlene Sitler, Interim Director, West Fresno County Migrant Project (MCC), Feb. 2, 1951, "The Mennonite Central Committee's San Joaquin Valley Migrant Project," pp. 1, 5, 9, IX-54 MCC-WCO box 1, MCC Reedley 1951, MCA-G.

71. Carl Wolgemuth, unit leader, Migrant Ministry, Coalinga, California, to Gordon Dyck, MCC, Akron, Pennsylvania, Dec. 14, 1955, MCC-WCO, box 2, MCC–West Coast: Correspondence 1955–Arthur Jost, CMBS-F. See Dwight Wiebe, VS & 1-W Office to VS Advisory Committee, memorandum and attachment, Nov. 9, 1959, MCC-WCO, box 2, MCC–West Coast: Correspondence 1959–Arthur Jost, CMBS-F.

72. Arthur, "Night Life," *Migrant Messenger*, Atwater, California (Aug. 1950), 5; Susan Suderman, report, Aug. 9, 1950, and July 27, 1950; Susan Suderman to Art, July 10, 1950; Susan Suderman, report, June 25, 1950, IX-54 MCC-WCO, box 2, Migrant V. S. Unit 1950, MCA-G. This was a common vocabulary among mission-minded Protestants in the American West. See, for example, Walker, "Protestantism in the Sangre de Cristos," 67–89.

73. H. J., editorial, *Migratory Moments*, San Jose, California, 1, no. 5 (Aug. 16, 1951): 2, IX-54 MCC-WCO box 1, MCC Reedley 1951, MCA-G.

74. Arlene Sitler, Interim Director, West Fresno County Migrant Project (MCC), Feb. 2, 1951, "The Mennonite Central Committee's San Joaquin Valley Migrant Project," p. 5, IX-54 MCC-WCO box 1, MCC Reedley 1951, MCA-G.

75. Judy to Mother, July 1958, IX-54 MCC-WCO box 2, Migrant V. S. Unit 1957–58, MCA-G.

76. *California News of the California Migrant Unit*, Stanislaus County, Sept. 1952, Oct. 1952, and Aug. 1953, IX-54 MCC-WCO box 2, Migrant V. S. Unit 1953, MCA-G.

77. Arthur Jost, "Report of the West Coast Regional Office," Dec. 6, 1952, p. 1, IX-54 MCC-WCO, box 1, MCC Reedley 1952, MCA-G.

78. *Mennonite Central Committee West Coast Regional Newsletter*, July-Aug. 1954, 2; "The Migrant Ministry in the Labor Camps: A Report of the Mennonite Central Committee Migrant Ministry in the Coalinga-Huron Area," April 1955, pp. 1–2, Correspondence, MCC 1954, drawer, FMCA.

79. "Dinuba-Reedley Area Meeting," 1; Falcón, *The Hispanic Mennonite Church*, 195; Dahl, "A History of the Spanish Mennonite," 27–34.

80. Dahl, "A History of the Spanish Mennonite," 5, 8–9, 58, 68. For a counterpoint, see Martinez, "Hispanics," 47–56.

81. Bechler, *The Black Mennonite Church*, 75–76, 110–12.

Chapter 6. From Sewing Circles to Missionary Societies

1. Rich, *Mennonite Women*; Goering, *Women in Search*; Unrau, *Encircled*.

2. Peters, "Women in the Christian Church," 157–58, 178; Redekop, *The Work of Their Hands*, 10; Rich, *Mennonite Women*, 202–203; Brereton, "United and Slighted," 146; Anderson, "Western Women," 101.

3. Braude, "Women's History *Is* American Religious History," 91–92, quote from p. 92; Brereton, "United and Slighted," 147. See also Lindley, *"You Have Stept out of Your Place."*

4. Rempel, "'She Hath Done What She Could'" (1995), 150−51, "Early Missionary Society," 39, and "'She Hath Done What She Could'" (1992), 24; "History from 1913" in *Diamond Jubilee 75 Years of Service,* p. 21, CB525 Reedley MB Church Records, box 5, Women's Missionary Service 1957−1970, 1985−1988, CMBS-F.

5. Rempel, "'She Hath Done What She Could'" (1995), 151, "Early Missionary Society Activity," 40, and "'She Hath Done What She Could'" (1992), 25. The story is retold in two anniversary publications of the Reedley MB Church. See *50th Jubilee,* 1905−1955, 46−49, and *The Church Alive,* 105−107.

6. "History from 1913" in *Diamond Jubilee 75 Years of Service,* 20.

7. Ibid.; Thirlwall, "Mennonite Quilts," 14−15; Rempel, "'She Hath Done What She Could'" (1992), 27.

8. "History from 1913," in *Diamond Jubilee 75 Years of Service,* 20−21.

9. *50th Jubilee,* 1905−1955, 47.

10. *The Church Alive,* 105, 107. Italics mine.

11. *50th Jubilee,* 1905−1955, 48.

12. *The Church Alive,* 107.

13. Penner and Frantz, "Through the Years," 7; Rempel, "'She Hath Done What She Could'" (1992), 25−27. It was the convention of the time for these women to identify themselves by their husbands' names. Where their given name is clear, it is used here.

14. Penner and Frantz, "Through the Years," 7.

15. Braude, "Women's History Is American Religious History," 91−92.

16. "History of the Sewing Circle of the M. B. Church of Shafter," CB530 Shafter MB Church Records, microfilm reel 77, frames 1402, 1404, and 1441, CMBS-F. By April 1939, singing became a regular feature of meetings.

17. Minutes March 2, 1939, CB530 Shafter MB Church Records, microfilm reel 77, frame 1439, CMBS-F.

18. Ibid., frames 1436, 1439−40, CMBS-F.

19. Minutes May 11, 1939, and May 25, 1939, CB530 Shafter MB Church Records, microfilm reel 77, frames 1450−51, CMBS-F.

20. Minutes June 19, 1939 and August 10, 1939, CB530 Shafter MB Church Records, microfilm reel 77, frames 1452, 1454, CMBS-F.

21. Sept. 29, 1918, Church Record Book, p. 37, CB553 Living Hope Church Records (Downey, CA), box 1, Church Record Book 1914−1924, CMBS-F.

22. May 25, 1919, Church Record Book, p. 42, CB553 Living Hope Church Records (Downey, CA), box 1, Church Record Book 1914−1924, CMBS-F.

23. Jan. 15, 1922, Church Record Book, p. 76, CB553 Living Hope Church Records (Downey, CA), box 1, Church Record Book 1914−1924, CMBS-F.

24. "The Women's Missionary Society," 1942 *Annual Reports Immanuel Mennonite Church, Los Angeles, California,* Jan. 11, 1942, 9; "Women's Missionary Sewing Society," *Annual Reports of the Immanuel Mennonite Church, Los Angeles, California,* Jan. 12, 1946; Ira J. Stevanus, "Report of the Women's Missionary Society," *Annual Meeting Sunday, January 15, 1950 Reports for 1949, Immanuel Mennonite Church,* 9, CB553 Living Hope Church Records (Downey, CA), box 1, Congregational Meetings/Annual Reports, CMBS-F.

25. "The Women's Missionary Society," 1942 *Annual Reports,* p. 9; "Women's Missionary Sewing Society," *Annual Reports of the Immanuel Mennonite Church, Los Angeles, California for the Year 1942,* Jan. 10, 1943, p. 10; Marie Bush, "Women's Missionary Sewing Society," *Annual Reports of the Immanuel Mennonite Church, Los Angeles, California for the Year 1943,* Jan. 9, 1944, p. 9; "Women's Missionary Sewing Society," *Annual Reports of the Immanuel Mennonite Church,* 1946; Martha Kersting, "Report of the Women's Missionary

Society," *Annual Meeting Sunday, January 16, 1949, Reports for Year 1948, Immanuel Mennonite Church*, p. 9; Ira J. Stevanus, "Report of the Women's Missionary Society," p. 9, CB553 Living Hope Church Records (Downey, CA), box 1, Congregational Meetings/Annual Reports, CMBS-F.

26. Anna M. Snyder, "Service Not a Substitute for Spirituality," *Missionary Sewing Circle Monthly* 21, no. 6 (Dec. 1948), IV-20-3 WMSC Publications, Missionary Sewing Circle Monthly 1945–48, MCA-G.

27. Minutes, February 15, 1940; March 21, 1940; March 4, 1943; April 1, 1943; June 24; and July 8, 1943, CB510 Bethany MB Church Records (Fresno, CA), box 5, Sewing Circle 1940–1946, CMBS-F; and Goertzen, *Bethany Church*, 3.

28. Minutes, March 21, 1940; June 4, 1942; and December 16, 1943, CB510 Bethany MB Church Records (Fresno, CA), box 5, Sewing Circle 1940–1946, CMBS-F.

29. Minutes, January 25, 1944, CB508 Dinuba MB Church Records, microfilm reel 4, frame 4270, CMBS-F; minutes, March 7, 1944; May 15, 1944; and October 17, 1944, CB508 Dinuba MB Church Records, Microfilm reel 4, frames 4272, 4277, 4286, CMBS-F; Froese, "Sewing Peace," 1–5.

30. *50th Jubilee, 1905–1955,* 47.

31. *M. B. Mission Society Yearbook,* 1940, CB525 Reedley MB Church Records, box 5, Women's Missionary Society 1940–1947, CMBS-F.

32. *M. B. Mission Society Yearbook,* 1940–1941, and 1942–1943, CB525 Reedley MB Church Records, box 5, Women's Missionary Society 1940–1947, CMBS-F.

33. *M. B. Mission Society Yearbook,* 1942, 1942–1943, 1944–1945, CB525 Reedley MB Church Records, box 5, Women's Missionary Society 1940–1947, CMBS-F; *M. B. Mission Society Yearbook* 1951–1952, CB525 Reedley MB Church Records, box 5, Women's Missionary Society 1947–1957, CMBS-F; *M. B. Mission Society Yearbook* 1957–1958, CB525 Reedley MB Church Records, box 5, Women's Missionary Society 1957–1970, 1985–1988, CMBS-F; *Scrapbook 1940–1955*, CB525 Reedley MB Church Records, box 10, CMBS-F; and *Scrapbook 1965–1977*, CB525 Reedley MB Church Records, box 11, CMBS-F.

34. *Annual Church Report,* March 1, 1945, to October 11, 1945; October 25, 1945, to October 17, 1946; October 24, 1946, to October 2, 1947; October 16, 1947, to October 7, 1948; October 21, 1948, to October 20, 1949; and October 20, 1950, to October 5, 1950, CB530 Shafter MB Church Records, microfilm reel 77, frames 1406–11, CMBS-F.

35. *Annual Church Report,* October 25, 1945, to October 17, 1946, CB530 Shafter MB Church Records, microfilm reel 77, frames 1407–1408, CMBS-F.

36. *Annual Church Report,* October 24, 1946 to October 2, 1947, CB530 Shafter MB Church Records, microfilm reel 77, frames 1408–1409, CMBS-F.

37. *A Summary Report for 1930–1950,* CB530 Shafter MB Church Records, microfilm reel 77, frame 1436, CMBS-F.

38. *50th Jubilee, 1905–1955,* 47.

39. Some sewing circles used "Women's Missionary Service" as part of their name, but the acronym WMS used here refers only to the MB Pacific District Conference organization. Rempel, "'She hath Done What She Could'" (1992), 35–41; *Yearbook of the 39th Pacific District Conference of the Mennonite Brethren Church of North America*, October 23–27, 1948, 37–38. Interestingly, in the three histories written by WMS about their organization, only one tells the story of resistance toward this organization. See Mrs. Henry Martens, "Fifth Anniversary," CB390 Women's Missionary Service Records, Scrapbook, vol. 1, 1948–1958, CMBS-F. The others are Mrs. Abe Leppke, "The History of the M. B. Missionary Service of the Pacific District Conference," and "10th Anniversary," CB390 Women's Missionary Service Records, Scrapbook, vol. 1, 1948–1958, CMBS-F.

40. Waldo Wiebe to Rev. J. B. Toews, Nov. 12, 1948, CB530 Shafter MB Church Records, microfilm reel 77, frames 1387, CMBS-F.

41. J. B. Toews to Rev. Waldo Wiebe, Nov. 18, 1948, CB530 Shafter MB Church Records, microfilm reel 77, frame 1388, CMBS-F.

42. Waldo Wiebe to Rev. J. B. Toews, Nov. 12, 1948, CB530 Shafter MB Church Records, microfilm reel 77, frame 1388, CMBS-F.

43. Rempel, " 'She hath Done What She Could' " (1992), 38–39.

44. Minutes, November 3, 18, and December 2, 1948, CB530 Shafter MB Church Records, microfilm reel 77, frame 1562, CMBS-F. Exodus 35:23–26 reads: "And all the skilled women spun with their hands, and brought what they had spun, in blue and purple and scarlet material and in fine linen. And all the women whose heart stirred with a skill spun the goats' hair" (NASB).

45. Minutes, December 1, 1949, CB530 Shafter MB Church Records, microfilm reel 77, frame 1570, CMBS-F.

46. Martens, "Fifth Anniversary."

47. Ibid.

48. "Report of the M. B. Missionary Society," *Yearbook of the 39th Pacific District Conference of the Mennonite Brethren Church of North America, October 23–27, 1948,* 37.

49. Ibid., 37–38.

50. Minutes, February 2, 1949, CB390 Women's Missionary Service Records, Executive Committee 1949–1960, CMBS-F.

51. Minutes, annual meeting, November 12, 1956, CB390 Women's Missionary Service Records, Annual Meeting 1948–1959, CMBS-F.

52. Minutes, annual meeting, November 15, 1949, CB390 Women's Missionary Service Records, Annual Meeting 1948–1959, CMBS-F.

53. Minutes, May 7, 1957, and May 14, 1957, CB511 Butler Avenue MB Church Records (Fresno, CA), box 3, Mary-Martha Circle 1957–1959, CMBS-F.

54. Minutes, July 2, 1957; September 26, 1957; December 12, 1957; April 22, 1958; and September 23, 1958, CB511 Butler Avenue MB Church Records (Fresno, CA), box 3, Mary-Martha Circle 1957–1959, CMBS-F.

55. Constitution [1954], CB390 Women's Missionary Service Records, Constitutions, CMBS-F.

56. Minutes, executive committee, November 13, 1954, CB390 Women's Missionary Service Records, Executive Committee 1949–1960, CMBS-F.

57. Arthur Jost to H. A. Dahl, Oct. 18, 1950, IX-54 MCC-WCO, box 1, MCC Reedley 1950, MCA-G.

58. Minutes, executive committee, January 12, 1955, CB390 Women's Missionary Service Records, Executive Committee 1949–1960, CMBS-F.

59. Minutes, executive committee, November 10, 1956, CB390 Women's Missionary Service Records, Executive Committee 1949–1960, CMBS-F.

60. P. A. Enns to Mrs. Henry Martens, March 28, 1959, CB390 Women's Missionary Service Records, Executive Committee 1949–1960, CMBS-F.

61. Examples of the variety of work are found throughout their minutes, such as minutes, November 9, 1959, CB390 Women's Missionary Service Records, Annual Meetings 1948–1959, CMBS-F.

62. CB390 Women's Missionary Service Records, passim, Annual Meetings 1948–1959, CMBS-F.

63. Sermon, "A Godly Mother," May 12, 1950, M37 J. B. Toews Papers, box 8, Sermons to Women's Missionary Societies, CMBS-F.

64. Sermons, n.d., M37 J. B. Toews Papers, box 8, Sermons to Women's Missionary Societies, CMBS-F.

65. *Annual Church Report*, 1950, and minutes, Mission Relief Workers, April 6, 1950, Shafter MB Church Records, microfilm roll 77, frames 1412, 1577, CMBS-F.

66. Minutes, Mission Relief Workers, May 18, 1950, CB530 Shafter MB Church Records, microfilm roll 77, frame 1580, CMBS-F.

67. *Annual Church Report*, 1950, CB530 Shafter MB Church Records, microfilm roll 77, frame 1412, CMBS-F.

68. Minutes, Mission Relief Workers, January 17, 1952, and April 3, 1952; report from Oct. 1951 to April 1952, CB530 Shafter MB Church Records, microfilm roll 77, frames 1640, 1645, 1657–58, CMBS-F.

69. *Yearbook, Missionary Sewing Circle*, 1955–1956, CB508 Dinuba MB Church Records, Missionary Sewing Circle Yearbooks 1955–1956, CMBS-F.

70. *Yearbooks, Women's Missionary Society*, 1952–1953, 1956–1957, CB525 Reedley MB Church Records, box 5, Women's Missionary Society 1947–1957, CMBS-F; and *Yearbook, Women's Missionary Society* 1957–1958, CB525 Reedley MB Church Records, box 5, Women's Missionary Society 1957–1970, 1985–1988, CMBS-F.

71. *Yearbook, Women's Missionary Society* 1962–1963, 1969–1970, CB525 Reedley MB Church Records, Women's Missionary Society 1957–1970, 1985–1988, CMBS-F.

72. Rempel, "'She Hath Done What She Could'" (1992), 51.

73. Minutes, executive board, April 4, 1961, Women's Missionary Service, Executive Committee 1961–1965, CMBS-F.

74. See also Froese, "Quilts, Bandages and Efficiency," and Guenther, "Evangelicalism in Mennonite Historiography," 15–32.

75. Calvary Mennonite Church, bulletin, July 30, 1950, III-5-2 Calvary Mennonite Church, box 3, Calvary Christian Fellowship Church Bulletins, 1950–57. MCA-G.

76. Calvary Mennonite Church, bulletin, Nov. 9, 1952, III-5-2 Calvary Mennonite Church, box 3, Calvary Christian Fellowship Church Bulletins, 1950–57. MCA-G.

77. Calvary Mennonite Church, bulletin, July 29, 1956, III-5-2 Calvary Mennonite Church box 3, Bulletins, 1956, MCA-G. Other sewing circles, such as in Upland, reflected on these themes in their scrapbooks where they sorted through thousands of stamps to raise funds for Japanese missions, as well as producing embroidered quilts and packed relief bundles of diapers, towels and stationary for their service projects. "Dorcas Stitchers Report," Jan. 1, 1958; Jan. 1, 1959; and Jan. 6, 1960, III-5-1 Mountain View Mennonite Church, Upland, CA, Annual Reports, 1958–1970, MCA-G.

78. Mrs. William Guengrich [Ida?], response to questionnaire for all district presidents, Feb. 12, 1957, p. 7. IV-20-22 WMSA Minnie Graber Collection, District Exec. Committees 1953–62, MCA-G.

79. Mrs. J. G. [Minnie] Graber to Sister Officers of the Fourteen District Executive Committees, Aug. 22, 1953, IV-20-22 WMSA Minnie Graber Collection, Misc. Corr. 1947–53, MCA-G.

80. Mrs. William Guengrich [Ida?], response to questionnaire for all district presidents, Feb. 12, 1957, p. 7, IV-20-22 WMSA Minnie Graber Collection, District Exec. Committees 1953–62, MCA-G.

81. Ida to Minnie Graber, July 24, 1958, IV-20-22 WMSA Minnie Graber Collection, Misc. Corr. 1956–58, MCA-G; and Ida to Minnie Graber, Sept. 26, 1957; July 2, 1956; Sept. 5 and 18, 1958, IV-20-22 WMSA Minnie Graber Collection, Misc. Corr. 1947–53, MCA-G.

82. Mrs. Garland Stevanus, "Report of the Women's Missionary Society," *Annual Meeting Sunday, January 18, 1953 Reports for 1952*, p. 8; Mrs. Henry Rempel, "Report of the Women's Missionary Society," *Annual Meeting Sunday, January 14, 1951 Reports for 1950*, p. 7; Mrs. Marvin Unrau, "Treasurer's Report of the W.M.S.," *Annual Report 1953*, Jan. 17, 1954, pp. 7–8; Selma Sprunger, "Treasurer's Report of the W.M.S.," *Annual Report 1954*, Jan. 28, 1955, p. 7; and Dorothy F. Quillin, "Report of the Women's Missionary Society," *Annual Report 1954*, Jan. 28, 1955, pp. 6–7, CB553 Living Hope Church Records (Downey, CA), box 1, Congregational Meetings/Annual Reports 1951–1955, CMBS-F.

83. Mrs. Marvin Unrau, "Treasurer's Report of the Women's Missionary Society," *Annual Report 1956*, Jan. 20, 1957, p. 8; Neoma Anderson, "Report of the Women's Missionary Society," *Annual Report 1957*, Jan. 19, 1958, p. 9; Neoma Anderson, "Report of the Women's Missionary Society," *Annual Report 1958*, Jan. 18, 1959, p. 8; and Linda Kliewer, "Report of the Women's Missionary Society," *Annual Report 1959*, Jan. 17, 1960, CB553 Living Hope Church Records (Downey, CA), box 1, Congregational Meetings/Annual Reports 1956–1960, CMBS-F.

84. Darlene Hinamon, "History of the First Mennonite Church of Reedley," research paper, Bethel College, Feb. 23, 1955, Student Papers, MCA-N; and "Worth While Circle," First Mennonite Church Reedley, Annual Reports, 1942, FMCA.

85. "Worth While Circle Yearbook 1945–46," MLA.CONG.88 First Mennonite Church (Reedley, CA), box 2, Misc. file, MCA-N; "Worthwhile Circle Yearbook, 1947–1948," p. 9, and "Worthwhile Circle Yearbook, 1949–1950," MLA.CONG.88 First Mennonite Church (Reedley, CA), box 2, Constitutions, Handbooks, Yearbooks, MCA-N.

86. Ruth Eymann, "Worthwhile Circle—June 1951–June 1952," *Program and Reports for the 1952 Annual Business Meeting of the First Mennonite Church Reedley, California*," p. 3; "Worthwhile Circle—June 1, 1952–May 31, 1953," *Program and Reports for the 1953 Annual Business Meeting of the First Mennonite Church Reedley, California*," p. 2; "Worthwhile Circle—June 1, 1953–May 31, 1954," *Program and Reports for the 1954 Annual Business Meeting of the First Mennonite Church Reedley, California*," p. 29; and "Worthwhile Circle—June 1, 1954–May 31, 1955," *Program and Reports for the 1955 Annual Business Meeting of the First Mennonite Church Reedley, California*," pp. 30–31; Nettie Auernheimer and Helen Sellers, "Worthwhile Circle—June 1, 1956–May 31, 1957," *Program and Reports for the 1957 Annual Business Meeting of the First Mennonite Church Reedley, California*," pp. 30–31; Clara Unruh and Helen Sellers, "Worthwhile Circle—June 1, 1957–May 30, 1958," *Program and Reports for the 1958 Annual Business Meeting of the First Mennonite Church Reedley, California*," pp. 31–32, MLA.CONG.88 First Mennonite Church (Reedley, CA), box 2, Program and Reports of Annual Business Meetings 1952–1958, MCA-N.

87. Ruth Eymann, "Worthwhile Circle—June 1, 1954–May 31, 1955," p. 30; Clara Unruh and Helen Sellers, "Worthwhile Circle—June 1, 1957–May 30, 1958," p. 31, MLA.CONG.88 First Mennonite Church (Reedley, CA), box 2, Program and Reports of Annual Business Meetings 1952–1958, MCA-N.

88. Ruth Eymann, "Worthwhile Circle—June 1, 1954–May 31, 1955," p. 30; Clara Unruh and Helen Sellers, "Worthwhile Circle—June 1, 1957–May 30, 1958," p. 31; Ruth Eymann, "Worthwhile Circle—June 1, 1953–May 31, 1954," p. 29; Nettie Auernheimer and Helen Sellers, "Worthwhile Circle—June 1, 1956–May 31, 1957," p. 30, MLA.CONG.88 First Mennonite Church (Reedley, CA), box 2, Program and Reports of Annual Business Meetings 1952–1958, MCA-N.

89. Mrs. Rueben Bergthold and Mrs. Paul Sellers, "Worthwhile Circle Report June 1, 1958–May 30, 1959, *Annual Report First Mennonite Church, Reedley, California, December 7*

& 8, 1959, p. 28, MLA.CONG.88 First Mennonite Church (Reedley, CA), box 2, Annual Reports 1959–1964, MCA-N.

90. "Women's Mission Society Yearbook 1958–1959" and "Women's Mission Society Yearbook 1959–1960," MLA.CONG.85 Mennonite Community Church (Fresno, CA), box 3, Misc. file, MCA-N; and "Early History of the Mennonite Community Church of Fresno," MLA.CONG.85 Mennonite Community Church (Fresno, CA), vertical file, Mennonite Community Church, Fresno, CA, MCA-N.

91. Ruth Koop, "Women's Mission Society Report," *Mennonite Community Church Fresno, California Annual Business Meeting December 31, 1956*, pp. 6–7, MLA.CONG.85 Mennonite Community Church (Fresno, CA), box 3, Council Meetings, Business Agendas, MCA-N.

92. Betty Friesen, "Women's Mission Treasurer's Report," *Mennonite Community Church Fresno, California Annual Business Meeting Agenda and Reports December 11 and 12, 1960*, p. 4; "Women's Mission Treasurer's Report," *Mennonite Community Church Fresno, California, Annual Business Meeting Reports December 11 and 12, 1960*, p. 6; and "Women's Mission Treasurer's Report," *Mennonite Community Church Fresno, California Annual Business Meeting Agenda and Reports December 10 and 14, 1959*, p. 6; Verna Epp, "Women's Mission Society Treasurer's Report," pp. 6–7; Ruth Koop, "Women's Mission Society Report," *Mennonite Community Church Fresno, California Annual Business Meeting December 31, 1956*, pp. 6–7. MLA.CONG.85 Mennonite Community Church (Fresno, CA), box 3, Council Meetings, Business Agendas, MCA-N.

93. Marianna Habegger and Nova Siemens, "Worthwhile Circle Report June 1, 1959 to May 30, 1960," *Annual Report First Mennonite Church, Reedley, California, December 5 & 6, 1960*, p. 27, MLA.CONG.88 First Mennonite Church (Reedley, CA), box 2, Annual Reports 1959–1964, MCA-N.

94. Dec. 1, 1937–Nov. 3, 1943; Nov. 14, 1949; May 15 and June 2, 1950, *Minute Book of First Mennonite Sewing Circle*, First Mennonite Church (Shafter, CA), (Unprocessed), MLA. There is a break in their records from the early 1940s-late 1950s. *Annual Report— First Mennonite Church Upland, 1956*, pp. 11–13; *Annual Report—First Mennonite Church Upland, 1957*, pp. 10, 12; *Annual Report—First Mennonite Church Upland, 1959*, Upland, CA, Yearbooks, Newsletters, Annual Reports, First Mennonite Church (Upland, CA), (Unprocessed), MCA-N.

95. Ralph E. Eymann, "Men's Brotherhood Report," *Program and Reports for the 1958 Annual Business Meeting of the First Mennonite Church Reedley, California*," p. 27, MLA.CONG.88 First Mennonite Church (Reedley, CA), box 2, Program and Reports of Annual Business Meetings 1952–1958, MCA-N.

96. Roland Stucky, "Men's Brotherhood Report," *Annual Report First Mennonite Church, Reedley, California, December 5 & 6, 1960*, p. 26, MLA.CONG.88 First Mennonite Church (Reedley, CA), box 2, Annual Reports 1959–1964, MCA-N.

97. Porterfield, *Feminine Spirituality*, 5, 14–15, 109–110; Scott, *Gender*, 1–27; Johnson, "'A Memory Sweet to Soldiers,'" 495–517.

98. Limerick, *Legacy of Conquest*, 18–19.

Chapter 7. Peaceful Patriots

1. Simons, "Reply to Gellius Faber," 668–70.

2. Juhnke and Hunter, *The Missing Peace*.

3. Bender, "The Anabaptist Vision," 3–24; Hershberger, *War, Peace, and Nonresistance*; and Yoder, *The Politics of Jesus*.

4. Zimmerman, "The Story of Kings View Hospital," 194.

5. See Gingerich, *Service for Peace*; and Hershberger, *The Mennonite Church*, 34–108; Hershberger, *War, Peace, and Nonresistance*, 233–67; Webb, "Mennonite Conscientious Objectors"; Stauffer, "The Rehabilitation of Men," 73–76; Ruth, "Avenues of Service," 200–202. Draft alternatives included I-A, regular military service; I-AO, noncombatant military service; and IV-E, CPS. For denominational statistics, see Toews, *Mennonites in American Society*, 173–74, and Charles, "A Presentation and Evaluation," 83–106.

6. Minutes, Church Council, March 10, 1941, Church Council Minutes [Binder], FMCA.

7. "Board of Deacons," and J. H. Lagenwalter, "The Minister's Report," *Annual Reports 1942*, Annual Reports drawer, Annual Reports 1942 file, FMCA.

8. Correspondent, correspondence, GH, June 2, 1944, Winton.

9. M. C., "Three Rivers Civilian Public Service Camp No. 107," ME, vol. 4, 716; Melvin Gingerich, "North Fork (CA) Civilian Public Service Camp No. 5," ME, vol. 3, 917; Melvin Gingerich, "Civilian Public Service Camp (Camino, California, USA)," GAMEO, 1953, www.gameo.org/encyclopedia/contents/C52_31.html; and Melvin Gingerich, "Livermore," ME, vol. 3, 378.

10. "Religious emphasis," *Welcome to Camp Snowline*, CPS Camp No. 31, Camino, California, IX-13-1 MCC CPS, Misc. Publications, MCA-G; and "Outside Speakers," *High Sierra Vistas Write-Up*, Dec. 1, 1942, IX-13-1 MCC CPS, "High Sierra Vistas," 1942–44, MCA-G.

11. Arthur Jost, "Vistas," *High Sierra Vistas* (Oct. 1942): 4. IX-13-1 MCC CPS, Bound Volumes, MCA-G.

12. Miles Eaton, "'My Father's House': Hinduism," *Snowliner*, June 30, 1943, p. 2, IX-13-1 MCC CPS, file 10, Bound Edition Vol. II and III, MCA-G.

13. Miles Eaton, "'My Father's House' [Zarathustrianism]," *Snowliner*, July 15, 1943, p. 3; "'My Father's House': Egyptian Teachings," *Snowliner*, Aug. 1, 1943, p. 2; "'My Father's House': Buddhism," *Snowliner*, n.d. [between Aug. 1 and Oct. 1, 1943], pp. 3, 5; "'My Father's House': Jainism," *Snowliner*, Oct. 1, 1943, p. 3, IX-13-1 MCC CPS, file 10, Bound Edition Vol. II and III. This was a camper-run paper, and when it came to the camp library, for example, some attempts were made to exclude "modernist" books in addition to Jehovah's Witness materials, despite their active presence in CPS. Leland Bachman, CPS Camp No. 31, Director, to Henry Fast MCC Akron, PA., Sept. 22, 1942; Henry Fast to Leland Bachman, Sept. 29, 1942; and William J. Ramseyer, Assistant Director Camp No. 31, to Robert Kreider, MCC, Akron, PA, Oct. 13, 1942, IX-6-3 MCC CPS and Other Corr. 1940–45, 31 Director 1942; and 31 Educational Director 1942, MCA-G.

14. Erwin C. Goering, Camp Director CPS No. 31, to Albert M. Gaeddert, Akron, PA., March 2, 1944, IX-6-3 MCC CPS and Other Corr. 1940–45, 31 Director II 1944, MCA-G. For an account of Mennonite "fellows" drinking at a local "beer joint," see Verney Unruh, Director, CPS Camp No. 31, to Elmer Ediger, MCC, Akron, PA., Oct. 15, 1946, IX-6-3 MCC CPS, 31 Director 1946, MCA-G.

15. William A. Baer, "But You Must Be Realistic!" *High Sierra Vistas* (Jan. 1943): 9, 11; Harold Vercler, "Faith of Our Fathers," *High Sierra Vistas* (Nov. 1943): 5; and "C.P.S. Present & Future," *High Sierra Vistas* (Dec. 1942): 8–9, IX-13-1 MCC CPS, Bound Volumes, MCA-G.

16. Bob McCullagh, "Our Responsibilities in CPS," *Sequoia Hi-Lites* (Sept. 1, 1943): 3, IX-13-1 MCC CPS, 15 Bound Vol. *Sequoia Hi-Lights*, MCA-G.

17. Covers from the *Snowliner*, Nov. and Dec. 1942, Feb. 27, March 13, April 10, 1943, IX-13-1 MCC CPS, 10, "The Snowliner" Bound Volumes I–III, MCA-G.

18. Covers, *Sequoia Hi-Lites*, CPS Camp #107, Three Rivers, California, Nov. [1943] and Feb. 2, 1944, IX-13-1 MCC CPS, 15 Bound Vol. *Sequoia Hi-Lites*, MCA-G. The classic articulation of American Civil Religion is Bellah, "Civil Religion," 1–21. Catherine L. Albanese calls the holiday cycle "cultural religion"; *America: Religions and Religion*, 465–68.

19. Leland Bachman, Camp 31 Director, to Mennonite Central Committee, Dec. 31, 1942, L. J. Anderson to "The Public Forum," *Placerville Times*, Dec. 30, 1942; L. J. Anderson to Director, Conscientious Objectors Camp, Camino, California, Dec. 29, 1942; L. J. Anderson to Gen. Lewis B. Hershey, Director of Selective Service, Washington, DC, Dec. 29, 1942, IX-6-3 MCC CPS and Other Corr. 1940–45, 31 Director II 1943, MCA-G.

20. Ruth, "Avenues of Service," 202–203.

21. Leland Bachman to MCC, Feb. 1, 1943; Paul Kermeit and George Miners to MCC and NSBRO [no date—attached to Bachman correspondence of Feb. 1, 1943]; Leland Bachman to Henry Fast, MCC, Feb. 6, 1943, and Feb. 23, 1943; W. J. Ramseyer, CPS Camp #31, Camino California to Albert Gaeddert, Moundridge, Kansas, March 5, 1943; Henry Fast to W. J. Ramseyer, March 26, 1943; Leland Bachman to Henry Fast, April 3, 1943, IX-6-3 MCC CPS and Other Corr. 1940–45, 31 Director II 1943, MCA-G.

22. "To Prune or Not to Prune: A Matter of Methods," *Snowliner*, Jan. 30, 1943, IX-13-1 MCC CPS, file 10, "The Snowliner" Bound Vol. I, MCA-G.

23. Erwin [C. Goering] to Esko & Co., June 18, 1943, IX-6-3 MCC CPS and Other Corr. 1940–45, 31 Director 1943, MCA-G.

24. Ibid.

25. Esko Loewen to Erwin Goering, June 24, 1943, IX-6-3 MCC CPS and Other Corr. 1940–45, 31 Director 1943, MCA-G.

26. P. C. Hiebert, et. al., Committee for General Welfare and Public Relations, "Providing for our Brethren Drafted into the Service of Our Country," *Year Book of the 34th Pacific District Conference of the Mennonite Brethren Church of North America*, November 26–27, 1943 (Hillsboro, KS: Mennonite Brethren Publishing House, 1943), 43.

27. Harold Gaede, CPS Diary 1944, April 4, 1944, M250, CMBS-F.

28. Ibid., Feb. 18, 1944; and "Of What Significance Fire-Fighting," *High Sierra Vistas* (Oct. 1942): 6, IX-13-1 MCC CPS, Bound Volumes, MCA-G.

29. "Report of the Minister-at-Large, Oct. 1, 1943 to June 2, 1944," *Program of the Forty-Fifth Session of the Pacific District Conference of the Mennonite Church of North America*, June 1944, pp. 10–11. See also Enns-Rempel, "The Pacific District Conference and CPS," 1, 7.

30. P. C. Hiebert et al., Committee for General Welfare and Public Relations, "Civilian Public Service," *Year Book of the 34th Pacific District Conference of the Mennonite Brethren Church of North America*, Nov. 26–27, 1943, p. 31; and Toews, "Civilian Public Service," 5.

31. Hiebert et al., "Civilian Public Service," 33; Harold Gaede, CPS Diary 1944, April 6, 1944, M250, CMBS-F.

32. Arthur Jost, "Easter at North Fork," *High Sierra Vistas* (April 1943): 3, IX-13-1 MCC CPS, Bound Volumes, MCA-G; Leland Bachman to Orie Miller, Feb. 13, 1943; Orie Miller to Leland Bachman, Feb. 23, 1943; Leland Bachman to Henry Fast, MCC, Feb. 27, 1943, IX-6-3 MCC CPS and Other Corr. 1940–45, 31 Director II 1943, MCA-G.

33. Roger Frantz to J. J. Toews, July 22, 1945, CB534 Wasco MB Church Records, box 3, Individual Files: Frantz, Roger & Katherine (& Children) 1940–1962, CMBS-F.

34. Program of the Fifth Annual Kern County Christian Fellowship Conference Held September 5, 6 and 7, 1942, minute book, pp. 128–29, 130, 132, 135, CB600 Kern County Christian Fellowship Records, CMBS-F.

35. Forsyth, "Motivational Bases."

36. J. J. Toews to Roger [Frantz], May 23, 1945, CB534 Wasco MB Church Records, box 3, Individual Files: Frantz, Roger & Katherine (& Children) 1940–1962, CMBS-F.

37. "Spud" to Rev. Toews, Nov. 6, 1945, CB534 Wasco MB Church Records, box 3, Individual Files: Graft, Tim 1958–1966, CMBS-F.

38. "Special Meeting of Church Council," 20 Sept. 1945, Church Council Minutes [Binder], FMCA.

39. "Home Church News," 1945, pp. 5–7, MLA.CONG.86 box 1, First Mennonite Church, Paso Robles, CA-Newsletters 1945–1967; and bulletin, Jan. 6, 1944, MLA. CONG.86, box 2, First Mennonite Church, Paso Robles, CA-Bulletins 1944, 1945, 1955 (scattered), MCA-N.

40. "The Pastor's Chat," *Herald*, First Mennonite Church, Upland, California, May 1943, p. 3; "Our Church at Work," *Herald*, First Mennonite Church, Upland, California, Aug. 1945, p. 2, Upland, California, First Mennonite Church (Unprocessed), "The Herald" Newsletter of Upland, CA, First Mennonite Church, 1937–44, 45, MCA-N.

41. Minutes, Church Council, Oct. 2, 1944, Church Council Minutes [Binder], FMCA.

42. Minutes, congregational meetings, Aug. 16, 1943, CB508 Dinuba MB Church, microfilm 3, frame 648, CMBS-F; *History of the First Mennonite Church*, 33–34; Goertzen, *Bethany Church*, 7–8; *A History of the Mennonite Brethren Church*, 18; Penner and Frantz, "Through the Years," 11; Loewen, *Reedley First Mennonite Church*, 51–52; and Reimer, *The Story of the Mennonite Brethren*.

43. Minutes, Church Council, Dec. 14, 1941, Church Council Minutes [Binder], FMCA.

44. This rate of compensation was common throughout the congregations. Minutes, congregational meetings, June 8, Sept. 14, 1944, CB510 Bethany MB Church Records (Fresno, CA), box 1, Congregational Meetings 1942–1952, CMBS-F; minutes, Aug. 30, 1944, CB530 Shafter MB Church Records, box 1, Church Business Meetings, 1943–1945, CMBS-F; minutes, Church Council, Oct. 2, 1944, CB525 Reedley MB Church Records, box 3, Church Council 1940–1944, CMBS-F.

45. Minutes, Dec. 14, 1941, CB530 Shafter MB Church Records, box 1, Church Business Meetings 1928–1943, trans. J. C. Penner, CMBS-F.

46. Minutes, Church Council, Aug. 31, 1944, CB525 Reedley MB Church Records, box 3, Church Council 1940–1944, CMBS-F.

47. Minutes, congregational meeting, Jan. 14, 1946, CB525 Reedley MB Church Records, box 3, Congregational Meetings 1946, CMBS-F.

48. "Kiwanians Honor Gaede," RE, Jan. 21, 1954, 1; "Dr. Gaede New Mayor of Reedley," RE, April 22, 1954, 1; "These are Your Council Candidates," RE, March 15, 1956, 1; *Reedley: A Study of Ethnic Heritage*, 108.

49. Gaede, "Roots of City Government," 5A.

50. Ibid., 4A.

51. Langley, "America and the Conscientious Objector," 4–5, 1–2, 7. Quotes from pp. 1–2, 7.

52. Balzer, "The Supreme Court," 116–17. Silas Langley gives a fuller account of these events in his article, "Conscientious Objection," 37–52.

53. Langley, "America and the Conscientious Objector," 46–47.

54. Ibid., 70–73, 77–78, 87–104.

55. Ibid., 8–9.

56. Examples of such testimony can be found in "Exhibit No. 5—Statement taken from petitioner by Mr. J. S. Hemmer, naturalization examiner," "Exhibit No. 6—Report of inves-

tigation of naturalization examiner, dated March 13, 1951," and "Exhibit No. 7—Statement of Mr. and Mrs. John George Thiessen," *Supreme Court of the United States October Term, 1953, Arthur Jost, Petitioner, vs. United States of America*, pp. 49–60. Of similar interest, see "Testimony of Otto B. Reimer," 83–85. Reverend Dan Friesen's testimony can be found in the same document, pp. 53–54, M24 Arthur Jost Papers, Legal Documents Supreme Court of the United States Sept. 1953-Jan. 1954, CMBS-F.

57. Appellee's Reply Brief [date?], pp. 4, 12, box M24, Arthur Jost Papers, Legal Documents: Fourth Appellate District, State of California Aug. 1952–May 1953, CMBS-F.

58. Appellant's Reply Brief [date?], pp. 1, 6, quote on page 6, box M24, Arthur Jost Papers, Legal Documents: Fourth Appellate District, State of California Aug. 1952–May 1953, CMBS-F.

59. Ibid., 7–9.

60. "Opinion." In *Arthur Jost vs. United States of America District Court of Appeal*, Fourth Appellate District, State of California, Civil No. 4400, p. 1, box M24, Arthur Jost Papers, Legal Documents: Fourth Appellate District, State of California Aug. 1952–May 1953, CMBS-F.

61. Ibid., 5.

62. Krimmer Mennonite Brethren came from the Crimea, hence the name.

63. "Petition for Rehearing," April 30, 1953, Arthur Jost Petitioner, pp. 2–7, 14, 27, box M24, Arthur Jost Papers, Legal Documents: Fourth Appellate District, State of California Aug. 1952–May 1953, CMBS-F. See also "Opinion," *Arthur Jost vs United States of America District Court of Appeal*, Fourth Appellate District, State of California, Civil No. 4400, p. 1; and "Brief Amicus Curiae of the American Legion, Department of California," District Court of Appeal, Fourth Appellate District, State of California, Civil No. 4400, pp. 9–12, box M24, Arthur Jost Papers, Legal Documents: Fourth Appellate District, State of California Aug. 1952–May 1953, CMBS-F.

64. "Appellant's Opening Brief," District Court of Appeal, Fourth Appellate District State of California, pp. 11–12, box M24, Arthur Jost Papers, Legal Documents: Fourth Appellate District, State of California Aug. 1952–May 1953, CMBS-F.

65. "Application for Leave to File Brief Amici Curiae: and Brief in Support of Appellant, Petition for Naturalization of Arthur Jost," in the District Court of Appeal, Fourth Appellate District, State of California, Brief Amici Curiae, by ACLU, Southern California Branch, p. 1, box M24, Arthur Jost Papers, Legal Documents: Fourth Appellate District, State of California Aug. 1952–May 1953, CMBS-F.

66. "Petition for Hearing," pp. 1, 6–7, box M24, Arthur Jost Papers, Legal Documents: Supreme Court of the State of California June 1953, CMBS-F.

67. "In the Supreme Court of the State of California Answer to Petition for Hearing," pp. 6–7, box M24, Arthur Jost Papers, Legal Documents: Supreme Court of the State of California June 1953, CMBS-F.

68. P. C. Hiebert to Arthur Jost, March 28, 1955, pp. 1–2, IX-54 MCC-WCO, box 1, MCC Reedley 1955, MCA-G. P. C. Hiebert had played a pivotal role in bringing the Harbin Mennonites to California. See chapter 1.

69. McMahon, *Dean Acheson*, 2–3,112–15; Langley, "Conscientious Objection," 45, 48–49.

70. Langley, "Conscientious Objection," 37–52.

71. Minutes, Board of Welfare and Public Relations Committee, Dec. 5, 1950, CB370 Welfare and Public Relations Committee Records, Board of Welfare & Public Relations Minutes/Reports 1950–1967, CMBS-F.

72. Ibid.

73. Ibid.

74. "A Statement by the Pacific District Conference Committee of Welfare and Public Relations to our Constituency Regarding the 4E Position" [1950?], p. 1, CB370 Board of Welfare & Public Relations Committee Records, Correspondence, 1950–1954, 1960–1962, CMBS-F.

75. Ibid.

76. "New Testament Scriptures which Clearly Set Forth the Doctrine of Non-Resistance," CB370 Board of Welfare & Public Relations Committee Records, Correspondence, 1950–1954, 1960–1962, CMBS-F.

77. O. B. Reimer to Pastor, March 30, 1951, CB370 Board of Welfare & Public Relations Committee Records, Correspondence, 1950–1954, 1960–1962, CMBS-F.

78. Toews, "Civilian Public Service," 1.

79. Zimmerman, "The Story of Kings View Hospital," 192–93.

Chapter 8. Socially Active Mennonitism and Mental Health

1. Starr, *Golden Dreams*, 19–20.

2. I am indebted to Dr. Paul Toews for this idea in a conversation in March 2002. Zimmerman, "The Story of Kings View Hospital," 192–93.

3. Schmidt, "Continuity and Change," 49–50, 62, 64.

4. "Psychiatric Hospital Concerns," *Year Book of the Pacific District Conference of the Mennonite Brethren Church of North America*, Nov. 26–28, 1937, trans. J. C. Penner, p. 27; "Report of the Mental Hospital Committee," *Year Book of the Pacific District Conference of the Mennonite Brethren Church of North America*, Nov. 25–27, 1938, p. 73. For more background, see the theme issue on Mennonite mental health services in *Mennonite Quarterly Review* 56, no. 1 (Jan. 1982), and Bender, "The Mennonite Mental Health Movement," 45–60.

5. For studies on American Mennonite mental health care, see Neufeld, *If We Can Love* and "The Mennonite Mental Health Story."

6. Arthur Jost, "The Mental Hospital Program of the M.C.C.," report to General Conference Peace Committee, 1948, April 27, 1948, p. 1, IX-54 MCC-WCO, box 3, Reedley Relief Center 1948, MCA-G; "Mennonite Central Committee West Coast Home for the Mentally Ill," pamphlet, IX-54 MCC-WCO, box 1, MCC–West Coast-MMHS, MCA-G; Stahly et al., "Mennonites and Mental Health," 118–19; Ediger, "Roots of the Mennonite Mental Health Story," 21–28; Jost, "Kings View Reedley," 78–79; "1945 Report of the Mental Health Hospital Study Committee," *Report to MCC West Coast Subcommittee Advisory Meeting*, March 24, 1947, Reedley, California, IX-10-4 KVH Records, Minutes and Reports—1946–51, MCA-G.

7. "Recommendations," in "Home for the Aged," *Yearbook of the Thirty-Seventh Pacific District Conference of the Mennonite Brethren Church of North America*, Nov. 28–30, 1946, 24–25; Neufeld, "The Mennonite Mental Health Story," 21.

8. Minutes, General Board, Oct. 29, 1946, CB400 MB Homes, Inc., Records, Minutes/Reports: General Board 1945–1950, CMBS-F.

9. Minutes, General Board, June 16, 1947, CB400 MB Homes, Inc., Records, Minutes/Reports: General Board 1945–1950, CMBS-F.

10. Elmer W. Ediger to Homes-for-Mentally-Ill Planning and Advisory Committee, report, April 8, 1947, IX-10-4 KVH Records, Minutes and Reports—1946–51, MCA-G.

11. "Historical Sketch of the Mennonite Brethren Homes, Inc.," p. 1, CB400 Mennonite Brethren Homes, Inc., Records, Historical Accounts, n.d., CMBS-F.

12. Arthur Jost, "M.C.C. Mental Hospital Project," *Yearbook of the 39th Pacific District Conference of the Mennonite Brethren Church of North America*, Oct. 23–27, 1948, 47.

13. Ibid.

14. Ibid., 48.

15. Arthur Jost, "The Mental Hospital Program of the M.C.C.," report to General Conference Peace Committee, 1948, April 27, 1948, p. 3, IX-54 MCC-WCO box 3, Reedley Relief Center 1948, MCA-G. For brief, sympathetic histories of Kings View, see Jost, "Kings View Reedley," 77–96, and Jost, "Fellowship in Service," 80–82.

16. Unruh, *In the Name of Christ*, 315–16; Stahly et al., "Mennonites and Mental Health," 123; Arthur Jost, "Kings View Survived Opposition and Floods," RE, Oct. 27, 1988, 60; and Zimmerman, "The Story of Kings View Hospital," 193.

17. Jost, "Kings View Reedley," 82–83.

18. *Resolutions*, 79.

19. Minutes, Committee for Bible Camps, May 9, 1961, CB410 Committee for Bible Camps Records, Minutes—Conference Camping Committee, CMBS-F.

20. Arthur Jost to Elmer Ediger, Jan. 19, 1948, IX-6-3 Mennonite Central Committee Correspondence 1948, Jost, Arthur, MCA-G. Resistance is also mentioned in minutes, General Board, Jan. 29, 1948, CB400 MB Homes, Inc., Records, Minutes/Reports: General Board 1945–1950, CMBS-F.

21. Jost to Ediger, Jan. 19, 1948; minutes, General Board, Jan. 29, 1948. Jost also described the struggle with the local community because of "general lack of understanding" and "prejudice." Arthur Jost, "The Mental Hospital Program of the M.C.C.," report to General Conference Peace Committee, 1948, April 27, 1948, p. 2. IX-54 MCC-WCO box 3, Reedley Relief Center 1948, MCA-G.

22. Arthur Jost to Elmer Ediger, April 8, 1948, IX-6-3 Mennonite Central Committee Correspondence 1948, Jost, Arthur, MCA-G.

23. Minutes, Kings View Homes Advisory Committee meeting, May 12, 1951, IX-10-4 KVH Records, Minutes and Reports—1946–51, MCA-G.

24. Arthur Jost to Rufus Frantz, Eugene, Oregon, April 29, 1948, and the Peace Committee to Pastors and Church Boards of the PDC, April 15, 1948, MCC-WCO, box 2, MCC–West Coast: Correspondence 1948—Arthur Jost, CMBS-F.

25. Arthur Jost to Rev. H. A. Fast, North Newton, Kansas, Aug. 30, 1948, MCC-WCO, box 2, MCC–West Coast: Correspondence 1948—Arthur Jost, CMBS-F.

26. Arthur Jost to Rev. Edward Diener, Roseland, Nebraska [date unknown], 1949, and Arthur Jost to Walter Wager, Architect on project, Oct. 21, 1949, MCC-WCO, box 2, MCC–West Coast: Correspondence 1949—Arthur Jost, CMBS-F.

27. Arthur Jost to MCC Executive Committee Members, Dec. 2, 1949, MCC-WCO, box 2, MCC–West Coast: Correspondence 1949—Arthur Jost, CMBS-F.

28. Elmer W. Ediger to Homes-for-Mentally-Ill Planning and Advisory Committee, report, April 8, 1947, IX-10-4 KVH Records, Minutes and Reports—1946–51, MCA-G.

29. Martha Lee Yoder, Social Worker, "Report to the Kings View Homes Board of Directors," Saturday, April 26, 1952, IX-10-4 KVH Records, Minutes and Reports—1952, MCA-G.

30. Arthur Jost to William T. Snyder, MCC, Akron, Penn., Feb. 6, 1950, MCC-WCO, box 2, MCC–West Coast: Correspondence Jan.–Feb. 1950—Arthur Jost, CMBS-F.

31. Delmar Stahly, Mental Health Service to John William Boyer, Phoenix, Arizona, Sept. 22, 1950, MCC-WCO, box 2, MCC–West Coast: Correspondence Sept.–Oct. 1950—Arthur Jost, CMBS-F.

32. Arthur Jost to Glenn Esh, Administrative Assistant, Relief Sector, MCC, Akron, Penn., Dec. 18, 1950, MCC-WCO, box 2, MCC–West Coast: Correspondence Nov.–Dec. 1950–Arthur Jost, CMBS-F.

33. "A Home for the Mentally Ill is Dedicated on the West Coast," *Mennonite Community* (April 1950): 13.

34. Arthur Jost to Richard Blosser of *Mennonite Weekly Review*, Dec. 2, 1949, MCC-WCO, box 2, MCC–West Coast: Correspondence 1949–Arthur Jost, CMBS-F.

35. Starr, *Golden Dreams*, 42; and Jost, "Kings View Homes," 5.

36. "Modern Construction Methods," 5, 8; P. C. Hiebert to Otto Reimer, Sept. 22, 1951, CB370 Board of Welfare & Public Relations Committee Records, Correspondence, 1950–1954, 1960–1962, CMBS-F.

37. Neufeld, "The Mennonite Mental Health Story," 20–21.

38. Henry A. Fast, "Mental Hospitals, Mennonite," ME, vol. 3, 654.

39. M. A. Kroeker, "Report on Kingsview [sic] Homes (Mental Hospitals)," *Year Book of the 45th General Conference of the Mennonite Brethren Church of North America*, July 21–26, 1951, 67.

40. Arthur Jost to Ray Horst, VS Section MCC, April 17, 1951, MCC-WCO, box 2, MCC–West Coast: Correspondence April–May 1951–Arthur Jost, CMBS-F.

41. "Gold Award Mental," 299.

42. Conference with Dr. Tallman and Arthur Jost, Jan. 19, 1950, MCC-WCO, box 1, MCC–West Coast–American Friends Service Committee 1950–1951, CMBS-F.

43. Arthur Jost to Frank F. Tallman, M.D., Director, State Department of Mental Hygiene, Sacramento, California, Jan. 3, 1950, MCC-WCO, box 2, MCC–West Coast: Correspondence Jan.–Feb. 1950–Arthur Jost, CMBS-F.

44. Minutes, study committee, Nov. 18, 1955; Arthur Jost, "Administrator's Report to the Kings View Homes Advisory Committee," Aug. 19, 1955, pp. 1, 3, 5, IX-10-4 KVH Records, Minutes and Reports–1954–55, MCA-G.

45. Arthur Jost, correspondence from Provo, UT, May 1943, *Christian Leader*, May 1943, p. 13.

46. Arthur Jost, "Kings View Homes," ME, Vol. 3, 177.

47. Jim S. Gaede, "Kings View Hospital Assignment Received," *Welfare and Public Relations Newsletter*, 1, no. 2 (May, 1962): 1.

48. "Kings View Hospital Report to Mennonite Mental Health Services," *Welfare and Public Relations Newsletter*, 1, no. 2 (May 1962): 4.

49. "Shall the Mental Hospital Program of the Mennonite Churches be Extended?" *Welfare and Public Relations Newsletter*, 1, no. 4 (Oct., 1962): 1. See also Yoder, "Kern View Bakersfield, California."

50. Delmar Stahly, MMHS Co-coordinator, "Analysis of the Bakersfield Mental Hospital Proposal," Jan. 5, 1963, Attachment III, *Resolution: Regarding the Bakersfield Psychiatric Hospital*, IX-10-4, Kern View Min. & Rep., 1962–65, MCA-G; "Fifth Mental Hospital Sets Jan. 17, for Groundbreaking," MCC *News Service*, Dec. 18, 1964.

51. Roy Just, "Expanding the Witness," *Welfare and Public Relations Newsletter*, 2, no. 1 (Feb. 1963): 1.

52. "Kern View Hospital," *Welfare and Public Relations Newsletter*, 2, no. 2 (June 1963): 1.

53. *Kern View Hospital Dedication Bulletin*, Oct. 16, 1966, IX-10-4, Kern View Misc., MCA-G.

54. Untitled [?], p. 3, Attachment II, *Resolution: Regarding the Bakersfield Psychiatric Hospital*, IX-10-4, Kern View Min. & Rep., 1962–65, MCA-G.

55. Kings View Homes, Inc., Board of Directors, "Program for the Bakersfield Psychiatric Hospital," pp. 2–3, 10–11, attached to *Resolution: Regarding the Bakersfield Psychiatric Hospital*, IX-10-4, Kern View Min. & Rep., 1962–65, MCA-G.

56. Jost, "Private Centers," 269–70. Mennonite Mental Health Services (MMHS), an arm of MCC, was formed in 1947 out of CPS funds. See Neufeld, "The Mennonite Mental Health Story," 18.

57. Neufeld, "Mennonite Mental Health Services," 42.

58. Jost, "Private Centers," 269–70, 274, 279.

59. Arthur Jost, "The Administrator's Report to the Kings View Homes Advisory Committee Meeting," Dec. 6, 1952, p. 4, IX-10-4 KVH Records, Minutes and Reports—1946–51, MCA-G.

60. Arthur Jost, "Report to the Semi-annual Meeting of the Kings View Homes Advisory Committee," Reedley, California, May 12, 1953, p. 3, IX-10-4, Kings View Homes Records, Minutes and Reports—1953, MCA-G.

61. Minutes, meeting held at MCC Offices, March 23, 1953, IX-10-4 Kings View Homes Records, Minutes and Reports—1953, MCA-G.

62. Arthur Jost, "Administrator's Report," Kings View Homes Board of Directors Executive Meeting, April 6, 1951, p. 2; Arthur Jost, "Devotional Program," p. 3, *Report to the Kings View Homes Advisory Committee Meeting*, Sept. 4, 1951, IX-10-4 KVH Records, Minutes and Reports—1946–51, MCA-G.

63. Minutes, executive committee of the Kings View Homes Advisory Committee meeting, March 3, 1952; Arthur Jost, "The Administrator's Report to the Kings View Homes Advisory Committee Meeting," Dec. 6, 1952, p. 1, IX-10-4 KVH Records, Minutes and Reports—1946–51, MCA-G.

64. Allen H. Erb, of study committee, "Supplement Kings View Homes Study Committee Report," Nov. 23, 1955, IX-12-1 Mennonite Central Committee Reports, Kings View Advisory Committee, MCA-G.

65. Arthur Jost to Delmar Stahly, Kings View Homes Inter Departmental Communication, March 2, 1960, IX-6-3, Kings View Hospital Administration 1960, MCA-G.

66. Beach and Davis, "The Short-Doyle Program," 398–402; Arthur Jost, "Administrators Report," May 3, 1957, p. 2, IX-10-4, Kings View Homes Records, Minutes and Reports—1957, MCA-G.

67. "Kings View Homes Psychiatric Services (partial condensation of brochure material)," May 18, 1957 p. 6, IX-10-4, Kings View Homes Records, Minutes and Reports—1957, MCA-G.

68. Arthur Laemmlen, Secretary of the Board, minutes of Board of Directors meeting, Dec. 13, 1958, p. 3, IX-10-4, Kings View Homes Records, Minutes and Reports—1958, MCA-G.

69. Arthur Laemmlen, secretary, Kings View Hospital Board of Directors meeting, April 2, 1959, p. 3, IX-10-4, Kings View Homes Records, Minutes and Reports—1959, MCA-G.

70. Ediger, "Influences on the Origin and Development," 42.

71. Arthur Jost, "Administrator's Report to the Board," Dec. 11, 1959, p. 1, IX-10-4, Kings View Homes Records, Minutes and Reports—1959, MCA-G.

72. Minutes, KVH Executive Committee meeting, July 19 and Aug. 15, 1960, IX-10-4, Kings View Homes Records, Minutes and Reports—1960, MCA-G.

73. Arthur Jost, "Kings View Hospital's Report to the Meeting of the Mennonite Mental Health Service," April 29–30, 1969, Book Lane Farm, Hagerstown, Maryland, p. 2; Arthur Laemmlen, Secretary of the Board KVH, "Kings View Hospital Board of Directors

Report to the Mennonite Mental Health Services Meeting," April 29–30, 1969, Book Lane Farm, Hagerstown, Maryland, p. 2, IX-10-4, Kings View Homes Records, Minutes and Reports—1960, MCA-G.

74. Charles A. Davis, M.D., Medical Director, KVH, "Kings View Hospital Annual Report of the Medical Director to the Board of Directors Meeting," Dec. 16, 1960, p. 3, IX-10-4, Kings View Homes Records, Minutes and Reports—1960, MCA-G.

75. Jackson C. Dillon, M.D., "The Medical Director's Report to the Kings View Homes Advisory Committee," Dec. 5, 1953, IX-12-1 Mennonite Central Committee Reports, Kings View Advisory Committee, MCA-G.

76. Arthur Jost, "Administrator's Report," Kings View Homes Board of Directors executive meeting, April 6, 1951, p. 2, IX-10-4 KVH Records, Minutes and Reports—1946–51, MCA-G. Bender, "The Development of the Mennonite Mental Health Movement," 97.

77. Minutes, advisory committee, Aug. 19, 1955, IX-12-1 Mennonite Central Committee Reports, Kings View Advisory Committee, MCA-G.

78. Jackson C. Dillon, M.D., KVH Medical Director, to Orie Miller, MCC, Akron, Penn., Feb. 22, 1957, IX-10-4, Correspondence—1957, MCA-G.

79. Arthur Jost to Delmar Stahly, memo, June 8, 1957, IX-10-4, Correspondence—1957, MCA-G.

80. Minutes, KVH Advisory Committee meeting, March 18 and July 30, 1956; Arthur Jost, "Report to the Mennonite Mental Health Services," Aug. 27, 1956, pp. 1–2; Clara Lee Edgar, Psychologist, "Psychiatric Research at Kings View Homes" [Sept. 1956?], pp. 1–4, minutes, steering committee, Kings View Homes, Nov. 20, 1956, IX-10-4, KVH Records, Minutes and Reports—1956, MCA-G.

81. Arthur Jost to Orie Miller, June 25, 1957, and Aug. 19, 1957, IX-10-4, Correspondence—1957, MCA-G.

82. Jack [Purves?] to Orie [Miller], Nov. 5, 1957, IX-10-4, Correspondence—1957, MCA-G.

83. Arthur Jost to Allen Erb, Lebanon Community Hospital, Lebanon, Oregon, Nov. 29, 1957, IX-10-4, Correspondence—1957, MCA-G.

84. Ibid.

85. "Exhibit 3," minutes, Kings View Homes Executive Committee meeting, Dec. 13, 1957; "The Administrator's Report to the Meeting of the Kings View Homes Board of Directors," Sept. 23, 1957, p. 3, IX-10-4, Kings View Homes Records, Minutes and Reports—1957, MCA-G.

86. Toews, A History of the Mennonite Brethren Church, 385.

87. Arthur Jost, "Report on the Kings View Homes' Project to the Meeting of the Mental Health Committee," Chicago, Ill., March 17, 1950, IX-10-4 KVH Records, Minutes and Reports—1946–51, MCA-G.

88. Eileen Moore, "Sequoia Safety Council Drive Successful," RE, Oct. 27, 1988, pp. 14M, 15M.

89. Ibid., p. 15M.

90. Ibid., p. 16M.

91. Minutes, special board meeting, June 6, 1957, CB400 MB Homes, Inc., Records, Minutes/Reports: General Board 1951–1957, CMBS-F.

92. Minutes, General Board, June 2, 1958, CB400 MB Homes, Inc., Records, Minutes/Reports: General Board 1958–1961, CMBS-F.

93. Minutes, General Board, Nov. 15, 1960, CB400 MB Homes, Inc., Records, Minutes/Reports: General Board 1958–1961, CMBS-F.

94. Arthur Jost, "Report on the Kings View Homes' Project to the Meeting of the Mental Health Committee," Chicago, Ill., March 17, 1950, IX-10-4 KVH Records, Minutes and Reports—1946–51, MCA-G.

95. "Report to the Administrator of KVH Executive Committee," April 2, 1958; "Report to MMHS," April 11–12, 1958, IX-10-4, Kings View Homes Records, Minutes and Reports—1958, MCA-G.

96. Arthur Jost, "Talk by Arthur Jost, Administrator, Kings View Homes, Reedley, California given at Buhler, Kansas," Jan. 13, 1953 [transcript of a tape-recorded speech], pp. 2, 5, 7, 11; Arthur Jost, "A CPS Unit Leader," A Symposium: Should the Churches Establish and Maintain Hospitals for the Mentally Ill? Akron, Pennsylvania, Feb. 15, 1945, pp. 5–7, M24 Arthur Jost Papers, Arthur Jost Mental Health Care Conference Presentations 1945–1998, CMBS-F.

97. Arthur Jost, untitled manuscript for MCC, July 7, 1955, p. 3, M24 Arthur Jost Papers, MHA 1950–1990, CMBS-F. See also Jost, "Mennonites and Mental Illness," 27–28; Jost and Neufeld, "Comprehensive Community Care," 85–87.

98. "Statement to the Subcommittee on Mental Health Services, California Assembly Committee on Ways & Means," Dec. 8, 1969, Santa Ana, California, M24 Arthur Jost Papers, Mental Healthcare: Government Testimonies & Appointments 1969–1975. For an alternative interpretation, see Bender, "The Development of the Mennonite Mental Health Movement," 75, 97. Bender based his research on Jost's reports to the Mennonite Mental Health Services, the agency run by MCC to oversee the Mennonite mental hospital system.

Chapter 9. Feeding the Hungry

1. Hostetler, "Mennonite Citrus," 8–9.

2. Horsch, "The Citrus Fruit," 7.

3. Ewy, "The Grape and Raisin Industry," 9.

4. "Annual Congregational Meeting 1919," History of F. M. C. Building Projects drawer, Congregational Minutes 1908–1922, trans. Louis Linscheid, 1981, FMCA.

5. Hiebert, Feeding the Hungry, 33–35; Unruh, In the Name of Christ, 13–14; Epp, Mennonite Exodus, 55, 59; Penner, "The Story of the Mennonite Central Committee," 169–72.

6. Enns-Rempel, "The West Coast Mennonite Relief Sale," 1; Enns-Rempel, "The Siberian Journey," 4–5.

7. Hiebert, Feeding the Hungry, 35; Enns-Rempel, "The Siberian Journey," 5–6.

8. "Oct.–Dec. 1919," Church Record Book 1914–1924, p. 47, CB553 Living Hope Church Records (Downey, CA), box 1, Church Record Book 1914–1924, CMBS-F.

9. Hiebert, Feeding the Hungry, 390; Reedley: A Study of Ethnic Heritage, 107.

10. "From a Rocking Chair," 2; Enns-Rempel, "The West Coast Mennonite Relief Sale," 1. Support continued into the 1920s, as evidenced by letters such as H. J. Krehbiel, correspondence, Jan. 4, 1923, TMenn, Reedley.

11. Enns-Rempel, "West Coast MCC," 2.

12. Enns-Rempel, "The West Coast Mennonite Relief Sale, 2–3. For a chronology of the West Coast MCC, see Enns-Rempel, "West Coast MCC," 1–5.

13. One-page untitled document to S. E. Eicker, Oct. 21, 1947, IX-54 MCC West Coast Regional Office, Reedley, California, box 3, Reedley Relief Center 1947, MCA-G.

14. Unruh, In the Name of Christ, 331.

15. Anonymous report to John A. Hostetter, Oct. 16, 1946, p. 1, IX-54 MCC-WCO box 3, Reedley Relief Center, 1947, MCA-G.

16. Ibid.

17. One-page untitled document to S. E. Eicker, Oct. 21, 1947.

18. Anonymous report to John A. Hostetter, Oct. 16, 1946, p. 2.

19. "From the Reedley Relief Center," Dec. 1, 1947, IX-54 MCC-WCO box 3, Reedley Relief Center, 1947, MCA-G.

20. Anna M. Snyder, "From Our Clothing Centers: Reedley, California," *Missionary Sewing Circle Monthly* 20, no. 5 (Nov. 1947), IV-20-3 WMSC Publications, Missionary Sewing Circle Monthly 1945–48, MCA-G.

21. Anonymous report, Dec. 1, 1948, p. 2, IX-54 MCC-WCO, box 3, Reedley Relief Center, 1948, MCA-G.

22. Anonymous report to John A. Hostetter, Oct. 16, 1946, p. 2.

23. Ibid.; Anna M. Snyder, "Reedley, California," *Missionary Sewing Circle Monthly* 19, no. 2 (Aug. 1946), IV-20-3 WMSC Publications, Missionary Sewing Circle Monthly 1945–48, MCA-G.

24. Anna M. Snyder, "Mennonite Relief Center Reedley, California," IX-54 MCC-WCO box 3, File Reedley Relief Center 1947, MCA-G; and Anna M. Snyder, "The Reedley Relief Center," *Missionary Sewing Circle Monthly* 19, no. 1 (July 1946), IV-20-3 WMSC Publications, Missionary Sewing Circle Monthly 1945–48, MCA-G.

25. For countries shipped to, see one-page untitled document to S. E. Eicker, Oct. 21, 1947, "From the Reedley Relief Center," and Snyder, "Mennonite Relief Center Reedley, California."

26. One-page untitled document to S. E. Eicker, Oct. 21, 1947.

27. "From the Reedley Relief Center," p. 1; anonymous report to John A. Hostetter, Oct. 16, 1946.

28. "From the Reedley Center," p. 2.

29. Arthur Jost to Charles Brannan, Secretary of Agriculture, Dec. 14, 1949, MCC-WCO, box 2, MCC–West Coast: Correspondence 1949–Arthur Jost, CMBS-F.

30. Ibid.

31. Arthur Jost to Paul Goering, N.S.B.R.O., Dec. 27, 1949, MCC-WCO, box 2, MCC–West Coast: Correspondence 1949–Arthur Jost, CMBS-F.

32. Paul L. Goering, NSBRO, to Arthur Jost, Jan. 11, 1950, MCC-WCO, box 2, Jan–Feb. 1950, CMBS-F.

33. Arthur Jost to Glenn Esh, Feb. 9, 1950; Arthur Jost to Relief Committee, Feb. 17, 1950, MCC-WCO, box 2, Jan.–Feb. 1950, CMBS-F; Arthur Jost to Glenn Esh, June 22, 1950, MCC-WCO, box 2, May–June 1950, CMBS-F.

34. William T. Snyder to Arthur Jost, Jan. 13, Feb. 18, Dec. 21, 1949, MCC-WCO, box 2, MCC–West Coast: Correspondence 1949–Arthur Jost, CMBS-F.

35. Memorandum, Arthur Jost to William T. Snyder, Mennonite Aid Section, Nov. 9, 1949, p. 1, MCC-WCO, box 2, MCC–West Coast: Correspondence 1949–Arthur Jost, CMBS-F.

36. Ibid., 2.

37. Minutes, Jan. 26, 1950, MCC-WCO, box 1, Displaced Persons in California, Advisory Committee, CMBS-F.

38. "Voluntary Service on the West Coast," IX-54 MCC-WCO, box 1, MCC Reedley 1950, MCA-G.

39. Gladys Buller, "My First Impressions," July 3, 1950, IX-54 MCC-WCO, box 1, MCC Reedley 1950, MCA-G.

40. Isabel Reidle, July 3, 1950, and Margaret Martin July 3, 1950, IX-54 MCC-WCO, box 1, MCC Reedley 1950, MCA-G.

41. Helen Tieszen, "An Evaluation of the Summer Voluntary Service Unit at Camp Paivika, Crestline, California," IX-54 MCC-WCO, box 1, MCC Reedley 1950, MCA-G, 1.

42. Ibid., 1–2.

43. Arlene Sitler to Beulah Stauffer, June 16, 1950, MCC-WCO, box 2, May–June 1950, CMBS-F.

44. "Crestline, California Evaluation of Voluntary Service Unit at Crippled Children's Camp, Aug. 1950," pp. 1–2, IX-54 MCC-WCO, box 1, MCC Reedley 1950, MCA-G.

45. Ibid., 2, 4.

46. Arlene Sitler to Ray E. Horst, Jan. 31, 1951, MCC-WCO, box 2, Correspondence—Jost Jan.–March 1951, CMBS-F.

47. Ray E. Horst to Arthur Jost, April 5, 1951, MCC–WCO, box 2, Correspondence—Jost April–May 1951, CMBS-F.

48. Beulah Stauffer, Akron, to Arlene Sitler, Reedley, April 6, 1950, MCC-WCO, box 2, March–April 1950, CMBS-F.

49. Arthur Jost to Orlo Kaufman, VS-MCC, Akron, May 7, 1951, MCC-WCO, box 2, Correspondence—Jost April–May 1951, CMBS-F.

50. Glenn Esh, Acting Director of Relief, MCC, Akron, to Arthur Jost, April 1, 1952, MCC-WCO, box 2, Correspondence 1952—Arthur Jost, CMBS-F.

51. Allen Linscheid to Glenn Esh, April 10, 1952; Glenn Esh, Acting Director of Relief, MCC, Akron, to Arthur Jost, April 1, 1952, MCC-WCO, box 2, Correspondence 1952—Arthur Jost, CMBS-F.

52. Wendell Metzler to Ada King, Aug. 26, 1953, MCC-WCO, box 2, Correspondence 1953—Arthur Jost, CMBS-F.

53. Minutes, Joint Relief Committee meeting, May 6, 1954, MCC-WCO, box 1, MCC West Coast Relief Committee and Relief Sale: Minutes and Reports 1953–1976, CMBS-F.

54. Minutes, Joint Relief Committee meeting, Jan. 22, March 11, and May 12, 1954, MCC-WCO, box 1, MCC West Coast Relief Committee and Relief Sale: Minutes and Reports 1953–1976, CMBS-F.

55. Minutes, relief meeting, Nov. 12, 1957, IX-54 MCC-WCO, box 1, West Coast Relief Committee Minutes 1950–1973, MCA-G.

56. Robert W. Miller to Arthur Jost, Nov. 27, 1957, MCC-WCO, box 2, Correspondence 1957—Arthur Jost, CMBS-F.

57. Arthur Jost to Orie O. Miller, Executive Secretary MCC, May 9, 1957, MCC-WCO, box 2, Correspondence 1957—Arthur Jost, CMBS-F.

58. Arthur Jost to William Snyder, June 26, 1957, MCC-WCO, box 2, Correspondence 1957—Arthur Jost, CMBS-F.

59. William T. Snyder to Arthur Jost, July 12, 1957, MCC-WCO, box 2, Correspondence 1957—Arthur Jost, CMBS-F.

60. William T. Snyder to Arthur Jost, Feb. 19, 1958, MCC-WCO, box 2, Correspondence 1958—Arthur Jost, CMBS-F.

61. William T. Snyder to Arthur Jost, Dec. 17, 1959, MCC-WCO, box 2, Correspondence 1959—Arthur Jost, CMBS-F.

62. Snyder to Orie Miller, Memorandum, Dec. 16, 1959, MCC-WCO, box 2, Correspondence 1959—Arthur Jost, CMBS-F.

63. Allen Linscheid, "MCC West Coast Relief Committee: A Perspective," p. 1, IX-54 MCC-WCO, box 3, West Coast Relief Committee, 1965, CMBS-F.

64. Arthur Jost to Brethren, July 25, 1960, MCC-WCO, box 2, Correspondence 1960—Arthur Jost, CMBS-F.

65. Ramon H. Jantz, Chairman of MCC-WCRC to MCC Constituent Churches on West Coast, Feb. 20, 1961, MCC-WCO, box 2, Correspondence 1961—Arthur Jost, CMBS-F; minutes, relief meeting, Nov. 12, 1957; minutes, West Coast Relief Committee, Dec. 8, 1960, IX-54 MCC-WCO, box 1, West Coast Relief Committee Minutes 1950−1973, MCA-G.

66. Executive Office (Snyder) to Relief Office (Hostetler), MCC Memorandum, Sept. 12, 1960, MCC-WCO, box 2, Correspondence 1960—Arthur Jost, CMBS-F; minutes, West Coast Relief Committee, Dec. 8, 1960, IX-54 MCC-WCO, box 1, West Coast Relief Committee Minutes 1950−1973, MCA-G.

67. Martha Zimmerman, Secretary of WCRC to Brethren In Christ & Mennonite Pastors in California, Dec. 12, 1961, MCC-WCO, box 2, Correspondence 1961—Arthur Jost, CMBS-F.

68. Minutes, West Coast Relief Committee, May 25, 1962, MCC-WCO, box 1, MCC West Coast Relief Committee and Relief Sale: Minutes and Reports 1953−1976, CMBS-F.

69. Minutes, West Coast Relief Committee, Nov. 16, 1962, MCC-WCO, box 1, MCC West Coast Relief Committee and Relief Sale: Minutes and Reports 1953−1976, CMBS-F.

70. Minutes, West Coast Relief Committee, Jan. 22, 1965, MCC-WCO, box 1, MCC West Coast Relief Committee and Relief Sale: Minutes and Reports 1953−1976, CMBS-F.

71. Minutes, West Coast Relief Committee, Nov. 13, 1964, MCC-WCO, box 1, MCC West Coast Relief Committee and Relief Sale: Minutes and Reports 1953−1976, CMBS-F.

72. John Hostetler to Allen Linscheid, May 26, 1964, MCC-WCO, box 2, Correspondence 1964—Arthur Jost, CMBS-F.

73. Minutes, West Coast Relief Committee, March 4, 1966, MCC-WCO, box 1, MCC West Coast Relief Committee and Relief Sale: Minutes and Reports 1953−1976, CMBS-F.

74. Minutes, West Coast Relief Committee, Feb. 16, 1968, MCC-WCO, box 1, MCC West Coast Relief Committee and Relief Sale: Minutes and Reports 1953−1976, CMBS-F.

75. "Project Bridgebuilding," MCC-WCO, box 1, Project Bridgebuilding, 1965−1968, CMBS-F.

76. Kraybill, "From Enclave to Engagement," 23−58.

Chapter 10. Protect and Assimilate

1. J. H. Lohrenz, "Fresno Mennonite Brethren Church," ME, vol. 2, 395.

2. Harold S. Bender, "Pacific District Conference (MB)," ME, vol. 4, 104; Lohrenz, "History of the Mennonite Brethren Church," 107−108.

3. Minutes, Oct. 1955 [front page]; Sept. 20, 1956; Jan. 7 and March 24, 1957; May 28, Sept. 3, Oct. 8, and Dec. 17, 1958; Jan. 12, Jan. 21, Feb. 11, March 18, April 21, Aug. 5, Aug. 12, Aug. 26, Sept. 2, Nov. 11, Nov. 18, and Dec. 31, 1959, CB511 Butler Avenue MB Church Records (Fresno, CA), box 1, Business Meeting Minute Book, CMBS-F.

4. Fast, "A Strategy for Church Growth," 22. Fast was pastor of Butler MB Church at the time of his study.

5. Ibid., 22.

6. Ibid., 20−27. Quote from p. 25.

7. "Church History," CB515 Kingsburg MB Church Records, box 1 [in front of first file in box 1], CMBS-F; minutes, congregational business meeting, Jan. 10, Jan. 18, May 28, Nov. 29, 1962, CB515 Kingsburg MB Church Records, box 1, Congregational Meetings 1962−1969, CMBS-F.

8. Minutes, congregational meeting, March 8, 1957; "Question of a New Church in

Wasco," March 8, 1957, CB534 Wasco Bible Church Records, box 1, Congregational Meetings 1957–1960, CMBS-F. It is about ten miles between the towns of Wasco and Shafter.

9. "Pastor's Report," Oct. 15, 1959, CB534 Wasco Bible Church Records, box 1, Congregational Meetings 1957–1960, CMBS-F. See also minutes, Church Council, Oct. 23, 1958, CB534 Wasco Bible Church Records, box 1, Church Council 1958–1961, CMBS-F.

10. Enns-Rempel, "Making a Home in the City," 214, 219–21. That would not be the end of evangelical influence on seminary development. In the early 1970s, one student at MBBS collected data on Pacific District Conference Mennonite Brethren churches to study church growth through a methodology borrowed from such leading evangelical church growth promoters such as Donald McGavern. See Wiens, "Growth Patterns."

11. Wiebe, *Remembering*, 5; Toews and Dueck, "Embodying the Vision," 104.

12. Toews, " 'A Shelter in a Time of Storm,' " 65–69, Toews, "Religious Idealism," 224–27; Wiebe, *Remembering*, 25–26.

13. Toews, " 'A Shelter in a Time of Storm,' " 69.

14. J. D. Hofer, Secretary-Treasurer, "Report of the Board of the PBI," *Year Book of the 35th Pacific District Conference of the Mennonite Brethren Church of North America*, Oct. 28–31, 1944, 23; Toews, "Religious Idealism," 222–24; G. W. Peters, "PBI of Fresno," ME, vol. 4, 103.

15. Toews, "Fundamentalist Conflict," 253–56.

16. Toews, *A Pilgrimage of Faith*, 173–74; Toews, " 'A Shelter in a Time of Storm,' " 64–65; Toews, *Mennonites in American Society*, 80–82.

17. Toews, *Mennonites in American Society*, 81.

18. Ibid.

19. For Mennonite Brethren education in America, see Peters, "The Coming of the Mennonite Brethren," 186–227. For Mennonite Brethren education in California, Toews, *A History of the Mennonite Brethren Church*, 257–82; Toews, *Mennonites in American Society*, 80–83, 282; Menno S. Harder, "Education, Mennonite," ME, vol. 2, 150; and Lohrenz, "History of the Mennonite Brethren Church," 112, 151.

20. "Brief Historical Sketch," and "Purpose of the School in General Terms," *Catalog of Pacific Bible Institute of Fresno, With Announcements for 1950–1951*, 7–8. For brief histories of PBI, see Wiebe, "The Birth of the Vision," 1–23; Toews, "Introduction," x-xv; Toews, "Singing the Christian College Song," 89–102.

21. Wiebe, "The Birth of a Vision," 2; "Recommendation for the PBI," *Year Book of the 35th Pacific District Conference of the Mennonite Brethren Church of North America*, Oct. 28–31, 1944, 27–28.

22. Toews, *A Pilgrimage of Faith*, 175.

23. *Pacific Bible Institute, Fresno, California, Catalog 1945–1946*, 3.

24. Ibid., 4.

25. Ibid., 7.

26. *Catalog of Pacific Bible Institute of Fresno, 1950–1951; Catalog of Pacific Bible Institute of Fresno, 1953–1954*; and *1959–1960 Catalogue [of] Pacific Bible Institute and Junior College*.

27. *Pacific Bible Institute, Fresno, California, Catalog 1946–1947*.

28. Redekop, "Mennonite Brethren Economic Developments," 128–32; Toews, "Religious Idealism," 222, 227–28. An example of involvement of Mennonites in business and the broader evangelical world is E. J. Peters, chairman of the Mennonite Brethren United States Conference Board of Education, 1954–1971. See Scrapbook: General Biographical 1905–1973; Scrapbook: Agriculture 1947–1965; Scrapbook: Boy Scouts, Fair Board, MEDA, Education 1948–1971, box 2, M189 E. J. Peters Collection, CMBS-F. See also the "Biography of E. J. Peters," which serves as introduction to the E. J. Peters Collection finding aid.

29. B. J. Braun, "Report by President of PBI and Junior College," *Minutes and Reports of the United States Conference of the Mennonite Brethren Church*, Aug. 18—19, 1959, 36—37.

30. Ibid., 37.

31. Minutes, representatives of Mennonite Brethren Bible College, Winnipeg, Tabor College, Hillsboro, PBI, Fresno, n.d., C240 Board of Education (United States Mennonite Brethren Conference) Records, box 2, Steering Committee for Coordination: Minutes/Reports 1955—1958, CMBS-F.

32. Frank C. Peters, President of Tabor College, to B. J. Braun, President of PBI, Oct. 22, 1955; and P. E. Schellenberg, President Tabor College, to S. W. Goossen, Acting President, PBI, Aug. 4, 1947, Fresno Pacific University President's Records, box 6, Tabor College 1945—1980, CMBS-F.

33. Frank C. Peters, President, Tabor College, to Rev. B. J. Braun, President of PBI, Oct. 22 1955, Fresno Pacific University President's Records, box 6, Tabor College 1945—1980, CMBS-F.

34. Ibid. On unification see also Arthur J. Wiebe, "Application for Accreditation" [Pacific College], Fall 1962, p. 2; Wiebe, *Remembering*, 55—85; and Enns-Rempel's thorough review of Wiebe's book, "Book Review," 9—10.

35. Arthur J. Wiebe, President, "Application for Accreditation," Fall 1962, pp. 2—3, Fresno Pacific University Provost's Records, box 1, Accreditation Application to CJCA/WASC, CMBS-F.

36. PBI *Catalog 1945—1946*, Fresno, California, p. 5; and "P.B.I. Directorate Report," *Year Book of the 46th General Conference of the Mennonite Brethren Church of North America*, Oct. 23—28, 1954, 44.

37. Joel A. Wiebe, Interim Director, "Report of the Pacific College," *Year Book of the 48th General Conference of the Mennonite Brethren Church of North America*, Nov. 12—16, 1960, 143.

38. "Special Report to the Board of Education as given to the Executive Committee of the West Coast Area Committee and to the General Chairman, Mr. E. J. Peters," July 18, 1957, pp. 1—2; "Report of PBI of Fresno Submitted to the Executive Committee of the Board of Education," May 5, 1955, pp. 1—2, C240 Board of Education (United States Conference of Mennonite Brethren) Records, box 6, West Coast Committee: Minutes/Reports 1955—1959, CMBS-F.

39. Toews, "Introduction," xii; Wiebe, "The Birth of the Vision," 6—8.

40. Lando Hiebert to G. W. Peters, PBI, Nov. 18, 1948, Fresno Pacific University President's Records, box 5, Prospective Faculty: A-R 1947—1952, CMBS-F.

41. Toews, "'A Shelter in a Time of Storm,'" 67; Wiebe, "The Birth of the Vision," 8; Reimer, "The Origins," 29; and "Minutes of the Annual Meeting of the Board of Education of the General Conference of the Mennonite Brethren Church of North America," Dec. 13—14, 1954, C240 Board of Education (United States Mennonite Brethren Conference) Records, box 1, Minutes, 1954, CMBS-F.

42. Minutes, meeting of the Board of Education, Feb. 20—22, 1960, p. 7, C240 Board of Education (United States Conference of Mennonite Brethren) Records, box 1, Minutes/Reports Feb. 1960, CMBS-F.

43. Toews, "The M. B. Biblical Seminary," 17, 19; Klassen, "The Biblical Seminary," 8, 10.

44. "Summarized Report of the Mennonite Brethren Conference Seminary Commission," held Oct. 27—28, 1948, Reedley, California, A350 General Conference Seminary Commission 1948—1949, CMBS-F.

45. "Principle Issues Involved in the Matter of Unification of Theological Training on the Seminary Level," n.d., C240 Board of Education (United States Conference of Men-

nonite Brethren) Records, box 2, Steering Committee for Coordination: Minutes/Reports 1955–1958, CMBS-F.

46. "Seminary Commission Meeting," Jan. 21, 1949, pg. 2, A350 General Conference Seminary Commission Records, 1948–1949, CMBS-F.

47. "Minutes, Seminary Commission Meeting," Jan. 1949 [no more specific date given], p. 4, A350 General Conference Seminary Commission Records, 1948–1949, CMBS-F.

48. Schmidt, "Continuity and Change," 104–105. Quote from p. 104.

49. Ibid., 114–15.

50. McGirr, *Suburban Warriors*.

51. B. J. Braun, "President's Report," Annual Meeting of the Board of Education, Jan. 23, 1957, C240 Board of Education (United States Mennonite Brethren Conference) Records, box 1, Minutes/Reports 1957, CMBS-F; "MBBS," *Year Book of the 47th General Conference of the Mennonite Brethren Church of North America*, Oct. 20–23, 1957, 81–82.

52. Minutes, Meeting of the Commission on Unification, Jan. 27–28, 1958; and "Findings of the Commission on Unification Submitted to the Board of Reference and Counsel of the General Conference," Jan. 27–28, 1958, Hillsboro, Kansas, C240 Board of Education (United States Mennonite Brethren Conference) Records, box 2, Steering Committee for Coordination: Minutes/Reports 1955–1958, CMBS-F.

53. "A Statement of Philosophy and Purpose of Mennonite Brethren Biblical Seminary," appendix 5, report by the dean of MBBS, Fresno, California, to the Board of Education, Aug. 19, 1960, C240 Board of Education (United States Mennonite Brethren Conference) Records, box 1, Minutes/Reports Aug.–Nov. 1960, CMBS-F.

54. Klassen, "Into Curriculum Structures," 28.

55. R. M. Baerg, "To the Executive Committee of the Board of Education of the U. S. Area Mennonite Brethren Conference," Fresno, California, May 19–20, 1964, pp. 2, 4, M189 E. J. Peters Collection, box 1, Board of Education correspondence: MB Biblical Seminary, CMBS-F. Baerg is simply making a suggestion to the board and does not offer here a possible new name.

56. Ibid., 4. As one student study of Mennonites put it, "The Seminary makes no apology for its evangelical position." Martens, "A Study of Mennonites," 71.

57. John E. Toews to J. B. Toews, Oct. 29, 1961; Jan. 30, Feb. 26, March 15, March 30, and June 1, 1963, M37 J. B. Toews Papers, box 4, Correspondence: Toews, John E. and Arlene (and Children), 1961–1997, CMBS-F.

58. Clarence Hiebert, Secretary, Coordinating Board of the USA Conference of Mennonite Brethren Churches, to J. H. Quiring, Chairman, Committee of Reference and Counsel, Mennonite Brethren Churches of Canada, Winnipeg, Manitoba, Dec. 10, 1965, M189 E. J. Peters Collection, box 1, Board of Education Correspondence: MB Biblical Seminary, CMBS-F.

59. J. B. Toews, "The Purpose of the Seminary," attachment to minutes, faculty meeting, Jan. 4, 1965, MBBS, Committee Records, box 1, Faculty Meetings Jan.–July 1965, CMBS-F; Toews, "The M. B. Biblical Seminary," 20–22; Toews, JB, 166–76; Toews, *A Pilgrimage of Faith*, 174–87; Bender, "The Anabaptist Vision"; Toews and Dueck, "Embodying the Vision," 105.

60. MBBS 1955–1956 [Catalog], 2.

61. *MBBS Catalog 1965–1966*, 17–18.

62. Toews, "The M. B. Biblical Seminary," 22–24.

63. Toews, "Recentering a Denomination," 3.

64. Ibid; Toews, "From Pietism to Secularism," 1–13. I thank Paul Toews for making this paper available to me.

65. Ibid., 4.

66. Klassen, "To Reclaim a Heritage," 2.

67. Enns-Rempel, "Pacific Bible Institute Once Owned," 1–2, 4; Enns-Rempel, "The Giffen Mansion," 1–2, 7.

Chapter 11. Labor Tensions

1. Isaak, *Our Life and Escape*, 67.

2. Dochuk, *From Bible Belt to Sunbelt*; and Gregory, *American Exodus*.

3. Dean, "Shirtsleeve Millionaires," 105, 110; and Edward J. Peters, "Vehicle Unloading Apparatus," patented Aug. 28, 1956, Patent Number: US002760656.

4. Dean, "Shirtsleeve Millionaires," 105–13. For the Eymann family and 1930s water, see chapter 1.

5. Ibid., 105, 108, 110.

6. Histories, memoirs, and biographies of this organization include Matthiessen, *Sal Si Puedes*; Horwitz, *La Causa*; Day, *Forty Acres*; Dunne, *Delano*; Levy, *César Chávez*; Taylor, *Chávez and the Farm Workers*; Meister and Loftis, *A Long Time Coming*; and Wells, *Strawberry Fields*.

7. Romo, "Mexican Americans in the New West," 136–37; Hine and Faragher, *The American West*, 548–50.

8. Mock, *Writing Peace*, 116.

9. Paul N. Kraybill to Guy F. Hershberger, March 29, 1974, Hist. Mss. 1-171, box 28, Guy F. Hershberger, 1896–1989, California Labor Concerns, Correspondence, 1974, MCA-G.

10. Ted Koontz to Guy Hershberger, April 1, 1974, Hist. Mss. 1-171, box 28, Guy F. Hershberger, 1896–1989, California Labor Concerns. Correspondence, 1974, MCA-G.

11. Guy F. Hershberger to Daniel Hertzler, April 19, 1974, Hist. Mss. 1-171, box 28, Guy F. Hershberger, 1896–1989, California Labor Concerns. Correspondence, 1974, MCA-G.

12. Robert M. Herhold, "To be a Man," *TMenn*, Sept. 5, 1972, 504. Two helpful essays on Chávez and religion are Lloyd-Moffett, "The Mysticism and Social Activism of César Chávez," 35–51, and León, "César Chávez and Mexican American Civil Religion," 53–64.

13. Harold R. Regier, "California Farmer/Worker Issue: Some Reflections," Hist. Mss. 1-171, box 28, Guy F. Hershberger, 1896–1989, California Labor Concerns, Correspondence, 1974, MCA-G.

14. "Personal Notes" [1974], Hist. Mss. 1-171, box 28, Guy F. Hershberger, 1896–1989, California Labor Concerns, Misc. Background Material, Etc., MCA-G.

15. "Reflections on Koontz and Hershberger Reports (Personal views of Guy F. Hershberger)," Hist. Mss. 1-171, box 28, Guy F. Hershberger, 1896–1989, California Labor Concerns, Misc. Background Material, Etc., MCA-G.

16. Hubert Schwartzentruber to Guy Hershberger, May 30, 1974, Hist. Mss. 1-171, box 28, Guy F. Hershberger, 1896–1989, California Labor Concerns, Misc. Background Material, Etc., MCA-G.

17. Ted Koontz, "Report to MCC Peace Section on Conversations in California Regarding the Farm Labor Situation March 12–16, 1974," pp. 1–2, Hist. Mss. 1-171, box 28, Guy F. Hershberger, 1896–1989, California Labor Concerns, Correspondence, 1974, MCA-G.

18. Ibid., 2.

19. Ibid., 4–5.

20. Ibid., 5, 7.

21. Ibid., 6–7. Quote from p. 7.

22. Ibid., 8.

23. "The Rise of the UFW: La Huelga Continues," www.ufw.org/_page.php?menu=research&inc=history/03.html (accessed April 30, 2007).

24. Ted Koontz, "Report to MCC Peace Section on Conversations in California Regarding the Farm Labor Situation March 12–16, 1974," p. 9, Hist. Mss. 1-171, box 28, Guy F. Hershberger, 1896–1989, California Labor Concerns, Correspondence, 1974, MCA-G. Fresno Pacific College, now Fresno Pacific University, was initially Pacific Bible Institute.

25. Ibid., 10.

26. Ibid., 10–11.

27. Harold R. Regier, "Report on California Farmer/Worker Issue Reedley/Fresno and Vicinity Visit," March 12–16, 1974, p. 11.

28. For background, see Snyder, *Anabaptist History and Theology.* For the Anabaptist vision, see Bender, "The Anabaptist Vision," 3–24.

29. Beth Sutter's Labor Study Diary, 1974, May 28, 1974, Hist. Mss. 1-171, box 28, Guy F. Hershberger, 1896–1989, California Labor Concerns, MCA-G. The dating system of this diary is sporadic. Though days that are more precise can be approximated by the content of the diary, the dates used here will be the ones from the diary entries. As the diary covers a period of thirteen days, it is still accurate.

30. Ibid.

31. Ibid.

32. Ibid.

33. Ibid. I have used the underlining as in the original source.

34. Ibid.

35. Ibid.

36. Ibid. Rev. Janzen repeated these points in Harold R. Regier, "Report on California Farmer/Worker Issue Reedley/Fresno and Vicinity Visit," March 12–16, 1974, pp. 8–9, Hist. Mss. 1-171, box 28, Guy F. Hershberger, 1896–1989, California Labor Concerns, Correspondence, 1974, MCA-G.

37. Beth Sutter's Labor Study Diary.

38. Ibid.

39. Ibid.

40. Bob Buxman, "Labor Practices of MB Farmers," M.Div. research project, Mennonite Brethren Biblical Seminary, 1978.

41. Harold R. Regier, "Report on California Farmer/Worker Issue Reedley/Fresno and Vicinity Visit," March 12–16, 1974, pp. 6–7.

42. The Lupe DeLeon and Neftali Torres report was not in any of the collections I found.

43. Minutes, United Farmworker-Grower Issues at Goshen College, July 30, 1974, Hist. Mss. 1-171, box 28, Guy F. Hershberger, 1896–1989, California Labor Concerns, Consultation on United Farmworker/Grower Issues (MBCM), 1974, MCA-G.

44. Toews, *Mennonites in American Society,* 238, 256–58.

45. Ibid., 261–62, 333–34. Quote from p. 334.

46. Harold R. Regier, "Report on California Farmer/Worker Issue Reedley/Fresno and Vicinity Visit," March 12–16, 1974, p. 11.

47. Ibid., 13.

48. Urry, *None But Saints.*

49. McWilliams, *Factories in the Field.*

50. Arthur Jost, Administrator West Coast Regional Office (MCC), to William Wiebe,

Chairman, Home Mission Board, Reedley, California, Feb. 1, 1951, MCC-WCO, box 2, MCC—West Coast: Correspondence Jan. to March 1951—Arthur Jost, CMBS-F.

Chapter 12. From Digging Gold to Saving Souls

1. Szasz, *Religion in the Modern American West*; Szasz and Szasz, "Religion and Spirituality," 359–91.
2. Driedger, *Mennonite Identity*, 111.
3. See, for example, Hine, *California's Utopian Colonies*; Miller, *The Quest for Utopia*; Bloom, *The American Religion*, 181–88; and Frankiel, *California's Spiritual Frontiers*.
4. Kraybill, "Modernity and Modernization," 95; Ainlay, "Communal Commitment," 142–46.
5. It can be argued that the "ecumenical" nature of evangelicalism was significant to the Mennonite Brethren success in California. See Guenther, "Evangelicalism in Mennonite Historiography," 35–53.
6. Kauffman and Driedger, *The Mennonite Mosaic*. Quote from p. 271.
7. Harms, *Geschichte der Mennoniten Brüdergemeinde*; Unruh, *Die Geschichte der Mennoniten-Brüdergemeinde*; Toews, *A History of the Mennonite Brethren Church*.
8. See especially Toews, *A Pilgrimage of Faith*, 205–328.
9. Urry, *None But Saints*; Urry, *Mennonites, Politics, and Peoplehood*.
10. Urry, "The Closed and Open," 479–82.
11. Ibid., 499–504. Quote from p. 500. See the table of the Wüst brethren pre-1860 and note that the vast majority are listed as teacher or merchant, after page 499.
12. Ibid., 578.
13. Klein, "Apocalypse Noir," 6.
14. The classic study of American millennialism is Tuveson, *Redeemer Nation*.
15. Toews, *Mennonites in American Society*, 34.

Epilogue. A New Breed of Mennonites

1. Dochuk, *From Bible Belt to Sunbelt*, 406; Starr, *Coast of Dreams*, 233–53, 498–99.
2. Carl Nolte, "Sprawl, Clutter Define Fresno: Civic Corruption Has Splotched the City's Image," *San Francisco Chronicle*, Sept. 1, 1999, 1, www.sfgate.com/news/article/Sprawl -Clutter-Define-Fresno-Civic-corruption-2911067.php#page-1.
3. Starr, *Coast of Dreams*, 497.
4. Ibid., 69–70, 489–503, 631.
5. Suter, "Embracing the Realities of Diverse Communities," 89–91. Employed by a biotech company, Ruth Suter was a member of First Mennonite Church of San Francisco, assistant moderator of the Pacific Southwest Mennonite Conference, and vice-chair of the Mennonite Church USA's Constituency Leaders Council.
6. Ibid., 88.
7. Pam, "Deeper Than Our Roots," 25.
8. Janzen, *Back to the City*, 61–64, 87.
9. Wright, "Mennonites in Southern California," 9.
10. Wright, "Mennonites in Southern California," 9–11.
11. James E. Horsch, ed. *Mennonite Directory 2001*, 105–108; *2000/2001 Planner Directory*, 118–26.
12. *2012/2013 Planner Directory*, Winnipeg: Board of Resource Ministries General

Conference of Mennonite Brethren Churches, Kindred Productions, 2012, 100–18, www
.mennoniteusa.org/online-directory.

13. Enns-Rempel, "West Coast MCC," 5; Froese, "Compassion and Culture," 129–48.

14. Enns-Rempel, "West Coast MCC," 5.

15. Martinez, "Reaching Out to Our Neighbors," 46, 50, 52–54.

16. Klassen, *Resolutions of the Pacific District*, 189–95.

17. Wright, "Mennonites in Southern California," 10.

18. Schmidt and Unger, "Telling the Good News," 43–45.

19. Toews, "Introduction," xii; Martens, "The Revision of the Fresno Pacific College
Idea," 119–21; Yoder, "From Monastery to Marketplace," 133–36.

20. Martens, "The Revision of the Fresno Pacific College Idea," 121–22, 126–30.

21. Toews, "The Evolution of the Fresno Pacific College Idea," 161; "The Fresno Pacific
University Idea," www.fresno.edu/about/fpu_idea (accessed July 24, 2013).

22. Loewen and Nolt, *Seeking Places of Peace*, 302–303; Janzen, *Entering the Wild*; Janzen,
"New Poems," 144; Hostetler, "The Story of *Mennonot*," 1–2.

23. Enns-Rempel, "West Coast MCC," 4–5.

24. "Kings View History," www.kingsview.org/?kv=about_us; "MHS Alliance," www
.kingsview.org/?kv=testimonials (both accessed July 24, 2013).

25. Peters, "Women of Commitment," 94–97. This caused some tension with the Wom-
en's Missionary Society (WMS), which met at the same time as the regional conference,
when changing the meeting times was met with resistance.

26. Toews and Enns-Rempel, "Adapting to the City," 152.

Bibliography

Archival Sources
Bancroft Library, University of California at Berkeley

William Neufeld Memoir. William Neufeld (BANC MSS 78/82c).
Kern County Land Co. *Californien als ein geeigneter Staat zur Etablirung von deutschen Kolonien: Kern County mit seinem fruchtbaren Ebenen und grossen Ansiedlung splatzen: die Kern County Land-Gesellschaft als Besitzerin von bewasserten Landereien, welche sie an deutsche Ansiedler zu verkaufen wunscht*
Bakersfield, California, 1895.

Center for Mennonite Brethren Studies, Fresno Pacific University

GENERAL CONFERENCE OF MENNONITE BRETHREN CHURCHES

Conference Yearbooks and Related Convention Records, 1878–
General Conference Seminary Commission 1948–1949
Mennonite Brethren Biblical Seminary, 1955–
Mennonite Brethren Missions/Services: Christian Witness
Reference and Counsel, Board of, 1928–1990

PACIFIC DISTRICT CONFERENCE OF MENNONITE BRETHREN CHURCHES—OFFICES

Bible Camps, Committee for, 1960–1967
Fresno Pacific University, 1944–
Home Missions, Board of, 1940–
Reference and Counsel, Board of, 1946– (Board of Faith and Life)
Welfare and Public Relations Committee, 1950–1967
Women's Missionary Service, 1949–
Yearbooks and Related Convention Records, 1912–

PACIFIC DISTRICT CONFERENCE OF MENNONITE BRETHREN CHURCHES—CONGREGATIONS

Bethania Mennonite Brethren Church, Escondido, California, 1908–1921
Bethany Mennonite Brethren Church, Fresno, California, 1939–
Butler Avenue Mennonite Brethren Church, Fresno, California, 1956–1988

City Terrace Brethren Church, Dinuba, California, 1913–1988
College Community Church, Mennonite Brethren, Clovis, California, 1962–1988
Dinuba Mennonite Brethren Church, Dinuba, California, 1925–
Heritage Bible Church, Bakersfield, California, 1917–1987
Kingsburg Mennonite Brethren Church, Kingsburg, California, 1962–1988
Living Hope Church, Downey, California, 1910–1985
Reedley Mennonite Brethren Church, Reedley, California, 1905–
Rosedale Bible Church, Bakersfield, California, 1910–1979
Shafter Mennonite Brethren Church, Shafter, California, 1918–1985
South Shafter Mennonite Brethren Church, Shafter, California, 1955–1987
Vinewood Community Church, Lodi, California, 1914–
Wasco Bible Church, Wasco, California, 1957–1991
Zion Mennonite Brethren Church, Dinuba, California, 1913–1988

PACIFIC DISTRICT CONFERENCE OF MENNONITE BRETHREN CHURCHES—OTHER

Kern County Christian Fellowship, 1938–1953, Record Group CB600
Mennonite Brethren Homes, Inc., 1945–present, Record Group CB400

MENNONITE CENTRAL COMMITTEE

West Coast Regional Office

UNITED STATES MENNONITE BRETHREN CONFERENCE

Board of Education, 1954–1979
United States Mennonite Brethren Conference Yearbooks, 1957–1965

PERSONAL PAPERS

M24: Arthur Jost Papers
M37: J. B. Toews Papers
M70: Helen C. Stoesz , *My Life Experiences from 1905–1936*
M189: E. J. Peters Papers
M239: Julius and Anna Siemens Papers
M250: Harold Gaede, CPS Diary 1944
M295: Dietrich J. and Lena Claassen Papers
M316: Henry J. Martens Research Collection, Kevin Enns-Rempel Papers

Center for Mennonite Brethren Studies, Tabor College

Martens, Henry J. 1867

First Mennonite Church, Reedley, California

First Mennonite Church Reedley Records

Mennonite Church USA Archives, Goshen College, Indiana

CONFERENCES

II-13: Pacific Coast Mennonite Conference, 1927–1979
II-15: Southwest Mennonite Conference, 1948–1994

CONGREGATIONS

III-5-1: Mountain View Mennonite Church, Upland, California
III-5-2: Calvary Christian Fellowship, Inglewood, California
III-57: Sharon Mennonite Church, Winton, CA California

MENNONITE MISSION IN LOS ANGELES

IV-7-1: Mennonite Board of Missions, Los Angeles 1921–1942

THE MENNONITE CENTRAL COMMITTEE ARCHIVAL COLLECTION, 1920–1995

IV-20: WMSC

IX-6-3: MCC Central Correspondence Files, "Kings View Hospital" 1947–1965

IX-6-3: MCC Central Correspondence Files, CPS Camps 150, 35, 107, 31, 1942–1946

IX-10: Mennonite Mental Health Services, Kings View Hospital, Reedley, California, 1946–1971

IX-10-4: Field Records, 1946–1971

IX-12-1: MCC Reports, "Kings View Homes Advisory Council and Building Committee, 1947–55"

IX-13-1: MCC CPS

IX-54: West Coast Regional Office, Reedley, California, 1947–1984

WOMEN'S DIARIES

Hist. Mss. 1-332 Agnes Albrecht Gunden (1888–1963)

Hist. Mss. 1-883 Dora Shantz Gehman (1897–1993)

PERSONAL COLLECTIONS

Hist. Mss. 1-723 Le Roy Bechler

Hist. Mss. 1-929 Glen Whitaker Collection, 1939–1935

Mennonite Church USA Archives, Bethel College, North Newton, Kansas

PACIFIC DISTRICT CONFERENCE

II.5.e. Vertical Files

II.5.j. Conference Files

CONGREGATIONAL RECORDS

MLA.CONG.4 Atwater Mennonite Church, Atwater, California

MLA.CONG.4a Bethel Mennonite Church, Winton, California, 1941–1965

First Mennonite Church, Shafter, California (unprocessed at MCA-N)

First Mennonite Church, Upland, California (unprocessed at MCA-N)

MLA.CONG.84 Immanuel Mennonite Church, Downey, California

MLA.CONG.85 Mennonite Community Church, Fresno, California

MLA.CONG.86 First Mennonite Church, Paso Robles, California

MLA.CONG.87 Willow Creek Mennonite Church, Paso Robles, California

MLA.CONG.88 First Mennonite Church, Reedley, California

PERSONAL MANUSCRIPTS

MS.236 Emma Mary Ruth Collection

MS.93 Menno Galle Collection

Small Archives Collections

SA 296 Phyllis Claassen

SA 1258 Oswald H. Goering

SA 1372 Katherine Esau, Botanist

Student Papers
Hinamon, Darlene. "History of the First Mennonite Church of Reedley." Feb. 1955.
Hirschler, Jo Lynn. "First Mennonite Church—Upland, California." Feb. 1958.
Janzen, Heinz. "The Mennonites in the San Joaquin Valley." May 1952. Correspondence.

VERTICAL FILES

First Mennonite Church, Upland, CA
Mennonite Community Church, Fresno, CA
Mennonite Sanitarium, Alta Loma, CA

Magazines, Newspapers, Yearbooks, and Reference Works

The Christian Leader
General Conference Yearbooks
Global Anabaptist Mennonite Encyclopedia Online (www.gameo.org)
Gospel Herald
The Gospel Witness, 1905—1908
Herald of Truth
The Mennonite (and *Supplements* 1912—1915)
Mennonite Brethren Biblical Seminary Catalog, 1955—1969
Mennonite Church Yearbooks
The Mennonite Community, 1947—1952
*The Mennonite Encyclopedia: A Comprehensive Reference Work on the Anabaptist-Mennonite Move-
    ment.* 4 Vols. Ed. Harold S. Bender et al. Scottdale, PA: Mennonite Publishing, 1955,
    1956, 1957, 1959.
Mennonite Weekly Review
Mennonite Yearbook, 1905—1971, passim (sometimes spelled "Year Book" in the original).
    This publication has a number of name changes, of which *Mennonite Yearbook* will be used
    to denote: *Mennonite Yearbook and Almanac* (1895—1930), *Yearbook of the General Conference
    of the Mennonite Church of North America* (1931—1946), and *Handbook of Information of the
    General Conference of the Mennonite Church of North America* (1947—present).
Pacific Bible Institute Catalog, 1944—1957. Alternative titles used include *Pacific Bible Institute,
    Fresno, California, Catalogue With Announcements for* [academic year listed], *Catalogue of
    Pacific Bible Institute* [academic year listed], [Academic Year] *Catalog, Pacific Bible Institute
    and Junior College*
Reedley Exponent, 1903—1954
Steinbach Post, 1915—1923
The Welfare and Public Relations Newsletter
Zionsbote

Sources Cited

50th Jubilee, 1905—1955: Mennonite Brethren Church Reedley, California. N.p., 1955.
Ahlstrom, Sydney E. *A Religious History of the American People.* New Haven, CT: Yale Univer-
    sity Press, 1972.
Ainlay, Stephen C. "Communal Commitment and Individualism." In *Anabaptist-Mennonite
    Identities in Ferment*, ed. Leo Driedger and Leland Harder, 135—53. Occasional Papers
    No. 14. Elkhart, IN: Institute of Mennonite Studies, 1990.

Albanese, Catherine L. *America: Religions and Religion.* 2nd ed. Santa Barbara: University of California Press, 1992.

Almirol, Edwin B. "Church Life Among Filipinos in Central California: Social Ties and Ethnic Identity." In *Religion and Society in the American West: Historical Essays*, ed. Carl Guarneri and David Alvarez, 299–316. Lanham, MD: University Press of America, 1987.

Anderson, Benedict. *Imagined Communities: Reflections on the Origin and Spread of Nationalism.* Rev. edition. London: Verso, 1991.

Anderson, Douglas Firth. "'A True Revival of Religion': Protestantism and the San Francisco Graft Prosecutions, 1906–1919." *Religion and American Culture* 4, no. 1 (Winter 1994): 25–49.

———. "Through Fire and Fair by the Golden Gate: Progressive Era Protestantism and Regional Culture." Ph. D. diss., Graduate Theological Union, 1988.

Anderson, Karen. "Western Women: The Twentieth-Century Experience." In *The Twentieth-Century West: Historical Interpretations*, ed. Gerald D. Nash and Richard Etulain, 99–122. Albuquerque: University of New Mexico Press, 1989.

Auernheimer, Roy. *Memories of a Farm Boy.* Newton, KS: Wordsworth, 1997.

Balzer, Joel. "The Supreme Court of the United States and the Naturalization of Pacifist Aliens, 1929–1955." M.A. thesis, Fresno State College, 1960.

Barrett, Lois. *The Vision and the Reality: The Story of Home Missions in the General Conference Mennonite Church.* Newton, KS: Faith and Life Press, 1983.

Beach, William B., Jr., and Anne Davis. "The Short-Doyle Program: Past, Present and Future." *California Medicine* 109, no. 5 (Nov. 1968): 398–402.

Bebbington, David. *Evangelicalism in Modern Britain: A History from the 1730s to the 1980s.* Grand Rapids: Baker Book House, 1992.

Bechler, Le Roy. *The Black Mennonite Church in North America 1886–1986.* Scottdale, PA: Herald Press, 1986.

Becker, Regina. *A Bundle of Living: Recollections of a Shafter Pioneer.* Shafter, CA: Shafter Historical Society, 1986.

———. *Our Heritage Memoirs: Family Register.* Shafter, CA: Belva M. Workentin, 1974.

Becker, Regina, comp. *Our Heritage.* Shafter, CA: n.p.,1981.

Bellah, Robert N. "Civil Religion in America." *Daedalus* 96 (1967): 1–21.

Bender, Harold S. "The Anabaptist Vision." *Church History* 13 (March 1944): 3–24.

———. "Foreword." For *Conscience Sake: A Study of Mennonite Migrations Resulting from the World War*, by Sanford Calvin Yoder, vii–xii. Scottdale, PA: Herald Press, 1945.

Bender, Titus William. "The Development of the Mennonite Mental Health Movement, 1942–1971." Ph.D. diss., Tulane University, 1976.

———. "The Mennonite Mental Health Movement and the Wider Society in the United States, 1942–1965." *Journal of Mennonite Studies* 29 (2011): 45–60.

Bergman, Phyllis, and Robert Toevs. *History of the Mennonites in the Paso Robles Area.* Compilation. N.p., 1988.

Berkeley, George. "Verses on the Prospect of Planting Arts and Learning in America." In *Berkeley! A Literary Tribute*, ed. Danielle La France, 3–4. Berkeley, CA: Heyday Books, 1997.

Bhabha, Homi K. *The Location of Culture.* London: Routledge Classics, 2004.

Bingham, Edwin R. "American Wests Through Autobiography and Memoir." *Pacific Historical Review* 56, no. 1 (Feb. 1987): 1–25.

Block, John. *Escape: Siberia to California—The 65 Year Providential Journey of Our Family.* N.p.: Fresno, CA, 1995.

Bloom, Harold. *The American Religion: The Emergence of the Post-Christian Nation.* New York: Simon and Schuster, 1992.

Blumhofer, Edith L. *Aimee Semple McPherson: Everybody's Sister.* Grand Rapids, MI: Eerdmans Publishing, 1993.

Boyer, Paul. *When Time Shall Be No More: Prophecy Belief in Modern American Culture.* Cambridge, MA: Harvard University Press, 1992.

Braude, Ann. "Women's History Is American Religious History." In *Retelling U.S. Religious History,* ed. Thomas A. Tweed, 87–107. Berkeley: University of California Press, 1997.

Brereton, Virginia Lieson. "United and Slighted: Women as Subordinated Insiders." In *Between the Times: The Travail of the Protestant Establishment in America, 1900–1960,* ed. William R. Hutchison, 143–67. Cambridge: Cambridge University Press, 1989.

Burkholder, Harold D. "The Pacific District Conference," *Mennonite Life* 6, no. 3 (July 1951): 24–27.

———. *The Story of Our Conference and Churches.* North Newton, KS: Mennonite Press, 1951.

Burns, Jeffrey M. "The Mexican-American Catholic Community in California, 1850–1980." In *Religion and Society in the American West: Historical Essays,* ed. Carl Guarneri and David Alvarez, 255–73. Lanham, MD: University Press of America, 1987.

Buxman, Bob. "Labor Practices of MB Farmers." M.Div. research project, Mennonite Brethren Biblical Seminary, 1978.

Campbell, Lee Price. "Seventy-Five Years on the Shores of the Peaceful Sea: A History of the Pacific District Conference of the General Conference Mennonite Church of North America." M.Div. thesis, Western Evangelical Seminary, 1973.

"A Centennial History of Mennonites in the Paso Robles Area." *California Mennonite Society Bulletin* 35 (Jan. 1998): 1–4.

Cha, Marn J. *Koreans in Central California (1903–1957): A Study of Settlement and Politics.* Lanham, MD: University Press of America, 2010.

Chan, Sucheng. *This Bitter-Sweet Soil: The Chinese in California Agriculture, 1860–1910.* Berkeley: University of California Press, 1986.

Charles, Howard. "A Presentation and Evaluation of MCC Draft Status Census." In *Proceedings of the Fourth Annual Conference on Mennonite Cultural Problems,* 83–106. North Newton, KS: Council of Mennonite and Affiliated Colleges, 1945.

The Church Alive in its 75th Year 1905–1980. Reedley, CA: 75th Anniversary Committee, 1980.

Dahl, Ruby. "A History of the Spanish Mennonite Brethren Churches in the Dinuba and Reedley Area." M.A. thesis, Mennonite Brethren Biblical Seminary, 1969.

Davis, Mike. *City of Quartz: Excavating the Future in Los Angeles.* New York: Vintage Books, 1992.

Day, Mark. *Forty Acres: César Chávez and the Farm Workers.* New York: Praeger, 1971.

Dayton, Donald W., and Robert K. Johnston. *The Variety of American Evangelicalism.* Knoxville: University of Tennessee Press, 1991.

Dean, Loomis. "Shirtsleeve Millionaires." Photographic essay. LIFE 31, no. 10 (Sept. 3, 1951): 105–13.

"Dinuba-Reedley Area Meeting Focuses on MB Hispanic Ministries." *Mennonite Brethren Historical Society of the West Coast* (California Mennonite Historical Society Bulletin) 4, no. 3 (March 1983): 1–2.

Dochuk, Darren. *From Bible Belt to Sunbelt: Plain-Folk Religion, Grassroots Politics, and the Rise of Evangelical Conservatism.* New York: Norton, 2011.

Dolan, Jay P. *The American Catholic Experience: A History from Colonial Times to the Present.* Notre Dame, IN: University of Notre Dame Press, 1992.

Driedger, Leo. *Mennonite Identity in Conflict.* Lewiston, NY: Edwin Mellen Press, 1988.

Dueck, Dora. "Images of the City in the Mennonite Brethren *Zionsbote,* 1890–1940." *Journal of Mennonite Studies* 20 (2002): 179–97.

Dunne, John Gregory. *Delano.* Revised and updated. New York: Farrar, Straus and Giroux, 1971.

Dyck, Cornelius J. "In the California Gold Rush." *Mennonite Life* 11, no. 1 (Jan. 1956): 25–28.

———. *An Introduction to Mennonite History.* 1967. 3rd ed. Scottdale, PA: Herald Press, 1993.

Ediger, Elmer M. "Influences on the Origin and Development of Mennonite Mental Health Centers." *Mennonite Quarterly Review* 56, no. 1 (Jan. 1982): 32–46.

———. "Roots of the Mennonite Mental Health Story." In *If We Can Love: The Mennonite Mental Health Story,* ed. Vernon H. Neufeld, 3–28. Newton, KA: Faith and Life Press, 1983.

Engh, Michael E., S.J. *Frontier Faiths: Church, Temple, and Synagogue in Los Angeles, 1846–1888.* Albuquerque: University of New Mexico Press, 1992.

Engel, Reuben. "History of the Church 1920s–1940s." In *The History of the Woodrow Mennonite Brethren Church 1910–1985,* 7–9. Woodrow, SK: Mennonite Brethren Church, Woodrow Gospel Chapel, 1985.

Enns-Rempel, Kevin. "Book Review." *California Mennonite Historical Society Bulletin* 31 (Dec. 1994): 9–12.

———. "California in their Own Words: First-hand Accounts of Early Mennonite Life in the Golden State." *California Mennonite Historical Society Bulletin* 29 (Oct. 1993): 1–2, 4–10.

———. "Churches that Died on the Vine: Short-lived California Mennonite Congregations." *California Mennonite Historical Society Bulletin* 49 (Summer 2008): 1–5.

———. "The Eymanns: Reedley's 'First Mennonite Family.'" *California Mennonite Historical Society Bulletin* 24 (April 1991): 6–8.

———. "From Russia with Pedagogy: The Origins of a Mennonite Educational Program in Reedley." *California Mennonite Historical Society Bulletin* 27 (Nov. 1992): 1–2, 6–10.

———. "The Giffen Mansion: Home of the Mennonite Brethren Biblical Seminary." *Mennonite Brethren Historical Society of the West Coast Bulletin* 21 (Dec. 1989): 1–2, 7.

———. "Health, Wealth, and Ministry: An Overview of Mennonites' Presence in California." *Mennonite Historical Bulletin* 68 (July 2007): 3–9.

———. "In Search of the 'Greatest Mennonite Settlement': The Career of Julius Siemens." *California Mennonite Historical Society Bulletin,* 26 (April 1992): 1–2, 6–10.

———. "Making a Home in the City: Mennonite Brethren Urbanization in California." In *Bridging Troubled Waters: The Mennonite Brethren at Mid-Twentieth Century,* ed. Paul Toews, 213–26. Winnipeg, MB: Kindred Productions, 1995.

———. "Many Roads to the San Joaquin Valley: Sources of Mennonite Settlement in the Reedley/Dinuba Area." *California Mennonite Historical Society Bulletin* 24 (April 1991): 1–4.

———. "The Mennonite Sanitarium at Alta Loma, California: 1914–1923." *California Mennonite Historical Society Bulletin* 25 (Nov. 1991): 1–2, 7–11.

———. "The Mennonite Settlement of Dos Palos." *Mennonite Brethren Historical Society of the West Coast Bulletin* 19 (April 1988): 3–4.

———. "Mennonites in California." Unpublished paper presented at Mennonite Central Committee U.S. board meetings, Nov. 2, 2001, Reedley, California. Copy in author's possession.

———. "Mennonites in the Escondido Valley." *Mennonite Brethren Historical Society of the West Coast Bulletin* 21 (Dec. 1989): 3–4.

———. "A New Life in the West: Settlement and Colonization on the Pacific Coast." In *Years of Fellowship: Pacific District Conference of the Mennonite Brethren Churches 1912–1987*, ed. Esther Jost, 71–85. Fresno, CA: Pacific District Conference of the Mennonite Brethren Churches, 1987.

———. "Origins of the Pacific District Conference." *Mennonite Brethren Historical Society of the West Coast Bulletin* 17 (April 1987): 1–3.

———. "Pacific Bible Institute Once Owned an Architectural Treasure." *Mennonite Brethren Historical Society of the West Coast Bulletin* 20 (April 1989): 1–2, 4.

———. "The Pacific District Conference and CPS: A Reciprocal Relationship." *Mennonite Brethren Historical Society of the West Coast Bulletin* 19 (April 1988): 1, 7.

———. "The Siberian Journey of M. B. Fast & Wilhelm P. Neufeld." *California Mennonite Historical Society Bulletin* 22 (April 1990): 4–6.

———. "They Came From Many Places: Sources of Mennonite Migration to California, 1887–1939." *California Mennonite Historical Society Bulletin* 28 (May 1993): 1–7.

———. "West Coast MCC: A Brief Overview of its Origins, Development and Activities." *California Mennonite Historical Society Bulletin* 32 (June 1995): 1–5.

———. "The West Coast Mennonite Relief Sale: The 'First' MCC Relief Sale." *Mennonite Brethren Historical Society of the West Coast Bulletin* 22 (April 1990): 1–3.

Epp, Frank H. *Mennonite Exodus*. Altona, MB: Friesen and Sons, 1962.

Erb, Alta Mae. *Studies in Mennonite City Missions*. Scottdale, PA: Mennonite Publishing House, 1937.

Ernst, Eldon G. "The Emergence of California in American Religious Historiography." *Religion and American Culture: A Journal of Interpretation* 11, no. 1 (2001): 31–52.

———. "Religion in California." *Pacific Theological Review* 19 (Winter 1986): 43–51.

Ernst, Eldon G., with Douglas Firth Anderson. *Pilgrim Progression: The Protestant Experience in California*. Santa Barbara, CA: Fithian Press, 1993

Esau, H. T. *First Sixty Years of M. B. Missions*. Hillsboro, KS: Mennonite Brethren Publishing House, 1954.

Ewy, Arnold C. "The Grape and Raisin Industry." *Mennonite Life* 5, no. 4 (Oct. 1950): 4–9.

Eymann, Harold. "Eymanns Here for Nearly a Century." *Reedley Historian*, Oct. 9, 1986, 9A–10A.

Falcón, Rafael. *The Hispanic Mennonite Church in North America 1932–1987*. Trans. Ronald Collins. Scottdale, PA: Herald Press, 1986.

Fast, Dennis. "A Strategy for Church Growth in the Butler Avenue Mennonite Brethren Church of Fresno, California." M.Div. Research project, Mennonite Brethren Biblical Seminary, 1980.

The First Mennonite Church, 1906–1956, Reedley, California, Fiftieth Anniversary Program and a Brief History of the Church. N.p., 1956.

Fjellstrom, Phebe. *Swedish-American Colonization in the San Joaquin Valley in California: A Study of the Acculturation and Assimilation of an Immigrant Group*. Studia ethnographica Upsaliensia 33. Uppsala: Institut for allmen och jamforande etnografi, 1970.

Forsyth, Dan. "Motivational Bases for Conformity to Religious Norms." Ph.D. diss., University of California, San Diego, 1983.

Frankiel, Sandra Sizer. *California's Spiritual Frontiers: Religious Alternatives in Anglo-Protestantism, 1850–1910*. Berkeley: University of California Press, 1988.

Frantz, Adolf Ingrid. *Water from the Well: The Recollections of a Former Plowboy*. Philadelphia: Dorrance, 1978.

Frodsham, Noel. "A Study of the Russian-Germans in Fresno County, California." M.A. thesis, University of Redlands, California, 1949.

Froese, Brian. "Compassion and Culture: Southeast Asian Refugees and California Mennonites." *Journal of Mennonite Studies* 24 (2006): 129–48.

———. "Quilts, Bandages and Efficiency: Mennonite Women's Missionary Societies and the Formation of a Modern Social-Religious Identity in California, 1930–1960." In *Historical Papers 2004: Canadian Society of Church History*, ed. Bruce L. Guenther, 15–32. N.p., 2004.

———. "Sewing Peace: Women's Missionary Societies, Churches, and the Californian Civilian Public Service Camps, 1940–1947." *California Mennonite Historical Society Bulletin* 40 (Spring 2004): 1–5.

———. "'Where the People Tell No Lies': Religious Images of California in Mennonite Memoirs." *California Mennonite Historical Society Bulletin* 38 (April 2003): 1–3.

"From a Rocking Chair: The First MCC Relief Sale." *MCC Contact* 12, no. 2 (April 1988): 2.

Gaede, Menno. "Roots of City Government." *Reedley Historian*, Oct. 13, 1983, 4A–5A.

Gasset, José Ortega. *Phenomenology and Art.* Trans. Philip W. Silver. New York: Norton, 1975.

Gaustad, Edwin S., and Leigh E. Schmidt. *The Religious History of America: The Heart of the American Story from Colonial Times to Today.* Rev. ed. New York: HarperSanFrancisco, 2002.

Gauvreau, Michael. "Protestantism Transformed: Personal Piety and Evangelical Social Vision, 1815–1867." In *The Canadian Protestant Experience, 1760 to 1990*, ed. George A. Rawlyk, 48–97. Montreal: McGill-Queen's University Press, 1990.

General Conference of Mennonite Brethren Churches. *Resolutions: Board of General Welfare and Public Relations.* Hillsboro, KS: Board of Missions and Services, 1989.

Gerbrandt, John J. *Destination California.* Photocopy of a typewritten manuscript, n.d.

"German Mennonites." *Reedley Historian*, Oct. 13, 1983, 3B.

Gingerich, Melvin. *Service for Peace: A History of Mennonite Civilian Public Service.* Akron, PA: Mennonite Central Committee, 1949.

Goering, Gladys V. *Women in Search of Mission: A History of the General Conference Mennonite Women's Organization.* Newton, KS: Faith and Life Press, 1980.

Goertzen, John. *Bethany Church: 50 Years.* Fresno: Bethany MB Church, 1992.

"Gold Award Mental Health Services for Rural Counties: Kings View Community Mental health Center Reedley, California." *Hospital and Community Psychiatry* (Oct. 1971): 299–301.

Goodykoontz, Colin Brumitt. *Home Missions on the American Frontier: With Particular Reference to the American Home Missionary Society.* Caldwell, ID: Caxton Printers, 1939.

Gregory, James N. *American Exodus: The Dust Bowl Migration and Okie Culture in California.* New York: Oxford University Press, 1989.

Guenther, Bruce L. "Evangelicalism in Mennonite Historiography: The Decline of Anabaptism or a Path Towards Dynamic Ecumenism?" *Journal of Mennonite Studies* 24 (2006): 35–53.

Harder, Leland, and Kevin Enns-Rempel. "The Henry J. Martens Land Scheme." In *Anabaptist/Mennonite Faith and Economics*, ed. Calvin Redekop, Victor A. Krahn, and Samuel J. Steiner, 199–222. Lanham, MD: University Press of America, 1994.

Hardwick, Susan Wiley. *Russian Refuge: Religion, Migration, and Settlement on the North American Pacific Rim.* Chicago: University of Chicago Press, 1993.

Harms, J. F. *Geschichte der Mennoniten Brüdergemeinde.* Hillsboro, KS: Mennonite Brethren Publishing House, 1925.

Hart, D. G. *Deconstructing Evangelicalism: Conservative Protestantism in the Age of Billy Graham.* Grand Rapids, MI: Baker Academic, 2004.

——. *That Old-Time Religion in Modern America: Evangelical Protestantism in the Twentieth Century.* Chicago: Ivan R. Dee, 2002.

Hasegawa, Melinda. "The Story of Hispanic Ministries: Becoming a Multicultural Church." In *First Mennonite Church: Celebrating Our Centennial—1906–2006: The Unfolding of Our Story,* ed. Corinna Siebert Ruth, 169–77. Reedley, CA: First Mennonite Church, Reedley, 2006.

Haslam, Gerald. *The Other California: The Great Central Valley in Life and Letters.* Reno: University of Nevada Press, 1994.

"Hennessy Accepts Murphy Dare." *Boston Evening Transcript,* Oct. 28, 1913, 3. http://news .google.com/newspapers?nid=2249&dat=19131028&id=BBsnAAAAIBAJ&sjid =cgMGAAAAIBAJ&pg=4653,5381686.

"Hennessy Makes New Graft Charges." *New York Times,* Sept. 10,1913. http://query.ny times.com/mem/archive-free/pdf?res=9C02E0DB123FE633A25753C1A96F9C94 6296D6CF.

Hershberger, Guy Franklin. *The Mennonite Church in the Second World War.* Scottdale, PA: Mennonite Publishing House, 1951.

——. *War, Peace, and Nonresistance.* Scottdale, PA: Herald Press, 1946.

Hertzler, Daniel. *From Germantown to Steinbach: A Mennonite Odyssey.* Scottdale, PA: Herald Press, 1981.

Hiebert, P. C. *Feeding the Hungry: Russia Famine, 1919–1925.* Scottdale, PA: Mennonite Central Committee, 1929.

Hine, Robert V. *California's Utopian Colonies.* San Marino, CA: Huntington Library, 1953.

Hine, Robert V., and John Mack Faragher. *The American West: A New Interpretive History.* New Haven, CT: Yale University Press, 2000.

History of the First Mennonite Church, Upland, California 1903–1984. Upland, CA: Floyd Brunk, 1984.

A History of the Mennonite Brethren Church of Rosedale, California: Its Organization and its Development 1909–1984. Rosedale, CA: Seventy-Fifth Anniversary Committee, 1984.

The History of Vinewood Community Church 1915–1991: Commemorating a Celebration of Faith. N.p., 1991.

Hofer, David L. *Accepting the Challenge: The Autobiography of David L. Hofer.* As told to Charlyn Bridges. Reedley, CA: Challenge Books, 2001.

Horsch, L. H. "The Citrus Fruit Industry of Southern California." *Mennonite Life* 2, no. 4 (Oct. 1947): 4–7.

Horwitz, George D. *La Causa: The California Grape Strike.* New York: Macmillan, 1970.

Hostetler, Lester. "Mennonite Citrus Fruit Growers." *Mennonite Life* 2, no. 4 (Oct. 1947): 8–9.

Hostetler, Sheri. "The Story of Mennonot." *Mennonot: For Mennos on the Margins* 1 (Fall 1993): 1–2, www.keybridgeltd.com/mennonot/Issue1.pdf.

Hundley, Norris, Jr. *The Great Thirst: Californians and Water: A History.* Berkeley: University of California Press, 2001.

Iorio, Sharon Hartin. *Faith's Harvest: Mennonite Identity in Northwest Oklahoma.* Norman: University of Oklahoma Press, 1999.

Isaak, H. P. *Our Life Story and Escape.* Dinuba, CA: N.p., 1976.

Jantzen, John B. *Frank F. Jantzen: Memoirs: As Recalled by His Children.* N.p., 1997.

Janzen, Jean. *Entering the Wild: Essays on Faith and Writing.* Intercourse, PA: Good Books, 2012.

——. "New Poems." *Journal of Mennonite Studies* 6 (1988): 144–51.

Janzen, Rod. "Back to the City: Mennonite Community Church Fresno, California 1954–2004." *California Mennonite Historical Society Bulletin* 43 (Winter 2006): 1–15.

————. *Back to the City: Mennonite Community Church Fresno, California, 1954–2004*. Fresno, CA: Mennonite Community Church, 2004.

————. "Jacob D. Hofer: Evangelist, Minister and Carpenter." *California Mennonite Historical Society Bulletin* 30 (May 1994): 1–2, 4–9.

Johnson, Marilynn S. *The Second Gold Rush: Oakland and the East Bay in World War II*. Berkeley: University of California Press, 1993.

Johnson, Susan Lee. "'A Memory Sweet to Soldiers': The Significance of Gender in the History of the 'American West.'" *Western Historical Quarterly* 24, no. 4 (Nov. 1993): 495–517.

"Joseph Summers." Obituary. *Herald of Truth*, Sept. 15, 1892.

"Joseph Summers—1823–1892." *Mennonite Historical Bulletin* 12, no. 2 (April 1951): 1–2.

Jost, Arthur. "Fellowship in Service: Social Ministries in the Pacific District." In *75 Years of Fellowship: Pacific District Conference of the Mennonite Brethren Churches 1912–1987*, ed. Esther Jost, 71–85. Fresno, CA: Pacific District Conference of the Mennonite Brethren Churches, 1987.

————. "Kings View Homes." *Mennonite Central Committee Services Bulletin* 4, no. 8 (Oct. 1950): 5, 8.

————. "Mennonites and Mental Illness—A Fifty Year History." *Journal of the California Alliance for the Mentally Ill* 3, no. 4 (1992): 27–28.

————. "Private Centers and Public Funding." In *If We Can Love: The Mennonite Mental Health Story*, ed. Vernon H. Neufeld, 267–81. Newton, KS: Faith and Life Press, 1983.

Jost, Arthur, and Vernon Neufeld. "Comprehensive Community Care." *Hospitals* (Journal of the American Hospital Association] 44 (March 16, 1970): 85–87.

Jost, Esther. "Kings View Reedley, California." In *If We Can Love: The Mennonite Mental Health Story*, ed. Vernon H. Neufeld, 77–96. Newton, KS: Faith and Life Press, 1983.

Juhnke, James C. *Vision, Doctrine, War: Mennonite Identity and Organization in America 1890–1930*. Scottdale, PA: Herald Press, 1989.

Juhnke, James C., and Carol M. Hunter. *The Missing Peace: The Search for Nonviolent Alternative in United States History*. 2nd ed. Kitchener, ON: Pandora Press, 2004.

Kauffman, J. Howard, and Leo Driedger. *The Mennonite Mosaic: Identity and Modernization*. Scottdale, PA: Herald Press, 1991.

Kauffman, Jess. *A Vision and a Legacy: The Story of Mennonite Camping, 1920–80*. Newton, KS: Faith and Life Press, 1984.

Kaufman, Edmund G. *The Development of the Missionary and Philanthropic Interest Among The Mennonites of North America*. Berne, IN: Mennonite Book Concern, 1931.

Kaufman, Edmund G., comp. *General Conference Mennonite Pioneers*. North Newton, KS: Bethel College, 1973.

Klassen, A. J. "The Biblical Seminary: A Brief Historical Survey." In *The Seminary Story: Twenty Years of Education in Ministry, 1955–1975*, ed. A. J. Klassen, 8–16. Fresno, CA: Mennonite Brethren Biblical Seminary, 1975.

————. "Into Curriculum Structures." In *The Seminary Story: Twenty Years of Education in Ministry, 1955–1975*, ed. A. J. Klassen, 25–34. Fresno, CA: Mennonite Brethren Biblical Seminary, 1975.

Klassen, A. J., ed. *Resolutions of the Pacific District Conference of Mennonite Brethren Churches 1911–1978*. Fresno, CA: Pacific District Conference of Mennonite Brethren Churches, 1979.

Klassen, Peter J. "To Reclaim a Heritage: The Birth of the Historical Society." *California Mennonite Historical Society Bulletin* 23 (Nov. 1990): 2.

Klein, Kerwin Lee. "Apocalypse Noir: Carey McWilliams and Posthistorical California."

Morrison Library Inaugural Address Series No. 7. Berkeley: Doe Library, University of California, 1997.

Kraybill, Donald B. "From Enclave to Engagement: MCC and the Transformation of Mennonite Identity." *Mennonite Quarterly Review* 70, no. 1 (Jan. 1996): 23–58.

———. "Modernity and Modernization." In *Anabaptist-Mennonite Identities in Ferment*, ed. Leo Driedger and Leland Harder, 91–109. Occasional Papers No. 14. Elkhart, IN: Institute of Mennonite Studies, 1990.

Krehbiel, H. J. *A Trip Through Europe, A Plea for the Abolition of War and A Report of the 400th Anniversary of the Mennonite Denomination.* Newton, KS: Herald Publishing, 1926.

Krehbiel. H. P. *The History of the General Conference of the Mennonite Church of North America.* Vol. 2. Newton, KS: H. P. Krehbiel, 1938.

Kreider, Robert. "Series Introduction." *Mennonites in American Society, 1930–1970: Modernity and the Persistence of Religious Community*, by Paul Toews, 11–12. Scottdale, PA: Herald Press, 1996.

Langley, Silas. "America and the Conscientious Objector in the Early Cold War: Arthur Jost vs. the United States." Paper for the Young Scholar's Award of the National Endowment for the Humanities, Fresno Pacific College, California, 1991.

———. "Conscientious Objection in the United States: Individual or Corporate? The Case of Arthur Jost v. The United States, 1954." *Mennonite Quarterly Review* 69, no. 4 (Oct. 1995): 37–52.

Leichty, Bruce. " 'Not Going to be a Kicker': A Bishop in California." *California Mennonite Historical Society Bulletin* 36 (April 1999): 1–8.

León, Luís D. "César Chávez and Mexican American Civil Religion." *Latino Religions and Civic Activism in the United States*, ed. Gastón Espinosa, Virgilio Elizondo, and Jesse Miranda, 53–64. New York: Oxford University Press, 2005.

Levy, Jacques E. *César Chávez: Autobiography of La Causa.* New York: Norton, 1975.

Lichti, Elsie. "Churches: Mennonites' History Traces Back to 1903." *Reedley Historian*, Oct. 11, 1984, 9B

Limerick, Patricia Nelson. *Legacy of Conquest: The Unbroken Past of the American West.* New York: Norton, 1987.

Lindley, Susan Hill. *"You Have Stept out of Your Place": A History of Women and Religion in America.* Louisville, KY: Westminster John Knox Press, 1996.

Lloyd-Moffett, Stephen R. "The Mysticism and Social Activism of César Chávez." In *Latino Religions and Civic Activism in the United States*, ed. Gastón Espinosa, Virgilio Elizondo, and Jesse Miranda, 35–51. New York: Oxford University Press, 2005.

Loewen, Harry, and Steven Nolt. *Through Fire and Water: An Overview of Mennonite History.* Scottdale, PA: Herald Press, 1996.

Loewen, Royden. *Diaspora in the Countryside: Two Mennonite Communities and Mid-Twentieth Century Rural Disjuncture.* Toronto, ON: University of Toronto Press, 2006.

Loewen, Royden and Steven M. Nolt. *Seeking Places of Peace: Global Mennonite History Series: North America.* Intercourse, PA: Good Books, 2012.

Loewen, Ted, ed. *Reedley First Mennonite Church: The First Seventy-Five Years 1906–1981.* North Newton, KA: Mennonite Press, 1981.

Lohrenz, John Howard. "History of the Mennonite Brethren Church of North America." M.A. thesis, Bluffton College, Ohio, 1919.

Loofbourow, Leon L. *In Search of God's Gold: A Story of Continued Christian Pioneering in California.* San Francisco: Historical Society of the California-Nevada Annual Conference of the Methodist Church, 1950.

Luthy, David. *The Amish in America: Settlements That Failed, 1840–1960.* Aylmer, ON: Pathway Publishers, 1986.

Maffly-Kipp, Laurie F. "Eastward Ho! American Religion from the Perspective of the Pacific Rim." In *Retelling U.S. Religious History,* ed. Thomas A. Tweed, 127–48. Berkeley: University of California Press, 1997.

Marsden, George M. "The Evangelical Denomination." In *Evangelicalism and Modern America,* ed. George Marsden, vii–xix. Grand Rapids, MI: Eerdmans Publishing, 1984.

———. *Fundamentalism and American Culture: The Shaping of Twentieth-Century Evangelicalism 1870–1925.* Oxford: Oxford University Press, 1980.

———. *Understanding Fundamentalism and Evangelicalism.* Grand Rapids, MI: Eerdmans Publishing, 1991.

Martens, Peter C. "A Study of Mennonites on the Pacific Slope." Master of theology thesis, San Francisco Theological Seminary, 1959.

Martens, Wilfred. "The Revision of the Fresno Pacific College Idea, 1979–1983: A Contextual and Linguistic Interpretation." In *Mennonite Idealism and Higher Education: The Story of the Pacific College Idea,* ed. Paul Toews, 119–32. Fresno, CA: Center for Mennonite Brethren Studies, 1995.

———. *River of Glass.* Scottdale, PA: Herald Press, 1980.

Martinez, Juan. "Hispanics in California: Myth and Opportunity." *Direction* 16, no. 1 (Spring 1987): 47–56.

———. "Reaching Out to Our Neighbors: Hispanic Mennonite Brethren Churches in California." In *75 Years of Fellowship: Pacific District Conference of the Mennonite Brethren Churches 1912–1987,* ed. Esther Jost, 46–56. Fresno, CA: Pacific District Conference of the Mennonite Brethren Churches, 1987.

Marty, Martin E. *The Irony of It All, 1893–1919.* Vol. 1 of *Modern American Religion.* Chicago: University of Illinois Press, 1986.

———. *The Noise of Conflict, 1919–1941.* Vol. 2 of *Modern American Religion.* Chicago: University of Illinois Press, 1991.

———. *Pilgrims in Their Own Land: 500 Years of Religion in America.* New York: Penguin, 1984.

———. *Under God, Indivisible, 1941–1960.* Vol. 3 of *Modern American Religion.* Chicago: University of Illinois Press, 1996.

Matsumoto, Valerie J. *Farming the Home Place: A Japanese American Community in California, 1919–1982.* Ithaca, NY: Cornell University Press, 1993.

Matthiessen, Peter. *Sal Si Puedes: César Chávez and the New American Revolution.* New York: Random House, 1969.

May, Lary. *Screening Out the Past: The Birth of Mass Culture and the Motion Picture Industry.* Chicago: University of Chicago Press, 1983.

McClure, Heath. "The Challenge of Yesterday: A History of the Mennonite Brethren Church at Rosedale, California." *California Mennonite Historical Society Bulletin* 33 (March 1996): 1–7.

McGirr, Lisa. *Suburban Warriors: The Origins of the New American Right.* Princeton, NJ: Princeton University Press, 2002.

McMahon, Robert J. *Dean Acheson and the Creation of an American World Order.* Washington, DC: Potomac Books, 2009.

McWilliams, Carey. *California: The Great Exception.* 1949. Berkeley: University of California Press, 1999.

———. *Factories in the Field: The Story of Migratory Farm Labor in California.* 1939. Berkeley: University of California Press, 2000.

———. *Southern California: An Island on the Land.* 1946. Salt Lake City, UT: Gibbs Smith, 1995.

Meister, Dick, and Anne Loftis. *A Long Time Coming: The Struggle to Unionize America's Farm Workers.* New York: Macmillan, 1977.

The Mennonite Mental Health Story. Fresno, CA: Mennonite Mental Health Services, 1972.

Miller, Timothy. *The Quest for Utopia in Twentieth-Century America, Volume I: 1900–1960.* Syracuse, NY: Syracuse University Press, 1998.

Mock, Melanie Springer. *Writing Peace: The Unheard Voices of Great War Mennonite Objectors.* Telford, PA: Pandora Press, 2003.

"Modern Construction Methods Produce Satisfactory, Low-Cost Building." *Mental Hospitals* 3, no. 1 (Jan. 1952): 5, 8.

Nachtigall, Gary B. "Mennonite Migration and Settlements of California." M.A. thesis, California State University, Fresno, 1972.

Nash, Gerald D. *The American West in the Twentieth Century: A Short History of an Urban Oasis.* Englewood Cliffs, NJ: Prentice-Hall, 1973.

Neufeld, Herb H. *Jacob's Journey: Escape from Communist Russia.* New York: Vantage Press, 2000.

Neufeld, Vernon H. "Mennonite Mental Health Services." In *If We Can Love: The Mennonite Mental Health Story,* ed. Vernon H. Neufeld, 31–53. Newton, KS: Faith and Life Press, 1983.

———. "The Mennonite Mental Health Story." *Mennonite Quarterly Review* 56, no. 1 (Jan. 1982): 18–31.

Neufeld, Vernon H., ed. *If We Can Love: The Mennonite Mental Health Story.* Newton, KS: Faith and Life Press, 1983.

Noll, Mark A. *American Evangelical Christianity: An Introduction.* Oxford: Blackwell, 2001.

Ollenburger, Ben C. *Ebenfeld: History, Interpretation, and Mennonite Brethren Identity.* Hillsboro, KS: Center for Mennonite Brethren Studies, 1994.

Our 50th Anniversary, November First, 1909–1959: Rosedale Mennonite Brethren. Bakersfield, CA: Rosedale Mennonite Brethren Church, 1959.

Pacific District Conference of the Mennonite Brethren Churches. *Home Missions of the Pacific District Conference, Mennonite Brethren Church of North America.* Fresno, CA: Pacific District Conference of the Mennonite Brethren Churches, 1949.

Pam, Chuwang. "Deeper Than Our Roots." In *Anabaptist Visions for the New Millennium: A Search for Identity,* ed. Dale Schrag and James Juhnke, 23–26. Kitchener, ON: Pandora Press, 2000.

Pannabecker, Samuel Floyd. *Open Doors: The History of the General Conference Mennonite Church.* Newton, KS: Faith and Life Press, 1975.

Parsons, Frances Berg. *Exiles of the Steppes.* Modesto, CA: N.p. 1982.

Penner, J. C., and Adolf I. Frantz. "Through the Years: A History of the Mennonite Brethren Church of Shafter, California Its Organization and Its Development 1918–1968." Photocopy of typewritten manuscript. Shafter, CA: Fiftieth Anniversary Celebration Committee, n.d.

Penner, Stephen. "The Story of the Mennonite Central Committee (MCC) at First Mennonite Church." In *First Mennonite Church: Celebrating Our Centennial—1906–2006: The Unfolding of Our Story,* ed. Corinna Siebert Ruth, 169–77. Reedley, CA: First Mennonite Church, Reedley, 2006.

Peters, Frank C. "The Coming of the Mennonite Brethren to the United States and Their Efforts at Education." Th.D. diss., Central Baptist Theological Seminary, 1957.

Peters, Marilyn. "Women in the Christian Church." In *Your Daughters Shall Prophesy: Women in Ministry in the Church,* ed. John E. Toews, Valerie Rempel, and Katie Funk Wiebe, 157–71. Winnipeg, MB: Kindred Press, 1992.

———. "Women of Commitment: A Rich Heritage & Promising Future." In *75 Years of Fellowship: Pacific District Conference of the Mennonite Brethren Churches 1912–1987*, ed. Esther Jost, 86–97. Fresno, CA: Pacific District Conference of the Mennonite Brethren Churches, 1987.

Porterfield, Amanda. *Feminine Spirituality in America: From Sarah Edwards to Martha Graham.* Philadelphia: Temple University Press, 1980.

Prieb, Wesley. *Peter C. Hiebert: "He Gave Them Bread."* Hillsboro, KS: Center for Mennonite Brethren Studies, Tabor College, 1990.

Program of the Forty-Fourth Session of the Pacific District Conference of the Mennonite Church of North America, June 17–20, 1943, held at First Mennonite Church, Reedley, California.

Redekop, Calvin. "Mennonite Brethren Economic Developments in the United States." In *Bridging Troubled Waters: Mennonite Brethren at Mid-Twentieth Century,* ed. Paul Toews, 117–45. Winnipeg, MB: Kindred Productions, 1995.

Redekop, Calvin, Stephen C. Ainlay, and Robert Siemens. *Mennonite Entrepreneurs.* Baltimore, MD: Johns Hopkins University Press, 1995.

Redekop, Gloria Neufeld. *The Work of Their Hands: Mennonite Women's Societies in Canada.* Toronto, ON: Wilfrid Laurier University Press, 1996.

Redekop, John H. "Mennonite Brethren in a Changing Society." In *For Everything a Season: Mennonite Brethren in North America, 1874–2002: An Informal History,* ed. Paul Toews and Kevin Enns-Rempel, 151–65. Fresno, CA: Historical Commission, 2002.

Reedley: A Study of Ethnic Heritage: A Study of Selected Ethnic Groups Playing a Major Role in the Historical Development of Reedley. Fresno, CA: Fresno Pacific College, Professional Development Division, 1988.

Reimche, Wilfred. "A History of the Woodrow Gospel Chapel, 1910–1940." In *The History of the Woodrow Mennonite Brethren Church 1910–1985,* 1–7. Woodrow, SK: Mennonite Brethren Church, Woodrow Gospel Chapel, 1985.

Reimer, Dalton. "The Origins of the Fresno Pacific College Idea." In *Mennonite Idealism and Higher Education: The Story of the Pacific College Idea,* ed. Paul Toews, 24–39. Fresno, CA: Center for Mennonite Brethren Studies, 1995.

Reimer, G. A. "Banking Was, Still is Bustling." *Reedley Historian,* Oct. 14, 1982, 10B.

Reimer, Otto B. "The Story of the Mennonite Brethren Church of Reedley, 1905–1980." Photocopy of a typewritten manuscript. N.p., n.d.

Reisner, Marc. *Cadillac Desert: The American West and Its Disappearing Water.* New York: Penguin Books, 1993.

Rempel, Arthur G. *Memories.* Unpublished typewritten manuscript. Walla Walla, WA: Arthur G. Rempel, 1993.

Rempel, Valerie. "Early Missionary Society Activity Among U.S. Mennonite Brethren Women." *Direction* 24, no. 2 (Fall 1995): 36–46.

———. "'She Hath Done What She Could:' The Development of the Women's Missionary Services in the Mennonite Churches of the United States." M.A. thesis, Mennonite Brethren Biblical Seminary, 1992.

———. "'She Hath Done What She Could': The Development of the Women's Missionary Service in the Mennonite Brethren Churches of the United States." In *Bridging Troubled Waters: Mennonite Brethren at Mid-Twentieth Century,* ed. Paul Toews, 149–64. Winnipeg, MB: Kindred Productions, 1995.

Rich, Elaine Sommers. *Mennonite Women: A Story of God's Faithfulness, 1683–1983.* Scottdale, PA: Herald Press, 1983.

Romo, Ricardo. "Mexican Americans in the New West." In *The Twentieth Century West: Historical Interpretations,* 136–37. Albuquerque: University of New Mexico Press, 1989.

Ruth, Corinna Siebert. "Avenues of Service at First Mennonite Church." In *First Mennonite Church: Celebrating Our Centennial—1906–2006: The Unfolding of Our Story*, ed. Corinna Siebert Ruth, 200–10. Reedley, CA: First Mennonite Church, Reedley, 2006.

———. "Early Families of First Mennonite Church." In *First Mennonite Church: Celebrating Our Centennial—1906–2006: The Unfolding of Our Story*, ed. Corinna Siebert Ruth, 70–85. Reedley, CA: First Mennonite Church, Reedley, 2006.

———. "'From the Dust Bowl to California.'" In *First Mennonite Church: Celebrating Our Centennial—1906–2006: The Unfolding of Our Story*, ed. Corinna Siebert Ruth, 122–28. Reedley, CA: First Mennonite Church, Reedley, 2006.

———. "The Stories of First Mennonite Church Members: Those Who Suffered Religious Persecution and Economic Hardships." In *First Mennonite Church: Celebrating Our Centennial—1906–2006: The Unfolding of Our Story*, ed. Corinna Siebert Ruth, 86. Reedley, CA: First Mennonite Church, Reedley, 2006.

Sánchez, George. *Becoming Mexican American: Ethnicity, Culture and Identity in Chicano Los Angeles, 1900–1945*. New York: Oxford University Press, 1993.

Saxton, Alexander. *The Indispensable Enemy: Labor and the Anti-Chinese Movement in California*. Berkeley: University of California Press, 1995.

Schlabach, Theron. *Gospel Versus Gospel: Mission and the Mennonite Church, 1863–1944*. Scottdale, PA: Herald Press, 1980.

Schmidt, Henry Jake. "Continuity and Change in an Ethical Tradition: A Case Study of North American Mennonite Brethren Church-State Rhetoric and Practice 1917–1979." Ph.D. diss., University of Southern California, 1981.

Schmidt, Henry J., and John Unger. "Telling the Good News: Home Missions in the Pacific District." In *75 Years of Fellowship: Pacific District Conference of the Mennonite Brethren Churches 1912–1987*, ed. Esther Jost, 33–45. Fresno, CA: Pacific District Conference of the Mennonite Brethren Churches, 1987.

Scott, Joan. *Gender and the Politics of History*. New York: Columbia University Press, 1988.

Shetler, S. G. *Church History of the Pacific Coast Mennonite Conference District*. Scottdale, PA: Mennonite Publishing House, 1921.

Simmons, John K., and Brian Wilson. *Competing Visions of Paradise: The California Experience of 19th Century Sectarianism*. Santa Barbara, CA: Fithian Press, 1993.

Simons, Menno. "Reply to Gellius Faber." In *The Complete Writings of Menno Simons c. 1496–1561*, 623–781. Scottdale, PA: Herald Press, 1984.

Smith, C. Henry. *Smith's Story of the Mennonites*. 1941. 5th ed., Newton, KS: Faith and Life Press, 1981.

Smith, Timothy L. "Religion and Ethnicity in America." *American Historical Review* 83 (Dec. 1978): 1155–85.

Smith, Wallace. *Garden of the Sun*. Los Angeles: Lymanhouse, 1939.

Smith, Willard H. *Mennonites in Illinois*. Scottdale, PA: Herald Press, 1983.

Snyder, C. Arnold. *Anabaptist History and Theology: An Introduction*. Kitchener, ON: Pandora Press, 1995.

Stahly, Delmar, et al. "Mennonites and Mental Health I. Mennonite Programs for Mental Illness." *Mennonite Life* (July 1954): 118–26.

Starr, Kevin. *Americans and the California Dream, 1850–1915*. New York: Oxford University Press, 1973.

———. *Coast of Dreams: California on the Edge, 1990–2003*. New York: Knopf, 2004.

———. *The Dream Endures: California Enters the 1940s*. New York: Oxford University Press, 1997.

———. *Embattled Dreams: California in War and Peace, 1940–1950.* New York: Oxford University Press, 2002.

———. *Endangered Dreams: The Great Depression in California.* New York: Oxford University Press, 1996.

———. *Golden Dreams: California in an Age of Abundance, 1950–1963.* New York: Oxford University Press, 2009.

Stauffer, William. "The Rehabilitation of Men in the C.P.S. Camps." In *Proceedings of the Conference on Mennonite Cultural Problems,* 73–76, July 22–23, 1943.

Stout, Harry S., and D. G. Hart, eds. *New Directions in American Religious History.* New York: Oxford University Press, 1997.

Suter, Ruth. "Embracing the Realities of Diverse Communities." In *Anabaptist Visions for the New Millennium: A Search for Identity,* ed. Dale Schrag and James Juhnke, 87–92. Kitchener, ON: Pandora Press, 2000.

Sutton, Matthew Avery. *Aimee Semple McPherson and the Resurrection of Christian America.* Cambridge, MA: Harvard University Press, 2007.

Sweet, Leonard I. "The Modernization of Protestant Religion in America." In *Altered Landscapes: Christianity in America, 1935–1985,* ed. David W. Lotz, Donald W. Shriver, Jr., and John F. Wilson, 19–41. Grand Rapids, MI: Eerdmans Publishing, 1989.

Sylvester, Katharine. *From Despair to Deliverance.* Enumclaw, WA: Winepress Publishing, 1999.

Szasz, Ferenc Morton. *Religion in the Modern American West.* Tucson: University of Arizona Press, 2000.

Szasz, Ferenc M., and Margaret Connell Szasz. "Religion and Spirituality." In *The Oxford History of the American West,* ed. Clyde A. Milner, Carol A. O'Conner, and Martha A. Sandweiss, 359–91. New York: Oxford University Press, 1994.

Taylor, Ronald B. *Chávez and the Farm Workers.* Boston: Beacon Press, 1975.

Thielmann, John H. *Escape to Freedom.* Sunnyvale, CA: Patson's Press, 1995.

Thirlwall, Lynda McIntosh. "Mennonite Quilts of Fresno County California: 1900–1940." M.S. thesis, California State University, Fresno, 1994.

Thirtieth Anniversary, 1910–1940. Los Angeles: Immanuel Mennonite Church, 1940.

Toews, J. A. *A History of the Mennonite Brethren Church: Pilgrims and Pioneers.* Ed. A. J. Klassen. Fresno, CA: General Conference of the Mennonite Brethren Churches, 1975.

Toews, J. B. *JB: The Autobiography of a Twentieth Century Mennonite Pilgrim.* Fresno, CA: Center for Mennonite Brethren Studies, 1995.

———. "The M. B. Biblical Seminary." In *The Seminary Story: Twenty Years of Education in Ministry, 1955–1975,* ed. A. J. Klassen, 17–24. Fresno, CA: Mennonite Brethren Biblical Seminary, 1975.

———. *A Pilgrimage of Faith: The Mennonite Brethren Church in Russia and North America.* Winnipeg, MB: Kindred Press, 1993.

Toews, Paul. "Civilian Public Service and the Transformation of American Mennonites." *California Mennonite Historical Society Bulletin* 19 (April 1988): 1, 5.

———. "From Pietism to Secularism via Anabaptism: An Informal History of the Changing Ideals and Relationship Between Fresno Pacific College and the Mennonite Brethren Church, 1944–1984." Unpublished paper, Feb. 1985, 1–19. Copy in author's possession.

———. "Fundamentalist Conflict in Mennonite Colleges: A Response to Cultural Transitions?" *Mennonite Quarterly Review* 62, no. 3 (July 1983): 241–56.

———. "Introduction." In *Mennonite Idealism and Higher Education: The Story of the Pacific College Idea,* ed. Paul Toews, x–xv. Fresno, CA: Center for Mennonite Brethren Studies, 1995.

———. *Mennonites in American Society, 1930–1970: Modernity and the Persistence of Religious Community.* Scottdale, PA: Herald Press, 1996.

———. "Recentering a Denomination: The Revival of Mennonite Brethren Historical Identity in the 1960s and 1970s." *California Mennonite Historical Society Bulletin* 23 (Nov. 1990): 3–4.

———. "Religious Idealism and Academic Vocation at Fresno Pacific College." In *Models for Christian Higher Education: Strategies for Success in the Twenty-First Century*, ed. Richard Hughes and William Adrian, 222–42. Grand Rapids, MI: Eerdmans Publishing, 1997.

———. "'A Shelter in a Time of Storm': The Establishment of Schools in the Pacific District Conference." In *75 Years of Fellowship: Pacific District Conference of the Mennonite Brethren Churches, 1912–1987*, ed. Esther Jost, 57–69. Fresno, CA: District Conference of the Mennonite Brethren Churches, 1987.

———. "Singing the Christian College Song in a Mennonite Key." In *Mennonite Idealism and Higher Education: The Story of the Pacific College Idea*, ed. Paul Toews, 89–102. Fresno, CA: Center for Mennonite Brethren Studies, 1995.

Toews, Paul, ed. "The Evolution of the Fresno Pacific College Idea." Appendix in *Mennonite Idealism and Higher Education: The Story of the Pacific College Idea*, 155–64. Fresno, CA: Center for Mennonite Brethren Studies, 1995.

Toews, Paul, and Abe Dueck. "Embodying the Vision: Higher Education." In *For Everything a Season: Mennonite Brethren in North America, 1874–2002: An Informal History*, ed. Paul Toews and Kevin Enns-Rempel, 95–107. Fresno, CA: Historical Commission, 2002.

Toews, Paul, and Kevin Enns-Rempel. "Adapting to the City: The Kerckhoff Community." In *For Everything a Season: Mennonite Brethren in North America, 1874–2002: An Informal History*, ed. Paul Toews and Kevin Enns-Rempel, 152. Fresno, CA: Historical Commission, 2002.

A Treasury of Historical Accounts 'Till 1913 Written by Pioneers of the Reedley Area. Comp. Katharine Nickel. Reedley, CA: n.p., 1961.

Tuveson, Ernest Lee. *Redeemer Nation: The Idea of America's Millennial Role.* Chicago: University of Chicago Press, 1968.

Unrau, Ruth. *Encircled: Stories of Mennonite Women.* Newton, KS: Faith and Life Press, 1986.

Unruh, A. H. *Die Geschichte der Mennoniten-Brudergemeinde 1860–1954.* Hillsboro, KS: General Conference of the Mennonite Brethren Church of North America, 1955.

Unruh, John D. *In the Name of Christ: A History of the Mennonite Central Committee.* Scottdale, PA: Herald Press, 1952.

Urry, James. "The Closed and Open: Social and Religious Change Amongst the Mennonites in Russia (1789–1889)." Ph.D. diss., Oxford University, 1978.

———. *Mennonites, Politics, and Peoplehood: Europe–Russia–Canada 1525–1980.* Winnipeg: University of Manitoba Press, 2006.

———. *None But Saints: The Transformation of Mennonite Life in Russia, 1789–1889.* 2nd ed. Kitchener, ON: Pandora Press, 2007.

van der Veer, Peter. "Introduction." In *Conversion to Modernities: The Globalization of Christianity*, ed. Peter van der Veer, 1–21. New York: Routledge, 1996.

Wacker, Grant. *Heaven Below: Early Pentecostals and American Culture.* Cambridge, MA: Harvard University Press, 2001.

Walker, Randi Jones. "Protestantism in the Sangre de Cristos: Factors in the Growth and Decline of the Hispanic Protestant Churches in Northern New Mexico and Southern Colorado, 1850–1920." Ph.D. diss., Claremont Graduate School, 1983.

Warner, Miriam E. "Mennonite Brethren: The Maintenance of Continuity in a Religious Ethnic Group." Ph.D. diss., University of California, Berkeley, 1985.

———. "Social Science Theory and a People Apart." *Direction* 17, no. 1 (Spring 1988): 17–29.

Webb, Paul Frank. "Mennonite Conscientious Objectors and the Civilian Public Service Camps of World War II." M.A. thesis, California State University, Fresno, 1988.

Wells, Miriam J. *Strawberry Fields: Politics, Class, and Work in California Agriculture.* Ithaca, NY: Cornell University Press, 1996.

Wenger, J. C. *The Mennonite Church in America: Sometimes Called Old Mennonites.* Scottdale, PA: Herald Press, 1966.

West, Nathanael. *The Day of the Locust.* 1939. New York: Penguin/Signet, 1983.

Wiebe, Arthur J. "The Birth of the Vision." In *Mennonite Idealism and Higher Education: The Story of the Pacific College Idea,* ed. Paul Toews, 1–23. Fresno, CA: Center for Mennonite Brethren Studies, 1995.

Wiebe, Joel A. *Remembering... Reaching a Vision for Service: A Fifty-Year History of Fresno Pacific College.* Fresno, CA: Fresno Pacific College, 1994.

Wiens, Roland M. "Growth Patterns of Mennonite Brethren Pacific District Mission Churches." M.A. thesis, Mennonite Brethren Biblical Seminary, 1971.

Woo, Wesley S. "Protestant Work Among the Chinese in the San Francisco Bay Area, 1850–1920." Ph.D. diss., Graduate Theological Union, 1983.

Worster, Donald. *Rivers of Empire: Water, Aridity, and the Growth of the American West.* New York: Oxford University Press, 1985.

Wright, Jeff. "Mennonites in Southern California: An Interpretive Essay." *California Mennonite Historical Society Bulletin* 36 (April 1999): 9–11.

Yoder, John. "From Monastery to Marketplace: Idea and Mission in Graduate and Professional Programs at Fresno Pacific College." In *Mennonite Idealism and Higher Education: The Story of the Pacific College Idea,* ed. Paul Toews, 133–51. Fresno, CA: Center for Mennonite Brethren Studies, 1995.

Yoder, John Howard. *The Politics of Jesus: Vicit Agnus Noster.* Grand Rapids, MI: Eerdmans Publishing, 1972.

Yoder, Larry R. "Kern View Bakersfield, California." In *If We Can Love: The Mennonite Mental Health Story,* ed. Vernon H. Neufeld, 185–205. Newton, KS: Faith and Life Press, 1983.

Yoder, Sanford Calvin. *For Conscience Sake: A Study of Mennonite Migrations Resulting from the World War.* Scottdale, PA: Herald Press, 1945.

Yung, Judy. *Unbound Feet: A Social History of Chinese Women in San Francisco.* Berkeley: University of California Press, 1995.

Zech, Kenneth. *Historic Reedley.* Reedley, CA: Reedley Historical Society, 1994.

Zimmerman, Martha. "The Story of Kings View Hospital and First Mennonite Church." In *First Mennonite Church: Celebrating Our Centennial—1906–2006: The Unfolding of Our Story,* ed. Corinna Siebert Ruth, 192–99. Reedley: First Mennonite Church, Reedley, 2006.

Index

Page numbers in *italics* refer to photographs.

Werner O. Packull,
Hutterites Beginnings: Communitarian Experiments during the Reformation
Benjamin W. Redekop and Calvin W. Redekop, eds.,
Power, Authority, and the Anabaptist Tradition
Calvin Redekop, Stephen C. Ainlay, and Robert Siemens,
Mennonite Entrepreneurs
Calvin Redekop, ed., *Creation and the Environment:*
An Anabaptist Perspective on a Sustainable World
Steven D. Reschly, *The Amish on the Iowa Prairie, 1840 to 1910*
Kimberly D. Schmidt, Diane Zimmerman Umble, and Steven D. Reschly,
Strangers at Home: Amish and Mennonite Women in History
Diane Zimmerman Umble,
Holding the Line: The Telephone in Old Order Mennonite and Amish Life
David Weaver-Zercher, *The Amish in the American Imagination*